T0244478

PUBLICATION SUPPORTED BY
FIGURE FOUNDATION

BISON
BOOKS

SKYWALKS

Robert Gordon's Untold Story of Hallmark's Kansas City Disaster

R. ELI PAUL

UNIVERSITY OF NEBRASKA PRESS | LINCOLN

The University of Nebraska Press is part of a land-grant institution with campuses and programs on the past, present, and future homelands of the Pawnee, Ponca, Otoe-Missouria, Omaha, Dakota, Lakota, Kaw, Cheyenne, and Arapaho Peoples, as well as those of the relocated Ho-Chunk, Sac and Fox, and Iowa Peoples.

Library of Congress Cataloging-in-Publication Data
Names: Paul, R. Eli, 1954– author.
Title: Skywalks: Robert Gordon's untold story of Hallmark's Kansas City disaster / R. Eli Paul.
Description: Lincoln: University of Nebraska Press, [2023] | Includes bibliographical references and index.
Identifiers: LCCN 2022017123
ISBN 9781496233134 (hardback)
ISBN 9781496234896 (epub)
ISBN 9781496234902 (pdf)
Subjects: LCSH: Kansas City Hyatt Regency—Trials, litigation, etc. | Liability for building accidents—Missouri—Kansas City. | Skywalks—Accidents—Missouri—Kansas City. | Gordon, Robert Charles, 1941–2008. | Lawyers—Missouri—Kansas City—Biography.
Classification: LCC KF228.H93 P38 2023 | DDC 343.77841107/8624—dc23/eng/20221101
LC record available at https://lccn.loc.gov/2022017123

Set and designed in Sabon Next by N. Putens.

To

Lori Cox-Paul

who made this book,

and so much more, possible

Most people, in fact, will not take trouble in finding out the truth, but are much more inclined to accept the first story they hear.

—THUCYDIDES, ancient Greek historian

CONTENTS

ILLUSTRATIONS

DRAMATIS PERSONAE

THE CASE

Rick Alm: Of the many print journalists Robert Gordon briefed about the *Federal Skywalk Cases*, Alm may have come closest to becoming a friend. A member of the select Hyatt investigative team of the *Kansas City Times* and *Star*, he kept in touch with the lawyer long after the story petered out. Alm later coauthored a book for the disaster's thirtieth anniversary.

Sally Firestone: Of all the surviving victims of the skywalks collapse, Firestone suffered the most grievous physical wounds. Molly Riley attended to the "girl in pink," presumably Firestone, as she lay immobile for hours in the skywalks rubble. Lantz Welch's primary client, Firestone eventually had the opportunity to tell her story before a sympathetic and generous jury in state court.

Robert Gordon: Colead counsel on behalf of the plaintiffs in the *Federal Skywalk Cases*, Bob Gordon seemed to possess limitless energy when digging into the documentary record to determine what he considered the truth. The sudden settlement of the case closed one door but opened another in the Kansas City attorney's struggle to present before the public a contradictory version of the disaster.

Donald Hall: Son of the founder and heir to the Hallmark fortune, Don Hall ran the family-owned "card colossus" during the design and construction of the Hyatt Regency Kansas City, the new jewel in the corporate crown. When questioned about the building project in any detail and under oath, the hands-on chief executive officer could remember but little.

Edward Pfrang: A highly regarded engineer with a team of professionals from the National Bureau of Standards, Pfrang brought an independent, no-nonsense approach to the scientific investigation of the skywalks collapse. As an expert in building technology, he only asked *what* was to blame for the skywalks collapse, not *who*, much to Robert Gordon's dismay.

Molly Riley: Robert Gordon's feisty client became the initial class representative in the *Federal Skywalk Cases*. At the July 1981 tea dance, Riley barely missed being crushed by the falling walkways, quickly pulled herself together, and diligently stayed on the scene for hours as an emergency nurse. Replaced as the class rep by Shirley Stover, then Deborah Jackson, she was crushed when the case was settled out of court.

Robert Sisk: Don Hall's college roommate at Dartmouth later became his personal lawyer. Sisk's highly regarded New York law firm took the lead in the defense of Hallmark Cards Inc. and forced other defendants named in the many lawsuits to follow its lead. He knew how to needle Robert Gordon while keeping a close eye on Gordon's later book project.

Lantz Welch: Welch was an exaggerated, cartoonish version of the ambulance-chasing, no-publicity-is-bad-publicity personal injury lawyer. Welch's goals for the Hyatt victims often clashed with Robert Gordon's, but he got results, including millions for his clients, millions for himself, and a magnificent lakeside castle, the house that Hallmark built. Gordon grew to admire the rogue.

Judith Whittaker: Associate general counsel for the Hallmark corporation, Whittaker was an accomplished lawyer with an eye for a federal judgeship and Gordon's nemesis. She often found herself as the only female corporate lawyer in the room. Whittaker outlawyered Gordon and came away with a huge victory, specifically Hallmark's survival as a profitable business. He thought she did so by skirting the law.

Paul Wolff: Gordon's high school classmate, Wolff went on to an Ivy League law school education and a high-powered career in Washington DC. When Wolff came on board to represent the federal class, bringing with him the nationally renowned Williams & Connolly firm, Gordon knew the plaintiffs now had the firepower equal to that of their deep-pocketed opponents.

Scott Wright: A newcomer to the bench and prone to spouting corn-pone aphorisms, Judge Wright of the U.S. District Court of the Western District of Missouri presided over the *Federal Skywalk Cases*. With his surprising and controversial certification of a federal class, the specter of corporation-killing punitive damages thereafter hung over the defendants. His close relationship with Robert Gordon was fraught with father-son overtones.

Irving Younger: Considered by many a leading scholar of the law and dangerous trial tactician but a paper tiger to others in the know, the lead counsel for the plaintiffs in the *Federal Skywalk Cases* never did his homework on the case—at least in Gordon's eyes. Younger's ulterior motives became clearer as the legal maneuverings progressed. Gordon ultimately made him a villain in his book.

THE BOOK

Julian Bach: Robert Gordon's second—and even more illustrious—literary agent was a step up in the New York pecking order from his predecessor. Bach initially thought the book would be submitted in 1986 but could only watch patiently from afar as the strained professional relationships between Gordon and the members of his writing-editing team deteriorated.

Burton Beals: The Simon & Schuster editor worked with his colleague Fred Hills to try and make "House of Cards" a reality. They got as far as the 1991 production of a promotional flyer for a book launch that never was. He described the Gordon manuscript as "extraordinarily complex," an understatement.

Knox Burger: Gordon's first literary agent was the head of a leading New York agency and a first-class curmudgeon. Burger paired Robert Byrne, another writing client, with Gordon. The trio went into the 1985 partnership expecting to produce a best seller in a few months. Burger and Byrne clashed with Gordon over style and substance and soon called it quits on the book project.

Robert Byrne: Gordon's first cowriter and a successful novelist in his own right, Byrne brought a level of practical expertise and proven accomplishments that any novice collaborator should have welcomed. His engineering background was a natural fit for telling the story of why the skywalks fell. An overly critical Gordon never granted Byrne a free rein on the project.

John Garrity: Gordon enlisted the local freelance journalist in 1986 as a work-for-hire ghostwriter and editor. Likewise a Julian Bach client, Garrity was unaware of Gordon's other collaborators but not surprised when he learned about them later. The fellow Kansas Citian experienced Gordon's eccentricities up close and personally but nevertheless capably readied a serviceable manuscript for a prospective publisher.

Robert Gordon: The lawyer's first rough manuscript was "When They Didn't Care Enough," its title a tortured play on the well-known Hallmark slogan. The next title was the more polished and prescient "House of Cards." Notwithstanding an outstanding pool of talent to shepherd a book project to completion, neither manuscript saw print. Gordon developed a powerful message, a convincing counternarrative to the Hyatt collapse story, but proved a poor messenger.

Paul Haskins: A veteran of the *Kansas City Times* who parlayed his Pulitzer into a better job with the *New York Times*, Haskins tried his hand after Robert Byrne at editing Robert Gordon. To the journalist's credit, he knew the Hyatt story inside and out, but the 1986 collaboration, which started out so promising and collegially, ended before year's end in bitter acrimony.

Fred Hills: Gordon's long-suffering editor at Simon & Schuster, the New York publishing house, Hills was attached to the project in 1987. He tried for years to get the obstinate author to tone down the vitriol and cut his manuscript to an acceptable, marketable length. Failing that, the senior editor gave Gordon the inevitable yet still devastating news in 1993 that S&S had dropped his book contract.

James Landis: Early on in 1984 Robert Gordon reached out to Landis, a literary agent with a sterling reputation at the William Morrow publishing house in New York. Although Landis passed on the book proposal, Gordon heeded some of his advice. Gordon followed up and contacted Kathy Robbins as an agent but ignored Landis's concerns about the manuscript's "bias."

Kathy Robbins: In the early stages of the book project Gordon reached out to the Robbins literary powerhouse for help. The hard-nosed agent and her stubborn prospective client were a poor fit, and both quickly moved on. The expert counsel Robbins gave him, that of engaging an experienced coauthor, was not lost on Gordon, although maybe never fully accepted.

Michel Scrivan: The mysterious, pompous, and verbose Hallmark executive met Robert Gordon at an outdoor party at the home of a Mission Hills neighbor but did not recognize him. Scrivan spoke out of school about the skywalks collapse to the attentive author-to-be. Gordon's scribbling of surreptitious notes during the lengthy conversation added some slapstick elements to a deadly serious story.

SKYWALKS

Prologue

The architects of the new hotel had set a goal for themselves to fulfill their client's wishes, and one command they were determined to obey was to create a spectacular main lobby. Physically the lobby needed to serve the mundane purposes of efficiently greeting, registering, and directing guests from their tower lodging on one side of the building to their meeting, recreational, and eating spaces on the other, a layout that hundreds of large conference hotels shared in common and one that rarely drew responses of surprise and wonder. The Hyatt Regency hotel in Kansas City, Missouri, would be different. The hotel would feature some gravity-defying architecture. Its five-story atrium lobby would have *skywalks*.

To the engineers poring over the blueprints, the word "skywalks" was translated from its elegant term to one more mundane—elevated walkways. This was just one more structural problem to solve: a span between the two functional areas of *x* length with a surface bearing load of *y*. The formula for the skywalks' support was merely a matter of materials and mathematical calculations.

To the contractors on the building project, their job in this particular instance was to turn the skywalks from an architect's notion and an engineer's set of figures into physical reality: steel deck topped with concrete for the floor, glass sides, and wooden railing. Installation would simply follow fabrication, but nothing was simple with the construction of this hotel. The project strictly adhered to a "design-build" plan, one intended to save time and money by eliminating a slew of potential bidders who would have painstakingly pored over a set of completed building plans to price and schedule the job. Design-build avoided this time-consuming bidding step, in part, by preparing detailed architectural, structural, and mechanical documents for the contractor in an almost "just-in-time" approach. By definition the design and construction phases overlapped, and the schedule tracked fast. The inevitable glitch that might have appeared early on a blueprint detail often revealed itself distressingly late, caught only after the thing was actually built and installed. The cost to stop and correct became that much higher.

To their client, the owner, the concerns of the designers, engineers, builders, and installers mattered less than the bigger goal—to complete the largest hotel project in Kansas City's history on time and on budget. The anticipated result was destined to be a grand addition to the city's skyline and a needed stimulus to its civic and commercial life. This structure, a crowning achievement of Don Hall, chief executive officer of the family-owned Hallmark Cards corporation and son of its founder, J. C. (Joyce) Hall, was meant to impress, inside and out, from top to bottom, and the finished product accomplished that. From a distance one gazed upon a forty-story building, the city's tallest at 504 feet, capped by its first revolving restaurant, appropriately named Skies.[1] Upon entering the hotel, one immediately encountered the "thin" skywalks, floating above the lobby, "invisible" as to their means of support, a dramatic architectural flourish and stunning in their design and execution. Nothing compared in the city. The owner left the details of how these marvels would be realized to others on the payroll.

To the executives who followed their boss's edicts, their priorities were clear: avoid delays, calculate and mitigate risks, and resolve inevitable disputes as they arose. Keep close tabs on the schedule. Keep closer tabs on the bottom line. This became an almost impossible task after October 14, 1979, when the lobby's atrium roof collapsed during construction and dropped tons of debris on the lobby floor below, barely missing the newly installed skywalks. Luckily, no workers were present when this after-hours accident occurred.

Downplayed at the time, the atrium roof collapse was nevertheless the turning point in the project. It is critical knowledge for understanding the later catastrophe of the fallen skywalks, which followed less than two years later when the hotel's lobby was packed with people, because it brought in 1979 all the interested parties—architect, engineer, contractor, subcontractor, and owner—together to discuss the perils that they now communally faced. But clearly the atrium's collapse did not prevent the skywalks from falling. Why? Who was to blame for the atrium error? How could it have been caught? Who was obligated to pay? If the atrium collapse delayed the project, could the opening-day schedule get back on track? Time was money, and hotel rooms had already been reserved and conferences booked. Were other areas of the construction site at risk?

To this group of interested parties came other associates to help sort out the project management, public relations, and legal complications, as much of a mess as the rubble strewn about the lobby floor, and this they quickly did. The Hallmark lawyers ramrodded the post-collapse meetings and soon pointed an accusatory finger at a subcontractor. The atrium roof support girders, made of steel, rested on a steel shelf, which itself was insufficiently fastened to the north wall on the east side of the lobby, a failing combination of too few bolts, too shallowly drilled into the concrete. But Hallmark kept the problem in-house, stonewalled their corporate insurer and its investigator, and quietly assigned the costs to the contractor and his subs. The company's public relations director put out a story to the local newspaper that drastically downplayed the hard facts of the roof collapse, citing merely that a steel beam had fallen at the job site but that the noninjury incident was insignificant and easy to correct. Just to be safe, Hallmark's risk manager found another insurance company to cover any future collapse. The pain was eased, the challenge was met, and the work resumed. The schedule barely hiccuped.

The grand opening of the Hyatt Regency was held a few months later on July 1, 1980. Red, white, and blue ribbons festooned one of the three skywalks, which the mayor and other dignitaries untied. As with any such project, construction workers toiled right up to the ribbon cutting. After the roof collapse, they had been ordered not to use the skywalks, as if they needed any such encouragement. One foreman on the job later expressed the consensus of his men: "Those hanger rods sure looked funny." Another foreman was more direct: "I didn't mind telling anybody, they [the skywalks] worried the hell out of me."[2]

Not everything in the new hotel worked quite right. The revolving restaurant did not yet revolve; that gimmick would finally become operable in early 1981. Hallmark as the owner formally turned over the keys to the managers from the Hyatt Corporation, as well as a punch list of problems that ranged from minor to major and numbered in the hundreds, once again not terribly out of the ordinary for a building project of this hotel's size and complexity. There was still the question among the staff of whether the fire alarm system in this $50 million "luxury facility" actually functioned.

To the people who flocked to the new hotel—tourists, conventioneers, civic groups, and celebrities—none of these warning signs mattered, not that they were aware of them. What mattered was the here and now, not the journey—how we got to this point—but this exquisite destination. Kansas City could boast of a shiny new thing, a lure for otherwise routine business meetings and corporate dinners, and a needed shot-in-the-arm to a flagging downtown, as one observer called it, a "$50 million investment in KC's future."[3] But it made an immediate impact on midwesterners as an ultrasophisticated venue. Why, even the renowned Henry Kissinger came to town to speak in the grand ballroom!

In 1981 the local Hyatt management came up with an idea, modeled on one at Hyatts in other cities, for how locals could share in the glamour, as well as for how regular foot traffic through the hotel's doors could be enhanced. Every Friday evening, "tea time" in a bygone age, the hotel would hold a tea dance in its spacious lobby, and in typical midwestern fashion the dance floor would be open to all. Big bands would play dance music for couples of all ages to fox trot, jitterbug, rumba, and waltz, some competitively. The skywalks that spanned the lobby offered unique vantage points to see and be seen. From the first dance in May, the weekly spectacle caught on immediately in Kansas City. Some two thousand dancers, musicians, partygoers, waitstaff, and onlookers jammed the atrium lobby and the adjacent bars and restaurants for hours of high-spirited fun.

On the hot summer evening of July 17, 1981, the revelry ended with the worst structural failure in the nation's history and the worst thing that ever happened in Kansas City. A shocked city was thrust into the spotlight in a way no one wanted, and a formerly benign word appeared in the national vocabulary, but not in the context its creators would have desired. After the world heard of the horrible hotel scene with its collapsed mass of twisted steel, concrete, dust, debris, water, blood and bodies, shrieks of victims, shrill of sirens, shouts of rescuers, and roar of jackhammers, *skywalks* took on another more menacing meaning.[4]

In the years to follow, the disaster followed a generally accepted narrative, one that gained credibility through repetition: on that fateful Friday evening, a 120-foot-long suspended walkway in Kansas City's newest and most exciting hotel, weighing about 64,000 pounds or 32 tons, pulled loose from its supports, pancaked below on another walkway of equal size, and together crashed onto a packed crowd of unsuspecting partiers below. There was no warning and no chance of escape for the 1,500 persons present. Ultimately, 114 people were killed and more than 200 injured, many for life. Some victims were trapped for hours while first responders struggled mightily amid the twisted rubble and chaotic conditions, in some instances resorting to emergency amputations, one with a chainsaw, to free victims. About a thousand emergency personnel and volunteers arrived on the scene, as did the city's mayor, who could be seen carrying a stretcher to get the wounded to emergency care. The city's hospitals received the alarm to prepare for a flood of patients, and they soon arrived. Within hours, more than a thousand people donated blood. Journalists rushed in and captured the hellish scene with words, photographs, and film, the most gruesome of which were never shared with the public. As word spread across the Kansas City metro area in an age before cell phones and twenty-four-hour news, family members anxiously sought information of any kind about loved ones at risk. All were witnessing the result of a man-made disaster of epic proportions, one that immediately mushroomed to a national story, and a universal question immediately arose. What caused the skywalks to fall?

Through the efforts of a hastily assembled team of investigative reporters from the *Kansas City Times* and *Kansas City Star*, an initial answer to the mystery soon surfaced. Several box-beam connections of thin, steel, vertical hanger rods that were spaced at intervals and had secured the walkways to the ceiling had failed, and a field examination by the press's own technical consultant quickly exposed the problem. Revealed by simple engineering calculations, government analysts later confirmed the system had no chance of supporting its own weight, much less the additional weight of people. Now the questions narrowed. Who was to blame for this building failure? Who was liable, financially and criminally, for the deaths and injuries that resulted?

A pack of local personal injury lawyers did not wait for answers. Quickly assessing the situation, they descended on the scene—some literally showing up at the hotel and the hospitals on the night of the disaster—to sign up victims as clients. The following Monday saw the first mad dash to the courthouse. A flurry of suits was filed in Missouri courts against a host of targeted defendants. Months of legal squabbling ensued.

Despite that fact, the sad stories of eyewitnesses to the carnage and its immediate aftermath took precedence over the distasteful and the dodgy. Collectively the tales were woeful, often horrific, and full of pathos, and they filled the pages of the local newspapers for months to come. Theirs became the ultimate narrative of the event, so much so that when memorialized thirty years later with a book, titled *The Last Dance*, the dramatic testimony of the victims, the survivors, the rescuers, and their families took center stage—as it deserved.[5]

Within the book's pages was a chapter on the reporting that had led to the awarding of a Pulitzer Prize, spotlighting the investigative journalists who within days had figured out and ably described the structural design failure. Later, in the wake of this turbulence, the local press uncovered the systemic and shameful lack of enforcement of the city's building codes. Toughening them up was one of the few positive outcomes of the whole affair.

Also mentioned prominently in the anniversary book was the role of two structural engineers who had worked on the project. They were eventually held responsible for the faulty design and subsequently lost their licenses to practice their profession. No mention was made of anyone tried and convicted of any crime because, as it turned out, no one was ever indicted. Nor was there much discourse within the book's pages on the many months of courtroom battles that began in earnest the Monday morning after the tragedy.

Because of this, Robert Gordon, a Kansas City attorney, made no appearance. Between the years 1981 and 1995, Gordon developed and refined a convincing, documented counternarrative to the causes of the collapse. At its heart his version held that negligent disregard for safety among authorities who should have known better was the real cause of the skywalks disaster, and those people, a list that extended beyond two engineers, should have been held accountable. He was unable to present that version in a public courtroom, however, although he certainly tried. For various reasons, many self-inflicted, he was unable to deliver his inflammatory findings in the form of a popular book, even though major literary agents and at least one New York trade publisher, Simon & Schuster, were committed to seeing it published.

Gordon's efforts—in court and then in publishing—guide the organization of the story my book tells. In fact, it is two stories, one of Gordon's failed "House of Cards" book project, which is preceded by his almost herculean legal struggles to place blame for the disaster where he thought it belonged. His years of legal efforts culminated bitterly for him in an unsatisfying out-of-court settlement, but it was that settlement that provided his book's raison d'être. To understand the later development of his "House of Cards" manuscript, one must therefore appreciate the earlier foundational proceedings known as the *Federal Skywalk Cases*. The connection between legal case and book project may seem obscure, but they are very much linked. Gordon's powerful message—his counternarrative to the Hyatt collapse story and its "thesis" on what happened and who was to blame—is the connection. He produced a powerful message, and it is only now being fully aired, reason enough for this book and Gordon as its central character.

Gordon's thesis was that Hallmark, which as the owner made all the important decisions regarding schedule and budget, should have realized that its hotel was unsafe. Its officials received a clear warning from the 1979 atrium roof collapse but did not heed that warning. The failure to deal correctly with the first collapse led to the second in 1981.

Hallmark never accepted this argument; the public rarely heard it. The Gordon thesis, however, was significantly vetted in two ways. First, Gordon's findings and conclusions formed the basis for the legal argument that the plaintiffs intended to make in court in the *Federal Skywalk Cases*. This version of the facts was effectively silenced by the out-of-court settlement in 1983. Second, the legal department of Simon & Schuster, the New York publisher that had contracted with Gordon, later scrutinized his manuscript, "House of Cards," and its controversial assertions and was left satisfied. The editors of Simon & Schuster were poised to proceed and publish the book, until—nothing.

In retrospect, Robert Gordon ultimately concluded that his attempt to tell the skywalks story was absurd, but never the story itself. Perhaps the ultimate absurdity is that, as central as he was to the aftermath of the Hallmark hotel disaster, he rarely shows up on anyone's radar anymore. He figured in none of the mandatory anniversary stories filed years later by local journalists. He took no part in any of the public commemorations by the survivors, and he did not emerge as a person of interest to historians. His thesis on the disaster's real cause, once furiously attacked and then commonly dismissed, has been forgotten. He had a tale that he ached to tell, but in the end, he kept it all to himself. Like the dust that was rapidly raised and that slowly floated downward after the doomed Hyatt walkways fell that summer night in 1981, the community had settled almost unconsciously on a less controversial and more expedient narrative. And because of that, no one came looking for Gordon, certainly not the archivists at the public library. But find him we did. Or to be more precise, his son found us.

IN AUGUST 2015 I RECEIVED A VOICEMAIL MESSAGE AT MY KANSAS City Public Library office from a man who identified himself as Andy Gordon. He said that he was looking for a place to donate his father's personal papers and case files. His father was the late Robert Gordon, a homegrown lawyer who worked on the "Hyatt case," and before his death he had written a book about it.[6] That was enough for me.

As the head of the Missouri Valley Special Collections, the history arm of this large, popular, urban library, I returned the call and set up an appointment to look at the "many boxes" of papers. I had several questions, but they could easily wait until a senior archivist and I met Andy face-to-face and evaluated the prospective donation for ourselves. The intervening time gave me the opportunity to cram for the meeting, which meant consulting the department's massive historical database, and going over in my mind the obvious questions: Who was Robert Gordon? What was his role in the Hyatt disaster? He wrote a book? What did the special collections already have in its thousands of linear feet of books, manuscripts, maps, newspapers, oral histories, photographs, and vertical files? A lot must exist, I mused; it was a national event in the 1980s for heaven's sake; what year was it exactly?

I briefly switched gears from historian to administrator: who else in Kansas City had collections on this subject? And of these local repositories, who else might be a competitor against the library in the acquisition of this one? I had no worries about the Kansas City regional branch of the National Archives, the office Andy had contacted first. Although the National Archives held the records for the relevant federal district court cases, papers from the private sector were well outside that institution's collecting purview. The archivist with whom Andy had talked had thoughtfully recommended Missouri Valley, so there would be no competition there. Nevertheless, this last question was the most bothersome to me. Maybe I should have moved up the meeting.

My search through the local history database for "Hyatt" revealed several bits and pieces but little in the way of unique primary sources, the type of materials that would draw researchers and scholars. And nothing turned up on "Robert Gordon." Past librarians of the Missouri

Valley Room, the dedicated public space for historical researchers in the library, had done a professional but fairly routine job of methodically recording the event at the time, clipping a hodgepodge of newspaper and magazine articles that flooded in tsunami-like. They had diligently amassed three-ring binders filled with photocopied articles from the *Kansas City Times* and *Kansas City Star*, and in these, I found Gordon.

The first mention appeared in February 1982, more than six months after the collapse. Just from this brief account Gordon stood out as a Kansas City attorney of some stature and accomplishment, but with maybe an air of controversy.[7] Of relevance to the library, however, he was someone whose personal papers could be of substantial historical significance. Subsequent articles did nothing to dispel the notion that Gordon was a key insider who witnessed and participated in the post-collapse legal wrangles that followed in the wake of the city's greatest disaster. As the major instigator and cheerleader for the formation of the "class action device," he idealistically advocated this course as "the fairest, most efficient, and economical way of processing the legal aftermath of this calamity." More to the point (especially to me), Gordon's team made bold claims in court of having "clear and striking documentary evidence of reckless conduct by at least some defendants." For a while, his side seemed to hold the whip hand, but the advantage did not last. Later in the year, only a month before the date set for trial, Gordon, seemingly almost in desperation, dropped a "sharply worded" brief on the court. The backroom poker game had moved to a gunfight in the town square. A headline fairly screamed, "Class Lawyer Seeks Sanctions in Skywalk Case; Judge Is Asked to Deny Hallmark, Crown Center a Trial Defense." Gordon alleged "a litany . . . of failures and deceptive maneuvers by Hallmark Cards Inc." He asserted specifically that Hallmark and its wholly owned subsidiary Crown Center had failed to produce critical documents during the discovery phase in a timely manner and its officials had lied under oath during pretrial depositions. The "documents" included a tape recording of a meeting held by Hallmark's upper-level management in November 1979 after the collapse of the hotel's atrium roof.[8] Wait, what? Another earlier structural collapse at the same hotel? How did this fit in the story? And there were tapes? Shades of Watergate came to mind—a local disaster and inevitable litigation had abruptly mutated into the Nixonian realm of stonewalling, cover-up, and smoking guns!

The tale from the library's news clips continued. Judging from the relentless newspaper coverage of the final days of 1982, all the lawyers found themselves caught up in a "flurry of activity." And it seemed as if the reporters, much less their readers, failed to keep up with the daily developments. Recent events had "generated enormous confusion in the mind of the public," so much so that everyone almost threw up his or her hands in surrender. I felt the same and had more questions than I did when I began. So, what happened with Robert Gordon and his explosive charges? How did the defendants respond? How did it all end? Where does Gordon's book, if it exists, fit into all this? Where is that tape recording, who's on it, and what does it say?

Only a bare outline of Gordon the man had emerged from my cursory research and but one solitary, grainy newspaper photograph of the author of these incendiary words. That seemed strange for someone who had kicked up so much dust in a midwestern city the size of Kansas City. Maybe his personal papers could make sense of him and his obviously controversial version of events, as well as this "complex web" of lawsuits, strands of which involved state, federal, and appellate courts, class-action and individual suits, out-of-court settlements, and debates on compensatory versus punitive damages.[9]

Something nagged at me, however. My feeling came from forty years' experience excavating the detritus of history in search of their hidden stories, a combination of anticipation and caution. This potential trove of primary documents looked more promising than most but possibly carried the risk of excessive expectations. A previously untold version of the Hallmark hotel disaster—a new narrative, the real story perhaps?—may soon be in the library's hands, if such a thing were really possible.[10] Anxiously, I awaited the day when I would field inspect the Gordon collection for myself and begin to learn its secrets.

That day came on September 21, 2015, as summer officially turned to fall. Accompanied by senior archivist Kate Hill, we drove to our midmorning appointment at the Gordon home, located just west of the Missouri-Kansas state line in Mission Hills, one of Kansas City's most elegant neighborhoods. The quiet, curved, tree-lined streets ran past one stylish mansion after another, many dating to the 1920s. Andy Gordon's Tudor-style "cottage" reflected a prosperous time when a garage for a family of means was attached and held two automobiles, not merely one. I now recalled that Andy had mentioned having moved his father's materials to the garage. I edged the car onto the circle driveway, which was just large enough to hold a modest fountain in its center, now shut down for the season. That's when people invariably called with their offers to the special collections, I thought, during cleaning seasons when it was "out with the old."

After we rang the doorbell, the owner appeared, we exchanged greetings and introductions on the front step, and the three of us immediately got down to business. Kate and I had been through this before. We followed the standard procedure that combined quick, hard-nosed collections appraisal with soft, soothing donor relations, always alert, however, to expect the unexpected. This time proved no different.

We moved a few steps from the front door of the house to the front of the garage. Andy opened both of its doors by hand. The nearer stall sat empty, the other, well, anything but. I detected a slight shudder from Kate, who stood beside me. I knew she was already calculating the number of acid-free boxes and length of open shelf space needed for this job. This potential "accession," in the professional parlance a formal acquisition to the Missouri Valley Special Collections, would outstrip the available supplies and space that she had on hand. My reaction was immediate and verbal, a mumbled "wow." A slave to bad analogies, I could only liken this block-like mass of big boxes, plastic tubs, and rusty file cabinets, piled as it was in a space meant for a car, to that of a Humvee—maybe not the original Hummer H1 but the smaller H3. Still big. But my thoughts dwelled less on where to park it than on what was under the hood.

Kate and I made an admittedly cursory look. Call it "historical triage," but that was all that was necessary. The collection was in no discernible arrangement—"no original order," as an archivist would say. The materials looked as if they had taken several tumbles over the years. Without the professional restriction when going through a prospective collection of "first do no harm," a credo that archivists share with doctors, we felt no compunction to poke and prod through the containers, and we found what we expected—legal papers and lots of them. We saw depositions, briefs, copies of court exhibits, and hundreds of folders with eye-catching labels: "AW [who?] Doesn't Know Who Designed Atrium or Skywalks," "HMK's [Hallmark's?] Destroyed-Redacted-Misplaced-Altered-Illegible Documents," "Hyatt Disaster—Corporate Liability for Punitive Damages," and the subtle but intriguing "Don Hall 12/12/79."[11] We found correspondence from Gordon to countless recipients, as well as lengthy notes on yellow, legal-sized, lined paper in his own hand, scattered hither and yon. The collection was what Andy had purported, and to the practiced eyes of professionals all of it related directly to the Hyatt lawsuit. That fact alone made it valuable to the mission of the library's special collections: the preservation of Kansas City history. A decision came quickly. I conditionally agreed on the spot to take the collection as it was, but we made another appointment to return with a larger crew, more boxes, and a pickup truck and trailer to haul them away.

As a senior manager, I realized that I needed a sign-off from my superiors before this was a done deal. I went immediately to the top, to Crosby Kemper III, the director of the Kansas City Public Library.[12] Kemper had hired me to head the special collections with the mandate of "grow the collections," and I had gladly obliged. In a recent undertaking I had gathered the resources to save the extensive Kansas City Stockyards collection from its off-site storage hell and finish its cataloging and processing. The papers from the very company that defined Kansas City as the classic "cowtown" were now open to scholars. In the past few years I had acquired a number of large archival collections from other iconic Kansas City institutions: the Savoy Hotel and Grill, which before its closure had boasted its claim as the city's oldest restaurant; the Kansas City Club, where an all-male membership for years had moved and shook the city's governance until the fashion for such organizations changed; the Kansas City Athenaeum, at one time the nation's fifth-largest women's organization and where the wives of the aforementioned club members carried out their gender-defined civic duties; and finally, the Folly Theater, a midcentury burlesque house turned X-rated movie theater, which earned later respectability as a carefully restored, modern performing arts center. That last collection came with a huge cache of stripper photos, a great treasure but a future problem, I anticipated, when it came time to create a digital collection open to all on the library's website. That concern now paled in comparison because I understood that, by taking the Gordon collection, the library and I could face great pushback by local powers-that-be.

I did not fear so much the reaction from the public than from the still very much alive Don Hall Sr., the Hallmark corporation, and the Hall Family Foundation, a major contributor to Kansas City's nonprofits. This was especially relevant because the foundation was a major funder of the library. How would these entities take it if the library accepted the papers of an apparent major critic, expended great resources to preserve and promote that collection, and made its potentially embarrassing contents accessible to the general public? I did my due diligence and gently pointed out this minefield to Kemper, who saw no problem with the acquisition if its disposition was handled correctly and fairly.

Kemper reached that decision naturally. As a member of the Kemper banking family, a longtime midwestern force to be reckoned with, he could stand toe-to-toe with any member of any other Kansas City first family. As the experienced director of a five-star urban library that played a huge role as an arbiter of civic engagement, he knew how to steer a middle course between a donor's desires and the free flow of information to the public. It also helped that he truly loved all aspects of Kansas City history, and he instantly grasped the significance of the Gordon collection. It must be saved. I assured him that I would indeed step lightly, but I left the meeting wondering how exactly I would do that.

It took two trips to pack and move the Gordon collection. Kate Hill and I came with two more archivists, Kara Evans and Joanna Marsh, and two hundred archival-quality banker boxes, each capable of holding one cubic foot of closely packed material. We set to work, bent and folded each heavy, flat, corrugated board into its final shape, opened the miscellany of Gordon containers, grabbed handfuls of paper, and packed them away, a repetitive yet methodical set of steps in this reboxing process. Working in the garage, open to the elements, each of us had dressed for the cool October weather in an assortment of sweaters, sweatshirts, and hoodies and, in turn, shed layers as the work progressed. One of the three millennials asked the rhetorical question of how this type of labor related to her advanced degree in history, library science, or what-have-you. A boomer myself, I had no good answer. "Good for the soul perhaps," I thought. The job took two three-hour-plus sessions, only interrupted by Andy occasionally checking on our progress and a crew from the library's facilities department. The crew members arrived toward the end of each session, loaded up the treasure, and drove off. The freight totaled 180 boxes.[13]

I had directed my colleagues beforehand to keep their eyes open during the excavations for one particular nugget—Robert Gordon's supposed book manuscript. In time a likely document turned up, a eureka moment given the mass of material in which it was concealed. The manuscript took the unassuming form of a spiral-bound typescript, which I eagerly opened to the title page, "When They Didn't Care Enough." Gordon's title, I immediately recognized, was a tortured play on words of Hallmark's famed greeting card slogan, "When you care enough to send the very best." By now I realized one thing about Gordon's personality—he took every opportunity to poke the bear.

I set the prize aside, not wanting to misplace it among all those identical white boxes. After all the earlier library research and the field trips handling the donation, the manuscript promised to be revealing reading, although until that time came, its literary and historical value remained questionable. How good could it really be if it was never published?

The realization soon came that the Gordon collection, his legacy to history, was something less than a successful lawyer's case files and more a struggling author's research files. And as I slowly learned the collection's secrets, I understood why "When They Didn't Care Enough"—later retitled "House of Cards"—struggled to see the publishing light of day.

The reasons were more complex than ones of profit and loss and the whims of the marketplace. The papers found in the Gordon collection, it turned out, were more important than a massive testament to a forgotten book project. Gordon had gathered and his heirs had bequeathed to the world nothing less than a new narrative for the Hallmark hotel disaster, its prelude and aftermath, and its causes, which were never fully explained. Although he had ample opportunities and expended great energy in his own peculiar, obsessive way, Gordon never revealed that untold narrative to the public, and his effort became a lesson to me on how difficult it is for the truth to come out. The purpose of *Skywalks*, the book whose genesis arose from the secrets in that archival collection, has been to rectify that oversight and to tell—finally—Robert Gordon's story.

1

The Tapes

After a grueling court hearing on October 5, 1982, followed by a long walk to decompress, Robert Gordon returned to his law office in the early evening only to find two cardboard boxes left by the door. Scrawled on each in black lettering was "HALLMARK DOCUMENTS." Gordon moved the boxes inside and opened one, and in his "usual contrarian manner" started with the contents on the bottom. He spotted a large, manila envelope, ripped it open, and found two tapes, one labeled "11-13-79 Meeting. Problems with the Atrium." The "problem," Gordon knew, was the massive collapse of the atrium roof at Hallmark's new Kansas City hotel in October 1979, less than two years before the 1981 skywalks disaster. He took the precious tape to a cassette player, inserted it, and pressed play. "The clarity was not great," he later remembered, but he could identify some voices, one being Hallmark Cards corporate lawyer Judith Whittaker and her "high pitched nasal tone." When the quality deteriorated further, he stopped the tape, turned it over, and listened again. He heard a quiet voice say—what exactly? "I would have sworn that I heard the skywalks being discussed," he explained. Both tapes were difficult to decipher, so he turned instead to the hundreds of pieces of paper he termed "unbelievable documents." Totally engrossed in his discoveries, by the time Gordon stopped to collect himself and really reflect on what he had heard and read, it was midmorning the next day.[1]

It was not just Whittaker's voice that grated on Gordon but the evidence he held in his hand, documents that disputed her recent deposition testimony under oath about this particular 1979 meeting. She had been asked about details of that specific meeting, held in the aftermath of the atrium roof collapse at the Hyatt Regency Kansas City, and had claimed, "I don't know. I don't recall." Yet Gordon had her handwritten notes on the collapse before him. She also had been asked if a tape recorder had been used and had answered, "Not that I recall," but he held an actual tape from that meeting. As colead counsel for the plaintiffs suing the Hallmark corporation in the *Federal Skywalk Cases*, Gordon immediately grasped how contradictory and devastating this evidence was against her and Hallmark, the hotel owner. The people responsible for building the hotel and opening it to the public had largely ignored the safety warnings that the roof collapse had flashed. The question of willful negligence that led to the skywalks disaster seemed to have been answered, at least to Gordon's satisfaction. It was premature, but victory seemed in sight.

Gordon, his legal team, and its predecessors had fought many "discovery battles" to reach this point. The initial request for the production of documents, including "sound recordings," had been filed on behalf of all state and federal court plaintiffs long ago in August 1981, only a month after the skywalks collapse. When the federal class, the group of victims that Gordon represented, was certified in January 1982, Gordon picked up the discovery baton but immediately hit a brick wall. He was not getting what he knew in his gut existed. In March his team asked for sanctions against the defense for its alleged failure to disclose documents. No sanctions followed after Irving Younger, the lead counsel for the plaintiffs in the federal case, held the motion in abeyance, in part after Hallmark reluctantly agreed to participate in depositions while awaiting an appellate court decision on the class certification. When the first federal court date (August 15) came and went, Hallmark again became recalcitrant. Gordon revived the sanctions motion in September with an eighty-six-page brief that forced the issue. And he piled on. "For the first time in this litigation," when met with resistance, "we adjourned a deposition and brought to the Court's immediate attention defendant's obstructionist behavior." It worked. Judge Scott O. Wright, who oversaw the *Federal Skywalk Cases*, responded angrily and threateningly, and Hallmark coughed up more records, including the all-important atrium roof collapse documents. Gordon concluded that the tapes turned up when they did because of his recent pressure.[2] Later he suspected that it was because he or the other plaintiffs' lawyers were about to stumble upon their existence anyway in upcoming depositions.

In an October 11, 1982, court hearing, which Gordon saw as "the crucial event in the skywalks saga," he gleefully brought to an astonished Judge Wright the news of the eleventh-hour document dump, "a thousand contemporaneous documents and two highly incriminating tape recordings" involving the atrium roof collapse. The *Kansas City Times* placed Gordon center stage in the drama. The attorney's accusations made the paper's evening edition: "Robert Gordon . . . said Hallmark should have disclosed the tapes' existence in January [1982], but he added the plaintiffs only learned of the tapes last week." Wright immediately understood the potential damage posed by the recordings. "This is a tape of everybody sitting around talking about how this thing [the atrium roof] fell, what caused it to fall, who was at fault and the whole bit." The "very upset" judge seemed angry enough that he might abruptly "strike the defense," or in other words "bar Hallmark . . . from presenting any defense in the federal skywalk cases" and declare a default judgment in favor of the plaintiffs.[3] Total victory.

The tapes possessed all the drama and consequence of a fictional "Perry Mason moment," the unexpected appearance of new evidence that definitively changes the outcome of the proceedings. Due to their lack of audio clarity, however, the related written documents made a more tangible, understandable, and immediate impact.[4] One such bombshell was an eleven-page memo written from notes about a meeting previously unknown to the plaintiffs held on October 19, 1979. Hallmark had called that meeting five days after the atrium roof collapse. Its author was the heretofore unknown—at least to Gordon and the plaintiffs—Pam Wight Curran, a former junior lawyer employed by Hallmark who served as the secretary of the critical meeting. More importantly, Curran also operated the tape recorder. Where had this witness been hiding all these months?[5] Another fact not lost on Gordon and Wright was that of the ten known witnesses present during the convening and taping of the November 13, 1979, meeting, nine had already been deposed for the *Federal Skywalk Cases*, and not one had mentioned Curran (who was also the spouse of a Hallmark executive) or her obviously conspicuous cassette recorder. Oops.

The testimony of Dick Heydinger, Hallmark's risk manager and the person responsible for seeing that the large, private corporation was properly insured, was most certainly impeached. When asked under oath at his deposition about this particular meeting, he could not even remember attending. He was also asked, "You say that quite frequently, that you don't recall things. Is there a problem with your memory?" His answer: "I don't recall." Yet the tape of that meeting indicated his active involvement, a setting where "he repeatedly interjected himself." To any but a partisan, his credibility was shot. With the surfacing of this new evidence and the threat of perjury staring him in the face, Heydinger's "lobotomized testimony," as Gordon termed it, would improve at the trial, rescheduled for January 1983.[6]

All that nonsense could be sorted out later, including whether Whittaker, Curran's boss, had perjured herself during her deposition. Right now this newly discovered memo about a meeting called to discuss the Hyatt hotel's "structural strength" prompted Gordon to conclude that "someone must have recognized the link between the design deficiencies in the roof connections and the possibility of design defects in the skywalks' connections."[7] Getting that unvarnished point before the public became more difficult after Hallmark officials hastily put together a press conference on the same day as the October court hearing and peremptorily released the incriminating tapes and documents. This puzzled the gathered reporters who had not covered the hearing earlier in the day, and the import of the materials was mostly lost on them. Hallmark succeeded in taking command of the story, downplayed the embarrassing news, and dealt Gordon's team a public relations blow. Up to this point, both he and the press were in the same boat, but only Gordon acknowledged it. "Hallmark had deceived all of us for over a year about what the victims' side considered the most important piece of evidence in the case," referring to the meeting tape.[8] In a couple of days Hallmark formally replied to a Gordon brief that had accompanied his court appearance. Attorney Whittaker still swore she was unaware of the recording or the tapes and that she had not read the related scribblings of her underling or other meeting participants who worked for Hallmark, even though, as Gordon knew very well, she herself had personally held the company's file labeled "Atrium of Hyatt—Collapse File."[9]

These denials by the defense seemed barely credible if one only took into account the practical aspects of the tape recorder in question. It was about seven and a half inches by five inches and nearly two inches thick and took a full-size cassette, about the size, Gordon estimated, of a paperback copy of the fat novel *Gone with the Wind*. One Hallmark lawyer dismissed the five-pound machine as no bigger than a pack of cigarettes, but from these dimensions it more closely resembled the size of a cigar box, in other words, something eminently noticeable.[10] During the meeting Curran had located it strategically on the conference table in order to pick up all voices. The kicker was the fact that the critical cassette tape had been recorded on both sides, and that obviously meant a manual, noisy switch-over in the middle of the group discussion. Yet Hallmark representatives maintained that no one had noticed the recording device for two and a half hours.

The local paper had a lot of new developments to digest, but Gordon expected its investigative team, with his assistance, to drop one last bombshell before the end of October. As he understood it, an in-depth piece being prepared would focus solely on Hallmark, the atrium roof collapse, and the new evidence that he would gladly interpret, which he spent considerable time doing. He assumed the article would include photographs of the atrium roof collapse and its bad connections, quotes from the recent documents that mentioned the related dangers of the skywalks, and memos about the attempt to hold down expenses at all costs.[11] It would be comparable to the paper's damaging investigative series on the Hyatt Corporation, the manager of Hallmark's hotel, published months before, and would similarly pull no punches.[12]

The end of October came and went, however, without this or any other shoe dropping, delayed perhaps because of the city's beatification of the legendary Joyce "J. C." Hall, Hallmark's founder and longtime leader, long retired, who died on October 29 at age ninety-two. "In lieu of photos of the first collapse at the Hyatt," recalled Gordon, "I stared at headlines like . . . 'Hallmark grew with KC into an American Dream-come-true.'" Other breathless banners were "Joyce C. Hall: A Mortal Man in the Realm of Myth" and "Associates Recall Hall's Unfailing Moral Integrity."[13] The text was no less laudatory of Hallmark: "Try to think of us without them." At the conclusion of one testimonial a bare mention was made of the controversy at hand: "It was a matter of tragic irony that the Hyatt Regency hotel disaster should have marred Joyce Hall's greatest visible gift to Kansas City, the Crown Center complex. But it is a measure of Kansas City's esteem for Joyce Hall that he will be associated not with the tragedy but remembered as a clever, industrious man who became the greeting-card king and, ultimately, a Kansas City institution."[14]

In the few months remaining before trial, Hallmark never suffered anything like the earlier investigative report that the Hyatt Corporation endured, and Gordon later concluded, maybe with some justification, that the ill-timed story about the company's shortcomings was intentionally spiked.[15] Whatever the case, it was another well-timed, if unplanned, public relations coup for Hallmark.

Gordon had no time to dwell on yet another hiccup with the press. Too much legal work had to be finished in November with but two more months to trial. The outlines of the trial arguments were clearly drawn. In a nutshell Hallmark held the position that it had no reason to suspect any problems existed in the skywalks or their structural support connections prior to July 17, 1981. Hallmark intended to portray itself as "just a passive investor" in the project.[16] This defense paled in comparison to the story the plaintiffs' lawyers planned to lay before the jury, detailing what *Hallmark did not do*: After the 1979 atrium roof collapse, Hallmark did not stop its "fast-tracking" method of building construction. Hallmark did not find outside professionals "who were competent, experienced, independent, and adequately remunerated for investigating, inspecting, calculating, and checking everything in the skywalks, especially in their connections." Hallmark did not find or fix the structural defects that would have been obvious to any qualified outsider. Hallmark did not load-test the skywalks either before or after the red flags raised after the roof collapse. On the other hand, what did Hallmark, which had "complete and absolute control" of the project, end up doing? Hallmark put budgets and schedules before caution. Hallmark took a calculated risk with the safety of its building and guests, covered in part by risk manager Heydinger cynically taking out additional insurance after the roof collapse. After the lawsuits came quickly and furiously, Hallmark broke the rules by delaying, obstructing, and in many instances stifling discovery completely. Hard questions by the plaintiffs' lawyers undoubtedly awaited Don Hall, Hallmark's chief executive officer and successor to his venerated father, Joyce, and his underlings at the upcoming trial. The questioning would be even sharper after the recent surfacing of damaging evidence.[17]

Make no mistake, Gordon wanted to go to trial, unless, of course, an exasperated Judge Wright drew the contest to a close and issued a summary judgment in the class's favor. On the other hand, Irving Younger and Paul Wolff, Gordon's allies on the plaintiffs' team and both affiliated with the famed Washington DC law firm of Williams & Connolly, showed little inclination for combat, although they now enjoyed the greater leverage to exert over the defendants that Gordon's research supplied. But what were they doing with it? The midwestern workhorse again accused the pair of East Coast thoroughbreds of not going all out: "Not a single document, not a single exhibit, not a single witness, not a single fact about the Skywalks itself has come from your firm's 'thousands of hours.'" He accused Wolff of what others had uttered earlier: "You have often done just about everything possible to create the impression that, indeed, you and Irving are just in this case for a quick settlement and a fast buck." He later confided to friend and mentor Arthur Miller, the notable Harvard jurist, "I have handled this without [Younger]. . . . He hasn't been here for six months. What a mistake he was."[18]

With or without Younger and Wolff's vigorous participation, Hallmark appeared to be cornered and on the ropes.[19] Perhaps it came as no real surprise that their lawyers slow-walked turning over the original tapes to Williams & Connolly until late November. The Washington lawyers immediately relayed the "hard to hear" tapes to Halvorson & Associates, a DC-area firm with a most relevant résumé. Robert H. Halvorson had enhanced Richard Nixon's Watergate tapes to make them audible for prosecutors, and if he hurried, the renowned audio expert might be expected to achieve similarly spectacular results in time for the trial.[20] What a bombshell that would be!

For his part Gordon continued on what he believed was a proven, successful plan of attack. He spent the better part of a month working on a follow-up sanctions report for the court, an expansion of his September 24 report and October 11 brief.[21] This would be, he knew, his magnum opus of pretrial writings, and on December 3, he did just that when he filed his sole-authored "Supplemental Points and Authorities Regarding Plaintiffs' Pending Rule 37 Motion."[22]

The *Kansas City Times* reported the next day on Gordon's brief, and how it did so should have alerted him to impending danger. John Dauner, the lone reporter covering the December 3 hearing, got a copy of the document and took it to his editor, who alerted Bill Johnson, Hallmark's head of public relations and main mouthpiece, all of which Gordon learned about well after the fact. Before Gordon ever got home that evening, he had calls from Dauner awaiting him, which he obligingly returned because, as he recalled in a moment of self-reflection, he worried that his brief had "obscured some basic points by overdocumentation." (This was an understatement.) He agreed to meet the reporter that night at his home.[23]

The next day's story was lengthy but underwhelming, far from damning to Hallmark, and greatly disappointing to Gordon. The headline focused on his seeking sanctions, and the story's lede, "The owners . . . should be denied the right to defend themselves," also rather missed the bigger point. Gordon's "sharply worded" text was disposed of as "a litany of allegations" made by a solitary lawyer. It carried a couple of blistering quotes from the brief but glided over his voluminous evidence of evasion. The motivations of the messenger, as perceived by the paper, cast an unnecessary shadow over the contents of his message. Hallmark's extensive response, Gordon thought, read more like a PR statement, and the article offered no follow-up comment from him or any of the principals on the plaintiffs' side.[24] So much for late-night consultations. Gordon probably felt like the author whose greatest work had been unread or, worse, read but misinterpreted. But the status of the *Federal Skywalk Cases*, more important than Gordon's hurt feelings, only became worse. Hallmark had its own bombshell to drop.

2

Molly Riley, a Class Act

Molly Riley lost her purse that night at the Hyatt, July 17, 1981. It contained her car keys, house key, wallet, credit cards, glasses case, and a pack of cigarettes. While waiting for her friend Gaye (Noland) Young to arrive at the dance, she had only smoked two and had used her limited amount of cash to buy three drink tickets to last the evening. Molly went to one of the seven lobby bars and exchanged the first for a glass of champagne, which, like beer and soft drinks, cost a dollar.[1]

It was the first time Molly had ever attended a Friday night "tea dance" at Kansas City's Hyatt Regency hotel, although to be fair the first ever had been held just two months before. The thirty-three-year-old divorced mother of two-year-old Matthew, exhausted from a long, hard week as a registered nurse, looked forward to an early start on her weekend. Her son safely with Molly's mother, the night promised to be a welcome respite from work and childcare, a chance "to dance and visit." As she entered the hotel at 5 p.m., she entered a spacious lobby area, fifty feet high with seventeen thousand square feet of floor space, much of it devoted to the tea dancers. She encountered a typical crowd for the popular event, older early birds dressed formally, the men in jackets and ties, the women in longer dresses. For a city in which African Americans made up a quarter of the population, the crowd of dancers was lily white. Once the after-work crowd showed up, the demographic trended younger, single, and still white, and people came in groups. Regulars may have been wearing their hotel-issued "I am a tea dance regular" button. It was "the place to be in Kansas City."[2]

For a hot night's breezy, light-hearted entertainment, the Hyatt dance faced limited competition. At the movies Burt Reynolds's summer blockbuster *The Cannonball Run* was doing good box office in area theaters, as well as across the country, as was the more urbane *For Your Eyes Only*, the latest James Bond entry starring Roger Moore as agent 007. Bill Murray, a recent graduate from TV's *Saturday Night Live* was transitioning to male lead in the comedy *Stripes* ("That's a fact, Jack!"), and Brooke Shields starred in the teenage romance *Endless Love*, which obviously appealed to a younger crowd than the average tea dancer. Homebodies could amuse themselves with that summer's craze—Rubik's Cube—the maddening plastic puzzle with its almost limitless twists and turns required to get the scrambled sides right with the world. The popular, fun-for-all-ages toy might have served as an apt metaphor for the aftermath of July 17, 1981.

For the more cultured, the summer season at Starlight, Kansas City's renowned outdoor theater venue, was in full swing. Roberta Flack was in the middle of a three-night singing gig after being a last-minute substitute for "The Way We Were" composer Marvin Hamlisch. On Monday the musical *Oliver!* was set to open with actor Christian Slater, age eleven, in the title role, four years before his movie debut.

Royals Stadium was a ghost town, not because the Major League baseball team was out of town but because the players had been out on strike since June 12. That explained why Rich Gale, one of the team's starting pitchers, was working as a bartender in the hotel—that and the fact that he earned a modest salary before the era of sports millionaires.[3] Happily for local sports fans, the Chiefs, the National Football League team, started practice on this particular day at William Jewell College, a short drive away in Liberty, Missouri. Like the Hyatt tea dances, Chief two-a-days were free, fun, and open to all.

Kansas City was on a roll, the culmination of thirty-plus years of postwar economic development. The timeline for the seventies was punctuated by notable civic achievements that would make any midwestern metropolis proud. In 1972 a new municipal airport came on line. Kansas

City International boasted an innovative layout of three "drive-to-your-plane" terminals. The Kansas City metro area, whose population fell out of the top twenty in the national ranking after the 1970 U.S. Census, was still a four-sport Major League city. The professional baseball and football teams moved in 1973 from the decrepit downtown stadium they shared to the beautiful, cutting-edge Truman Sports Complex in the sprawling suburbs. The move paid off in 1980 when the Kansas City Royals hosted the franchise's first World Series. The Kansas City Chiefs, located in the adjacent Arrowhead Stadium, were expected to follow their neighbor's winning ways. Kemper Arena, completed in 1974, the home of the National Basketball Association's Kansas City Kings and, for a while, the Scouts of the National Hockey League, served as ground zero for the 1976 Republican Convention. The modern-looking building and winner of several architectural design awards drew raves for its lack of interior columns and unobstructed views due to large exterior steel trusses from which its roof was suspended. For four days the indoor arena and, by extension, the city were in the national spotlight during this historic event, the last contested presidential convention in modern times, and all went swimmingly during the occasion, a booster's dream. Providentially, no one was in the Kemper, which sat seventeen thousand, on the evening of June 4, 1979, when its space-age roof collapsed.[4] This man-made disaster embarrassed the locals but did little to tamp down the decade's boosterism, although going into the 1980s it should have served as a warning to the city fathers about their infrastructure.

The new decade, one could only believe, would see more such advancements, and the Hyatt Regency Kansas City qualified as one. The Hyatt joined two big hotels that had opened in the last decade, and its 733 "deluxe" rooms would surely translate into more convention business for the city. For the metro area, the Hyatt's workforce of nine hundred newly hired employees equated to a medium-sized company moving to town. But this hotel meant more than economic development. "Since the openings of large, luxury hotels are few and far between," opined a *Kansas City Star* editor in July 1980, "they always generate glamour and a special excitement of their own."[5]

Molly Riley witnessed this excitement herself as she asked directions for the gift shop, bought some matches, and settled into a nearby seat to have a smoke and people-watch, especially the dancers in the spacious atrium lobby. She recalled passing the time with some people sitting nearby as she waited for Gaye. In the next couple of hours, the gregarious Molly talked to Gary Morton, who was a bartender at the event, Dianne and Ed Welch, who survived the night, and Mark Williams, the last person to be found alive under the skywalk rubble. Williams, whose father was a personal injury attorney, filed the first damage suit in the aftermath and settled before the end of the year for a figure between $2.2 and $3 million.[6] Molly also talked to Jacqueline S. "Jackie" Brooks, Williams's date, who was also at her first tea dance. Brooks, whose career goal was to work in the hotel industry, was there to celebrate with Williams the job she had just landed with the Hilton company. Before leaving for the dance, she had told her mother, "Mom, I'll bet you wish you could go, too." The twenty-four-year-old was killed in the collapse, her body nestled next to Williams. Molly would later remember the flowers in her hair.[7]

After Gaye's arrival, the two moved about the hotel and continued to mingle with their fellow revelers. They both spent time on the second-floor skywalk looking at the dancers below before returning to the first floor in hopes of finding an empty table underneath. Failing that, they moved across the lobby in another futile search, hopeless in the standing-room-only mass. About seven o'clock, still early, Molly and Gaye decided to leave and retraced their way toward the elevated walkways. Riley had just laid an empty drink on a table under the skywalks, turned away, and headed slowly toward the hotel exit:

> I was facing the dance floor, watching the dance contest. Suddenly there was a tremendous swirling wind that had glass and other things in it. I remember feeling a sense that something dreadful was happening. I couldn't open my eyes. I was propelled forward and down. I heard people screaming. Finally, I heard an unbelievably loud, horrible sound. That's all I remember, except that I remember trying to open my eyes, and I could not. And then there was silence.

> I don't remember exactly, for a few minutes, but when I was able to look around, I looked back to where I had been standing, and it appeared as if everyone behind me had been killed. Both skywalks were on the ground. There were pieces of people coming out from under the debris. There was blood. There were people caught in between the skywalks, and I believed at that moment that my best friend and, indeed, everyone behind me, was dead.[8]

In due course, as time stood still, she took stock of her own injuries: "I had tremendous neck pains, back pain. I had a headache. I was extremely nauseated. I had cuts on my left leg, cuts and glass on the bottom of my feet and my knee. I had small cuts from glass in my hair, and I was covered with glass and silt."[9] Later these would be termed by those who were not there as "small dollar amount injuries."[10]

To her satisfaction, "I realized, once I was able to turn, that I was alive. . . . I was moving. I didn't think about anything else." But think she did. Immediately her nurse's training kicked in as she shifted reflexively from victim to rescuer. "I grieved momentarily for Gaye because I fully believed that she was dead, and then I did what came naturally, and that was to try to help the people that were injured and dying."[11] Four hours elapsed before Molly left the hotel, at which point "the injured, for the most part, had been taken to hospitals. There were seven that I knew of that had become trapped, and no patients coming out, and we knew it would be a while until they got the seven free, so I felt that there were adequate medical staff to care for the seven, and I felt that I could leave."[12]

Now the professional caregiver had to care for herself. An ambulance driver took the worn-out nurse to St. Joseph's Hospital, a couple miles away. She felt terrible, her eyes bothered her, and she thought that she still had glass in them. Her head hurt, her knees and feet were bleeding, and tremors had commenced. The driver helped Molly make it through the hospital entrance, where a patient-care aide sat her down and checked her into the emergency room. "I was in a daze," she recalled. "Everything I was wearing was ruined. My dress was covered with blood, my slip, my hose were torn from the glass, and they were full of blood." Her attending physician wanted her to stay overnight, but Molly refused. "I was very upset. . . . I was frightened. I wanted to go home." She called her brother Sean, who picked her up and took her home to Prairie Village, a modest suburb across the state line in Kansas. The lost house key meant that they had to break into her house, a trifling yet another upsetting moment. "I was frightened. I asked him to stay with me for a while. I turned on all of the lights I could find."[13] By now Friday night had turned into the wee hours of Saturday morning.

Coincidentally, it was Riley's day off from work, and she spent it in bed. "I didn't sleep at all."[14] She worried about her car, abandoned at the hotel. It might get towed, so she had her brother Sean retrieve it. It was another expense due to her lost keys because it required calling a costly locksmith to the scene. She had a date that night with a hospital pharmacist. She canceled it. On Sunday, which was a scheduled workday, she again stayed in bed; it was the only time she ever missed work because of her injuries, mental or physical, suffered at the Hyatt. During the day she pulled herself together and made at least two calls, one to her parents, the other to Bill Whitaker, an attorney she knew. Molly Riley, a victim and rescuer, was about to become a crusader.

If she was looking for a personal injury lawyer, William P. Whitaker might not have been the ideal choice, but he was the lawyer she knew and trusted. He had done some legal work for her a few years before, and before that they had even gone on two or three dates. A graduate of the Wharton School of the University of Pennsylvania, where he majored in economics, and the law school of the University of Missouri–Kansas City, in later years Whitaker combined the two fields and became a noted local entrepreneur and general counsel. He ran a series of biotechnology start-ups that he helped found.[15] If not as her lawyer, Whitaker could at least serve as a trusted advisor and recommend the right attorney.

What Riley wanted "first of all" and for years to come was to use legal means to "punish those people responsible." Her secondary concern was the recovery of damages, those that related to her physical and mental well-being. She came to appreciate the concept of punitive damages assessed against those responsible for the "killing and mutilating of all of the people that were involved."[16] Later, while being hammered under oath by aggressive inquisitors, intent on tripping her up, she would never mince words about her motivations.

Meeting over lunch early the following week, Whitaker and Riley discussed the best way to handle a lawsuit. He knew an attorney who specialized in class-action law work on the behalf of large groups of victims, someone experienced with determining responsibility, assigning blame, exacting punishment, and squeezing damages from corporate malefactors. His name was Robert Gordon. He was a Kansas City lawyer, and coincidentally Gordon and Whitaker shared an office suite as partners.

Prepped by Whitaker, who put the notion of a class action in his head, Gordon welcomed Riley to his office later in the week. Although they had spoken on the phone earlier, Gordon heard her story again.[17] He remembered meeting a small woman with reddish hair and green eyes that darted "here and there." As with their earlier, brief conversation, Molly chattered eagerly and when face-to-face leaned toward Gordon "as a conspirator might, telling you what *really* happened that night."[18]

It was a grim story. After the skywalks fell, the swirling dust forced Molly to keep her eyes shut. She thought to herself, "I want to hold Matthew [her son] just once more." When she opened her eyes and turned to the rubble, she saw the bodies and the blood. She thought, "I'm a nurse; they need me." She went over to one of the bodies, still living, whom she named "The Girl in Pink." Trapped from the waist down, the young woman faced the floor and had trouble breathing. Blood streamed down her face, further impeding respiration. Molly and Phyllis Banks, another tea dancer and a fellow nurse whom Molly knew, took turns holding her head while rescuers worked frantically to free her. At 8:09 p.m. she was carried to the hotel's convention exhibit hall, which served that night as an emergency medical center. "The Girl in Pink" turned out to be Sally Firestone, who survived, although her injuries left her paralyzed for life.[19]

Molly saw chunks of people—arms, legs, gray hair attached to crushed skulls, brain matter, a severed head. She witnessed doctors amputating a victim's leg with a chainsaw. A lifeless body passed by her on a stretcher, the battered face covered with a cocktail napkin. "I was shocked at what this thing could do to the human body," she said. Shock turned to joy and relief when she later spotted Gaye outside the hotel, standing behind a police line. Blood poured down the face of her friend, the matron of honor at her wedding, but she lived.[20]

Molly was the first Hyatt eyewitness with whom Gordon had met and spoken, and although her physical wounds might have appeared superficial, her experiences were deep and damaging. This initial, private encounter impressed Gordon profoundly, maybe because Molly was equal parts rescuer and victim. That dual role carried far more weight with him, one suspects, than even the tidal wave of stories that poured from the newsrooms of the local media.

IN THE TRAGEDY'S IMMEDIATE AFTERMATH, THE MORNING *KANSAS City Times* and the afternoon *Kansas City Star*, the city's somewhat bizarre, double-entity but singly owned newspapers of record, took the lead. They shared the same quarters, the same publisher, and the same point of view. The rivalry between the two papers and their separate staffs of journalists more resembled that of two gentlemanly English cricket clubs than the cutthroat competition of a "Front Page" pack of reporters. Together the dailies devoted vast amounts of column inches to the Hyatt story in the week between the disaster and the Gordon-Riley meeting, and like the majority of their readers, Gordon had no direct connection to the event, but he was a voracious and close reader of current events. Bringing his own outlook as a member of the bar and of Kansas City society, certain details in the hundreds of pages of newsprint would have jumped out and given him pause, if nothing more than to file away for later reference in his exceptional memory.[21]

Before Gordon met Riley, the *Kansas City Times*, beginning with its Saturday morning edition, published six issues containing Hyatt news, as did the *Star*. The latter did not put out a Saturday issue but carried the banner for the huge, two-hundred-page-plus Sunday, July 19 paper. Although the separate staffs immediately pooled resources to cover the largest local story in decades, little redundancy appeared in the cascade of stories. As is still the case today in a world of fractured news media, the departments of the local television stations routinely followed the lead set by their cousins in print. If all Gordon knew was what he read in the papers, to paraphrase Will Rogers's old saw, then he knew a lot about what happened on July 17. But he could not have helped having further questions. And he did.

The community, meanwhile, found itself in the midst of a legal frenzy. The Hyatt disaster lured lawyers to the scene as quickly as their finned counterparts to bloody chum. "Kansas City lawyers specializing in personal injury work said they expect their phones to start ringing early Monday morning," reported the morning newspaper on Monday, July 20. One of those lawyers was Lantz Welch. A local personal injury lawyer, Welch was never shy around reporters. He warned hospitalized victims to beware of early contact with adjusters, a privilege enjoyed by representatives of insurance companies and an advantage not shared with law firms. In those naive, ethical years, lawyers were prevented from advertising their services to the public. They were barred from gigantic, garish billboards along busy highways and loud pitches during late-night television shows. Welch, who danced around the ethical edges, contended: "The argument they [the insurance companies] present to the bereaved is, 'Why should you give up one-third of what you have coming to some lawyer?' But the key is: Who knows what a victim has coming? . . . No one really knows." The quotable attorney, however, may have had a clue on a monetary figure, as did the newspaper, which anticipated "a rush of lawsuits" to total in the "hundreds of millions of dollars." To no one's surprise, Welch joined in the rush and ended up with twenty-five victims as clients. He was only beginning to get his name in the paper.[22]

At Truman Medical Center in Kansas City, where fifteen Hyatt victims remained hospitalized, an official reported: "Jim Bartimus of the Lantz Welch law firm in Kansas City was distributing a letter [noted elsewhere as a 'witness information form'] to the injured asking if they would be able to furnish information. . . . A number of our patients complained and said they did not wish to be approached. He didn't have our permission, so we asked him to leave."

Bartimus admitted to a reporter that he passed out the forms but denied that he was asked to leave the hospital. Not to put too fine a point on the account, by the time the administrator arrived on the scene, Bartimus had already finished passing out the forms and was voluntarily leaving the hospital. Welch, quoted again in the paper, "believed that what his associate did not only was proper, but essential to the case," adding, "I don't think it is anyone's business how I conduct my investigation as long as I don't disrupt their hospital. That's what being a lawyer is all about." This was an old dodge—looking for "witnesses." It was a means for the ethically challenged to get around the prohibition of direct, hard-sell advertising for clients. Welch and company soon expanded their efforts to the newspapers themselves by placing a small but impossible-to-miss ad that ran in both Kansas City papers for six days, headlined in all-caps "EYEWITNESSES—HYATT REGENCY." Responded Welch to a reporter's raised eyebrow, "I'm advertising because I believe very strongly in investigation. . . . If a lawyer is not very careful in the way he gathers information, he could be accused of being an ambulance chaser. I don't intend to have that happen."[23] This outlandish statement probably made Gordon laugh out loud over his morning coffee.

Within a week a *Kansas City Times* columnist laid bare the situation, what he termed "disaster's unhappy aftermath": "Now the Hyatt is a magnet for something else. The accident, quite simply, is attracting vultures. Out-of-town and hometown lawyers alike have become visible after the disaster and are expecting clients from among the injured and survivors of the dead. With the promise of huge lawsuits and million-dollar settlements, there can be no doubt that the Hyatt Regency hotel disaster will prove to be an enormous financial windfall to many members of the legal profession."[24] On Thursday alone, three more lawsuits, to the tune of $10 million, $5 million, and $4 million, were filed in Jackson County Circuit Court in Kansas City.[25]

In Gordon's "cast of characters" for his later narrative, he made a great distinction between him and the Welches of the world. He never considered himself one of these mercenaries, later stating unequivocally, "My involvement with this disaster was in the courtrooms and not in the hospital rooms." Although Welch came off as something of a court jester in the subsequent legal jousting and in Gordon's version of events, his firm later received its own windfall, a significant cut of a dramatic, $15 million settlement for one of the Hyatt's most egregiously injured survivors.[26]

Others besides Welch commented about what to expect. Philip H. Corboy, a renowned Chicago rainmaker who specialized in high-dollar personal injury cases, gave an outsider's unvarnished take on the upcoming legal process: "Disaster cases filed in federal courts around the country are usually consolidated, just for the purpose of discovery—the pretrial activity on the part of the lawyers to find out what happened, what the damages are, and what the case is worth."

Here was Corboy's money quote: "About 90 percent of them eventually settle out." He spoke from experience as the legal representative for several families after a 1979 airplane crash that claimed three hundred victims. According to his scenario, one case would eventually decide liability. That would be easy in the Hyatt case: "What you have there ... somebody did something wrong." After that, the "fault percentages" and the sum of "contributions" by the defendants would be worked out. That task would be harder: "Defendants will eventually try to supply to the jury the computer way of providing damages. They will try to make it a cold, calculating unilateral exercise in adding up figures.... The plaintiff's lawyer has a completely different job.... [T]he real job is to show that a human life has been taken."

At some point the defendants would start to make settlement offers to the plaintiffs. "The whole function of the consolidation is to hopefully reach a settlement without having to try all these cases," said Corboy.[27] The "consolidation" of the discovery process did indeed occur in the *Federal Skywalk Cases*, and Gordon played a central role during its course.

These few cautionary tales of local lawyers paled in number and breadth to those of the many Hyatt victims. Robert Gordon and his wife, Josie, felt bad for a couple they considered victims as well, who must have been personally devastated by the disaster. Josie quickly dashed off a personal note to Don Hall and his wife, Adele, handwritten and not ready-made from a Hallmark store, that expressed the Gordon family's sincere sympathy for the incredible burden now shouldered by their neighbors, the

Hall family. The Gordons did not travel in the same circle as the Halls, although their paths occasionally crossed at large social functions. "They didn't know us," said Josie, but in the small world of galas, openings, and dinners, "know of" is quite likely. Little Bobby Gordon grew up next door to William F. Hall, the brother of Hallmark founder Joyce Hall, and even referred to the old man as "Uncle Will," so there was some degree of history and familiarity between the households. Adele responded to their note in kind.[28]

Newspaper editorialists, who felt the same sense of sympathy, offered similar sentiment, plus a heap of praise: "The agony and sorrow of last weekend must be doubly difficult for those who have done something first rate and who find themselves in the midst of tragedy. Lesser men would give up. But when Don Hall speaks of 'high ideals and a mission,' the words can be believed. One need look no further than Crown Center to find their substance."[29]

On the same day of Josie's note, Diane Stafford, a *Kansas City Star* reporter, charitably reflected on the high regard that the Halls of Hallmark enjoyed. "It is some awful, evil irony that has forced the horrors of the Hyatt Regency hotel disaster on Donald Hall and Hallmark Cards Inc." Their "money, vision and civic pride" had brought attention and acclaim to Kansas City. Maybe even a bit of the "hall of fame" quality that the Hallmark brand possessed had rubbed off on the gritty midwestern metropolis. These niceties penned by Stafford were followed with her hard-nosed observations and pointed questions. In the last fiscal year, the private corporation had more than $1 billion in estimated sales and profits of $80 million. The Hall family, who owned about 75 percent of the company stock, controlled "one of the largest and certainly the most visible of Kansas City corporations." So it took no great analytical tools to conclude, "Hall has personal clout in accordance with the enormous economic clout Hallmark wields in the area." But the reporter shrewdly hinted that the company that "sets the standard for corporate conscience by which all other Kansas City firms are judged," might need to draw on all its banked civic goodwill in the troubled days to come, especially as she and her readers awaited answers to hard questions: "Were corners cut?

was the workmanship shoddy? was the design flawed? were the materials poor?"[30] These would become Gordon's questions as well.

The sympathetic tone of the newspaper continued when Don Hall sat for his one and only interview after the Hyatt disaster. When asked about Hallmark's financial strength, he answered, "Our insurance is good. There is no question about that." He went on to voice his company's can-do attitude in the face of adversity, which the reporter dutifully relayed: "Hall and others in the company, which prides itself in providing 'the very best'—be it a 75-cent greeting card, office or residential space, a deluxe hotel room, or a television show—already were turning to getting on with the company's commitment to reopening the Hyatt Regency as soon as possible and continuing the development of the Crown Center complex."

Also interviewed was James C. McClune, president of Crown Center Redevelopment Corporation, who remarked on the building project as if answering one of Stafford's hypothetical questions: "You hire who you are sure is competent, and rely on them." McClune added that he could not remember any problems "during construction or since, that were out of the ordinary or that would not be expected in the construction of a building of that magnitude."[31] (Interestingly, Robert Berkebile and Herbert Duncan, two of the architects for the doomed building, said the same thing in an interview held about the same time: "We didn't encounter problems until this disaster.") Soon it became apparent that the highly placed McClune, the head of the "Hallmark subsidiary that owns the hotel property," along with his outside and in-house architects, were suffering from severe cases of selective amnesia.[32] These public statements were soon contradicted—red flags to a lawyer of Gordon's caliber—and revealed as major gaffes, and by July 22, all Hallmark officials and employees had been advised by counsel to make no further public comment.[33]

IF HALLMARK OFFICIALS COULD NO LONGER MAKE PUBLIC STATEMENTS, outsider observers had no such restrictions. Stanley Chesley spoke from Cincinnati, Ohio, where he represented victims of the high-profile Beverly

Hills Supper Club fire that in 1977 killed 162 persons in Louisville, Kentucky. He also had represented several clients from the MGM Grand Hotel fire that killed eighty-seven in Las Vegas in 1980. It was crucial, he said, "that attorneys and investigators for the victims—not just those working for the potential defendants—have access to the hotel." Chesley added that "a very key piece of evidence" remained inside the Hyatt—the third walkway. "Under no circumstances," he said, "should the hotel be allowed to remove it until all parties involved have a chance to inspect it."[34]

By now Hallmark's actions were speaking louder than its words. In the dark of night and away from prying eyes, Hallmark removed the intact third skywalk that still graced the hotel lobby and hauled it in sections to a nearby warehouse. This was the walkway offset from the two that had fallen. Don Hall gave the order over Mayor Richard L. Berkley's vehement objections. The "early morning rebuff," as it was characterized, enraged the mayor, and he said so in a restrained way in the morning paper. "The third-floor walkway should have been left there a little longer. Certainly, there could be some scientific analysis and benefit derived from leaving it there and testing it."[35] This was seconded by two structural engineers from the Washington headquarters of the National Bureau of Standards, in town at the behest of U.S. senator Thomas F. Eagleton (D-MO), to inspect the wreckage, now considered evidence; however, the engineers were kept away by the owner from a close, hands-on examination of the remaining skywalk. Berkley added, "It gave the wrong impression, the way it was handled," and "this kind of action does not build public confidence."[36]

Confidence might have been shaken further if the public knew of the recent actions of Robert A. "Bob" Kipp, Kansas City's city manager. Mayor Berkley had reached out to City Manager Kipp for support against Hallmark's removal of the third skywalk, but Kipp, too, had rebuffed him, citing Hallmark's right to do what it pleased with its "private property." During these critical, post-collapse days, Kipp also helped scuttle Berkley's heat-of-the-moment proposal to form a citizens' investigative panel to discover the causes of the collapse. No, advised the manager to the city council, it would open the city to lawsuits.[37] Kansas City operated under a "weak mayor," strong city manager form of governance, put in place a half century before to counter corrupt machine-era politics. Hired by the city council, the manager answered directly to the council, not the mayor, who only wielded one vote on the thirteen-person body. City departments, such as the Public Works Department (under whose authority the city building inspectors fell), answered to the city manager as their boss, not the mayor. In this instance, with the council firmly in Kipp's corner, Berkley was hamstrung, and no such public investigative body was formed. Years later, Robert Gordon learned of Kipp's whereabouts immediately after the skywalks collapse. In a situation room filled with Hallmark senior executives and lawyers, Robert Kipp was the sole public servant present. Gordon concluded that Hallmark had a powerful friend in city hall.[38]

A couple of days before the controversial skywalk removal, Hallmark had also "removed in the pre-dawn hours" the debris from the skywalks collapse, which was "taken to a secure location." This action did not produce the same level of blowback, but together with the skywalk removal others cried foul, particularly lawyers for the plaintiffs. Their reactions ranged from disappointment to outrage: "The dismantling of the third 120-foot-long skywalk removed from the scene what some people believe may be vital evidence about the collapse of two similar walkways. . . . Another plaintiff's attorney, Lantz Welch, said he 'would have gotten a temporary restraining order' if he had known about the walkway removal during working hours . . . adding that he was 'surprised and a little angry' about the unannounced removal."[39]

The editorial board of the paper, always aware of Hallmark's eminence in the community, avoided mentioning the corporation by name and weighed in more delicately: "The seeming haste in moving the debris also is not likely to engender public trust. And there is the delicate matter of taking down the remaining skywalk. An air of secrecy seemed to surround these operations. If this was unintentional, it nevertheless has a devastating effect on public confidence. We assume no one has anything to hide."[40]

Hallmark bent slightly to public pressure. At week's end its Crown Center Redevelopment subsidiary and Max Foust, a local attorney representing several of the plaintiffs, agreed to the provisions of a court order that protected "every steel rod, washer, nut, bolt, piece of concrete, steel, wood, glass and all other items of debris as well as portions of the skywalks" from being destroyed, permanently altered, or removed from their new warehouse storage. Foust referred to the action as a "precautionary measure."[41]

However, these were not the only things that Hallmark had mishandled. As Gordon continued to read and analyze the breaking stories in the newspapers, his skepticism about the troubled hotel and the people who owned it—people he thought he knew—only grew. If in the week after the disaster Hallmark representatives acted as if they had something to hide, maybe they did. The collapse of the skywalks, shockingly, may not have been an isolated incident. Government officials responsible for public safety, baffled as they were in the immediate aftermath of the disaster, looked for earlier clues, and they soon found them and wasted little time in making them public. Their revelations put Hallmark, the hotel builder and owner, in a critical light and helped explain their self-imposed gag order. For a major construction project that had experienced "no problems," Vernon Strahm, the regional administrator for the federal government's Occupational Safety and Health Administration (OSHA), begged to differ. His records showed that a steel beam broke loose and fell to the lobby floor during the hotel's construction. This accident "may have indicated structural or design flaws in the facility." His investigators had come on the scene in late October 1979 in the wake of a worker fatality, a tragic but apparently unrelated incident. What really caught the attention of OSHA was more than the fall of a single beam. The investigators encountered the rubble of a massive, recent, "unusual" roof collapse in the hotel's atrium lobby. "There must be some structural or architectural failure when something like that happens," said Strahm. Needless to say, as a result of their 1979 inspection, OSHA issued a fistful of citations to the contractors for safety violations.[42] The government official did not have to spell out the implications for the 1981 disaster; he left the reporters to do that.

More details about the 1979 atrium roof collapse soon followed, and it was a blockbuster that appeared as front-page news: "Eight months before the Hyatt Regency hotel opened its doors to guests last summer, a large section of the atrium roof crashed four stories into the lobby. . . . The collapse occurred across the lobby from where two skywalks broke from their moorings." The newspaper confessed that the reporting at the time of the October 14, 1979, collapse had been spotty: "It was reported only that a single 16-foot steel beam had fallen. But OSHA records show that a large section of the roof fell in." The reporters now working the story turned up a couple of workers who saw the severity of the damage, which confirmed the public's worst fears about something amiss with the construction of the new hotel: "John Holmes, a construction foreman, said that after the roof collapsed, the skywalks were closed off to workers 'just as a precaution.' An iron worker at the Hyatt Regency construction site, John Turner said, 'It looked like the whole back, eastern (section) collapsed.' OSHA's records confirm this." Holmes also recalled that the atrium roof, which already had received its concrete pour, had been in place for a month before it fell several stories to the floor below.[43]

The newspaper backed this up with its own expert, Bogdan O. Kuzmanovic, a nearby University of Kansas professor and highly respected structural engineer. Kuzmanovic used the term "major collapse" when he examined OSHA's photographic record of the site. He thought holistically, explaining that no single explanation would ever suffice for the Hyatt disaster and that "difficulties with design, construction, inspection, and possibly materials combined to cause the collapse."[44] Curiously he left out a major component of a building construction project when he did not include as a possible contributor to the collapse a fifth element—project management. That oversight would be left for Gordon to address later.

When the reporters asked Hallmark's director of public relations to square this major collapse with his original press release that only a single beam had fallen with minimal damage, the executive replied, "I work for a greeting card company. I'm not an engineer." Then he took no more questions.[45]

After a week of such news, Robert Gordon, who often came to conclusions swiftly if not prematurely, may have entered the Molly Riley meeting with his own developed sense of outrage. He had learned things that cast a shadow on Hallmark, the corporation with the "high ideals," and on its leader, "our leading citizen," as the mayor called him.[46] Most troubling to Gordon, a lawyer who routinely sniffed out bad behavior by big businesses, was a growing suspicion that an unsafe building had been opened to the public. If that was true, then the owner, architect, general contractor, and other principals had been negligent in a knowing manner, pure and simple. But as the playwright and wit Oscar Wilde said a century before, "The truth is rarely pure and never simple."[47]

3

Robert Charles "Bobby" Gordon

Like Molly Riley, his prospective client, Robert Gordon saw the world in black and white. Good lawyering meant following rules, and he hated when they were broken. If lawyer and client shared anything at all, they were perfectly aligned in a desire for justice. Also, as it turned out, neither liked bullies. Each possessed the innate ability to suffer slings and arrows, although maybe not quietly, yet still stand up to those more powerful. As the representative of the Hyatt victims, Molly later exhibited that fortitude when she faced a roomful of hostile lawyers during her deposition. Bob Gordon did that and more for the next decade, until he could do so no longer.

Their one meeting was enough to get the ball rolling. Before it ended, Riley, Whitaker, and Gordon had decided to proceed with a class action, and the lawyers crafted a letter to serve as a contract. Molly agreed to its terms and paid $40 for the filing fee, which was soon applied on Thursday, July 30, when her suit was filed in state court.[1]

A victim with a story in search of an advocate had found a more-than-willing fighter, ready and able to enter the fray. The lawyer, who had no real connection to the events of July 17, found himself caught up in a gripping narrative and a legal case that inevitably would become the great cause of his life. But just who was this Robert Gordon, and what else could he possibly hold in common with his new client?

The contrasts between attorney and client were stark. Margaret Mary "Molly" Riley was born in 1948, therefore a baby boomer, Gordon in 1941 from the generation before. A native of North Kansas City, a town located north of the Missouri River within sight of downtown Kansas City's skyscrapers, Riley had gone to Catholic schools, St. Patrick's elementary school in her hometown and St. Teresa's Academy all-girls high school in Kansas City proper. She attended the University of Missouri–Kansas City, the city's commuter school, for two years before leaving. In 1972 she earned an associate degree in nursing from an area community college and immediately went to work at a local hospital.[2]

A native Kansas Citian, Robert Charles "Bobby" Gordon was a 1959 alumnus of Southwest High School, the most prestigious public school in Kansas City. Distinguished alumni included Hollywood director Robert Altman, H&R Block founder Henry Bloch, novelist Evan Connell, and actress Betty Lynn, better known as the character Thelma Lou in *The Andy Griffith Show*. *New Yorker* humorist Calvin "Bud" Trillin, six years Gordon's senior, once referred to their alma mater as "a high school that had a strong resemblance to the high schools in the sort of Hollywood movies that featured Andy Hardy—or, as it turned out, the sort of movies that featured Paul Newman and Joanne Woodward, since Southwest was the school attended by the children of Mr. and Mrs. Bridge." A smart student, Gordon left to attend the University of California at Berkeley, a section of the country he adored. In 1953 the adolescent Gordon had attended with his local troop the national Boy Scouts of America jamboree in California and on the way had the opportunity to see the Bay Area. "Stayed in San Frisco [*sic*] almost all day long. Loved it," he wrote in his official "Jamboree Diary." He never lost his affection for the area. His son observed knowingly that he was "a West Coast type of guy."[3]

In his college career at Cal, Gordon earned an honors degree in political science and another from Boalt Hall, the university's prestigious school of law.[4] After graduating in 1966, his father, M.C., had wanted him to go into the family's clothing manufacturing business, the Burlington Overall Company. The company's main product was bib overalls made of denim and favored by farmers, laborers, and tradesmen. In 1913 Gordon's maternal grandfather had built a new factory in the heart of Kansas City's then-burgeoning garment district and moved his business and most of his employees there from Burlington, Iowa. His name was Hyman Naman, a Lithuanian Jew who had immigrated to the United States in the late nineteenth century. This grandfather and a veiled reference to his ethnicity only appear once in the family papers that compose part of the larger Gordon collection and, when mentioned in one of Robert's letters, only as "H. Naman."[5] One can make whatever one wants from that fleeting reference.

Gordon's law school education was originally intended to bring needed legal skills to the company. Nevertheless, he would have no part of his father's business other than sitting behind his grandfather's oak desk in his law office.[6] He did return to Kansas City, though, and forged a career in the law, first serving as a clerk to William Henry Becker, chief judge of the U.S. District Court of the Western District of Missouri (1966–67), and then joining the practice of the prestigious firm of Watson Ess Marshall & Enggas. His legal specialty became corporate fraud and antitrust or, in his own words, "going after commercial wrongs committed by corporations."[7]

In 1969 he married Josephine "Josie" Pickard, a Vassar graduate whose Kansas City family was one of wealth and standing, exemplified perhaps when they donated a painting by Camille Pissarro, a master of French impressionism, to the Nelson-Atkins Museum of Art. The announcement of the Gordon-Pickard engagement and subsequent wedding appeared prominently in the local high society weekly, still a viable part of the ecosystem that catered to the city's upper crust. They went on their honeymoon to—where else?—San Francisco and Carmel, California. Theirs was a happy marriage, made more so by the addition of two children, whose births and toddler activities also warranted mention in the society notices.[8]

As a contrast to this model of family bliss, Molly married Franklin Donald Tomc in May 1978, gave birth to a son, Matthew, and divorced in October the next year. A dock worker at the Proctor & Gamble plant, Tomc paid $230 a month in child support. The exes rarely communicated, even to discuss their son. "We don't talk. . . . He doesn't call," Molly said. Tomc's check supplemented the single mother's take-home pay as a registered nurse, a little over $1,000 a month, but her income barely covered her and her son's monthly expenses, the two largest being a house payment of $467 and a car payment of $162. Since leaving home she had lived in a succession of apartments and small houses, and her current residence was a single-story cottage of a little over a thousand square feet, with two bedrooms, one bathroom, and a single-car garage.[9]

The Gordon family of four lived in a mansion of more than 6,800 square feet with nineteen or so rooms, five of them bedrooms. Built a year before Molly's in 1928, the house on Verona Road sat on an acre-plus lot in a coveted section, then and now, of Mission Hills, Kansas. Gordon once described a home filled with "2 kids, 2 basset hounds . . . 7 cats," not to mention the nanny, the model electric train, and the overflowing shelves of books on military history. The handsome English Tudor was one of the venues for the annual Wellesley Garden Tour and also the kitchen tour sponsored by the Kansas City Art Institute. Activity, love, laughter, and intellectual conversation, like the behavior of gas molecules within a confined space, filled the household. It was here with his family, watching television that night, that he first heard the news of the Hyatt collapse.[10]

To an outside observer, Robert Gordon enjoyed a wonderful life. He was great with the kids, Josie later recalled, "the best dad ever." But the man who apparently had his fair share of life's bounty also had more than his share of quirks and eccentricities, readily apparent and usually accepted by others. For one birthday his daughter gave him a greeting card—made by Hallmark, appropriately—that began, "Every family has at least one man who is prudent, moderate in his habits and who always behaves properly!" which set up the punch line inside: "But it's more fun having one like *you*!"

Molly Riley may have noticed an oddity or two in her visit to the office in the Country Club Plaza, Kansas City's tony center of upscale shopping, fancy restaurants, and professional offices. The lease for the office suite was in Gordon's name, and its interior decoration reflected his tastes and peculiarities. One indicator was the container of pencils that sat on his receptionist's desk, each sharpened to the exact same height, like a column of soldiers standing at attention.[11] Less subtle was Gordon's passion for military history, which reflected his enjoyment of combat or at least his admiration for soldiers and fighters. Allusions abounded in his own writings—and, judging from transcripts of court proceedings, his everyday conversations as well—with awkward references to D-day, George Patton, and Winston Churchill. His office, decorated in a style he termed "early foxhole," was packed with wartime memorabilia, including military uniforms, models, recruiting posters, and toy soldiers that he hand-painted himself. On one side of his office library, Gordon had a wood-burning fireplace, adorned above by a photograph of Churchill. In an example of his boundless enthusiasm and ample resources, he once purchased a large assortment of "military miniatures" for the sum of $4,617. A colleague remembered seeing him once walking outdoors near his office dressed in a vintage World War II American army uniform. This was also his preferred dress for the occasional costume party. His wife, Josie, evidently took such things in stride. A *Star* society reporter once caught the pair at a Kansas City gala in their "creative black tie," him again in uniform and her in evening gown with a black sash bedecked with historic military medals. "We're representing the Banana Republic," she quipped.[12]

Gordon found great delight in movement or the machines that made it possible. He loved trains, planes, and automobiles, particularly sports cars. An enclosed porch in his mansion held his extensive model train layout. He was a licensed pilot and flew rented planes. Optimistically he hoped someday to own his own flying machine. A copy of an early will went so far as to bequeath to Josie's brother "any airplane or helicopter owned by me at my death."[13] But with this love came heartache. A friend reminisced about the time "Bob landed his plane on the highway" during an emergency, a possible source of considerable embarrassment and some irony because his son Andy later became an accomplished commercial airline pilot. The same friend also remembered the fits that one particular Jaguar gave Gordon. Its continual maintenance problems, all too common with the British luxury car, caused so much grief that he gave up and backed it into the extreme end of the garage, where the Jag sat undisturbed for years until the house around it sold.[14]

Odd outerwear and comic antics served as cover for a more vulnerable soul. "Quixotic" springs to mind as an appropriate descriptor for this worldly lawyer. The adjective carries a primary meaning of "exceedingly idealistic," one expressed beautifully in a lyric by singer-songwriter Gordon Lightfoot in his song "Don Quixote," which went, "Through the woodland, through the valley, comes a horseman wild and free; tilting at the windmills passing, who can the brave young horseman be."[15] The dictionary, however, tacks on secondary, less romantic meanings to the word, such as "unrealistic" and "impractical," of which readers of the Cervantes classic readily attribute to its main character. Gordon did so himself, when he begged a television announcer during the Hallmark affair to "not conclude that I am some half-crazed character out of a Cervantes novel who has nothing better to do than go spinning through the universe trying to right every wrong."[16]

Sometimes he did just that, however, and his work on the *Federal Skywalk Cases* may not have been the first instance of his crusader spirit, these words of protestation aside. In 1968 violent riots wracked Kansas City, as with many American cities, in the aftermath of the Martin Luther King assassination. To quell the civil unrest the police ham-handedly carried out wholesale roundups of inner-city residents, usually Black, whether they were rioters or not. Gordon saw this and brought his legal skills to bear to do pro bono work on behalf of wrongfully arrested members of the African American community. He had once thought of being a civil rights lawyer and simply felt it was the right thing to do.[17] In the politely racist environment of Kansas City (at the best of times), this may not have been seen as a socially acceptable act by his peers in the Mission Hills enclaves. All these attributes of a quixotic personality make an interesting combination for a protagonist, a person for whom one can root and express dismay simultaneously.

In his writings Gordon often wore his heart on his sleeve, something one does not normally associate with the temperament of members of his profession, or with the "Mr. Bridge" disposition portrayed by expatriate novelist Connell and still current then in upper-class Kansas City.[18] In November 1980, months before the Hyatt entered their lives, Gordon's daughter, Tracy, and son, Andrew, received a seven-page, typed, single-spaced letter from "Your Old Man"—Gordon was but thirty-nine—written from Berkeley, California. It came immediately after he attended that year's annual football game between his beloved UC Bears and their archrival, the Stanford Cardinals, and he was in an upbeat, nostalgic mood. He mentioned that the date, November 22, held special significance to their father. It was the anniversary of the assassination of his hero, John F. Kennedy, in 1963, Gordon's first year at law school. His dark thoughts of that time were tempered with "one of my most treasured memories," another day spent, years before, at Memorial Stadium. In spring 1962 the University of California had celebrated its centennial, and the young president of the United States had come to make a speech to honor the event. "You will never have an opportunity," wrote Gordon, "to see the excitement and interest that his presence and his thoughts created. Nor will you ever hear, in person, his classic oratorial cadenzas."[19]

Gordon's touching picture of that "almost magical day" switched gears to a blow-by-blow account of the recent football game, unexpectedly won by his outclassed Bears. For this most faithful and proud alumnus, it was a joyous day indeed. "We made all people who root for the underdog instead of the favorite, for the weak instead of the strong, for the common soldier instead of the plumed knight, and for the desperate and the cornered, instead of the cocksure and the strutters, believe in themselves again." The astonishing victory was "a new footnote to that still small list that inspires all men and women by shining example," and his list included the Spartans at Thermopylae, English archers at Agincourt, Ethan Allen's Green Mountain boys, Andy Jackson's irregulars against the best of the British army, the American "miracle on ice" hockey team at the 1980 Olympics, and David on the biblical field facing Goliath. Gordon pointed out to his kids a personal example of his own victory over daunting odds: "Maybe, it may also in some small way be similar to your old man in the Rebar case when I finally obtained a previously unheard-of default judgment in a class action. Homework, perseverance, and confidence in a single point of civil procedure (which all the other attorneys had given up on as a 'waste of time'), coupled with smug over-confidence by the steel companies is what, at long last, defeated those rascals." In a couple of years, Gordon the spirited idealist would again face, as he wrote to his children, "the greatest of odds and the most powerful of opponents."[20]

Inspired by JFK and sympathetic to underdogs, other clues to Gordon's political leanings appear in his early published writings. In 1964, while still in law school, he commented in a letter to the editor of the *Kansas City Star* on the John Birch Society, an extreme right-wing, pro-conspiracy, anti-government political organization that was garnering much press. The inquisitive Gordon had attended a meeting "out of curiosity," initially "amused at the blatant absurdities" mouthed by the chapter's followers. Disgust followed amusement, then fear "that these blind extremists may somehow gain real power." The dedication and the ultra-patriotism of the Birchers, "wrapped . . . in the American flag," made them especially dangerous, Gordon thought, and he advised against driving the group underground, "where their activities would not be accessible to public view."[21]

In a brief essay for the local *Kansas City Bar Journal*, law student Gordon expounded on a subject in which he had firsthand knowledge—"free speech"—the controversy about the public use of "four-letter words" that had embroiled the University of California campus and attracted national attention. His description of the initial offender, a young man who "suddenly sat down on a busy Berkeley street corner with a large sign emblazoned only with America's most taboo four-letter word," sounded like someone who had seen the incident himself. The college-gridiron-loving Gordon especially noted how others "proceeded to use the word in a variety of ways which included a football-type spell-out." ("Give me an 'F'!") He concluded the piece with his own noncontroversial, middle-of-the-road attitude: "If the means of your speech make the message offensive to those who may not wish to hear it, then you have abused your First Amendment rights." In other words, "The audience also has rights that must be protected, and that unrestrained liberty to use any genuinely offensive speech can degenerate too easily into license for the few and misery for [the] many."[22] There is no evidence that Gordon, no matter how offensive or obnoxious his opponents found him, ever strayed from these views.

Perchance the most revealing of Gordon's college writings is his undergraduate honors thesis, an exposition on the Lord Acton principle, "Power corrupts, absolute power corrupts absolutely." He runs through a quartet of great political philosophers—Plato, Hobbes, Locke, and Rousseau—but clearly favors John Locke and his views on the restraint of power. One can later detect Gordon's affinity, like the seventeenth-century Enlightenment thinker, to "channel the evil reservoir of power through an aqueduct of sufficient ingenuity so that the power is usable and the evil filtered out."[23] Filtered out, say, by the use of punitive damages? That opportunity would knock in the future on another door.

To those who knew professionally this solitary specimen of a rare species among Kansas City attorneys, Gordon became an object of curiosity, regard, and scorn, sometimes by the same individual in the course of a single conversation. He was the butt of one particular piece of local lore, which occurred when he served as a young law clerk for Judge William Henry Becker. As due his seniority, the judge had the first prime parking stall outside the then–federal courthouse in downtown Kansas City, a stately, old building since converted to condominiums. Gordon would surreptitiously use the privileged space when Becker was absent to work at home, as he often was. One day Becker, unannounced, drove to the office, came to his spot, and found another car parked there. He complained about it to the nearest security officer and demanded that the offender immediately be towed. "Bobby" somehow got wind of the judge's arrival, frantically "went down by way of the freight elevator," and moved his car. Meanwhile, the judge slowly circled the block, returned to find his spot now open, and pulled his car in. A summoned tow truck arrived shortly thereafter and mistakenly "towed the judge's car to Grandview!" (a distant Kansas City suburb). What happened next is unknown, but as an epilogue, over the years the humorous tale became apocryphal, institutional folklore, and the Gordon role would be attributed to later novitiates clerking under other judges.[24]

As Gordon crossed paths or, more likely, butted heads with his contemporaries, words to describe him could have filled one of his ubiquitous yellow legal pads. "Dogged," wrote one admiring journalist, a trait one desires in their lawyer, as is "combative," a word his son used. Other descriptors were less flattering. As if following a musical scale from a lower to a higher register, the words included "insecure," "offensive," "reckless," and "irrational." One lawyer called him "an acquired taste."[25] Another normally tight-lipped attorney who faced off against Gordon was critical of his verbosity and speculations and thought him untrustworthy, adding, "I tried to never meet alone with him, either in a room together or on the phone."[26] Many came up with the same word for Gordon during his quest for the truth behind the worst American building collapse until the fall of New York's Twin Towers—"obsessed."[27] Maybe the best word to describe him, voiced by witnesses ranging from courtroom opponents dealing with his strident accusations to modern archivists dealing with his mountain of papers, was "exhausting." A difficult person with whom to remain on good terms, Gordon once told a correspondent, "I have at times been quite outspoken about my colleagues, and I consider their antipathy sufficient reward."[28] Little wonder this gadfly never ran out of people to dislike and vice versa.

In one especially litigious, close-to-home episode, Gordon took on the role of a personal injury lawyer. He pressured a Minnesota sporting goods company to pay damages to his son, Andy, for injuries suffered from the company's defective slingshot. The outraged father was willing to settle for the purchase price of the offending toy ($21.95) and Andy's pain and suffering ($500); he did not include the resultant medical expenses ($41.25), which had been paid by others. The victim no longer remembers how this spat resolved itself.[29]

But Gordon also left clues that a hard, prickly shell covered a soft center that desired love and acceptance. His papers hold a scattering of newspaper comic strips and magazine cartoons that resonated and merited saving. In one yellowed clipping one of the characters in the *Peanuts* cartoon strip grimaces and says, "You can understand why the others get annoyed with Charlie Brown. He bores them because he wants so much to be liked." But few found Gordon boring. Years later his ex-wife, Josie, remembered that he could discuss any topic and bring something interesting to the conversation, either an interesting tidbit of background information or a fitting anecdote for the occasion. From the first, she found him "brilliant" and, combined with a great sense of humor, "one of the funniest people I ever knew." At a dinner party, "I wanted to be seated near him. His end of the table was having all the fun."[30]

If Gordon's personal eccentricities and nonconformity attracted attention, so did his work habits. Thank-you notes from local reporters whom he had assisted in understanding the intricacies of the *Federal Skywalk Cases* recalled the many late hours he kept at his office. David Hayes, a *Times* reporter, often found Gordon "poring over documents or depositions long after midnight." And he had a trait that endeared him to any reporter on deadline: "It didn't seem to matter at what time of day or night it was, we always seemed to be able to reach you."[31] A glance at Gordon's time records for this period shows that this observation was nothing if not understated.

Such devotion to work also carried a downside, one that Gordon himself wryly observed. "When asked my son/daughter's age/birthdate, I have to calculate it by what class action I was handling at that time."[32] His son, Andy, made the point more painfully: "Dad, I don't get to see you a lot. It's hard on me and maybe Tracy . . . whenever you come home you just go to sleep. This case means a lot to you but don't be away all this much. . . . No fun! The end. From Andy. My birthday you know."[33]

From Kent Granger, a fellow lawyer and his best friend at the time, came a handwritten note, probably passed to Gordon during one of their interminable deposition hearings, "Dear Bob—For the rest of this case I will stipulate you are abusing your wife & children."[34]

Nothing, it would seem—no family obligation, no hobby, no other case—absorbed Gordon as much as the *Federal Skywalk Cases*. A competitive streak emerged, coupled with "a keen desire to beat the best of the best."[35] During his direct involvement from mid-1981 to early 1983, Gordon almost single-handedly pored through more than a million pages of documents gathered in a common depository for the case, and this self-assigned colossal task may say more about his personality than any other behavior. The document depository is a strange venue to learn about and take the measure of a man, but where else reveals a person's character more than where they feel the most comfortable? This was a place that only a historian at heart could love: file cabinet after file cabinet stuffed with paper, documentary treasures awaiting discovery and copying. Before they secured access, reporters considered the depository a Fort Knox. Lawyers, on the other hand, saw it as a place to avoid, a dungeon to send their underlings.[36]

This episode revealed Gordon's work ethic, his methodology for case preparation, his attention to detail, and his unswerving focus. What actions led to the collapse of the skywalks? Who were the actors responsible? Somewhere in the many crammed cabinets, missing pieces of the puzzle waited for discovery, and answers would emerge. No others shared this obsession, and it never proved contagious. This set him apart, and he knew it. In a reflection that sounded more like dogged historian Robert Caro, known for his edict to researchers to "turn every page," Gordon proudly stated, "For sheer intellectual pleasure, I've never known anything to compare with the excitement and challenge of using a defendant's own documents to prove the plaintiffs' case. Finding the right piece of paper in a vast, uncharted depository is like discovering a 70,000 carat, canary-yellow, flawless diamond in a flea market. In my experience, the success of any case against a major corporation always depended on the documents."[37]

This was grunt work of the type that his peers routinely assigned to "their rawest legal recruits or even to non-lawyers, young paralegals." Gordon did most of the document examination himself. He spent hundreds of hours on the task, and he brought his own unique twist to the process. He remembered the day he began, following a personal quirk by inspecting "the last folder at the back of the bottom drawer of the owner's final file cabinet" first.[38] His knowledge of the secrets found in the depository was a tactical strength and offered an early advantage. In the long run it proved of no strategic importance.

Most important to the story at hand, Gordon became the unassailable expert on the minutiae of the skywalks case, an incredible resource for others, and its natural chronicler. Maybe because of his odd mix of personal history, singular strengths, and character flaws, he felt compelled to speak truth to power. He was in a position to do so and at times even be heard. He was a privileged insider who was uniquely positioned, "wild and free," as Lightfoot sang, to formulate and champion a unique, contrarian view of what caused a modern building to fall and crush the life from 114 people. His considerable personal wealth provided a certain level of independence from the pressures exerted by a restrictive legal community and granted him the rare freedom to stir the pot, something few others shared his propensity to do. Fewer still, especially among his fellow members of the bar, seemed to share his respect for following the rules. He was quite the concoction, equal parts bomb-thrower and rule follower, draped in a seersucker suit.[39] His fateful participation in the legal aftermath of the city's greatest man-made catastrophe provided the platform for all to view the considerable talents and obvious blemishes of this driven man.

Robert Gordon, a man who may defy categorization, would need all the advantages he could muster as he set forth to engage powerful opponents on behalf of Molly Riley and others. Together they entered the fray as underdogs who, as a lawyer and a nurse, often looked out for others of their kind. It was possibly the greatest trait shared by the pair—Gordon's Don Quixote and Riley's Sancho Panza—as they girded for battle before a field of giants.[40] How would the deeply held principles of these two fare in a federal district court?

IT SHOULD COME AS NO SURPRISE THAT ROBERT GORDON, SOMETHING of a perfectionist but always a lawyer, kept close track of his time. The term "billable hours" is one that any layman knows and understands. Time is money, and for those in the legal profession a careful reckoning of one's professional time spent on a case translated into cold, hard cash. Recordkeeping joined death and taxes as certainties in a lawyer's life.

The tracking and billing of time to clients required some skill. The goal was the creation of an accurate and useful time record that ideally combined a careful balance of accuracy, brevity, and clarity. Expended time was calculated in fractions of an hour, and Gordon did his in six-minute increments, or tenths of an hour, which was at the far end of such computations, but not considered excessive. Best practices called for contemporaneous, daily timekeeping or, in other words, recording immediately after the completion of a specific task, say, reading a deposition, writing a brief, or consulting with a client. This resulted in an itemized list of tasks and their concomitant portions of time. Daily recordkeeping was considered the standard; weekly or, heaven forbid, monthly reckonings were to be avoided at all costs (since one might forget a task and underbill!). The objective was tracking time, not reconstructing it. The experts on such matters also recommended against "block billing" or the listing of all of one's day's tasks as a single entry and then giving only the total number of hours spent that entire day.[41] Although Gordon followed the norm and faithfully recorded his activities on a daily basis, he also did block billing.

How Gordon kept time is something of a mystery. He could have used a daily tally sheet or a clipboard with a time sheet or a time notebook or just one of his ubiquitous, yellow legal pads with his handwritten jottings. This was before the day of personal computers and sophisticated software programs that offered spreadsheets with fancy templates developed solely for this market, but nevertheless, his final, typed-up paper product survived and can be found in his archival collection.[42] It is a remarkable historical document, as exemplified by its very first entry relating to the *Federal Skywalk Cases*: "December 5, 1981 (Saturday): Research our class briefs per Court's request; later in day tried to help Mogin (W&C), who is totally ignorant of class action case law and managed to lose copies of all the cases & briefs that I had previously given him when he was here in Nov.; went to pick up copies of Molly's & Wolff's depos; read them; sent them to D.C. [hours =] 4.6."

Gordon's self-titled "daily time records" began on the aforementioned date and ended on January 31, 1983. The document ran for ninety-five pages, and each daily entry is typed and single-spaced, jammed with information. Countless individuals were mentioned by name, in this instance Molly Riley, his client, and Paul M. Wolff, a Washington DC lawyer also representing the Hyatt plaintiffs. Legalese abounds, such as "class briefs" and "depos," in other words, depositions. Although one might question their lack of brevity (entries often run into dozens, if not hundreds of words) and correctness (in the above example the purported ignorance of Paul Mogin, a Gordon ally at the Williams & Connolly law firm), his accounting did follow the professional recommendation for clarity to the point of indiscretion. Mentors on such matters cautioned their students to always keep in mind that their time records would be read by others. Gordon blithely ignored this restraint, and his critical appraisals of others are sprinkled throughout the pages. The document therefore became something of a daily reflection, created as events were swirling about. The entries reflected the ebb and flow of the case, its highs and lows, turning points and dead ends, at least as their author perceived them at the time. One is left with the impression that what remains for our prying eyes is more "dear diary" than tedious time card, the latter the type of document that by and large would receive little consideration by a historian. Generated by a garrulous insider to the federal case, the result is a valuable testament in real time to the legal events that transpired after the hotel disaster.

Returning to his entry for that particular December day, Gordon put in more than four hours, which may not seem like much until one realizes that it was on a Sunday and probably while at home with the family. Nearly all of his weekends during the case were spent this way.

The statistics are impressive and alarming and remind one less of venturing forth on a fanciful, quixotic quest and more of commencing a manic, single-minded undertaking. For the calendar year of 1982, Gordon spent a total of 4,369 hours on the case. Compare this to a "normal" work year that consists of a 40-hour work week for fifty-two weeks, or 2,080 hours. His busiest month was October 1982, for which he logged 496 hours, an average of 16 hours a day. He recorded work for every day of that month, all thirty-one, which was not unique to October. Gordon also worked on the case every day in the months of January, March, April, June, July, August, September, November, and December.

He routinely put in significant numbers of hours on holidays—New Year's Day, Memorial Day, the Fourth of July, Labor Day, Thanksgiving, and Christmas. If 1982 had been a leap year, he would have worked, no doubt, on February 29. He worked on his own birthday (February 22), as well as those of his wife, daughter, and son.[43] To say Gordon devoted all his waking time to this case is no overstatement, and one wonders at the source of his stamina. Later he recounted—in the third person—his time-saving tricks to "maximize all available time" on the case:

> Among other devices, he saved half an hour a day in transportation time by keeping an office on the Plaza close to his home. He slept at the office 16 nights to save even more time. He completely eliminated lunches. . . . He did not attend a single social function. He kept many document files at his home for studying at any available time. He also purchased a copy machine for use at home. . . . He used portable tape recorders at home and in the car to insure that thoughts and strategy were preserved without taking time to write the information out. He ceased reading all books, periodicals, and even daily papers, except for Hyatt-related articles.[44]

Gordon would need all these tricks and more.

4

One in a Hundred Lawsuits

From the time the triumvirate of Riley, Whitaker, and Gordon aspired to a class action until the end of the year, less than six months, their main goal—and obstacle—was to see the formation and certification of that federal class. Gordon referred dryly to his legal activities in the last half of 1981 as his "phase 1." In carefully and methodically preparing their lawsuit in those initial weeks, Gordon and Whitaker took three steps: researching and drafting the original class action complaint; crafting the questions that they intended to ask the defendants; and imagining the types of documents that they would request from them when given the opportunity.[1] Sooner rather than later, Gordon would need the information only his opponents could provide, and he would rely on the "discovery" process primarily to get it. As he defined, discovery was

> a process that compels an opponent to disgorge the facts, usually under oath, before trial. Discovery is designed to speed up a trial, or force a fair settlement, by making lawyers do the hard work of determining the truth now, not later. There are several basic tools for discovery. One device is "interrogatories," which are precise written questions seeking specific information. Another commonly used initial discovery mechanism is a "request for production of documents," which allows attorneys to study and copy the other side's

materials, such as notes, memos, contracts, letters, and tapes, which were relevant. "Relevance" was broadly defined to mean almost anything relating to the lawsuit or any of the issues it raised.[2]

Gordon knew from past experience that contemporaneous documents would be vital, "the best evidence in the case." From them he expected to learn what happened prior to the disaster, to establish who was responsible for the collapse, to determine the legal liability of those accountable for "the damage to the members of the class," and, finally, to award the amount of compensatory and punitive damages, if any, that were "just and proper."[3] For Gordon, the case always hinged on the documents.

The case also depended on creating and certifying the class, which according to Gordon's rough estimate might encompass as many as 2,700 individuals.[4] To adjudicate merely a fraction of their potential complaints in the courtroom would be nigh unto impossible and likely grind the system to a halt. The "mere" hundred lawsuits filed within the first two months after the disaster threatened the fair and equitable outcome for all those concerned. Judge Scott O. Wright of the Western District of Missouri, who was relatively new to the bench and had randomly drawn the case to hear, saw the problems in characteristically practical terms:

> It was obvious that the issues of liability and punitive damages would be identical in all the cases, so it would be extremely inefficient to try those issues over and over. On top of that, there would be a constant battle to see whose case would be tried first, second, third, and so on, and there would be inconsistent results if each case was tried individually. I also was concerned that, if there were limited funds to pay all of the claims, some of the victims and their lawyers might get a windfall while others got left out in the cold.[5]

Molly Riley had no intention of being left out in the cold and welcomed the opportunity to serve as the vehicle for turning her case into a class action. A determined Riley took seriously the role of "representative" of the class, and in the few weeks of late July and August alone she conferred with her counsel six times in person and on the phone, an impressive number of legal consultations.[6]

Besides providing exemplary client service, Gordon and Whitaker looked beyond their office suite for help, and they quickly got it.[7] Gordon recognized the feasibility of using the class device for mass accidents, but "why, then, haven't I ever heard of a successful mass tort class action?" To a layman the difference between a mass tort and a class action was a distinction without a difference. But a logic existed for this case. A large number of people at the same event and at the same place had "suffered the same type of wrong at the same moment." The same set of facts had affected all the Hyatt victims. The only variable was the extent of one's injuries, which would determine the damages awarded; however, that financial variable was a sticking point for the personal injury lawyers. For some victims the damages could be in the millions, but they could be a relative pittance for others without representation.[8]

Gordon then reached out to Harvard law professor Arthur Miller, a friend and, more importantly, a heavyweight in the field, to answer that question. Miller was legendary because he "literally wrote the book on federal practice and procedure," and his renown extended exponentially beyond legal circles when in the nineties he frequently appeared as a learned, reassuring, white-haired talking head on the fledgling cable channel Court TV.[9] A decade earlier Gordon had met Miller while attending a summer Harvard Law School seminar, and they renewed their friendship whenever their business paths crossed. They had also worked together on a couple of earlier class actions. Gordon thought Miller took an "avuncular interest" in his efforts. "I found him as congenial and unstuffy as he was brilliant and creative."[10]

Miller welcomed the challenge of overcoming existing case law that Gordon's query posed but dashed cold water on the idea: "I'm an optimist, Bob. And I don't want to discourage you, but speaking frankly, your chances of getting a skywalks class are about one in a million." Nevertheless, Miller and Gordon talked through a possible strategy, which hinged on two legal requirements: "manageability" and "superiority." Would a class action help a judge "manage" or dramatically lessen his congested case load? Would a class action be a "superior" means, based on speed, efficiency, and fairness, to resolve a complicated dispute? And here was the kicker. A limited pool of recoverable money for the plaintiffs—and that appeared to be the case here—might also nudge the court toward their argument and improve the odds for a class formation.[11] As noted, Judge Wright found the argument persuasive.

Miller's involvement paled in comparison to that of Paul M. Wolff, another friend. When Gordon reached out to Wolff, a high school buddy, he was making an overture to the big guns of Williams & Connolly, one of the premier law firms in Washington DC and, hence, the nation. Paul M. Wolff responded immediately and favorably. "We've got all the know-how, experience, and experts you could ever want all lined up. I'm delighted you called me. I'd love to represent the class."[12] Wolff graduated from Southwest High School in Kansas City in 1959, the same year as Gordon, and their presence graced several pages of that year's *Sachem*, the SWHS yearbook. Both served on the student council, and as juniors, both attended Missouri Boys State, a weeklong gathering of the state's "best and brightest" for a crash course in competitive leadership and government skills. Both were members of their school's senior business committee, under which Gordon worked on the "prom" and "publicity" subcommittees and Wolff on the more serious, one might imagine, "commencement" subcommittee. Although both made the honor roll, Wolff may have been the better scholar because he added "seven semesters" to his senior summary, along with his selection to the National Honor Society. On the other hand, Gordon may have been the more well-rounded student with a varsity letter in tennis, first place in the "I Speak for Democracy" contest, and a part in that year's school play.[13] The performance of "The Man Who Came to Dinner" starred an immobile, house-bound member of the New York elite who, among other indignities during his forced stay in small-town America, suffered the persistent entreaties of a sweet but bumbling "Dr. Bradley" (played by Gordon) to read, coincidentally as it turned out in real life, his ponderous book manuscript.[14]

After their graduation, Gordon was off to the West Coast and the University of California, Wolff in the opposite direction to the University of Wisconsin, where he graduated Phi Beta Kappa, then to Harvard Law School. After returning to his hometown to practice law, Gordon ended up living a mile and a half from his old high school. Wolff stayed on the East Coast, a world away from Kansas City. In 1981, when his old classmate made contact, Wolff was well on his way to a highly regarded, decades-long career in the law.[15] Gordon hoped that baiting this hook might also snag Edward Bennett Williams, founder of Williams & Connolly and the biggest fish of all.

Williams had a well-earned reputation as a hard-nosed, take-no-prisoners litigator who insisted on "taking every case to its ultimate conclusion." In his early years he had garnered great publicity, whether he won or lost, by representing such notorious defendants as teamster boss Jimmy Hoffa, mobster Charles "Lucky" Luciano, and Senator Joseph McCarthy. By the early 1980s his clientele was more upscale and corporate, such as the influential Graham family that owned the *Washington Post*, and the fees were huge. He had even parlayed his wealth into major ownership stakes in the Washington Redskins football team and later baseball's Baltimore Orioles. Within the Washington beltway the well-connected and politically powerful Williams was considered the "consummate insider." In the *People* magazine parlance of the 1980s, he was a "superlawyer," the head of the "hottest trial firm in Washington, if not the country." One associate declared, "Being in the courtroom with Williams was somewhat akin to having your breath sucked out by a tornado."[16] He was a larger-than-life character in a town that bred them by the litter. Unfortunately for Gordon, a lingering, severe illness rendered Williams's incredible talent unavailable for a leading role in the Hyatt case, but to Gordon's great relief a close second stepped in as a substitute.

Irving Younger, new to the firm, was at age forty-eight a leading scholar, renowned trial tactician, and spellbinding orator of wit and theatrics in both the court and the classroom. In 1981, as a newly named partner, he worked as a Williams & Connolly litigator and held an adjunct professorship at the Georgetown University Law Center. The author of several influential books, he wrote the standard textbook on evidence law, and his "Ten Commandments of Cross-Examination" were known to all trial lawyers.[17] Even the man-on-the-street could recite a variation of its most famous edict. "Don't ask a question to which you do not know the answer." Younger's heading up the plaintiff team as its lead counsel brought a combustible mixture of celebrity, gravitas, and vigor to the team that few lawyers in the nation equaled. His presence also brought a response of fear and loathing from certain Kansas City lawyers. "Who the hell is this uppity professor!" exclaimed personal injury attorney Lantz Welch. Regardless of the pushback, the fact remained that within a month Gordon had signed up a stellar lineup of high-powered advocates—the respected Miller, the hometown-boy-made-good Wolff, and the flamboyant Younger.[18] In the years to come, Gordon would put together other "dream teams."

The group soon got to work. On August 3 Gordon and Bill Whitaker met with Wolff in Kansas City to strategize. (Younger could not make the trip from Washington due to a scheduling conflict, which Gordon only learned when picking up Wolff at the airport. Later, Gordon would view the unexpected and poorly excused absence by Younger as an ill omen.) The trio discussed the pros and cons of state versus federal court; whether to consolidate the discovery of documents with other plaintiffs; which particular documents to request; and the scope and content of the interrogatories, of which nearly four hundred were sent to Hallmark in August. The eager Gordon could not wait to start digging into documents on a fact-finding mission. "Unlike dozens of other lawyers who were simply initiating litigation," he later wrote, "I wanted the class to start finding out immediately what the defendants' files revealed about who and what might be responsible for the collapse."[19]

Following up on these master-plan tactics kept Gordon and Whitaker busy. None of this mattered if the class did not get certified, which meant that reaching that objective was the highest priority. But certification came with the greatest pushback. "Unfortunately, most members of the local plaintiffs' bar had already decided, amongst themselves, how the Skywalks' litigation was going to be handled," remarked Gordon, "and they did not take kindly to the prospect of there being some other method."[20] On September 1 the "other method," unorthodox as it was, emerged. Molly Riley's complaint, originally "commenced" in state circuit court, was soon voluntarily dismissed and "recommenced" in federal district court, filed on her behalf and "all others similarly situated" against Hallmark and Crown Center Redevelopment Corp, its wholly owned subsidiary. The two corporate entities and the other defendants were cited for "gross negligence" and a litany of offenses, repeating the things that the newspaper investigators had already brought to the public's attention: changing the skywalk design; using suspension rods threaded like "common bolts"; using insufficient anchor bolts, nuts, and washers; failing to provide "redundancy"; and failing to properly inspect or test the skywalks. Estimated compensatory damages suffered by the class members, according to the complaint, totaled in excess of $100 million. The dreaded punitive damages—a monetary punishment rarely covered by insurance—would be at least another $250 million, for a total of $350 million. Riley's was the fifty-fourth skywalk case to be filed but the first and only one to request that a class action be granted. By early October a hundred lawsuits had been filed, but this was not the month's most surprising development.[21]

5

Hallmark's Kansas City

Much to the public's disbelief and consternation, the Hyatt Regency hotel reopened for business on October 1, when emotions were still raw. Anticipating this backlash, Paul Gigot of the *Wall Street Journal*, an outside observer if ever there was one, had exposed to a national readership what many locals were thinking: "The Halls had become an object of anger and suspicion." Hallmark, he bluntly wrote, had responded to the tragedy "with uncharacteristic silence." He quoted an editor of the *Kansas City Star* who commented, "They've done some very un-Hallmark things."[1] Gigot would only have needed to look at recent local history to understand what his source meant by that.

Hallmark Cards had spent decades building a national brand and a sterling reputation, particularly in its headquarters city, and the locals had responded approvingly. If the rough-and-tumble Kansas City Stockyards defined the first century of Kansas City (1850–1950), then the refined Hallmark was what the city aspired to be in the next.[2] The card company offered the locals a sophisticated image of high quality, good taste, artistic refinement, and business integrity as no other institution. Here was the ideal corporate citizen to represent Kansas City to the nation, something to counter a crass legacy as a wide-open city of Prohibition-era political bosses and mobbed-up gangsters.

It took years for Joyce C. Hall, Hallmark's founder and master salesman to carefully construct the brand, but he put together the pieces early. By 1950 Hall's enterprise had been in existence for thirty years and led the entire market in greeting cards; "a million greetings a day," advertisements proclaimed. He employed 2,300 people in the Kansas City area, making the company one of the largest private employers and an economic powerhouse. Want ads for good jobs in his offices, studios, and printing plants ran in the paper every day. More creative artists were on staff than any other American business, it was claimed, except for Walt Disney's animation studio in Hollywood. Like Disney, a good friend with similar midwestern, hardscrabble roots, Hall had created an empire in new media from nothing. Both were entrepreneurs whose names became associated with quality products. Neither were shy to broadcast that fact. Hall publicly hobnobbed with presidents and prime ministers, and in one audacious marketing move he bought several works painted by Winston Churchill for a series of Christmas cards. When the world looked favorably on Hall, it viewed Kansas City likewise.

In another example from 1950, Kansas City celebrated its centennial, and what began as a local observance expanded beyond the organizers' dreams, all due to Hall. Before its award-winning forays in television, initiated the next year with the first production of the *Hallmark Hall of Fame*, Hallmark had sponsored prime-time radio programs. *Hallmark Playhouse*, a show of "great stars in top dramas," aired nationally on the CBS network on Thursday nights, and Hall stepped in to use his program to showcase his city to the nation. The broadcast moved from Hollywood to Kansas City, bringing along stars Robert Young, Jane Wyman, and a "brilliant array of talent" to head a dramatic, one-hour rendering of Kansas City history. On the evening of June 1, listeners in fifteen million homes—one of which might have included a ten-year-old Bobby Gordon—tuned in to "City of the Future," as the episode was titled, and it was a big hit, at least locally.

A couple of days later an appreciative *Kansas City Star* editorialist rhapsodized about Hall and "the spirit of a Kansas City business that would go to such effort and expense to let the world know about its home town." Civic-mindedness and integrity, such was the Hallmark way. "We can't recall such an effort and purpose by a local business anywhere else." The company stood alone in the eyes of the public, and even Gordon, later its harshest critic, believed in the intervening decades that "no corporation, certainly no other company in the Midwest, had a stronger civic conscience."[3] Business had grown along with reputation. By the time of the Hyatt disaster, the number of greeting cards printed daily exceeded ten times the output of a 1950 day. Cards were sold in twenty-one thousand retail outlets in more than a hundred countries in twenty languages.[4] But Hallmark's success and the city's reflected glory did not always travel in tandem.

ONCE THE NINETEENTH LARGEST U.S. CITY IN ITS 1920S HEYDAY, Hallmark's Kansas City had fallen to twenty-seventh with little to stop the downward trajectory. In 1980 the city, bleeding population to the suburbs, had shrunk to 450,000 souls, even after recent decades of massive land annexations.[5] White emigration to the suburbs, energized by racial unrest, school desegregation, and fear, had accelerated in the sixties and seventies. Racial and economic boundaries within the city limits were hardening, and the Crown Center complex, a "city within a city," became an island fortress to counteract these fluid times and changing fortunes.[6]

Over the years the company had added significant parcels of "midtown" land to buffer the corporate headquarters, including Signboard Hill, a public eyesore to its immediate west. The natural limestone bluff hosted a mess of garish billboards that had sprouted like weeds across the street from the increasingly obsolete Union Station (1914) and the decrepit Liberty Memorial (1926), dedicated long ago to the doughboys who had served in World War I. Pershing Boulevard, the renamed Twenty-Fourth Street, served as an east-west connector for these worn-out landmarks, as well as an unattractive gaggle of other old buildings. Main Street, Grand Avenue, and McGee ran north-south through the city and knitted together the neighborhood. In 1967 the visionary J. C. Hall drew up the master plans for a major urban renewal. The city quickly approved the Crown Center Redevelopment Plan, and his son, Don, considered an "agent of change," was charged with executing it. The Hall argument was "Let one firm replace 85 acres of blight with a model urban community."[7]

The urban landscape was in a state of flux, "the shiny and the shabby," as one modern geographer described it.[8] Only a mile west of Hallmark and its Missouri center of operations, one crossed the state boundary into Kansas and another Kansas City, a point of constant confusion to disoriented out-of-towners since time immemorial and a source of resentment, at least by the locals who suffered from the unintentional slight.

A dozen blocks to the north of Crown Center, downtown and still in Missouri, ran Twelfth Street east and west, which aptly symbolized the new Kansas City trying to overcome its old habits. This thoroughfare in the central business district hosted a raft of seedy bars, shabby burlesque houses, and peep shows under the control of the local mob. This was a lingering vestige of the old, wide-open, sin-and-gin town of Boss Tom Pendergast, his political machine, and its organized crime associates of the interwar period, an R-rated neighborhood in stark contrast to the G-rated plans of Hallmark. A landmark building on Twelfth Street, as well as a prospective but weak competitor to the hotelier Halls, the Muehlebach Hotel (established 1915 with a 1952 annex) reminded one of downtown's former grandeur and preeminence in city affairs. But the old hotel was a poor fit with nearby Bartle Hall, the shiny new convention center built in 1976 to halt the downtown slide.[9] If Kansas City was to revive its convention business, it needed bigger and splashier accommodations, even if they cannibalized their predecessors.

To the east of Hallmark by half a mile ran Troost Avenue, and another half a mile past that the famous Eighteenth and Vine jazz district. Both were shadows of their former selves. The thriving white businesses that had lined the avenue in its heyday and the famous Black jazz clubs at the "Vine" were long gone, replaced by the "Troost Wall," an invisible but known-to-all north-south boundary that kept white and Black communities apart in Kansas City.[10] Since the urban riots of 1968, the word "Troost" became a synonym to whites of their most fearful images of their fellow Black Kansas Citians.

Far to the south on Main Street, a couple of dozen blocks and a world away from these problems, was the Country Club Plaza, a swank retail mecca since the 1920s, where Robert Gordon and other successful professionals in the 1980s had their tastefully appointed offices. An earlier pioneer of urban planning by the name of Jesse Clyde Nichols—also known as J.C.—may have inspired the younger Hall with his innovative mix of shops, offices, apartments, and abundant parking that for half a century had appealed to well-to-do Kansas Citians. Between the venerable Plaza and the brash suburban malls dotting the metropolitan area, few consumers missed the grand old downtown department stores that were now boarded up or bulldozed away.

A closer and more appropriate southern boundary to Hallmark, though, may have been the nearest secondary school, Westport High School, established 1908, located at Thirty-Ninth Street and McGee. Westport High proved that midtown still boasted a sizable student body, but its demography was changing fast. The enrollment was less than 10 percent African American in the mid-1960s but more than 50 percent by 1980, the result of a combination of active desegregation efforts and white flight responses.[11]

Evidence is scant whether the organizers of the Hyatt tea dances took these demographic factors into consideration. They seem to have made no attempts to court a minority audience to the hotel or its attractions. On the pages of *The Call*, Kansas City's African American community newspaper, a reader saw no advertisements for upcoming tea dances like those that graced the major dailies. Joelouis Mattox, an occasional columnist for *The Call*, "wondered" if the dances "were attracting blacks," and on the evening of July 17 went to see for himself. His was one of the few African American perspectives of the post-collapse sights.[12]

Missing connections with a friend working at a nearby Crown Center shop, Mattox walked to the Hyatt at 7:30 p.m., escaping by minutes from becoming a victim himself. The scene, he described later, was "frantic, but not chaotic. . . . There were people with bandages sitting on the sidewalk in front of the IBM building [across the street to the west], and injured people being brought out of the hotel on stretchers. I asked two bystanders what had happened. They said they didn't know."

So, Mattox calmly stepped through a broken lobby window to view the catastrophe and learn for himself. "[I] saw two men pinned beneath an I-beam. One was dead, and the other was alive. Four firemen were working furiously with hacksaws and sledgehammers trying to free the man that was alive. I asked if I could help. One of the firemen said 'go over there.' He pointed to the north end of the lobby."

Moving through the devastated lobby, Mattox saw his second dead person, and near the gift shop, three more.

> A broken pipe near the ceiling was spewing water into the lobby. There was blood and water everywhere. . . . I saw a black lady in a hotel uniform standing by a raised pallet that had seven or eight covered bodies on it. I went over to the lady and asked what had happened. She said, "Sir, two of the catwalks fell." Before I could ask her anything else, a fireman brought another body and put it on the platform, and she went about covering it. I went over to a black firefighter, a Battalion Chief [Arnett Williams], and asked him what I could do.[13]

Mattox walked halfway up the lobby's grand staircase and turned to take in the entire picture. "I saw the sunken semi-circle that once was an elegant lobby bar. It was unrecognizable, littered with forklifts, stretchers, intravenous devices, towels, balloons, and cocktail glass. I saw smoke and flames coming from jackhammers and blowtorches being used to free people from their predicaments."

Mattox also saw body parts sticking out from the rubble. His fellow people of color whom he encountered that night, and as *The Call* also reported, largely fell into the categories of hotel employees and first responders, not tea dancers. The paper went on to reassure its readers, "None of the victims killed were believed to have been black," and graciously offered its deepest sympathy to those who had suffered so terribly.[14]

THE CROWN CENTER COMPLEX, WITH THE HYATT REGENCY AS ITS capstone, was an invaluable asset both to its owners and to the city, and assets must be protected. By the mid-1970s the budget for the Crown Center development had reached $350 million, for this time an immense sum for a private developer, and the master plan was largely completed, with the exception of a second convention hotel. The local and national media proclaimed, "Crown Center is turning slums and ancient buildings into . . . a national showcase," offering "new answers to old urban problems." And the architects of this urban redevelopment marvel were people "who care enough to build the very best."[15]

Envisioned by Joyce Hall, an authentic American genius and the founder of Hallmark, this family-friendly, intentionally insular city-within-a-city provided a magic kingdom of shopping, dining, lodging, and entertainment.[16] Prestigious multistory office buildings, tasteful retail shops and boutiques, and high-rise apartment towers eventually dotted the Hallmark landscape, accompanied by well-camouflaged parking garages that separated traffic between pedestrians and automobiles. Grand Avenue was seen as almost a Hallmark private drive, which annoyed other businesses.[17] The mixed-use redevelopment was highlighted by such outside amenities as an attractive central square and Olympic-sized ice-skating rink.[18] The Crown Center logo even drew upon the famed, five-pointed Hallmark crown itself, a symbol of quality, to form the letter "w" in the word "crown."

Since the immediate aftermath of the disaster, corporate officials knew their actions—or inactions—had soured the public on the vaunted Hallmark reputation for caring and quality. As the media pressed corporate officials, Jim Dawson, a vice president in marketing, spelled out the key questions a week after the disaster in an internal memo. In the memo, a testament to the company's acute sense of self-awareness and self-preservation, and revealing in the use of "you" and "we," Dawson posed five brutal points to senior management:

Why were we so secretive in the two late-hour removal operations?

Why did we not get concurrence from all interested parties, including the Mayor? Why did you say you did when the interested parties say you didn't?

Why were federal investigators denied access to the debris? Why didn't they know it was being moved?

Why hasn't any Hallmark official or expert come forth to explain positively why it's taking the actions it's taking? There must be reasons (legal, insurance, financial, etc.) that are very honest and believable. What are they?

Why aren't you coming forth with any information until you're forced to? Are you trying to hide something?[19]

These questions remained largely unanswered in the contentious months that followed the disaster.

Reopening a scant ten weeks after the collapse seemed insensitive, uncaring, and mercenary—very un-Hallmark—but, public sentiment be damned, the company needed to staunch the flow of red ink. In the interim the hotel had lost $5.5 million, a substantial sum, and gained a new walkway. Along the west wall a new north-south walkway—it was termed a "terrace," not a "skywalk"—replaced the two that had fallen and the dismantled third. It was ground-supported by ten massive steel-reinforced concrete columns on the floor, not the original hanger rods of one and a quarter inch in diameter from the ceiling. An observant reporter at reopening day irreverently commented that the walkway's most conspicuous users were not guests but hotel employees.[20] William S. "Bill" Johnson, a Hallmark executive, spoke on behalf of Don Hall, who had been "personally assured that this hotel has been brought to one of the highest levels of safety possible." This very public act of turning "a mausoleum back into a hotel," tastelessly rushed as it seemed to outside observers, did not square with the carefully crafted image of a caring, quality-conscious institution.[21]

On October 27 Gordon filed a twenty-three-page memo in support of class certification. It was written for an audience of one, Judge Wright, and Gordon's argument appealed to the judge's sense of fairness and addressed the elephant in the room: the limited fund problem. Even at this early stage everyone assumed that most, if not all, of the defendants were holding the weak hand in this high-stakes poker game. If awarded, the compensatory and punitive damages demanded in the hundred lawsuits filed to date would "far exceed the total amount of insurance policies issued by all the potential insurers."[22] Running out of money would obviously affect the plaintiffs, but the huge sums bandied about also scared the wits out of the defendants. Any payments to plaintiffs not covered by the insurance companies would have to come out of their own hides. This could be hundreds of millions of dollars or more, beyond the net worth and solvency of all but Hallmark and Hyatt. Even for these giants, it was a matter of survival. This disaster could deal a fatal blow to their brands and the public's trust in their products. Gordon's call for a class action meant the likelihood of fair outcomes for the victims, but it could also spell financial ruin for their adversaries. Wright needed time to weigh all this, but the practical judge did not need a lot of convincing. Excessive legal fees peeved Wright, who had come from private practice himself. He liked the fact that his court would have the authority to limit fees paid to the plaintiffs' lawyers, which made him—and, by extension, Gordon and his "carpetbagger" friends from Washington—sworn enemies of a host of other lawyers who envisioned hefty contingency fees dancing in their heads.[23]

Until that decision came down, Gordon was not the only one eager to dig into the evidence. The walkway rubble that Hallmark officials had carted away in the dead of night and "drawings, specifications, inspection reports, test reports, and construction logs" were finally going to be examined by outside, objective engineers.[24] The National Bureau of Standards (NBS), no longer limited by the owner to only distant, visual observations, had begun its intensive hands-on investigation into the skywalks collapse. In a probe that lasted through the late summer, fall, and early winter of 1981, the NBS began its comprehensive analysis by faithfully replicating the structural materials and assemblies used in the actual walkways, testing them, and then cross-examining carefully selected specimens from the debris. The investigators wanted to take some critical materials—box beam pieces, lengths of ceiling support rods, and concrete core samples—from their Kansas City home in a Hallmark warehouse to Washington for further analysis, but permission to remove them came only after an order from the state and federal courts. On November 5, after an inspection by lawyers, custody was transferred to the NBS. The pertinent specimens, about 1,400 pounds in all, were then "wrapped for shipment" and "wax seals" affixed to this precious cargo for its trip by van with NBS drivers to the government laboratories in Gaithersburg, Maryland, outside Washington DC.[25]

If this nonregulatory agency of the U.S. Department of Commerce was known for anything by the public, it was for "weights and measures" and the development of quality standards for commercial materials and products. The bureau had a reputation for being "neutral" and "totally independent," as did Edward O. Pfrang of its Center of Building Technology, an "experienced analyst of structural failures" and now the chief investigator of the Hyatt collapse.[26] Pfrang and his colleagues brought great resources to work the problem: why had the skywalks hanger system failed on the second and fourth floors but not on the third? But they were scientists with labs, not policemen with subpoena power.[27] When Pfrang stated, "We're looking at everything that relates to the skywalks which may have affected their structural ability," he had a narrow field of vision. On the contrary, Gordon and other inquisitors, if given their preference, wanted to know *who* caused the disaster, not *how* it occurred. The answer to the latter was by now pretty well established.[28] Either way, the NBS's conclusive findings, promised to the public in early 1982, would undoubtedly cast a negative light on someone and further roil the waters.

Kansas City had suffered a public relations black eye and a blow to its civic pride, which was only aggravated further by outside journalists like Gigot and distant public officials like Pfrang. It seemed so unfair. Little wonder that soon after the July 1981 collapse the Greater Kansas City Chamber of Commerce rallied behind the home team, in this case, the Kansas City business community. Its good name needed to be restored and quickly. Hallmark's hotel disaster was a disaster for everyone.

The Chamber of Commerce came to city hall with a salve, a "five-man committee of experts" to review—behind closed doors—key information about the collapse and then follow with recommendations for any needed changes in the city ordinances relating to construction. Mayor Berkley strongly lobbied for including a couple of impartial "citizen advisors" on the committee to represent the public. He instinctively knew that his constituents needed reassurance in the aftermath of the catastrophe, but his sensible call was rebuffed. The city council, which wanted no part in a blame-game investigation, welcomed the cover that the Chamber offered and approved its plan, citing the organization's "independent evaluation" as a factor in its hurried deliberations. Robert A. Long, the chairman of the Chamber, promised that the investigation would be done by "people who know what they're doing" and would not be a "whitewash job." Each member pledged that any business relationships with Hall or Hallmark, "big customers of mine" reported one, "would not stand in the way of a thorough airing of any problems they might uncover." One problem was the committee's limited charge: to keep tabs on the current inspection process as it led up to an upcoming reopening. Another was the composition of the all-male committee, the members of whom were affiliated with the construction industry. Ensuring the quality of the repair work and, one hoped, the safety of future hotel patrons were their top priorities. Determining the cause of the collapse was outside their purview, which may have seemed counterintuitive since they were reviewing corrective measures to prevent another disaster. Nevertheless, the committee strictly abided by that self-imposed restriction. An editorial writer for the *Kansas City Times*, also chafing from its reporters being barred from all committee deliberations, gently hinted at a perceived rush to judgment. ("We hope we are wrong, but there appears to be an eagerness on the part of many involved to rush along.")[29] Other than the owner, the Chamber, and the city council, this "neutral party" approach pleased no one, but the committee's activities in the next few months guaranteed a distraction. When the committee toured the Hyatt lobby floor during a well-publicized field trip, a gaggle of cordoned-off reporters, photographers, and cameramen could only watch from afar.[30]

It took the committee only ten weeks to formulate a favorable, all-clear preliminary statement, which it made before the city council on October 1, a mere four hours before the first guests arrived at the remodeled Hyatt Regency. The conjoined events created a small stir in the newspapers. The question of safety was officially settled by the powers-that-be. "No building anywhere has ever been so thoroughly studied for safety or, most likely, ever will be again," embellished a Chamber spokesman. Don Hall, a Hallmark official said, was satisfied that the hotel was safe for occupancy. It should have been because the hotel owner ended up spending $5 million more on repairs.[31]

So blessed, the hotel's reopening itself was a quiet affair—"no fanfare, no balloons, no brass bands," pointed out a hotel spokesman.[32] A month later, in a show of support, the Greater Kansas City Chamber of Commerce held its annual banquet at the troubled hotel. All in attendance were ready to put the past year behind them and look ahead to 1982. The outgoing chairman told the evening assembly of nine hundred that they were the "weavers of the fabric that goes into one's life" and that the coming year called for "busy weavers." The Chamber's final report of its hotel investigation, now largely an afterthought, followed a familiar pattern and came out earlier the day of the banquet. To no real surprise, the committee answered no serious questions and offered no recommendations for actions by the city government. Nor was the report part of the evening's gala program for this crowd of forward-looking businessmen. A University of Kansas engineering professor, after a careful read of the report, remarked on the hotel's "all-around sloppiness in construction, supervision, and design."[33] The committee's findings, therefore, convinced no one, except its authors and other Chamber members, and Robert Gordon not at all.

On the same day that the final report came out, Monday, November 2, Gordon spent the day working in the document depository—drudgery he enjoyed—and struck pay dirt. He found, to his satisfaction, "contemporaneous documents . . . revealing reckless disregard for the safety of those who had been urged to walk on and beneath 120 tons [actually 64 tons if one only considers the two fallen skywalks] of steel and concrete." Describing the finds later, he rather immodestly quoted Winston Churchill: "This was a pure case of serendipity, the making of unexpected lucky discoveries, but it should be added that these happen only for prepared minds capable of recognizing what accident sets before them." Setting aside his earlier reservations, Gordon made up his mind about whom to blame, something the Chamber committee had studiously avoided. From this date forward, he wrote, "it was always evident that Hallmark's knowledge of the failure to test the skywalks was due solely to its refusal to authorize the necessary funds." To this experienced hand at uncovering corporate malfeasance, "The proof of that was as solid as anything plaintiffs' counsel [Gordon] had ever encountered." But every discovery of his also came with frustration, an instance that played itself out time and again in the next year and, really, for the rest of his life. At this stage the facts that Gordon uncovered and, to him, their obvious meanings had a limited audience: basically, his legal team and no one else. The public was left in the dark; for facts it was dependent on an environment of hurried reporting, warmed-over press releases, superficial investigations, and mixed messages (for example, "Hyatt Flaws Fixed," as one newspaper headline blared). Here he was sitting on a trove of revelatory papers, "seventeen file cabinets," he later recalled, "eventually filled with documents containing the best written record of what had caused so much suffering."[34] His goal, if he had his way, was to get these incriminating pieces of evidence before the public in a courtroom, the preferred pathway to the truth. The legal activity involving Gordon, Molly Riley, and the plaintiffs' team picked up.

6

The Deponent

On December 3, 1981, Molly Riley gave her deposition before a roomful of lawyers in courtroom 7, United States Courthouse, 811 Grand Avenue, Kansas City, Jackson County, Missouri. Present for the plaintiff were Robert Gordon, Bill Whitaker, and in from Washington DC, Irving Younger and Paul Wolff. Representing the defendant, Hallmark, were two top-notch firms: Stinson, Mag & Fizzell of Kansas City (attorneys John C. Aisenbrey and Robert L. Driscoll) and Hughes, Hubbard & Reed, New York, New York (Richard C. Yeskoo). Eighteen others represented a host of other plaintiffs and defendants.[1] Riley's examination, largely carried out by David R. Morris, Max W. Foust, and John Elliott Shamberg, personal injury attorneys who wanted to kill the class, began with the standard question, "Will you please tell us your full name?" Riley's answer to that was followed with their statement, "Molly, we have a room full of attorneys here today." If this palpable comment was meant to intimidate the young, single, female witness, it failed.

The deposition started at 10:45 a.m. and went past 3:30 p.m. Riley did not take lunch and only took three or four five-minute breaks during the proceedings. In the course of the day Riley went on to tell her story of how and why she came to "represent everyone that was physically touched by that disaster." She added more context to the version that Gordon had heard in July:

> I phoned him [Whitaker] and said that—that he missed some evening, and he said what, and I said I was down at the Hyatt, and he was surprised, expressed surprise, I don't remember his words. And I said I saw in the paper where your ex-wife had been hurt down there, and I was wondering how she was because she was in the hospital. And he asked me what had happened to me and what happened down there. And I told him that I was extremely upset and extremely angry, and I told him I wanted to see to it that something like that could never happen again, that I wanted to file a lawsuit.[2]

She admitted to the room a prior relationship with Whitaker, her counsel, who had represented her in a guardianship case a few years before. But was it more than business? When queried about a "social relationship" between them, Riley asked for clarification: "Would you define 'social' for me?" Did she ever date him? Her answer was yes, in 1975, and "it was two or three dates." How this was relevant was never made clear, as were dodgy questions about her income sources, personal finances, her divorce, the relationship with her ex-husband, current dating history (a pharmacist whom Riley steadfastly refused to name), and her son's childcare on the night of the disaster. Such verbal exchanges, considered decades later through a more enlightened lens, revealed less about the facts of the case than they did about the existing power dynamics of the time, a middle-class woman holding her own in a room of upper-class sexists.[3]

Throughout the 184 pages of the long deposition, Riley's questioners poured out a continuous stream of innuendo to impugn her motives. Her role as rescuer scored her no points. (A Hallmark lawyer derisively referred to nurse-rescuer Riley as "Miss Nightingale.")[4] Some victims, who had suffered terrible physical losses, were asking for millions in damages; her injuries—her terrible experiences that night—were denigrated. Her dollar amount request, "$10,000 at least," seemed piddling in comparison, implying that her suit was a nuisance at best. She became the butt of sarcasm and insult. One lawyer wondered if she would accept an offer of "ten thousand one-dollar bills."[5] The hints were obvious: Molly Riley, gold-digger. Riley, chiseler.

But the figure did matter to her. "I am asking for special damages that I have already shown you the bills for, and corresponding compensatory damages for the pain and suffering that I am continuing to endure." Why did she care about punitive damages, and did she even know their meaning? "I believe those to be damages that punish," Riley replied, "They are to punish those responsible for what happened that night." The lawyers raised the subject of attorney costs to assail her integrity. "They [her attorneys] advised me that I would be ultimately responsible for the costs and expenses and that it would possibly be in the thousands," explained Riley calmly. Could she really pay them? "The agreement was that my attorneys would advance the expenses for me." Foust and Shamberg hammered her about legal expenses. "I am not stupid," countered Riley. "I was well aware of the costs involved." In a statement that could indicate either resignation or determination, she said, "I will try to find the money and pay it."[6] The thrust of this line of the inquiry was to scream sham arrangement, pointedly questioning the motives of the class representative and her counsel, but the blows did not appear to land.

Riley effectively counterpunched, even after being badgered by a male lawyer on his high horse: "What makes you think you are so eminently qualified to represent . . . the awesome responsibility of looking after all of these people that you want to be the representative of," which again reflected as much as anything the sexism of the day. Five months after initiating this action, Riley had an answer to that question: "I understand a Class Action lawsuit to be a suit where an individual or individuals represents an entire group of people, not just themselves as individuals. . . . I am a representative of the members of that Class, that we all have the same things in common, and that I am ultimately responsible for the expenses incurred in the suit in trying to represent everyone in the Class . . . to represent these people who have a common bond with myself, to the best of my ability."

Riley clearly comprehended her role and had no reservations in expressing it or her motivations, which were more than a payoff: "I felt that I wanted, again, to see that this never happens again, that the people or persons responsible be brought to justice, and that all people are equally represented, and I decided that a Class Action, after it was fully explained by Mr. Gordon and Mr. Whitaker, is what I wanted to do." But the issue of money never strayed far from the discussion. When asked whether she had any interest in settling her personal claim, she succinctly answered, "I wouldn't be interested." Later asked this same question again by a different attorney: "I am not personally wanting this case to be settled from my own end. I want these people to be brought to justice, and I want them to never be able to do this to people again." Compensation was not her "prime motive" for filing the lawsuit. She understood the stakes in the starkest of terms: "My best interests aren't why I filed this lawsuit." Gordon had warned her that lawyers on the other side would do a "high pressure job" on her, they did, and she came through intact with her calm, collected demeanor and the courage of her convictions.[7] Molly Riley proved a model class action representative. This stressful day in the hot seat, before a largely hostile audience, turned out to be a dramatic high point for her.

Other than as a participant observer, Gordon left no indelible record in the Riley deposition, but he was busy, as his time records for the month attested. On December 6, three days after Molly's deposition and at the beginning of his self-described "second phase" of the class action lawsuit, he logged as his main activity "class action hearing preparation." Two days later, still drafting, revising, and reviewing his motion for class certification, Gordon also "pulled together 25 best pun. dam. [punitive damage] documents on Crown Center/Hallmark just in case Court wants to see what is the factual belief that defts [defendants] consciously disregarded known dangers." Two more days and he was in federal court.[8]

Irving Younger led the argument before Judge Wright in favor of certification, and he was in fine form. Wright later recalled that Younger "was an absolute master when he was 'on stage' inside the courtroom." The orator stressed that initial claims now exceeded $3 billion, although insurance barely covered 10 percent of that figure. Early damage settlements threatened to deplete the limited amount of money available to pay later claimants. He was not remiss in acknowledging Gordon's diligence with the document depository. Gordon, he said, had "come upon documents which apparently have not yet come to the attention of the other intervening plaintiffs" represented by the personal injury attorneys who had filed in state court. The importance of these pieces of discovery evidence could not be overstated. "They represent a persuasive showing that there is a substantial case to be made on punitive damages against at least some of these defendants." Younger summed up: "So powerful are these documents . . . I could be ready to try this case on punitive damages on a class-wide basis on Monday, May 17, 1982."[9] Gordon may have gilded the lily when he followed on Younger's heels with a seven-page letter to Wright that explained, as he noted in his diary, "in greater detail what I had found re: pun. dam. [punitive damages]" Gordon pointed to the liability of "Crown Center & Hallmark due to its disqualification of General Testing Labs & Eldridge a year before Skywalks collapsed because of the 'poor work, poor performance,' [and] 'disastrous conduct' by those companies."[10]

The argument for creating a class—simplification, speed, and fairness—proved persuasive because on January 25, 1982, Judge Wright issued his order in favor of the plaintiffs. The benefits to the court were obvious. Who had ever experienced so many cases of such magnitude and potential damages all at once? Wright liked the notion of one case replacing dozens and not clogging his docket until the millennium. He ruled that it would be a mandatory class action, which meant that "everyone would be bound by the resolution of the case on the issues of liability and punitive damages." He later wrote, "Once those issues were decided in the first phase of the case, each individual claim would either settle or go to trial over compensatory damages."[11] The notion also appealed to the ex-marine's egalitarian nature that the large but limited funds available from the strapped defendants—if a judgment presumably went against them—would be shared by all plaintiffs and not totally exhausted by the early, big winners. It was almost as if a guilty verdict was a foregone conclusion. The defendants would be found liable, and they would pay enormous damages. Six months after Molly Riley sought shelter from her personal storm in the Gordon-Whitaker law office, the *Federal Skywalk Cases* had set sail.

7

The *Federal Skywalk Cases*

The coming year—1982—turned out to be the defining period in Robert Gordon's life, a year in which, as he once described it, he lived "several lifetimes."[1] The *Federal Skywalk Cases* was the most important legal case on which he had ever worked or ever would. Never were the stakes so high or the adversaries so low. His personal life was set aside for the duration. Concerns about health only mattered if they threatened the time and energy to keep going. There would be no stopping until the matter was resolved. There were always documents to analyze, briefs to write, witnesses to depose, colleagues to consult, and opponents to counter. Each day brought another in a relentless series of challenges, obstacles, pushback, stonewalling, double-dealing, disappointments, strategizing, and the thrust and parry of legal battle. Stunning victories were invariably accompanied by crushing defeats, and vice versa. Yet the fighting persisted, the outcome always remaining in doubt until near the end. And after the struggle formally ended, Gordon refused to let it go.

The courtroom victory that certified the class surprised even the most optimistic of the plaintiffs' team. "In the aftermath of the court's January 25, 1982, ruling," wrote Gordon later, "the class team was euphoric." The normally buttoned-down Cambridge professor Arthur Miller called to congratulate. "He sounded as jubilant as a new father," and, in the sense that he helped bring the notion of a class action to life, he deserved to be.[2]

Earlier in the month the insurance companies that were on the hook for damage claims announced that they were committed to a $151 million pool for out-of-court settlements.[3] None applied to punitive damages. This amount would figure in all subsequent negotiations and would be a self-fulfilling prophecy in the final outcome.

The trial was tentatively scheduled for August 16, 1982, and was estimated to last three to six months. More than 250 witnesses were expected to be called and five thousand exhibits presented. In response, Gordon immediately ramped up his operation. He leased more office space and acquired more equipment—furniture and file cabinets, word processors and "super-fast, heavy-duty copiers," more phones, a postage meter, a beefed-up burglar-and-fire alarm system, and "private areas to think."[4]

The joy and determination of one side was mirrored by the vehement protests and equal resolve of the other, particularly the personal injury lawyers who usually toiled in the Missouri state court, a venue considered more generous in its awards than its federal counterpart. Although consolidating dozens of lawsuits, many filed in state court, into one federal class action was a bold stroke, even noble in its intent, the personal injury lawyers considered the action appalling. Their hopes for big paydays and million-dollar windfalls were seriously threatened. Eagerly anticipating a third of each client's recovery from these sure-thing damage cases, they had no intention of swapping huge, multiple fees for a one-time recovery at hourly billable rates. The class action might serve the victims well, but their lawyers not so much, at least in the collective opinion of this branch of the legal community.

Though seething, the "plaintiff intervenors," who literally intervened in this legal proceeding as interested third parties, wrote a polite but inflexible letter to Judge Wright stating their intractable position. The three signatory attorneys still "firmly" believed class action was not in the "best interests of victims seriously injured or dependents of those killed," without stating the obvious—that nor was it in their own best interests. They were offended that their motivations in opposing the class had been questioned because "no one representing such people"—least of all these gentlemen—"could put selfish economic interests above the interests of these victims." They continued in the same vein, "Our opposition to the class has always been based on the conviction the seriously damaged victims will be compensated more fully and expediously [*sic*] for their actual damages without a class action."[5] No one bought their argument.

Wright's ruling was immediately appealed to the U.S. Court of Appeals for the Eighth Circuit in St. Louis, Missouri, through a writ of *mandamus*, Latin for "we command." In this instance the personal injury lawyers were seeking a peremptory order, or command, from the higher appellate court to the lower district court to decertify the class. The subsequent battle would take months to play out.[6] This sword of Damocles hung over everyone for the next six months, the fate of the federal class action suit seemingly hanging by a thread.

In the meantime, the mob took their ire out on Molly Riley, unemployed since the day of her deposition when her hospital employer forced her to resign, and successfully challenged her role as the class representative.[7] The reason was "lack of diversity," which meant in this context, diversity in citizenship that the federal court demanded. Riley resided in Kansas, as did one of the defendant companies, and that was a problem. One or the other would have to be dropped from the civil action, and it turned out to be Riley. This was more a nuisance because another victim could step into the breach as the class representative, which soon happened, but it came as a blow to Riley and Gordon. Still a plaintiff, she kept up on the proceedings that followed, and Gordon regularly updated her in the following months.[8]

With the odds against them, lawyers for the defendants followed a playbook of delay and disruption. They petitioned to get Judge Wright thrown off the case or, if that failed, a change in venue. Either tactic appeared to the plaintiffs as a declaration of weakness. "There is no risk of change of venue," said Younger dismissively, "since the publicity on this case is already so massive."[9] Wright remained on the case, and the case remained in his court for the immediate future.

The challenges to Riley and Wright aside, the threat of ruinous punitive damages if the defendants lost was real and intense. Hallmark, with its deep pockets, tried to distance itself from its Crown Center Redevelopment

Corporation by claiming CCRC was an independent entity solely involved and responsible for this individual project, a tactic that would have transferred the basis for punitive damages from the billion-dollar parent to a $40 million division.[10] Throwing the latter to the wolves would have been a small price to pay.

Meanwhile, more embarrassing details emerged. Evidently, Eldridge, the general contractor on the hotel project, had long been bankrupt and kept afloat—and captive—by Hallmark, which meant that the owner had essentially taken on that responsibility during the construction project. In Gordon's view, Hallmark became its own general contractor after Eldridge went broke, and in so doing, the owner removed an integral safety feature—a critical check and balance. Their entwined relationship made it even more difficult for Hallmark to distance itself from the disaster, but it never ceased to try, especially in the public's mind.[11]

The seemingly scattershot approach to a defense, however, followed a common theme—if not eliminate the class, then pick away relentlessly at the size of the class and by extension the potential punitive damages. Hence, individual settlements with Hyatt victims resumed post-certification at full speed. "The defendants knew that if there was going to be a punitive damage trial in August," wrote Gordon, "they should not forego any chance to settle as many cases as possible, since each remaining victim's cause of action represented another basis for the jury to increase the total punitive award." This was a big tell on how the defendants played the weak hand dealt them, basically an early but unspoken concession to an eventual unfavorable verdict. The press, the public watchdog for these maneuvers, never caught on.[12]

Little wonder that the focal point of the mob's wrath finally fell on Robert Gordon, the greatest champion of punitive damages. Appointed by Wright as a logical choice to serve as colead counsel for the plaintiffs in the federal case, Gordon was not a member of their good-old-boys club and, therefore, was an easy target for his adversaries. His forte was not personal injury cases, as theirs was, and hence in their eyes, his experience was unqualified. Oddly, they saw his past experience in a dozen class action cases as irrelevant in this a class-action suit. Ignored or forgotten were his earlier class-action successes in the litigation against such obscure names as Fine Paper, Sugar Antitrust, Folding Carton, Reinforcing Steel Bar, Corrugated Box, and Topsy's, a chain of popcorn stores. None of the verdicts drew front-page coverage, but their outcomes composed a significant portion of his professional success. One colleague described him as "one excellent class action lawyer."[13] To modern eyes, Gordon was being swift-boated almost a quarter century before the term entered the American lexicon.[14] If not fit for the *Federal Skywalk Cases*, who was?

Prone to intemperate remarks, Gordon did nothing to ease the anxieties of the defendants' attorneys. He made it clear in his public statements that the ultimate point of the class-action suit was "to seek punitive damages to make sure those found responsible for the tragedy pay for it." He hoped that severe punishment would put the fear of God in anyone in the future daring to put up an unsafe building. For Gordon this position was no mere bargaining chip—he believed it. Fortuitously for his continued involvement, the formal objections went nowhere after an increasingly irate Wright came to Gordon's defense and denied the motion to disqualify, noting that "character assassinations have been legion."[15]

Attacks from his legal brethren were especially galling to Gordon, who prided himself on following the rules, and such ethical tactics placed him at a disadvantage. As his son Andy later noted, "My dad thought he was playing chess."[16] Gordon realized that he did not practice the type of law that a viewer of classic TV's *Perry Mason* would recognize, but neither did his attackers. He also could understand, maybe even accept, their collective efforts to destroy the class. That was part of the game, but never the breaking of established rules.

One new ruling came from Judge Wright, and Gordon took great pleasure in carrying it out. Wright's January certification decision shifted the responsibility of handling discovery from the group of personal injury lawyers to the federal class lawyers. Gordon, who needed no encouragement, was in his element, and he defined the next six months of documents work as his "second phase" of the case.[17] But he needed help and immediately urged his allies at Williams & Connolly to move to Kansas City and "get cracking on discovery." When asked when the big guns from DC would set up shop locally, Irving Younger replied, "Soon."[18] But Gordon's plea went unheeded, so he got "cracking" instead.

The time for further discovery—document requests and witness depositions—was finite, a matter of a few months. Wright's timetable for the case mandated the conclusion of this phase by July. Therefore, "to do the dizzying job correctly," Gordon strategized, "I could not merely read tons of documents day and night. Indices, files, cross-references, and digests for retrieval also had to be prepared." Foremost in this system were his "hot files," where he placed the most important documents, each with a brief explanation of how that document helped prove their case. This group had its counterpart: documents that hurt their case. Whether he was speaking from humility or hubris, Gordon claimed, "Throughout the entire course of the skywalks litigation, my Ouch File contained only one document, the minutes of the December 12, 1979, design review meeting at Hallmark." This was the meeting highlighted by Don Hall's presence and his only documented "safety" lecture. This document seemed to indicate that, after the atrium roof collapse, the structural engineers had checked *all* the atrium connections and found them safe, thereby largely absolving Hallmark of negligence. This was the Hallmark skywalks defense in a nutshell: "It had known nothing negative or even suspicious" about the steel-to-steel vertical connections or the steel hanger rods and box beams. This document stuck in Gordon's craw. To him—and maybe him alone—the meeting minutes seemed too convenient, and he suspected their message had been massaged. Gordon spent considerable time discrediting the contents, until eventually, to his satisfaction, he "discovered some major problems with Hallmark's favorite piece of paper."[19] He would save that for the trial.

IN THE MIDST OF THIS HYPERACTIVITY THE NATIONAL BUREAU OF Standards reappeared and came out with its findings, fulfilling its promise "to give the Kansas City public an explanation of the hotel disaster" and its "most probable cause."[20] The 258-page report covered the bureau's extensive laboratory tests, going into great detail about things but not about people. At its driest, the report stated where the disaster began:

"Failure of the walkway system initiated in the box beam-hanger rod connection at location 9UE (east [E] end of middle box beam in fourth floor [U or upper] walkway)." The nut-and-washer assembly on the rod had pulled through this box beam. Lost support at this location transferred load instantaneously to other locations, which failed in turn, with devastating effects to the upper skywalk, then to the skywalk below. A rare mention of people, not things, was the conclusion the engineers made about the number of persons—the "live load"—on the skywalks at the time of the collapse. Discounting eyewitness estimates and relying on television videotape shot prior to the collapse, they estimated about forty people on the second-floor skywalk and a total of sixty-three on both.[21] The report did not say how many of this number survived.

Other than that portion, as an engineering study, it was not easy reading for the layman and required translation. In his subsequent press conference in February 1982, Edward Pfrang refused "to point the finger at anyone" but lobbed a couple of grenades anyway. The original design of the walkways had violated all applicable building codes, much less its inferior replacement. The change in the hanger-rod, box-beam design from a continuous to an "interrupted" rod had made the skywalks "easier to build" and "less expensive," but from day one the load on the fourth-floor rod connections was twice what its original plans called for. They were ticking time bombs.[22]

Such statements were big news, but seven months after the disaster with the memories still painful, if the public expected to find out who was to blame, they were mightily disappointed. The victims who were looking for the names of persons to hold responsible, or even the names of any of the project principals, saw none in the government document or heard none during the press conference. Pfrang emphasized to an incredulous press corps, "It was not within our charge to assess blame, liability, or negligence on anyone's part"—in other words, to find managerial mistakes. Readers only learned the "how"—what caused the catastrophic failure of the hotel's walkways. "Cause was one thing," observed Gordon, "culpability was another." The report answered none of Gordon's specific questions: *Who* designed the fatal hanger-rod to box-beam connections? *Who* should have seen and caught the deficiencies? *Who* failed to heed any of the potential danger signs and failed to follow up?[23]

Others spotted the same deficits in the report, including an expert witness for the personal injury attorneys. Ed De Vilbiss, a professor of architecture at Kansas State University, described the Hyatt collapse as "not an engineering error," but a construction management one. "Our attention," stated De Vilbiss, "has been misdirected by the focus of the Bureau of Standards on the engineering aspects." Much later, before an assistant U.S. attorney, De Vilbiss doubled down: "H/CC [Hallmark Cards/Crown Center Redevelopment Corp.] gambled that they could substantially weaken the management of the construction administration and still build a safe building. They lost. The poorly designed interlocking contracts were implemented with the conscious decision to hire a contractor that . . . intended to run the project with roughly half of the professional staff proposed by other contracting firms that were considered. H/CC proceeded under the delusion that they were capable of filling in for the contractor's deficiencies."[24]

Returning to Gordon's basic question, "How could the 1979 problems in the [atrium] connections have failed to highlight the need for quality assurance?" Without subpoena power, however, "the NBS never intended to, nor could it, address or assess the non-mechanical managerial mistakes." That could only come, Gordon believed, from "full fact-finding in the lawsuits and a public trial."[25]

After its initial splash, *Investigation of the Kansas City Hyatt Regency Walkways Collapse* found a large niche audience as a key text for future students of the disaster, whose teachers focused, as in 1982, more on engineering and less on management. Take, for example, this later, anonymous engineering student on an internet forum, obviously familiar with the report's contents, who boiled down the building's structural mistakes in plain English:

> The original plan was for the tie rods to pass through the upper most platform and that platform would be held up by a nut on the

> tie rod, which was threaded. Then the tie rod would continue down and support the deck below in the same manner. This design forced the tie rod to be threaded the entire length as the nut would have to be run up the rod to the top level. The contractor [Havens Steel, the subcontractor who fabricated the steel] proposed a change to avoid using a fully threaded rod. It was not a cost saving measure; it was the real-world problem coming out that the threaded tie rod was bound to be damaged in the process since the assembly was going to be built and hoisted into place. The contractor proposed this change, and the engineer [Gillum-Colaco] approved the submittal. . . . In the new design the rod supported the top deck, and then a second rod supported the second deck by hanging from the top one. The problem here is it forces the top deck assembly to support not only its weight but also the weight of the lower deck. The box beams that were used were not designed to do this.[26]

This interpretation was all true and helpful for engineering students and the general public in their understanding. A couple of generations later, however, explanations still centered on the "how," not the "who."

Setback

However the NBS report helped or hindered his case, Robert Gordon pressed on, but he soon hit another impasse. The defendants' lawyers blocked their clients from testifying at depositions until the U.S. Court of Appeals for the Eighth Circuit rendered its decision on the class-action challenge. Gordon immediately informed Judge Wright of this flaunting of the rules. The judge ordered Gordon to "immediately file a request to hold defense counsel in contempt of court." Gordon gladly complied, and a contempt hearing followed in early March.[1] Wright, according to Gordon, "wanted action, and 'action' to him meant depositions." The defense counsel underplayed the affair, calling it "the normal give-and-take of litigation," and avoided punishment when Younger played good cop to Gordon's bad and withdrew the complaint.[2] Although irritated by Younger yet again, Gordon had accomplished the bigger goal. Depositions proceeded.[3]

Gordon took his first deposition later in March. Richard C. Heydinger, Hallmark's risk manager, testified under oath for five days. Arnold Waxman, Hallmark's project engineer, followed, and his deposition lasted a grueling thirteen days. Gordon's standard operating procedure in conducting depositions required those all-important, associated documents. Referring to defendants in depositions, and these two fellows doubtlessly came to mind, Gordon observed, "The only way to break them down is to confront them with contemporaneous documents that will 'refresh' their well-coached, lobotomized memories."[4] He also likened his technique self-deprecatingly to being "basset-like" and "plodding." (Gordon owned two of the droopy-eared hounds.) Another clue to his manner came from a skywalks-related deposition in which he was not present. Two lawyers sparred over the line of questioning one was taking:

LAWYER ONE: "Excuse me. Would you mind asking questions somewhere else than leaning over the witness's shoulder?"

LAWYER TWO: "Well, I am trying to read the document [that was before the witness] and ask questions at the same time. If you can figure out another way to do it, I would be more than happy to."

LAWYER ONE: "You can look at it and take a half step back."

LAWYER TWO: "I don't think that is necessary. You are starting to sound like Bobby Gordon."[5]

His slow, dogged approach, he said, "eventually unearthed entire categories of documents" relating to the atrium roof collapse, which he then squeezed from the defense. Depositions begat documents, and in turn, "piles of damning documents out of Hallmark" kept "a witness honest during a deposition" and the defense on its toes.[6]

Gordon was on his toes, too, and a pattern emerged in the deposition process. "Depos and discovery went hand-in-hand," he said. "Hallmark held back its most incriminating documents until the eve of that person's deposition." As an example, before the Waxman deposition, "hundreds of pieces of paper that I had never seen before were dumped onto the deposition table just as I was about to begin questioning Waxman." To make matters even more complicated, documents that belonged to one Hallmark executive often were jumbled together with the same type of documents from other execs. Rest assured, Gordon managed to go through the pile before the sessions concluded, but it was always difficult to assign individual documents to one person or another.[7]

After the National Bureau of Standards had determined what Gordon termed the "technical cause" of the collapse, he knew he needed to find any internal criticism "or mere suspicion" of the general design of the atrium, and better yet of the skywalks, to knock down Hallmark's "know-nothing defense." The bulk of his questioning worked this angle, and his last questions to Heydinger illustrated this tactic, as well as the wave of collective amnesia suffered by Hallmark deponents:

Q: "Has anybody at any time ever told you that there was a connection between the two situations, one being the pulling away of the skywalks (from the north wall of the atrium wall), and the other being the collapse of the atrium roof on October 14, 1979?"
A: "Not that I recall."
Q: "Have you ever seen any documents that made a connection between the two?"
A: "Not that I recall."[8]

Gordon also confirmed a couple of details in the developing timeline of the pending disaster. Heydinger's meeting notes after the atrium collapse backed up Gordon's supposition that the principals were aware of "design and construction defects in the lobby."[9] After the atrium roof collapse, Hallmark lawyers prevented an investigator from their insurance company from doing an immediate field exam and only relented months later after debris cleanup and roof reinstallation made it moot. After the roof collapse, Hallmark also fortuitously bought a second insurance policy to cover future unforeseen building failures. Unrelated to the timeline and on a whim, Gordon asked one meeting participant whether recording devices had been present at critical times. The expected answer from this insider would have been a definite "no." The actual response—"Not that I recall"—sounded suspicious.[10]

Minor frustrations aside, Gordon counted on "everything about the disaster coming out at trial," and he was doing his part in getting ready for the August court date. The same could not be said for Younger and Wolff, and Gordon came to the crushing conclusion that his partners were more interested in avoiding a trial and reaching a settlement. The pair never moved to Kansas City, ostensibly waiting for the Eighth Circuit Court's ruling about the class, and confined their visits to the occasional "whirlwind" meeting and mandatory court appearance. They left Gordon holding the bag by making him conduct their depositions. Younger, in particular, never familiarized himself with the documents, "the nitty-gritty, little details on which a lawyer builds a case," and seemed more interested in the publicity the case generated.[11] Profiled in a national law journal, one passage especially infuriated Gordon: "For several years Younger has been thinking about how to handle mass tort cases, a process of analysis that led him to writing the brief in the Kansas City case." To which Gordon seethed, "Actually, Younger had not even read the brief until after it was finished and filed here."[12]

Others were even less charitable. Richard Routman, a Kansas City attorney who served with Gordon as a cocounsel on the plaintiffs' team, accused Younger to his face. "Everyone I speak to thinks that you are just in it for as much money and as little work as possible."[13] Spoken in anger and frustration, it had the ring of truth.

In late April and knee-deep in the Waxman deposition, Gordon learned that Williams & Connolly had worked up an initial out-of-court settlement with the defendants. Hallmark, he was informed, would pay all the compensatory damages to victims who had been either physically or emotionally harmed. "Even those who suffered no physical injury will receive a thousand dollars apiece." The company would also pay punitive damages of $10 million, an "absurdly low" sum in Gordon's estimation, and "not a penny [of] that will come out of Hallmark's coffers." Gordon, who constantly and vigorously voiced his opposition to this or any other settlement, considered it a "cheap option." Not only would Hallmark get off easy, but it would "avoid the adverse publicity of a public trial and the danger of a jury's verdict," along with the enormous punitive damages expected as a result.[14] Plus, as two newspaper analysts declared, a settlement would end any "further examination of how the accident happened or who was responsible." Thomas E. Deacy Jr., a lawyer for the Hyatt Corporation and a realist, disagreed. "I don't think civil litigation is for the purpose of informing the public and satisfying the public's interest in what brought something about," he said. "The proper function of the civil courts is to decide controversies."[15] Another function apparently was to put the proper spin on the outcome, and a small catch popped up in the fine print.

Punitive damages could not be called that but had to carry the innocuous term of "supplementary compensation." That face-saving, public relations detail mattered not a whit to the agreeable Younger, who thought Judge Wright would approve the settlement. The more pressing concern for the plaintiffs' lead counsel was the impending appellate court decision. A ruling not in the plaintiffs' favor meant the decertification of the class. Was this Younger's real reason for his haste, or was an early settlement his goal all along? Gordon came to believe the latter, which only buttressed his misgivings about Younger and Wolff.[16]

A meeting in Wright's chambers followed, and in the *Kansas City Star* front-page news story that followed, the reporter cast Gordon in a dim light using fewer than a dozen words. "Mr. Gordon," read the article, "said he believes the amount of the proposed settlement—reportedly $23.5 million, *with $3.5 million as legal fees for the class-action team*—is too low" (italics mine).[17] This was incorrect. Gordon had said the $20 million figure, and only that amount, was too low. Legal fees were not part of their conversation. When the reporter combined both figures together and attributed it to Gordon, he lumped together *all* the class counsel as greedy guns-for-hire, which galled Gordon to no end. He complained immediately to the paper about this "hatchet job," and the *Star* promptly issued a "clarification," one that came off as something less than a retraction.[18] It read in toto: "An article in *The Kansas City Star* on May 3 may have implied that Robert C. Gordon, a Kansas City lawyer, was the source of information that attorney fees of $3.5 million would be taken out of a proposed $23.5 million settlement in the class-action lawsuit stemming from the Hyatt Regency disaster last summer. Attorney fees were not mentioned in an interview with Mr. Gordon for that story."[19]

Someone had mentioned these fees, and whoever did had neatly placed Gordon, to his embarrassment, in the same category as the Lantz Welches of the world. Score one for the defense in the battle for the hearts and minds of Kansas City readers. This would not be the last local newspaper story that Gordon would clip out, stew over, and rage against in 1982.

Settlement negotiations threatened to bring discovery and depositions to a halt, and everyone involved knew what an extended hiatus meant, especially the personal injury lawyers in state court who had turned over the discovery process to Gordon's team. A settlement on punitive damages now, said attorney Max Foust, normally an implacable Gordon foe, "would be the most effective way to cover up everything."[20] And there would be nothing to hinder the defendants from continuing their unchallenged and very public denials of culpability.

To add to his distress, not only was Gordon in limbo, he was tossed out of his old law firm. His partners had cast a collective vote "yea" for the settlement in Gordon's absence while he was engaged in taking a deposition. He received a letter from Anderson, Granger, Nagels, Lastelic & Gordon that, as of June 1, there would be no more Gordon on the letterhead. "I had been booted out of my law firm for not supporting Hallmark's settlement proposal," Gordon would observe later.[21] The firm was also aggravated, according to Gordon, that he had classified his five hundred hours of case work prior to December 1981 as *pro bono publico*, in other words, no fees. This was too much altruism for his colleagues, one partner saying that Gordon "now speaks only for himself, as he did often while he was with this firm."[22]

Not surprisingly, Gordon continued working on the case, proud of the tangible accomplishments by the group to date in the discovery phase: twenty-four depositions, 7,300 pages of testimony, more than five hundred exhibits. And he had cracked an even tougher nut. "Hallmark," he said, had been "forced to disgorge about eighteen thousand previously withheld documents," and he was not done yet.[23] In late May Judge Wright issued a court order that directed the defendants to produce more documents that Gordon had targeted, specifically those that revealed their "appraisals of their respective responsibilities for design, construction, inspection, testing, maintenance, and use of the skywalks."[24] The greatest danger, the one that had loomed over everything, now materialized.

On June 7, 1982, the Eighth Circuit, in a two-to-one decision, overruled Judge Wright and "vacated," or decertified, the mandatory class and, with that, formally dissolved the case. The majority ruled that the class had incorrectly included cases filed in state court before the class was certified, which, in their opinion, violated the federal Anti-Injunction Act.[25]

If the legal ruling was unclear to the layman, the real-world implication was not. "Naturally," declared Gordon, "Hallmark pulled the plug on its class-wide settlement overture to Younger." As the one-year anniversary of the skywalks collapse approached, a shaken but undeterred Gordon set a new course: "My task now was to keep trying to get the facts about the collapse and hope for a voluntary class." In the meantime, Hallmark was taking no chances and "settling right and left" with victims in order to reduce the size, if not eliminate the formation, of a new and modified class.[26] The race was on.

A BURST OF MEDIA ATTENTION FOLLOWED THE FIRST ANNIVERSARY of Hallmark's hotel disaster. As one local columnist wryly observed, "Journalists cannot leave anniversaries of tragedies alone," and this time was no different.[27] The paper focused on the "tangle of legalities" and provided up-to-date statistics to emphasize the point. About $25 million had been paid in damages so far to 162 claimants, the *Kansas City Times* reported, with $5 million to $7.5 million of that going to their attorneys. Although not a beneficiary of this big payday, Gordon appeared in the feature story anyway, reflecting his heightened public profile, and gave, for him, a mild quote. "If our community is to gain anything from this dreadful experience, it is critically important that the public and the press receive forthright and accurate information."[28]

Molly Riley, still firm in her opinions, appeared in the same article and held little back. The strong words voiced by the former class representative for the *Federal Skywalk Cases* indicated that the horrors experienced by the victims, the survivors, and the first responders remained fresh in people's minds, and Riley had more to share about that night:

> There was this woman around my age trapped in between the first and second floors. The medic said, "Forget her. We can't get her out." And she heard that. This girl had a piece of concrete impaled in her chest for two hours, and she was given up for dead. . . . No amount of money is going to pay her husband or her kids, if she's got them. I feel that she and so many others will have suffered and died for

> nothing. But maybe the litigation can be used to deter companies from ever building a building like this. That is my motive [for a trial]. It's not the money. I just keep seeing that woman.[29]

Others demurred and only wanted July 17, 1982, to pass quietly. Mayor Richard Berkley, who had been a stretcher bearer in the hotel one year before, walked a political tightrope. The mayor grieved as many others but did so privately. "My feeling," Berkley said, "is that people will certainly be aware of the date and handle it in their own individual way." He planned no civic observance, thought the media was making more of the occasion than was warranted, and saw the city well on its way to "normalcy." Robert McGregor, the new president of the Chamber of Commerce of Greater Kansas City and a less astute politician, placed his emphasis squarely on the highly competitive convention business and its place in the local economy. "If we're going to continue to promote Kansas City as the most important place in the middle of the country, we need quality hotels. We need that hotel."[30]

Looking back with grief and unanswered questions and looking forward to healing and forgetting, these polar opposite attitudes became the dual forces, the standard yin and yang, of those who wanted to move on and consider the disaster as an unfortunate one-off and those who wanted to remember and get to the bottom of what essentially remained a mystery. This dichotomy of public, all-too-human responses holds as true for today's man-made catastrophes as it did in Kansas City in the 1980s.

For Gordon, meanwhile, few facts were in the public domain, and the condition did not look to improve. Information necessary to tell something resembling the full story resided in the document depository, but its secrets had yet to be revealed. It was closed to all but the attorneys and their paralegals. Even worse for getting facts out to the public, the Eighth Circuit Court had decertified the class, and a trial was uncertain. The August trial date was definitely off the calendar. The plaintiffs' team was at an admitted "low ebb."[31]

The appellate court's decision did not mean an end to individually filed federal cases, however. Several cases remained filed in federal court for

Wright to adjudicate, not to mention those in state court by other judges. The discovery process—and Gordon's work as deposition coordinator—continued in what he in time called his "third phase" of the case. After Hallmark and its retinue saw the class action crippled and the immediate danger abated, they breathed a sigh of relief and now complied almost willingly with Gordon's nonstop document requests.[32] Together with the raft of depositions still scheduled, Gordon was swamped with work.

As the initial blow from the Eighth Circuit wore off, the plaintiffs' team spied an opening. A modification to the class might mollify the court, and this they promptly made. The "newly modified class," voluntary, not mandatory, offered an "opt-out" clause, by which members could drop out from the class, settle one's own claim, and grant relief to the defendants.[33] It seemed a good strategy at the time, maybe the only one, but the proposed loophole came back to bite the team later. Gordon wrote the legal brief arguing this point. Although anonymous, he is the obvious author because its concluding paragraph contained a tortured metaphor, a quirk that characterized his future writings: "Just because the class 'vehicle' may have temporarily lost a fender on its detour to St. Louis should not result in its ultimate discard to the junk yard. The vehicle can be readily repaired in order to maintain its steady course toward an early trial date."[34] This entire passage was reprinted in the paper, which only encouraged later flights of literary fancy.[35]

As Gordon wrestled one problem to the ground, another arose. None of the defendants hailed from Iowa, and Shirley Stover, an Iowan who had been buried by concrete at the Hyatt and rescued, brought the necessary geographic "diversity" to the case. She had filled Molly Riley's shoes as the class representative, but she would not remain so in the new and supposedly improved class. In an August hearing to discuss the merits of the yet-to-be-certified version, Gordon predicted in court that Hallmark would try to buy off Stover by settling her claim in order to undermine the class once again.[36] His counterpart for Hallmark strenuously objected to this insult before Judge Wright, maybe too much, because that is exactly what happened.[37]

In early September Stover settled for $3.25 million. Lacking a suitable class representative, Judge Wright denied the formation of a new class, although he left the door open. He did consolidate the remaining federal cases and set a court date for January 10, 1983, with or without class-action status.[38] Robert L. Collins, the Stover lawyer, defended his actions by citing his responsibility to his client and the irresponsibility, as he saw it, of Williams & Connolly, who seemed to have disappeared from the scene. A disgusted Collins spared no criticism of Irving Younger's work as lead counsel for the plaintiffs, and that of Younger's colleague and Gordon's boyhood chum Paul Wolff. The latter, said Collins, "elected to vacation in Europe at a time when, I am told, he was scheduled to be taking depositions in Kansas City." And communicating directly to Younger in a scorching letter, "You have failed to honor your commitments to Bob Gordon (by whose grace you were ever even remotely involved in the Hyatt cases), the Court, and the victims of the Hyatt disaster."[39]

Gordon, desperately needing help from Younger and Wolff with discovery and trial preparation, continued to urge that they move to Kansas City. He even solemnly swore that, if they came, "I shall not ever bring up complaints and irritants." After this plea again fell on deaf ears, he responded in the only way he knew how—by putting in more hours at the office. The phrase "slept at office" began to crop up in his daily diary.[40]

In late September the plaintiffs' lawyers found another young woman to be its class representative. The third time was a charm with Deborah Jackson, a resident of Utah and an Iowa native who brought the necessary diversity of citizenship to the class. On July 17, 1981, the thirty-year-old had come down from her hotel room to the lobby in perfect time to witness from a safer distance the skywalks collapse. She suffered, according to her critics, "insignificant" physical and "alleged" mental injuries. As a guest of luxury hotels, Jackson was cursed. Only two years before, she had escaped the MGM Grand Hotel and Casino fire in Las Vegas, Nevada, which devastated the structure and claimed eighty-five lives, but this fact played no part in the judge's deliberation. Wright certified Jackson and the new, voluntary class in late October.[41] Punitive damages were back on the table.

WHILE THE PERSONALITY CLASHES LARGELY REMAINED BEHIND THE scenes, all the courtroom fits and starts became fodder for the newspapers, and it usually played poorly for the federal plaintiffs' counsel. Gordon always believed his side was at a distinct disadvantage to the Hallmark public relations machine when it came to press dealings. Nevertheless, he single-handedly tried to overcome this deficit and level the playing field. He knew a way to bring the press around—if not exactly to his side, then maybe a step closer to the "truth," and for Gordon the truth lay with the documents. But they remained unavailable to reporters in the depository. What if, together as allies, they could pry the door open on behalf of the public?[42]

It was always an uneasy alliance. Gordon, in a low moment and from the perspective of hindsight, perceived an "anti-class-action, anti-punitive-damage, and anti-federal-court slant of many of the stories" he read in the morning *Times* and the afternoon *Star*. While he was portrayed as anything but an unbiased source, he indeed knew the details of the case. He was a fact-checker's dream, and this appealed to the reporters. Equally important, he was always available at any time, any day, for a call or a conference. Between the months of June and October 1982 Gordon spoke or met with at least twelve different local reporters, nine from print media and three from television. During this period his daily time record—a truly remarkable and detailed historical document—noted more than 150 phone calls, individual meetings, group conferences, and bull sessions, several extending into the wee hours of the night. This figure does not include contacts with outside publications, such as the *Wall Street Journal*, or background meetings he held for local news editors, the reporters' bosses.[43] Robert Gordon became by necessity a one-man public information office.

The "paper" (Gordon's term, shared by all Kansas Citians who lumped the *Star* and *Times* together) was his primary means for shaping the story. Formerly employee owned, since 1974 the two newspapers had been the property of Capital Cities Communications, a New York media powerhouse that would be gobbled up a decade later by the Walt Disney Company. "CapCities" was a strong corporate owner, on the surface immune from midwestern parochial pressures and powerful enough to stand up to Hallmark, a fellow "co-establishment leader" in Kansas City. In contrast, the local television and radio stations possessed only a fraction of the power, influence, and protection enjoyed by the paper. Gordon knew the paper was "the only vehicle for disseminating relevant information," that is, for getting out damaging information from the documents before the public eye.[44]

Still, Gordon was not all that confident. Although the paper had been correct early on with the structural engineering causes of the skywalks collapse and still basked in the glow of its well-deserved Pulitzer win in April for its coverage of the Hyatt story, it had dropped the ball starting with the National Bureau of Standards report.[45] "The paper's equation of the rod and beam failure with the legal and moral reason for the skywalks disaster," wrote Gordon later, "was as wrong as concluding that the O-ring alone was responsible for the *Challenger* tragedy," a reference to the 1986 space shuttle failure. He could only shake his head about how the reporters missed the point that "the responsible party could be someone other than, or in addition to, the contractor, the architect, the engineer, the subcontractor, or the fabricator." But maybe, with some guidance, he could help redirect their slant and shape the public's perception away from the notion that Hallmark, the owner, was merely an innocent bystander.[46] Everyone had assumed that all relevant documents would be made public in the August trial, but with that date off the books, circumstances demanded a change in plans. If this pack of journalists listened and learned, concluded Gordon, and if they could be trusted to do the right thing, they could reinvigorate the investigation, craft a different narrative, and set the record straight. Most importantly, they had to dig through the evidence themselves, and that meant having access to the document depository.

Gordon took on the task officially in early July when he counseled with the paper's top in-house lawyer. Together they planned a one-two punch for the argument in favor of opening the records. First came a characteristically lengthy, forty-page pleading from Gordon to Judge Wright, filed in mid-July. The paper made sure to cover this with a prominent story, headlined "Class Action Lawyers Ask Judge to Open Hyatt Case Documents to Public."[47] A lead editorial followed a couple of days after that—and two days before the anniversary of the disaster. Gordon could not have asked for better words and deeds by his biggest ally: "Nothing contributes more to the creation and coloring of tragic legend than a sense that the truth has not come out, that facts are burrowed away. . . . Nobody wants to prolong the Hyatt agony for Kansas City. But it could be long lasting in the dark recesses of suspicion and rumor."[48]

The defendants quickly replied, both to the press and to the court. The press could not be trusted with this responsibility, their lawyers argued, and this reckless action would only result in the dissemination of inadmissible documents that lacked context and relevance, and they would, therefore, be prejudicial to a fair trial. The general counsel for the *Star* and *Times*, championing the public's right to know, came out in support of Gordon's motion and countered the defendants by playing the Pulitzer card. The paper had earned the prestigious award "in part because of the thorough and accurate manner in which they analyzed complex drawings, diagrams, and other documents. It would be the intention of the editors to continue that careful approach." Moreover, he promised, "the newspapers would allow the documents to speak for themselves." He did not mention Gordon's role as the paper's potential document whisperer, however. In September Wright ruled in favor of a compromise that opened a significant portion of the records, now totaling a half-million documents. To satisfy Hallmark's objection, the compromise granted reporters access to only those documents already in Gordon's possession, which was a significant portion in quantity and quality. Nevertheless, the rush was on.[49] By this time the most widely anticipated document, generated by Gordon himself, was wending its way to the document depository—the deposition of chief executive officer and chairman of the board Donald J. Hall of Hallmark Cards. Gordon had finally caught up to his most prized quarry.

9

Betrayal

The deposition of Don Hall began on August 30, 1982, and was held at a Howard Johnson's on Sixth and Main streets in downtown Kansas City. Compared to Molly Riley's deposition in December 1981, it lasted four days longer and amounted to 829 pages of court-reported transcriptions versus her more modest 184-page document. In stark contrast, the questions directed toward the corporate leader read as more polite and less aggressive than those the young nurse fielded. Hall was not asked whom he was dating or how much money he made. His answers—when he provided substantive answers—also contrasted with those Riley gave. Where her responses appeared hesitant early in the session but grew more confident and passionate as time went on, his were brief, measured, and rarely straightforward, and his lawyers blocked many of the questions. By the thirty-first page of the document, Gordon later observed, one lawyer had "made an objection or coached the witness at least once on every page." What further exasperated Gordon, and presumably his fellow inquisitors who asked the bulk of the questions, was Hall's apparent loss of memory on some aspect or another for just about every subject brought up. "I don't recall" became such a common refrain by this apparent amnesiac that, when asked by an outsider how one particular session went, Gordon answered, "I don't recall."[1] (See this volume's appendix.)

Hall's poor memory notwithstanding, Gordon dutifully notated the entire document afterward, and his typed notes, though lacking in lawyerly decorum and brimming with sarcasm, are priceless reading. He frequently called bullshit on Hall:

> B.S. Denies that he used his right to speak up at design review meetings and disapprove designs.
>
> B.S. Hall denies he ever learned there were structural problems in the Atrium. This is followed by 3 pages of objections from lawyers.
>
> B.S. Claims to never have heard of any design problems with the skywalks or construction problems.
>
> More B.S. Never knew skywalks were pulling away.
>
> In regard to discussion of inspection of design at meetings, Hall gives his usual, escape-hatch, B.S. answer that he heard nothing but conversation regarding aesthetic design and functional layout.
>
> Hall: "My wish, which I have expressed before, at that meeting [on December 12, 1979], as I recall, was that everything that would be critical to safety or loss of life in that building be rechecked from every standpoint." B.S.[2]

Gordon zeroed in on the public statement that Hall made in the immediate aftermath of the skywalks collapse to carry out his own "extensive investigation" into its causes.[3]

> GORDON: "Do you recall, Mr. Hall, stating to that reporter or anyone else, following the collapse, that you pledged that there would be a full and open inquiry and investigation into the cause of the skywalks failure?"
>
> HALL: "I think I might have said something to the effect that we would attempt to find out the cause. I don't remember the words."
>
> GORDON: "Have you attempted to find out the cause?"
>
> HALL: "We have, under the auspices of our attorneys, attempted to find out."
>
> GORDON: "Have you learned the cause?"

At this point Hall's lawyer objected, and after a brief period of back-and-forth, Gordon continued. "When you pledged to the public, and others, that you were going to conduct a full and total inquiry, did you not mean that if you learned the results of that inquiry, you would let the public know?" Again, the defendant's lawyer objected, but Hall replied, "I don't recall what I meant, frankly, in regard to the public."

Gordon pressed on. "Is, is it your intention to make those results available to the public?"

Hall answered, "I would again have to defer to counsel on that, but I would hope that eventually, after the legal actions now in process can be disposed of, that the public would have complete knowledge of what happened in the skywalks."

At this point, John Townsend, Hall's lawyer, asked the court reporter to "show an expletive deleted, on the record."[4] Just a guess, but one wonders if Robert Gordon, after hearing of Don Hall's "hope" for "complete knowledge," said "bullshit" under his breath, or if opposing counsel only thought he did.

Juvenile remarks aside, a few revelations emerged in the critical area of Hallmark's role in project management, even though Hall continued to distance himself from the decision-making process on the Hyatt project.[5] Some grudging progress was made in dispelling "any lingering notion that Hallmark and Crown Center could be considered independent of one another," although Hall adamantly denied that Hallmark or its subsidiary Crown Center Redevelopment Corporation "made an effort to determine how anything was to be built." More light shone on Hallmark's dominant relationship with Eldridge, its bankrupt and hostage general contractor, although Hall denied having anything to do with its selection. He testified that he had little role, if any, in the design review meetings he attended, going so far as to say, "I did not make any design decisions at all." Gordon noted, "Though he remembers being at the 12/12/79 meeting, doesn't remember discussing the skywalks design or construction problem." Moreover, when asked something as innocuous as how often he had visited the site to acquaint himself with construction progress, Hall replied with a variation of his usual refrain: "I would have no very good guess on that topic." Such answers really got under Gordon's skin.[6]

The head of Hallmark even tried to appear removed from the power of the purse. "Hall won't say HMK wanted the Hyatt completed on time, within budget; only that CCRC did, and it was not a concern, it was an interest."[7] His denials of personal involvement and corporate oversight were stunning admissions and, if true, revealed a detached, hands-off chief executive officer bordering on the negligent, complacent, or incompetent. One doubts anyone in the room believed the denials, least of all Gordon, who said later, "Nobody asked me, but frankly, if it had been my hotel and my money, I would have expected to have the final say-so on what the structure was going to look like, how it was going to be used, and how much it was going to cost me."[8]

As the gathering adjourned and left the room one day, Gordon spotted some torn-up scraps of paper in a wastebasket and fished them out. On a hunch he took them home and had his daughter, Tracy, and son, Andy, piece them back together like a jigsaw puzzle. One note passed from a Hallmark lawyer to another read, "If I were DJH, after this experience I'd issue an order that *NO ONE* write or send me anything." Again, those pesky documents.[9]

Although the reluctant witness survived his five-day ordeal, anyone leaving the Howard Johnson's might have wondered how well a similar performance would play on the witness stand before a jury. Its members might expect more from the man whose entire business was based on remembering.

Gordon had limited time to ponder the future since he continued to find himself caught in each day's "rush of events," as another participant in the *Federal Skywalk Cases* described this frantic time.[10] Besides his September deposition load of Hall et al., Gordon was helping the newspaper reporters make sense of the contents of the document depository by holding long tutorials for members of the investigative team. His hard work produced mixed results in October, a tumultuous month. After wading through "100,000 pages of hotel construction documents" and "15,000 pages of depositions," in early October, a *Star* and *Times* team of four investigative reporters and a specially assigned editor put out their first set of front-page articles under the banner of "The Hyatt Papers: Documentation of a Disaster."[11] The articles carried headlines with provocative phrases meant to grab the reader—"thin, invisible walkways" and "signals of trouble were missed" and "inspection problems plagued Hyatt construction." The "red flag" of the 1979 atrium roof collapse received the play it deserved but, in Gordon's judgment, once again left Hallmark, the owner, off the hook. Citing the design review meeting minutes for December 12, 1979, when Don Hall was present, and his still-warm deposition in hand, the paper blandly reported that he had "expressed concern about future loss of life in the hotel and directed that key structural connections be identified for future inspections." The reporters and their editors spent their precious column inches on *how* the Hallmark-Hyatt collaboration reached the decision to put the skywalks in the hotel rather than *who* actually made the critical decision. Everyone was slippery on this point, an example of the old cliché of failure being an orphan. Still, the paper was inching tentatively beyond the subject of design and engineering failure to the fringes of project management, like a skittish beast approaching a dangerous waterhole. Gordon found the progress slow and agonizing, but he was promised the investigative series had long to run and major bombshells to drop.[12] That never happened.

Nor did other papers of record follow the bread crumbs that Gordon spread before them. Interestingly, a duo of *Wall Street Journal* reporters followed a parallel track in October with their own post-document-depository, front-page story. They, too, dug into the depositions and consulted heavily with Gordon on their meaning and import. The theme of their "Haunted Hotel" article was "a history of oversights, misunderstandings, and safety problems." Gordon felt more heartburn when the respected national newspaper characterized the atrium roof collapse as merely a fallen "roof beam." As with their Kansas City counterparts, the WSJ reporters likewise cited the December 12, 1979, meeting that Hall attended and also his deposition and, again, counter to Gordon's take on the documents, let the owner off easy. "The court records make clear that during construction Hallmark officials urged the safest possible building."[13] The article paid little heed to Gordon's developing thesis of management failures during a series of blunders. These weak efforts by the press, at least in Gordon's opinion, proved initially irrelevant because he thought he had something better than newspaper stories. He had tapes.

THE OCTOBER 5 "DISCOVERY" ON HIS LAW OFFICE DOORSTEP OF THE boxes of critical tape recordings and related documents of the 1979 post-atrium-roof-collapse meetings provided Gordon with the fodder for the sanction report on which he spent the remainder of the month and the next. He now had the evidence, he thought, to show that the 1979 and 1981 hotel collapses were "more than 2 closely-related accidents," that "they were, in fact, one long accident." Maybe more importantly he had several individuals saying something quite different on tape and in meeting notes than what they had sworn to in later depositions. And the depositions continued, including his personal examination of Judith Whittaker, making an encore appearance in light of the new, damaging revelations.[14] In the flush of this positive turn in the fortunes of his case and ever the idealist, Gordon believed his written analysis might ensure victory, either in the form of a summary judgment in the plaintiffs' favor or as an overwhelming argument at jury trial.

That analysis was his "Supplemental Points and Authorities," filed in early December as the 1,554th document in the *Federal Skywalk Cases*. It had grown to a ninety-two-page tome of single-spaced, annotated arguments, counterarguments, excruciating details, tangents, obscurities, and rhetorical cul-de-sacs that dropped anchor in Wright's court and would weigh down the zealous lawyer's subsequent nonfiction narratives of the final days of the case. Exhibits consisting of about a hundred documents and 1,347 pages accompanied the brief—a non sequitur if ever there was one. Gordon's name appeared on the signature page as the sole author.[15]

Gordon's brief drew upon contemporaneous notes from the November 1979 meeting and its recording, which now seemed to contradict testimony given under oath by certain defendants in their depositions. He alleged, using the defendants' own words, that after this mishap they became aware that the skywalks, specifically their horizontal wall mounts, which had visibly pulled away, were unsafe. Although this defect was later corrected, the owner failed to carry out more extensive inspections, Gordon argued, due to "budget considerations," which presumably would have caught the other less visible but worse skywalk support failures of the vertical double-hanger-rod to box-beam connectors. Gordon found this inaction almost incomprehensible, not only to him but to "those who have lived in this community and had come to trust Hallmark as a company whose very name conjures up the image of quality and concern for only the very best." No effort was made to follow the format of the earlier, dispassionate National Bureau of Standards investigative report. A year's worth of frustration poured out when he charged that Hallmark officials had "evasively responded to questions or falsely stated under oath that they did not recall information and knowledge which the documents demonstrate they did possess."[16] The last glove came off, and Gordon named names. He pointed the finger of blame for this "pattern of obstruction, delay, and evasion" at "the one person chiefly responsible for the Hyatt project itself," and that was chairman of the board, chief executive officer, Hallmark owner, and founder's son Donald Joyce Hall.[17]

How can one describe this legal magnum opus? It was verbose, repetitive, strident, lacking in nuance, persuasive if one concentrated on the argument, exhaustive in detailing his opponents' bad behavior, exhausting if one was wading through it and trying to hit a newspaper deadline, and eye-glazing to an amateur. Nothing was sugar-coated in its severe text, sprinkled throughout with words such as "chaos" and "outrageous" and "bad faith" and "defendant's long-running farce."[18] He threw everything into this piece of unfiltered writing except brevity and bullet points. It survives as a dense legal argument, not as a gripping, well-paced narrative, which, it turned out, characterized much of the structure and tone of his later, obsessive writings on the Hallmark hotel disaster. If he could have turned this brief into Strunk-and-White precise prose, or nurtured a sympathetic journalist as his Boswell, he had a real story to tell. But it needed to be understandable and convincing to a confused public, and it was not. Of potentially great promise, "Supplemental Points" could have been the last installment of "The Hyatt Papers," the investigative series that the paper had so mysteriously mislaid. The promised pretrial public exposé of Hallmark's true role in the disaster and its ongoing misinformation, deflection, and evasion, as told through Gordon's timeline of intentional obstruction and abuse of the discovery process, never saw print.

The details of the atrium roof collapse, bolstered by the new documents that exposed Hallmark's continued efforts to disconnect the dots between 1979 and 1981, drove Gordon's narrative *über alles*. How could one ignore 2,700 square feet of roof, its structural steel beams, steel columns, and poured concrete slab that had fallen? To understand the skywalks collapse one only needed to look at the earlier roof collapse, "the single most important prior event in this case," and the tentpole of Gordon's evolving thesis. Moreover, the October 1979 incident exposed the building as "inadequate and unsafe," its builders having possessed a "foreknowledge of disaster." Withholding the damning documents for a year had "prolonged the entire discovery process" with needless hours of depositions spent trying to pin down witnesses who were now pinned. Hallmark had used the time to assault the mandatory class, settle with representative Stover, and plan who-knows-what-other tricks. Gordon never anticipated that the company would "hide the facts," that is, not play by the rules, but this was not a civilized game of chess. He urged the court to punish this blatant, willful rule-breaking and the egregious failure to comply with discovery court orders and the Federal Rules of Civil Procedure. Grant the plaintiffs a default summary judgment in favor of the plaintiffs, he implored.[19] His breathless, unapologetic shot at immediate victory included everything but the kitchen sink.[20]

This was where the episode of *Perry Mason* would have ended as the epilogue wrapped up the loose ends before the credits and closing theme. It would have concluded with a summary judgment against Hallmark, an assessment of crushing punitive damages, and a hint of future perjury indictments and convictions. But no such storybook ending followed. Instead, when it mattered, Gordon's loose alliance with the newspapers abruptly ruptured, and the latter appeared to close ranks around the hometown company.

THE DECEMBER 3 BRIEF DID NOT HAVE THE IMPACT GORDON HOPED because something else soon overshadowed it. On December 6 the *Kansas City Star* proclaimed what Hallmark called a "global settlement" between the company and the personal injury lawyers and their clients in state court. In a surprising move, all parties had agreed to the formation of a competing state class, one that also included those members of the federal class. In this settlement Hallmark denied liability, although it agreed to pay damages. A fund would be set up to pay out $20 million in punitive damages to claimants. A check of $1,000, payable immediately, would go to anyone present at the 1981 tea dance, even if they were not physically injured. The provisions of the rushed agreement would be finalized on January 5, 1983, five days before the federal trial began.[21] The ramifications of the state class action were enormous.

Up to this point, the federal class represented more than 1,500 victims of "emotional distress," but not for long if a no-questions-asked payday of a quick $1,000 came with the recipient formally leaving the federal class. If settled by January 5, it would leave too few plaintiffs to form another class in federal court. This would once again destroy the federal class, probably forever, scuttle the trial, and allow the defendants to avoid larger punitive damages that had once seemed inevitable in federal district court. The $20 million, a fraction of the amount the federal plaintiffs intended to demand, would be all that Hallmark (really its insurers) would have to pay to satisfy its punitive damage obligations. To top it off, the only people who would draw from the $20 million would be those who chose to go to trial in state court, which meant at this late date a limited number of seriously injured victims and their lawyers. An emergency hearing in Judge Wright's chambers was called for the next day, December 7.[22]

For Gordon, this was truly a day of infamy. Younger and Wolff rushed in from Washington to join Gordon in court. But it was Joseph A. Sherman, an attorney for Havens Steel, who during the course of the heated proceedings dropped the biggest bomb. He told Wright that Younger and Wolff, contrary to their position today in opposition to the state class formation, had initiated secret meetings with Hallmark and the state lawyers to do just that—allow the class, settle the case, and collect their fees. The meetings had run from late October to mid-November. The negotiations with Younger and Wolff apparently hit an impasse after the latter attorney's insistence on $150 million to settle the case. Gordon, who knew nothing of these negotiations, was thunderstruck. What sort of "monstrous mischief" was this? Whose side were they on? Why would Younger, who represented the victims, retreat from a position of strength and sell them out? Sell *him* out? All his work to date looked like a complete and utter waste of time. How could any plaintiffs' lawyer in the *Federal Skywalk Cases*, especially this pair of hypocrites, now effectively oppose the actions in state court? The answer was simple; they could not. All the momentum in the case abruptly shifted with this one revelation. Wright was caught so off guard that he became barely more than an embarrassed spectator for the rest of the session. The schemer Younger, too, was apparently caught short. The law professor thought he had a gentleman's agreement with the other side to keep things hush-hush. Neither side would publicly mention their earlier discussions.[23] Tawdry details about the haggling over money dribbled out later in the month and further damaged the veracity of Younger and Wolff.[24] By that time it was apparent to all that the team of plaintiffs' lawyers had lost the moral high ground and fought from a position of weakness, reacting to forces beyond their foresight and control. No matter their scattered fire and continued bloody skirmishing, the case—the war—was lost.

Gordon knew deep down that it was hopeless from here on out. The suspense was over; little doubt remained in the outcome. There would be no trial, no airing of the truth for the public, no satisfaction for the victims, no real punishment of their victimizers. The opposition had come up with new rules, followed them precisely, and was in complete control. Gordon was checked and checkmated, his subsequent moves meaningless. Yet, he could not bear to say this out loud, nor could he chronicle the moment in his daily diary. A year later he privately discussed these final days with Judge Wright, who wised up the lawyer: "Well, Bob, I'll tell you something. After they pulled that deal over in State Court, we didn't have anything left."[25] As it turned out, Wright would offer no further resistance to a swift conclusion of the case, no matter the outcome.

When he later composed his retrospective for this dark period, Gordon still could not face up to the fact that this was the day of doom, that he—and the plaintiffs—had been betrayed. His narrative, as did his fealty to following the rules of the game, demanded that he keep moving pieces until all of his were captured. The scuffles for the remainder of December and early January, although they claimed front-page real estate in the paper, were beside the point. For Gordon, his moment in the sun had passed. Distraught, exhausted, emotions raw, his role reverted to that of a background character in the final scene before curtain.

Rubbing salt in an open wound, yet another disturbing article appeared in the *Times*, one that, as Gordon said later, "undercut my whole discovery sanction request." The very first sentence set him off: "The owners of the Hyatt Regency hotel apparently were assured by the engineers that the skywalks were structurally sound and could safely hold large numbers of people, according to an early draft of a transcript of a tape recording of a meeting held in 1979."[26] An early draft? Where did the *Times* reporter get a transcript of the November 13, 1979, meeting? Who made it? It was easy to see why Gordon became incensed. After months of sharing documents and his insider's knowledge of the case, eagerly lapped up by a host of reporters and editors, he had to learn about an important, 144-page transcript by reading about it like anyone else in the morning paper?[27] No one had alerted him to its existence, much less its reporting. The author, a member of the investigative team for "The Hyatt Papers" who had just days before received a tutorial on the December 3 brief, had not even bothered to call for a comment before running the story.[28] Gordon felt ambushed and further betrayed.

A careful reading of the original article by cooler heads might concur. The reporter employed the term "owners" or "Hyatt owners" when referring to Hallmark, which seemed like a subtle but deliberate obfuscation, and he did not inform his readers about who drafted the transcript and supplied it to him. This ambiguity regarding sourcing caused other attorneys to contact Gordon and mistakenly accuse him of the leak.[29] It would only come out later that the source was related to Hallmark.

The article went on to state that "the skywalk connections had been checked," which may have led the reader to think all had been inspected instead of only a few spots, and certainly not the critical vertical hanger-rod connections. Also, last October, when the tape was released to the media, Hallmark contended that it was "of poor quality and mostly intelligible," but nothing in the article indicated how those technical defects had been overcome to produce a transcript. Gordon believed the author knew better on both counts, and it was the last straw. Little wonder he lashed out, but he could only do it personally and with his only remaining weapon—words in a letter.

Gordon responded with a blistering, almost manic dispatch on December 13 to Rick Serrano, the author of what Gordon characterized as the offending, "thinly disguised" ad for Hallmark.[30] With everything else going on during December's "rush of events," Gordon felt compelled to compose a lengthy screed, nine pages of single-spaced typescript and the culmination of his growing frustration with the press, made especially acute by the total defeat now in sight. Not that the reporter did not deserve it, but he conveniently served as the stand-in for all his colleagues, every journalist who had let Gordon down.

"No one tried to reach me," wrote Gordon, not even one phone call.[31] "You reduced the highly incriminating words on contemporaneous documents to a mere 'contention by Mr. Gordon,'" an admittedly biased advocate but one who felt he deserved a response. "I thought that I had earned a modicum of your trust in me—at least enough to require that you find out what I honestly thought of that specious draft transcript." Gordon obviously had trusted Serrano, who had been given keys to the lawyer's office in August.[32]

Then came the rapid-fire accusations with guns blazing: "There is a waste bucket full of errors contained in your article." One of the more glaring: "You know damn well" that only the horizontal end connections of the skywalks had been inspected and repaired after the October 1979 roof collapse, not ceiling connections. More importantly, "The heart of the whole case against Hallmark is what did it do when it was put on actual notice on 10-14-79 that the Atrium area and the Skywalks were defectly [*sic*] designed, improperly installed, or both. You have known since August, when I gave *you* a copy of defendant's contract with H. R. Inspection, it did squat."

But to Gordon, the "most egregious" of the errors was Serrano's failure to compare the Hallmark transcript against Gordon's brief: "Rather painstakingly, I went over each and every line in that brief with you and Mr. [John] Dauner on Friday (12-2-82) [*sic*—December 3] night to be sure that the significance of the documents was clear and so that you could see for yourselves exactly where the statements appear in Hallmark's own contemporaneous documents. Apparently, this was all a great waste of time."[33]

Throw in words like "irresponsibility," "galling," and "absurdity," and one gets the picture of the level of Gordon's rage. But perhaps what upset Gordon most was the Fourth Estate's disregard for the Holy Scripture, the documents relating to the case. Gordon had helped open the hallowed document depository and revealed its secrets. Hallmark had "coughed-up" twenty-one thousand pieces of paper since his September 24 sanctions motion, which he had devoted hours of his life to decipher for their benefit. And at the final test, to his utter befuddlement and fury, these novitiates had gotten the lesson wrong or, worse, ignored its meaning: "Hallmark avoided, evaded, and trifled with specific Court Orders to produce these very documents for over a year. What I cannot comprehend is why the *Star* and the *Times* do not also feel abused in this matter. You were lied to as much as we were."

Serrano responded with a phone call, to which Gordon noted, "He doesn't blame me for being PO'd [pissed off]." The reporter deflected by "wanting me to know that story & Tr. [transcript of the tape] came to him from Bill Johnson (HMK's in-house PR man) & direct instructions to do story came from M[ike]. Davies," editor and president of the *Kansas City Times*.[34] Interestingly there is little indication that the paper in its later reporting ever followed up meaningfully on this letter, hand-delivered as it was to the reporter and his superiors, even though it was chocked with sound bites.[35] Maybe it was snubbed because, as the local press plainly saw, Gordon had moved from center ring to sideshow. He could be ignored as easily as the warning at the end of the letter, which contained a cultural reference that has only half stood the test of time. "Eventually, all the truth will out and the *Star* and *Times* will either look like Bebe Rebozo or Ben Bradlee. The choice is yours." Since the 1970s the name of Bebe Rebozo, crony of disgraced President Nixon, has faded away. That of Ben Bradlee, *Washington Post* editor of Woodward and Bernstein, remains well known and highly regarded by later generations. Unfortunately, Gordon never had a newspaper editor of Bradlee's stature and strength on his side.

ONCE HE FINALLY STOPPED VENTING, GORDON COULD HAVE SKIMMED the paper and seen the dominoes begin to fall, in particular, the public notice about when and where Hyatt victims could pick up their $1,000 checks. In only four days, more than six hundred people would do just that, siphoning off plaintiffs from the federal class. "At the rate Hallmark was settling," guessed Gordon, "there soon would not be enough people left to comprise a federal class."[36] It took little more than a month for his fears to be realized.

Meanwhile, the defeated man continued to go through the legal motions, and an outside observer would have seen no slacking off in the herculean effort to prepare for trial. Between December 14, the day after the heartburn with Serrano et al., and the scheduled day of the January trial, Gordon never spent less than twelve hours a day on the case. On Christmas Eve he put in fifteen hours, Christmas Day, sixteen, New Year's Eve, sixteen more, and on the first day of 1983, fifteen. He kept up a manic pace on self-appointed tasks, such as writing a follow-up "reply brief" to rebut Hallmark's counter to his December sanction report. (His goal on this assignment was to keep his reply under fifty pages.) He prepared massive "interrogatory charts" for use in the courtroom, an unwieldy visual aide that consisted of eight panels, each four feet by six feet. They highlighted how the many witnesses for the defense had contradicted, maybe perjured, themselves in their answers under oath.

He contacted witnesses for the plaintiffs to make sure they showed up. He stressed about not having in hand a true transcript of the 1979 meeting, although Halvorson himself was prepared to testify that the tape had been spliced and maybe doctored. Any spare minute left over from these activities allowed for further organization and reorganization of the many documents he intended to have on hand at the trial. Nothing deterred his final preparations, not even in early January, when the state circuit court approved the state class settlement.[37]

Events of the few days before trial quickly passed Gordon by. Settlement talks occurred without him, even though they were common knowledge to all, and he lashed out in the press to Rick Alm, one of the reporters who still showed some sympathy for Gordon's predicament. "If they settle this federal trial for anything less than a total admission of guilt by Hallmark, it's going to be the same feeling you had when they pardoned Nixon or when the truth of the Kennedy assassination was lost in the death of Oswald." The system, argued Gordon, needed to be allowed to work.[38]

On Monday morning, January 10, 1983, Gordon showed up to a packed federal courthouse for the first day of trial, documents and exhibits in tow, only to find out that there would be no trial.[39] Younger and Wolff, neither of whom had returned his calls over the weekend, were in chambers with Judge Wright, along with lawyers from the other side. As the resident loose cannon, vehement in his opposition to settling, Gordon was intentionally excluded by the lawyers of both sides.[40] The adversaries had met privately over the weekend to hash out an agreement, and Younger, as lead counsel, negotiated for the plaintiffs. They ended up settling the *Federal Skywalk Cases*, and the judge entered the court to proclaim that fact to the world.[41] Wright, whose later memoir was titled *Never in Doubt*, nonetheless had "mixed feelings" about how the case ended but, looking back after a quarter century, was more than ready for "closure" and to move on. His court order that followed later in the month called the settlement "fair, reasonable, and adequate."[42] The contest was officially over.

The federal court settlement paralleled the one rushed through state court. In both, a class member could choose a $1,000 payment in exchange for a full release of claims against the defendants. Or class members could elect to negotiate a full settlement of their claims through arbitration, the costs of which were paid by the defendants. These members were also eligible for "supplemental compensation" (a fig leaf term for "punitive damages"), a figure not to exceed $3.5 million. It would be paid out in two ways: as a figure one half of their compensatory damages determined by arbitration or, if a plaintiff rolled the dice, as a later award by a jury in federal court.[43] An enterprising reporter got the immediate reactions of five victims to the settlement, one of whom was Molly Riley. Unlike the others, she was not ready to put the tragedy behind her. Overnight the idealist had become a cynic. "The public really needed to know what happened, and I don't think it will ever come out."[44] For the victims, the outcome was not a cathartic moment.

Gordon retreated from the courthouse to his office and immediately began the dismal process of boxing up his precious documents and putting his office back in order. No one from the paper called to disturb his work. Three days later he moved his case files to off-site storage.[45]

1. Before the skywalks fell, a young Robert Gordon (*far left*) appeared to have it all. Here on a ski trip with his beautiful wife, Josie (*far right*), lifelong friend Dick Woods, and Woods's wife, Gina, Gordon's wonderful life later included two adored children, a magnificent home, and a thriving Kansas City law practice. Courtesy Missouri Valley Special Collections, Kansas City Public Library, Kansas City, Missouri.

2. Molly Riley in her nurse's scrubs, about 1981. Riley innocently began the evening of July 17, 1981, as one of many Hyatt tea party revelers and ended it hours later, exhausted after shifting from the role of injured victim to trained nurse and first responder. She became a client of Robert Gordon and a hero in his story. Courtesy Molly Riley Tomc.

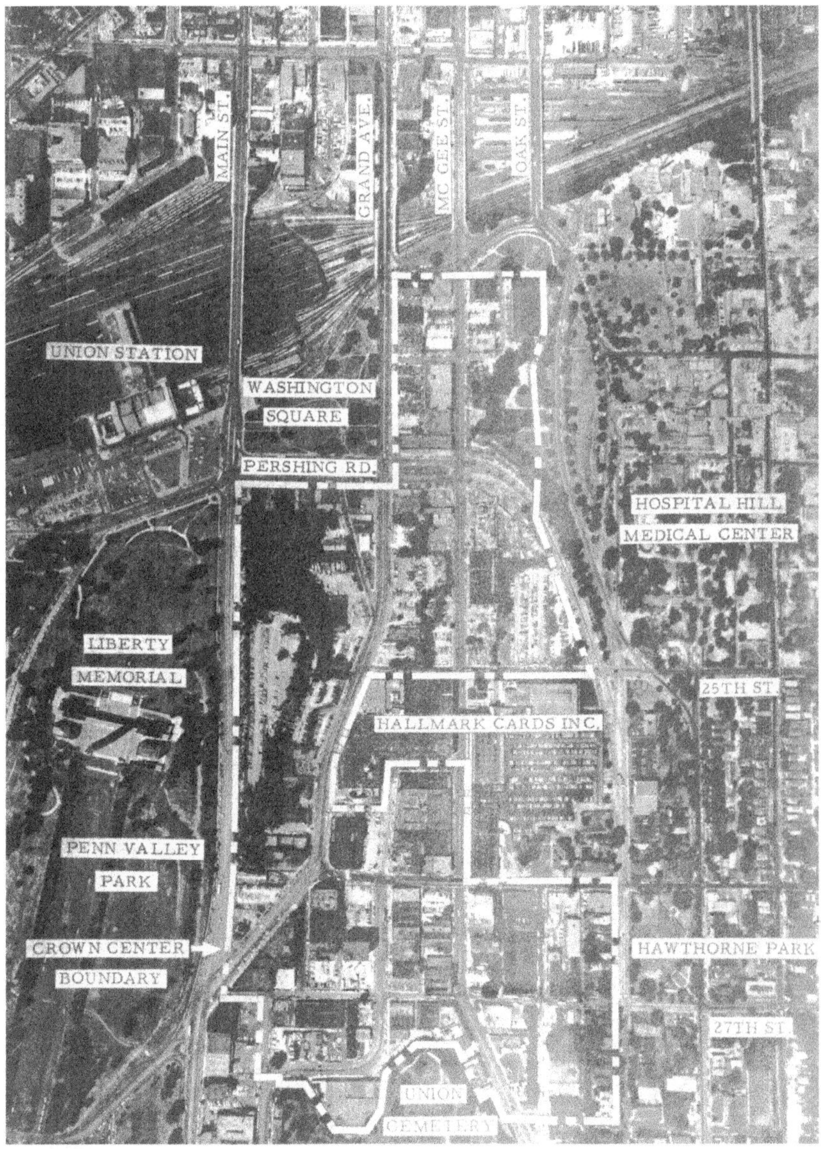

3. Hallmark property boundaries, Kansas City, Missouri, n.d. In the 1960s Hallmark Cards ventured outside the realm of their greeting card empire into urban renewal and the development of Crown Center. Courtesy Missouri Valley Special Collections, Kansas City Public Library, Kansas City, Missouri.

4. Crown Center consisted of an expansive, eighty-five-acre project that encompassed retail and office space, luxury hotels and high-rise apartments, and the company's corporate headquarters. Hallmark officials considered the new Hyatt Regency as their crowning achievement. Courtesy Missouri Valley Special Collections, Kansas City Public Library, Kansas City, Missouri.

5. The Hyatt Regency Kansas City was designed, built, and owned by Hallmark Cards, which turned over the day-to-day operations to the Hyatt Corporation in 1980. The top of the hotel boasted a revolving restaurant called Skies. Courtesy Missouri Valley Special Collections, Kansas City Public Library, Kansas City, Missouri.

6. Two years before the skywalks disaster, the hotel suffered another catastrophe when during construction the roof of the atrium lobby collapsed. Note the worker for scale. Courtesy Missouri Valley Special Collections, Kansas City Public Library, Kansas City, Missouri.

7. The October 14, 1979, atrium roof collapse sent tons of steel support beams and concrete debris hurtling to the floor below. Courtesy Missouri Valley Special Collections, Kansas City Public Library, Kansas City, Missouri.

8. In Robert Gordon's opinion, the atrium roof collapse and the hotel's rushed design and construction gave a clear warning of other lurking dangers, which project managers largely failed to heed. Courtesy Missouri Valley Special Collections, Kansas City Public Library, Kansas City, Missouri.

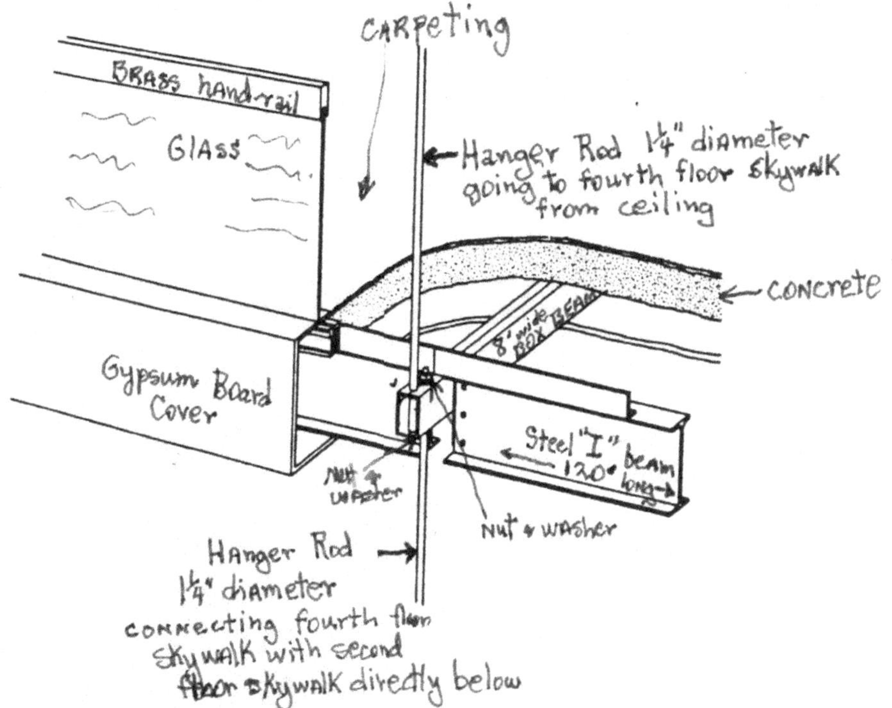

Simplified detail of walkway structural system and architectural treatment.

9. Robert Gordon modified a drawing from the investigative report of the National Bureau of Standards to create a more-detailed version of the vertical hanger-rod support system for the skywalks. Courtesy Missouri Valley Special Collections, Kansas City Public Library, Kansas City, Missouri.

10. Box beam "9UE," as later designated by the National Bureau of Standards, was the ninth in a series of skywalk connections, located on the east side of the upper (fourth-floor) skywalk. NBS engineers pinpointed the initial structural failure to this connection. When 9UE gave way, other skywalk connections could not compensate for the additional stresses of the massive load. Courtesy Missouri Valley Special Collections, Kansas City Public Library, Kansas City, Missouri.

11. The hotel lobby, shown before the collapse, was a dramatic gathering place that could accommodate hundreds of people. A sunken bar anchored the lobby's center. Courtesy Missouri Valley Special Collections, Kansas City Public Library, Kansas City, Missouri.

12. After the collapse of the two skywalks, it took time for the first responders to register what happened. The fourth-floor skywalk failed first, quickly pancaking on the one immediately below. An estimated sixty-three people were standing on the pair and had no chance for escape. Courtesy Missouri Valley Special Collections, Kansas City Public Library, Kansas City, Missouri.

13. Rescue efforts began immediately to remove people trapped under the sixty-four thousand pounds of debris. Large cranes were brought in to remove heavy sections. The last skywalk section was lifted away the next day, and thirty-one bodies were removed. Courtesy Missouri Valley Special Collections, Kansas City Public Library, Kansas City, Missouri.

14. Survivors of the tea dance disaster stumbled outside the hotel, where they were joined by hundreds of first responders, good Samaritans who came to help and donate blood, and shocked onlookers. Courtesy Missouri Valley Special Collections, Kansas City Public Library, Kansas City, Missouri.

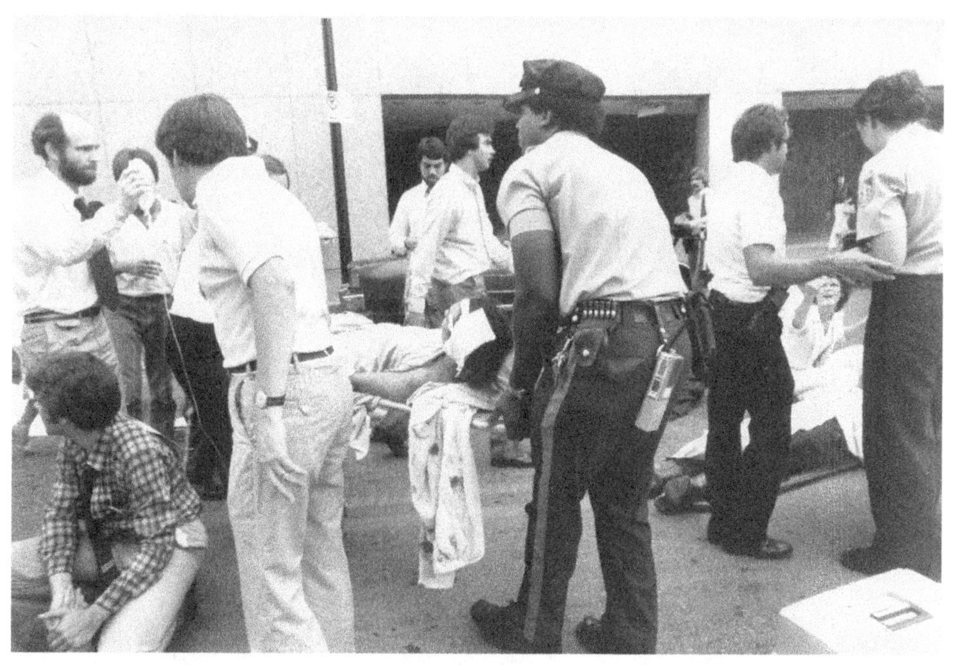

15. As first responders rushed to help the injured, horrified Kansas Citians were asking tough questions. What caused the skywalks to fall? Who was to blame? How could this have happened to fellow citizens of our city? Courtesy Missouri Valley Special Collections, Kansas City Public Library, Kansas City, Missouri.

16. Donald J. Hall, president and chief executive officer of Hallmark Cards, 1978. His company enjoyed a national reputation for quality, excellence, and caring, as exemplified by its acclaimed *Hall of Fame* television productions, but the Hyatt collapse and the ensuing litigation threatened that brand. Author's collection.

17. A World War II Marine Corps aviator, country lawyer and prosecutor, and finally a federal judge, Scott Wright presided over the *Federal Skywalk Cases*. His blistering censures, controversial decisions, and cornpone witticisms routinely shook up those in his courtroom and judge's chambers. Robert Gordon accepted the judge's eccentricities, as well as his rulings. Courtesy Missouri Valley Special Collections, Kansas City Public Library, Kansas City, Missouri.

18. Irving Younger, lead counsel for the plaintiffs in the *Federal Skywalk Cases*, brought his considerable flair and academic reputation to the class-action lawsuit, but in Robert Gordon's mind, he gave it little personal attention. Gordon reluctantly concluded that Younger had been angling for a quick, lucrative, out-of-court settlement from the onset. Courtesy Library of Congress, Bernard Gotfryd photograph collection, LC-DIG-gtfy-04671.

19. In 1986 three colleagues accompanied Judith Whittaker, Hallmark's deputy chief counsel, in the Jackson County, Missouri, courthouse, one of the many legal venues where she and Robert Gordon crossed paths. Gordon ultimately proved no match for Whittaker and the street fighting that characterized the *Federal Skywalk Cases* and later legal skirmishes with the Hallmark company. Courtesy Missouri Valley Special Collections, Kansas City Public Library, Kansas City, Missouri.

20. Robert Gordon, in his signature seersucker suit, shared a convivial moment with Richard Berkley (*left*), mayor of Kansas City, Missouri, and an unidentified woman. By now Gordon's writing career had commenced. Courtesy Tracy Gordon.

21. A professional writer and editor with an engineering background, Robert Byrne specialized in disaster-themed novels. On paper he was the perfect partner to rewrite Robert Gordon's work of nonfiction, but their collaboration, as with all of Gordon's team-ups, met with no success. Author's collection.

HOUSE OF CARDS

The Most Outrageous Cover-up Since Watergate . . .

Now, the whole shocking truth about the tragedy is finally revealed in a book that is sure to stir up controversy—and headlines—across America. In *House of Cards*, Robert Gordon, an attorney appointed by a federal judge to represent the victims in a class action suit, has re-created the Hyatt disaster—and the whole sordid tale of pride, greed and negligence that led to the collapse and subsequent attempts to hide the facts. With all the compelling narrative power of *A Night to Remember*, he describes the hotel and the people who came there to dance amid splendor and luxury in the spectacular atrium—and vividly captures the moment of collapse and the heroic rescue efforts amid a scene of unbelievable chaos and destruction. And with carefully documented proof, he reveals the ways in which those responsible for the tragedy manipulated the media and hid behind legal smokescreens in the greatest cover-up since Watergate.

22. Simon & Schuster went so far in 1991 to produce a brochure and order form for Robert Gordon's *House of Cards*. The publisher advertised a book of 304 pages at a price of $19.95. This excerpt of the brochure copy promised a "sordid tale" of the "whole shocking truth." Courtesy Missouri Valley Special Collections, Kansas City Public Library, Kansas City, Missouri.

23. A pensive Robert Gordon dropped off his daughter, Tracy, on her first day of college at University of California–Santa Cruz, September 1989. In this critical year, Gordon left the law and concentrated on getting his manuscript through Simon & Schuster's rigorous editorial process. Courtesy Tracy Gordon.

24. It took thirty-four years to design, build, locate, fund, and dedicate a skywalk memorial to those killed. For the centerpiece of the memorial, artist Rita Blitt created a sculpture titled *Sending Love* that suggested two tea dancers in one last, loving embrace. Courtesy Lori Cox-Paul.

10

Writer

Robert Gordon was at a loss after the case was settled out from under him. No legal avenue remained open, no day in court where he could lay out the facts as he understood them and tell what really happened.[1] Being so out-lawyered was even more galling because he believed that the story currently before the public, with its most damaging facts obscured by the dust kicked up by the lawyers, was as flimsy as a house of cards. Stopped in his tracks on what to do next, the battle-scarred but stubborn attorney nevertheless refused to let go. He was determined somehow to tell the story of what really happened with the Hyatt skywalks. This would prove largely a solitary endeavor.

The defeated lawyer made a life-changing decision. He abruptly switched gears, abandoned his law practice for the moment, and ventured forth into an alien field. He would become an author. His literary goals were twofold: first, nothing but the truth for the victims, which he knew he had uncovered in the Hallmark documents and depositions, and second, nothing but public condemnation for those persons who had escaped justice. Specifically, he believed he could lay the blame on Hallmark, grossly negligent in its mad dash to keep the hotel project on time and on budget. If successful, this would also restore the tarnished Hyatt brand, a secondary concern but one that he saw as only fair. Gordon's access to the sheer volume of evidence, his widely acknowledged command of the facts, and his public image as an inner-circle player and a lone wolf beholden to nobody made him, on the surface, an ideal, authoritative chronicler. As he proudly told someone he meant to impress, "I no longer need to rely on legal cases for a living. I have no fear of reprisal as do most practicing attorneys." His means for righting the wrongs he perceived would be a book that told the "unvarnished skywalks story."[2] But first, some unfinished business remained at the courthouse.

On January 20, 1983, Gordon returned to court for a wrap-up hearing on the proposed settlement, a fait accompli, where he had to endure listening to Hallmark's New York counsel "load up the official record with a ton of self-serving misinformation."[3] As part of the settlement agreement, Hallmark had agreed to pay further damages in the public-relations-friendly form of $6.5 million to local charities, making the lemons of punitive damages into the sweetest of lemonade for their corporate image. The *St. Louis Post-Dispatch*, from its cross-state perspective, proclaimed the company's $6.5 million "donation" an "extraordinary act of penance" that would "reaffirm Hallmark's place in the front rank of that city's corporate citizens." Even more importantly, the total settlement in federal court of $10 million ($6.5 million plus $3.5 million) was perfectly manageable for the defendants, as it had been when that identical figure had been bandied about in May 1982 for punitive damages. Throw in the to-be-determined fees to the plaintiffs' lawyers for which the defendants were responsible and the $20 million settlement fund in state court, and the grand total so far was a far cry from the financial abyss that Hallmark stared down months before. Their prescient insurance policies, meanwhile, already covered the $50 million that had been paid to date to victims or their families.[4]

After enduring his gloating foe's victory lap taken in court, Gordon was begrudgingly granted a few minutes of commentary, and he pulled himself together to get in a couple of zingers, one being, "If the hotel had been occupied at the time of that first collapse, it would have killed four times the number of people who died when the skywalks fell." The only real satisfaction he felt that depressing day, however, was his success in getting his precious sanction reports, something of a counternarrative to that of the victors, submitted as part of the record.[5]

All told, the defendants would end up paying out about $150 million to the victims, of which $35 million went to the personal injury attorneys. The fees and reimbursable expenses for all the federal class counsel, Gordon included, totaled less than a tenth of that latter figure. For those still debating the merits of the federal class concept, the total stood in stark contrast to the multimillions that the personal injury lawyers in state court took as their share of the spoils. And as for the final settlement figure, distant observers at the *National Law Journal* had once estimated that a settlement for a mandatory federal class could have been double that—$300 million.[6]

On the last day of January, the federal district court issued its order approving the settlement. Gordon met again that day with Molly Riley to explain what all had happened. He spent the next decade working on that explanation. Riley through Bill Whitaker spent the next three months wrangling over a settlement, and for a time it looked as if they might go to trial on April 18 on an accelerated docket. A week before that happened, the two sides reached an agreement, and her claim was settled.[7] Molly Riley, whose involvement with the *Federal Skywalk Cases* officially ceased, took little satisfaction from this hollow victory. It was never about the money, she later said, and she needed to move on with her life. She had a small child to raise and a nursing career to attend to.[8]

To an indignant Gordon, sick of the legal scheming and manipulation, everyone with dirty hands in the disaster had eluded punishment. Still seething a month later, he confided to Arthur Miller, "Bitter? You bet I am. I've been involved in losing causes before, and I'm sure it will happen again, but this case was like no other. 114 people were murdered."[9]

Publicly he tempered such rash remarks, and as the newspaper summarized, "While he supported the final settlement, he would have preferred to see the case go to trial." Years later, he sounded almost magnanimous: "For all the Watergate legends about investigative coups, I no longer believed that the media is set up to solve lengthy and complex problems," especially those relating to the legal system.[10]

Winning a relatively large settlement for the plaintiffs was little consolation, as was the court-approved fee for his professional services and expenses accrued in the past year. Gordon received a check from Hallmark's Crown Center Redevelopment Corporation for $450,000, a princely sum for that time but a mere pinprick to the giant corporation.[11] Still, the welcome income allowed Gordon to take a "sabbatical" from his law practice.

To Gordon's disappointment, it was a case of justice denied. As unsatisfactory as this denouement was, it essentially drew the Hyatt skywalks disaster to a close for a city grown weary of reliving that painful night, as well as observing the courtroom antics, public accusations, private rumors, and bad national press. The unofficial and unreported consensus in the legal community was that the multimillion-dollar award, large as it was, should have been many times higher. The defendants, whispered some, may have indeed been criminally negligent and gotten off the hook, but these unsettling questions remained unanswered because the full case against Hallmark and its project partners would never be heard by the public in federal court. In the wake of the settlement the newspaper soon lost interest in the story, disbanded its Hyatt investigative team, and assigned its reporters elsewhere. There was no more juice to squeeze from that orange. The generally accepted narrative, simple and less nuanced, was now preserved in amber, and little incentive existed to dispute its insufficient storyline. The hotel had long since reopened to the public and reintegrated into the community, although the Friday night dances were no more. Kansas Citians, by and large, were ready to move on and put this blot on their city behind them, with one notable exception: Robert Gordon.

FOR A BOOK PROJECT, GORDON NEEDED TO PRODUCE A SERVICEABLE manuscript, and with that as his North Star, Gordon began his self-transformation from lawyer to writer at, of all places, a suburban cocktail party. The late July 1983 event began pleasantly enough as a mild diversion and then turned into something of a madcap affair. Gordon and his wife, Josie, attended a surprise birthday party for a neighbor. It was a forty-ish crowd, a couple of dozen people roaming the grounds of a sprawling, ranch-style house in toney Mission Hills, all engaged in a lengthy scavenger hunt. Outside activity of any kind on a typical hot, humid Kansas City summer's night undoubtedly meant thirsty work. After three hours of such fun, the crowd was ready for cocktails and conviviality, to be concluded with a buffet dinner at 11:30 p.m.[12]

As with any large party, some of the attendees were strangers to one another. A mutual acquaintance—who possessed some discretion—introduced the Gordons to another person. "Bob and Josie, I would like you to meet Michel. Michel works for Hallmark," adding tongue-in-cheek, "Bob is a writer."[13] Suddenly the evening became more interesting, and Gordon began to engage the man in conversation, which he kept at for the next two hours. Michel A. Scrivan (pronounced "scruh-VON"), Hallmark executive, remained clueless for the entire evening to the identity of this newfound friend who never gave his last name.

Coincidentally the hotel disaster was back in the news, although it vied with yesterday's Kansas City Royals debacle, the infamous George Brett "pine tar" game in New York. Closer to home than Yankee Stadium, the U.S. Attorney's Office for the Western District had recently announced that it was joining an ongoing investigation by the Jackson County, Missouri, prosecutor into possible criminal culpability in what was known as the Hyatt case.[14] Tonight, therefore, the disaster seemed an appropriate topic for casual conversation over drinks, a subject and a setting that raised no suspicion with Gordon's quarry. Scrivan volunteered his prediction: "Nothing, absolutely nothing will come of it. Hallmark knows how to handle itself." (To Gordon's later chagrin, this proved all too true. Nothing ever came of this half-hearted probe by prosecutors, but that was in the unknowable future.) "After all," continued Scrivan, a native of Poland who spoke with a French-tinted accent that emphasized his haughtiness, "we certainly took care of all the other lawsuits."

A total cipher to Gordon, this Scrivan was truly a mystery man. Who was he? What did he do at Hallmark? For someone who had the company's organizational chart in his head, the name flew completely under his radar.[15] This self-described "insider" supplied those missing details and much, much more before the evening ended.

Scrivan's innocuous title at Hallmark was "facilities engineer director," but what did that mean? The company hired him, he said, sometime after the 1980 MGM Grand Hotel fire. That hotel disaster had killed eighty-five people and preceded the Hyatt collapse by eight months. Regarding his role at Hallmark, he was vague, maybe intentionally. His previous job at American Airlines sounded similar, "director of facilities maintenance," and he had somehow been involved, he claimed, in dealing with the consequences of AA's doomed "Flight 191," the horrendous crash of a DC-10 at O'Hare Field in Chicago in May 1979, the deadliest air accident ever in U.S. history.[16] Disaster management done discretely, it seemed, was Scrivan's forte.

Opposite this European sophisticate, Gordon took on the ruse of "a typical Mission Hills resident," someone, he condescendingly pronounced, who had read some, but not all, of the skywalks stories, which had left him confused "as to just what was going on." Yet, he continued to "rather fervently" have faith, as he had been "raised to believe" that "Hallmark is synonymous with quality." The tragedy was someone else's fault, probably those "St. Louis engineers," a refrain that echoed Kansas City's longtime prejudice against its larger, cross-state rival. The two metropolises, located on the eastern and western edges of Missouri, sat like anthropomorphic bookends that face away from each other.[17]

Scrivan took the bait and responded to Gordon's "innocent" questions with a flurry of provocative if not outrageous statements. What about the construction of the hotel? His answer: it was "lousy, shitty workmanship." What about the skywalks? The faulty hanger-rod, box-beam support system, said Scrivan, had been "visible to the naked eye" well "before the collapse."[18] Wasn't the general contractor in the end responsible, asked Gordon? "You have to understand how a corporation protects itself from legal liability," replied Scrivan. "By using Eldridge, Hallmark set up a barrier between itself and people who could sue us." But you used outside architects and engineers? What about their work? "We did a lot of it," he answered. "We could have done all of it, but you see what happened. We were smart to use some outside people." Such maneuvers, Scrivan spelled out to his supposedly naive listener, gave Hallmark "the legal advantage we got by not saying that we were really the ones designing and building it." In other words, paraphrased Gordon, Hallmark "tried to remove itself from direct liability from the project's very beginning and did so rather cleverly." No matter what Scrivan disclosed, though, Gordon's response remained the same, with fingers crossed behind his back: "I steadfastly refused to even consider the possibility that . . . the Hallmark company and/or Kansas City's only billionaire [Don Hall] . . . could have done anything wrong."[19]

The jaw-dropping quotes came fast and furious, and Gordon needed time to catch his breath. Here his actions moved from the subtle to the ridiculous:

> Every now and then I would pretend I had to go to the bathroom or to get another drink just so I would have a chance to scribble down some notes on what he was saying. Unfortunately, [our hostess] is one of those scrupulously neat housewives who think that one's house—at party time at least—should more resemble an unlived-in display model rather than a real home. After wasting several minutes just trying to find a pen or pencil, and some paper, I ended up jotting down his remarks on the cash bills I had with me, the inside cover of one of the few books I could find, and, yes, even some toilet paper. Finally, I found some Big Red [Big Chief?] tablet paper in the bedroom of the host's son.

Finesse had given way to slapstick. The party, the conversation, and the undercover operation only ended sometime after 1:00 a.m. when Scrivan and his wife left. Not to miss an opportunity, Gordon hitched a ride home with them because even the patient Josie had left long before. There was no time to extend the dialogue since, as it turned out, the Scrivans only lived three blocks from him.[20] There is no record that the two men ever spoke again.

Gordon took these frantic notes and immediately crafted an eight-page, single-spaced, detailed, overwrought memo-to-file on this bizarre episode, all the while shaking his head about what he had heard. From the mouth of this supposed corporate insider, to whom he attached such adjectives as articulate and arrogant, egotistical and pretentious, but most importantly, loquacious, Gordon now had an old suspicion confirmed. During the discovery phase, Hallmark-connected witnesses had skillfully tormented him in their depositions, and it was now clear that they had been coached to follow a series of "dodges and deceptions." Don't mention certain things. Don't remember too much. "Act really stupid, dumb like you can't remember things that you know perfectly well or what people have told you or what you've read in memos," or so said the quite believable Scrivan.

Moreover, Gordon concluded, Hallmark had learned nothing from the debacle except that "a backwater, unsophisticated company," according to this indiscrete employee, "could deal, quite easily, with a bad thing and emerge from it a better company." By "better," Scrivan cynically meant "it could now use its power to expand" and not just be "a big fish in a small pond." And within the executive suite, the company was indeed moving upward and onward. Don Hall was a good manager but a poor leader; he could not be blamed for creating the problem, said Scrivan, only for not fixing it: "He should have set personally very high standards for safety. Instead, highest priorities were meeting time schedules and not going over budgets. . . . But they didn't mean to hurt anybody." Intentions aside, Hall was not going to get a second chance. Soon he would be moving out of the presidency and getting bumped up to be Hallmark's largely figurehead chairman. "Someone else is going to run the company," predicted Scrivan correctly. Like the "careless people" in F. Scott Fitzgerald's *The Great Gatsby* who had "smashed up things and creatures," the owners of Hallmark had "retreated back into their money or their vast carelessness or whatever it was that kept them together, and let other people clean up the mess they had made."[21] By the time Gordon finished the report to himself, he had the themes for his book: poor leadership, bad project management, misplaced priorities, avoidance of responsibility, shift of blame, justice not served.

For Gordon, it was an auspicious beginning for his transition from lawyer to writer. This was getting exciting. But how would he use this seriocomic, possibly libelous incident in his book, especially since it merely reinforced what he already believed?[22] It was time to write.

THE HISTORICAL RECORD IS THIN ON EXACTLY WHEN GORDON TOOK pen to paper on his book. He mentioned in April 1985 that he had been working on it for twenty-eight months, which would give a start date sometime in early 1983. Another mention is his obscure note ("possible chapter title: 'Don Hall Reviews'") that appeared on an undated document created in September 1982, long before the facts of the case were known, much less the outcome decided. The most demonstrative evidence is an author's questionnaire that gave 1982 as the start date and that, intriguingly, the idea came from Judge Wright. But these thin references may merely indicate when Gordon first entertained the thought of doing a book, as authors tend to do. Not until the litigation ended and he was free to follow his muse did he mention to others that he intended "to spend the rest of the year" writing, in hindsight something of an understatement.[23]

An independent sort, Gordon did seek and receive assistance from others, although at this early stage it took the form of collegiate-level research and background writing. In the summer of 1983 Gordon had Charles Stanford, a graduate student in English from the University of Missouri, help in making the National Bureau of Standards final report "interesting and understandable." Kathryn Anne Miller, another English major from the University of Kansas, interviewed a number of Hyatt victims on Gordon's behalf.[24] Neither made a significant impact on Gordon's initial writing attempt, which reflected his voice entirely.

As with his memo-to-file on the Scrivan affair and the many legal briefs that preceded it, when Gordon started writing, the words gushed forth. The index to his files conveniently served as the "outline of my book."[25] Chapter after revised chapter of raw manuscript flowed during this early, hyperactive phase of the book project, so much so that it creates an archival quandary to arrange the surviving, undated documents in some sort of logical, progressive order of literary development.

From the historical debris that remains, Gordon's writing process consisted of composing by hand on the lined, yellow legal pad ubiquitous to his profession. Using a wide-tipped, black ink pen, he had a large, forceful, cursive script, and words flowed rapidly and uninterrupted to quickly fill a page. He left the typing and later the word processing, an infant technology making great strides in the early 1980s, to a baffling succession of secretaries and assistants. On draft after draft of typescript he would make his additions, corrections, and edits in a clearly recognizable hand. No page of his or the writings of others ever left his desk without a flurry of marginal notes, critical comments, underlining, and exclamation points. The books in his private library suffered the same fate.

Untrained and unversed in the skills of writing popular nonfiction, Gordon received inspiration from older classics and the best sellers of the day. Thornton Wilder's novel *The Bridge of San Luis Rey* (1927), particularly its prologue, deeply influenced him. The story centered around a fatal bridge collapse—on a Friday in July, no less—that sparks an extensive investigation by its central character. This solitary individual, a dedicated priest, makes it his extended mission to gather scattered evidence to determine the reasons for this incomprehensible accident that killed innocent people. He is relentless. "In compiling his book about these people, Brother Juniper seemed to be pursued by the fear that in omitting the slightest detail, he might lose some guiding hint." Years later he has methodically and radically figured out what it all means and gathers his findings in a massive compilation, a "literary monument," the conclusions to which the authorities strongly object. If Gordon considered his life as one that followed this plot, then its ominous ending should have given him pause. In the novel the indefatigable investigator's book never sees print, a single forgotten manuscript copy survives in a library unread, and this being colonial Peru, the doomed author, a man of God, is burned at the stake as a heretic and dies a martyr.[26]

Only one element was missing from Wilder's story—indifference by the bridge builder—but this was a central theme in the works of Robert Byrne, a noted American novelist of the day with whom Gordon collaborated for a while. Byrne, for whom one reviewer coined the term "disaster maven," specialized in tales of structural catastrophe and had recently produced a string of successes with such terse titles as *The Tunnel* (1977) and *The Dam* (1981). The breathless blurbs for *Skyscraper* (1984), Byrne's latest book, revealed a kindred spirit: the skyscraper being "a monument of the man who had it built, the pressures to cut corners that weigh on architects and engineers, and the cumulative power of inevitable human and mechanical errors" and its hero, "an engineer [who] soon finds that the building's flaws are worse than he imagined and that the conspiracy to keep him from the truth about the building is, if anything, more dangerous than the building itself." Byrne's inspiration for this novel was the Hyatt Regency disaster and for its theme the search for the cause of an engineering failure. The influential Byrne probably established the approach and set the tone for the sections of Gordon's manuscript that focused on the skywalks engineering, their collapse, and the decision makers behind them.[27]

For the legal sections, which took up the bulk of his manuscript, Gordon himself acknowledged his debt to Alan Dershowitz's *The Best Defense* (1982).[28] The American legal system was deeply flawed, "corrupt to the core," stated the Harvard-based law professor, whose specialty was taking on unpopular cases that spotlighted its structural corruption. Here was an in-your-face lawyer and wildly successful author that Gordon could emulate, someone for whom the best defense was a good offense—or just being offensive. Advocates of Dershowitz's provocative, originally laudatory approach later became dismissive of the lawyer, aggravated by his picking poor defendants. Think of Dershowitz's later advocacy for O. J. Simpson, Jeffrey Epstein, Donald Trump, and Harvey Weinstein.[29] Nor did his aggressive approach wear well over time. This flaw was perhaps not yet apparent to Gordon, his admiring fan.

In his correspondence Gordon often cited favorably David McClintick's *Indecent Exposure*, a 1982 *New York Times* best seller that traced in excruciating—yet exhilarating—detail the notoriously shady movie industry and one of its wayward Hollywood moguls, David Begelman.[30] McClintick's story provided a template that meshed perfectly with Gordon's: a simple explanation emerges as the cause of a major problem, in this case, a film head's act of embezzlement, which later turns out to be only "the tip of the iceberg" of a bigger cover-up and scandal that the intrepid reporter and fledgling book author in due course unravels; his revelations rattle both Hollywood and Wall Street. Although Gordon identified with this scenario, he could only dream of a similar outcome: the arrogant get their comeuppance; the guilty lose their reputations or their jobs or both; powerful yet irresponsible firms falter and fall. With its brisk sales and national notoriety, *Indecent Exposure*, with its strong point of view, omniscient narrator, and clever dialogue, became a testament to the power of the printed word, only surpassed by another title that by this time cast a giant shadow across the world of popular culture.

That book, *All the President's Men* (1974), was everything that Gordon wanted his to be.[31] It had the same elements: a national story that grips the nation, powerful institutions that are not what they purport, and resolute investigators breaking down a stone wall of silence and obstruction to uncover a massive scandal. Although no "Deep Throat" made a dramatic appearance in Gordon's narrative, he could offer up the scene of guilty parties likewise caught on a smoking-gun tape. Woodward and Bernstein showed that a story about investigating and exposing the truth was more film-worthy than the crime itself, and the lawyer made notes. For his own opus, Gordon toyed for a while with opening up with the tense, iconic scene from *All the President's Men*. Instead of a security guard making his rounds, noticing something amiss, and discovering the Watergate burglars, Gordon offered up a night watchman at the Hyatt hotel construction site who set the narrative wheels in motion when he stumbled across the atrium roof collapse on that October night in 1979. Later research cast doubt on that scenario, so Gordon dropped it and developed another.[32]

The night watchman failed to be included in Gordon's "cast of characters," a compilation that began early on during the class-action lawsuit and included the persons who in due course appeared by name in his narrative. This took the form of an intimidating list of 158 names, presumably for the benefit of a confused reader. They ranged from Don Hall, the head of Hallmark and the builder of the Hyatt Regency, to Danny Hafley, a young construction materials inspector who, along with dozens of others, missed the fatal flaws of the hotel—and everyone in between.[33] Only ten persons on Gordon's list were women, seven lawyers and three from the media, and no persons of color. However, this was a Kansas City case, and it involved elite individuals and prominent institutions that formed the highest reaches of society, of which Gordon could be considered a close associate if not a dues-paying member.

Sixty were identified as lawyers, several of whom in Gordon's opinion were nothing more than glorified ambulance chasers. They represented hundreds of plaintiffs and defendants and were recipients, as one wag put it, of "The Lawyers' Relief Act."[34] When a character first appeared, a thumbnail description accompanied the name, meant to keep one distinct from another but usually resulted in their quick sort into one camp or another, that is, either pro-Gordon (and therefore pro–class action) or not. Interestingly, for such a personal account as Gordon's manuscript ended up being, the list did not include any family members, nonbusiness friends, or longtime intimates.

By December 1983 Gordon was working from a nine-page outline for his book that took the form of a numerical list of "post 7-17-81 files." By January 1984, a year after the *Federal Skywalk Cases* settlement, he had already drafted at least ten chapters for review. The manuscript carried the unwieldy title "When They Didn't Care Enough," a not-so-subtle play on the well-known Hallmark slogan, "When you care enough to send the very best."[35] The accompanying subtitle was less opaque and to the point: "The Story of the Worst Structural Disaster in American History." Over the years Gordon went back and forth on several variations of the main title. He settled on "House of Cards," going so far as having the title registered prematurely in 1989, where a comprehensive library catalog described the forthcoming book as "a behind-the-scenes look at the corporate misconduct that caused the tragedy." For his eventual, breathless subtitle he abandoned all subtlety and identified his prime antagonist by name: "The Cover-Up Behind the Worst Structural Collapse in American History—Hallmark's Hyatt Regency Skywalks Disaster."[36]

The promise of the title—exposing a cover-up—versus the reality of the manuscript's first version may have disappointed its early readers.

Jill Tvedten Long, the daughter of Kansas City fireman and Hyatt victim John Tvedten Sr., had the opportunity to read an early draft and offer comments. She spoke authoritatively for so many others who had suffered a great loss and who were dissatisfied with the conventional narrative characterized by the glaring absence of responsibility. She had blunt questions: Who was to blame? Who were these people, and why had they avoided responsibility? How could it have been the fault of just two structural engineers since they did not design the support system, nor did they fabricate it, install it, inspect it, or sign off on it? Long rightly concluded that the general public "will want to know about the victims, why the skywalks collapsed, who is responsible for the collapse, and Hallmark's cover-up attempt." She gently hinted about the major flaw in the narrative, that the audience she represented would not be nearly as interested in the subsequent legal issues as the lawyer-turned-author. "We may have different goals for this book," she wrote.[37] Her goal may have tilted toward vengeance, his toward the truth. Nevertheless, it would have paid for Gordon to heed her advice.

11

House of Cards

The early constructive criticism from Jill Tvedten Long regrettably did not slow Gordon from the course he had plotted for his book. In the spring of 1984, Gordon believed he was ready to reach out to major agents and publishers. In the months since the class-action settlement, he had "wanted to write, as much as possible, while everything was still very fresh in my mind" and now heeded a personal recommendation from the aforementioned David McClintick of *Indecent Exposure* fame to reach out to James Landis of William Morrow & Company in New York. A persistent editor who had spent four years shepherding to publication Robert Pirsig's classic but unconventional *Zen and the Art of Motorcycle Maintenance* (1974), the highly regarded Landis later left the company to become a recognized novelist in his own right under the name "J. D. Landis."[1]

Gordon sent Landis a seventeen-page book proposal for "When They Didn't Care Enough," alternatively titled in this instance "A Calculated Risk: The Story of the Hyatt Skywalks Catastrophe." Gordon stressed the size and scope of his research. "My research assistant and I have personally interviewed over a hundred victims and/or their rescuers, a dozen public officials, and several of the attorneys who represented various defendants in the case," as well as Judge Wright and anonymous "courthouse personnel." Not that it mattered to the experienced editor, but Gordon helpfully added, "I am working basically from both a general outline and from 368 specific subject matter files," along with "my personal diary," plus a "chronology of important events" and a "cast of characters." He anticipated completing the first draft of the entire book by late summer 1984.[2]

After his review Landis paid Gordon a backhanded compliment when he described the writing as "more than competent," but promptly passed on the book. He cited the manuscript's "bias," which would become a common refrain from other publishing professionals. More importantly, editor Landis suggested he backtrack a step and get a literary agent, and he recommended several, one of whom Gordon contacted and engaged, Kathy P. Robbins.[3]

Robbins, who later represented the author "Anonymous" (revealed to be journalist Joe Klein of the Clinton-era sensation *Primary Colors*), showed interest. Robbins was described by others as "temperamental, forceful, engaging, smart, creative, warm, and tough," everything an aspiring author could desire from an agent in New York's rough-and-tumble literary world. Her newly created agency, with its growing stable of political journalists, specialized in nonfiction books about current events by insiders, a perfect fit, it would seem, for Gordon.[4]

To her credit Robbins made the logical suggestion that Gordon work with a seasoned coauthor, the single act that in itself should have ensured the project's ultimate success. Actually, with Landis's damning "more than competent" remark fresh in everyone's mind, Robbins held firm that she would only take on this project if Gordon worked with a writer. By September Gordon was dutifully awaiting her list of prospects while reporting to her that the book was "two-thirds finished." The only remaining part "concerns the legal aftermath of the collapse," to which he confidently added, "Naturally, that is the area where I am most knowledgeable as to what really happened."[5]

Two collaborators emerged: the aforementioned Robert Byrne and Knox Burger, a replacement for Robbins. Who came first is unclear, but maybe they came as a matched set because Burger was Byrne's agent. Byrne came with impressive credentials, including a midwestern upbringing and a college degree in engineering. Born in 1930 and raised in Dubuque, Iowa, he went on to receive a degree in civil engineering from the University of Colorado. He got a taste for writing from an earlier career, a long stint as editor of *Western Construction*, a San Francisco trade magazine. Success from his first books allowed him to quit his day job and focus on writing full-time.[6]

Byrne seemed to be the ideal partner. The three recent novels he had under his belt shared with this project the theme of man-made structural disasters. To top it off, Gordon may have already been acquainted with Byrne's work through a positive review published in the *Kansas City Star* only two months before the Hyatt disaster. The book reviewer ended his piece, unsettling when read in retrospect, with this endorsement: "With plenty of nail-biting drama, violent death, and a graphic explosion of human folly, *The Dam* is a disquieting reading experience for devotees of prophetic fiction."[7] When Gordon contacted him, Byrne was still living in the Bay Area of California.

Byrne enthusiastically signed on and saw nothing but blue sky above. The topic was right up his alley. In his first letter to Gordon, Byrne exclaimed, "There is no question in my mind that a book is possible here that would have a shot at being the main selection of the Book of the Month Club, as well as one that would reach the *New York Times* best-seller list."[8] This would have launched Gordon's book into the stratosphere since the Book of the Month Club once boasted half a million members. The table seemed set for a topical best seller that possessed incredible advantages: a plugged-in New York agent as Gordon's point person; an accomplished author and something of a subject matter specialist as a partner; bountiful amounts of time and money to expend on the project; a mastery of the primary sources; an event still fresh and current to the public; and a Woodward-and-Bernstein-style exposé that no one had yet broken. All the elements were in place for a dynamite book save one, a factor that the principals did not foresee: Gordon's inability to collaborate.

Before ever seeing the manuscript, Byrne volunteered, "I have an idea of the book's organization and content. . . . I'm sure I could come up with a book with terrific impact." Byrne came on strong, maybe too strong, one thinks, for Gordon's taste. Nevertheless, by November 1984 the two were pounding out the terms of Byrne's work-for-hire by Gordon and passing a draft contract back and forth to each other. And back in Kansas City, Gordon had three more chapters under his belt.[9]

At the same time that Gordon was gaining a coauthor, he was jettisoning his original agent. In December he asked Robbins for the return of all copies of his materials and abruptly ended their business relationship. His reasons, he stated, were "his inability to reach her and her lack of attention to the book." In the age of snail mail, she replied rather promptly—the next week—and cited *his* failure to return *her* calls. She had read his latest chapters to be sure, making no direct comment on their quality, but insisted that "you need to work with a writer." She was willing to continue on the project "only if you're willing to collaborate," which gave away her worry that the deal with Byrne or any other author was not progressing. "We may indeed not be a match as client and agent," she wrote, a statement that others would echo in the following years. Gordon replied soon thereafter, employing a rather sheepish tone to blame the missed phone calls on an unnamed female secretary since fired, but pushed back on Robbins's advice. "I must do this book in my own amateurish, clumsy manner." He concluded with, "My apologies for your having wasted so much time and effort."[10] This exchange with a strong woman professional emitted from Gordon more than a whiff of male chauvinism.

The Byrne collaboration began in earnest after Gordon made a down payment of $25,000 for six months of service, real money in 1985, when a senior reporter or junior editor was fortunate to make that much in a year. Byrne intended to devote his time entirely to "the skywalks book," and his first tasks would be to put together a formal book proposal and rewrite Gordon's existing chapters, which now amounted to four hundred typed, double-spaced pages. Gordon anticipated sending the remainder by April 1, 1985. (He always seemed to be "two-thirds finished.") Byrne also offered to do any additional research as needed, even coming to Kansas City to conduct interviews, but Gordon scotched that idea.[11]

The early optimism soon faded. The new year brought the full weight of the second major player to the project, Knox Burger, head of a leading New York literary agency. Burger, a "crusty" but influential veteran editor-turned-agent, possessed a sterling reputation as a skilled reader with an eye for talent. To his everlasting fame, he had published Kurt Vonnegut's first short story. Vonnegut himself spoke for all when he said that Burger, a curmudgeonly father figure to the famed author, had "discovered and encouraged more good young writers than any other editor of his time." It appeared that, somewhat miraculously, beginner Gordon had traded up in powerhouse agents.[12]

Burger did not have to wait long for the Gordon-Byrne book proposal. Like Robbins, Burger did not mince words in a lengthy letter to Byrne that set the tone for the year: "You've been patient and resilient in the face of my sending you back to the drawing board twice already on this proposal. . . . And your difficulties are compounded by having to deal with Mr. Gordon."[13]

Burger articulated his many concerns, for one the book's ending. "It's tough if the story has to end on a bitter, the-company-really-won note." He also complained that Gordon "may be riding his hobby horse too hard or at too great length." Later chapters that dealt with the court case, so dear to Gordon's heart, were "overly detailed" with "no real outline and an insufficient sense." The tone in these chapters was "a little flat, bland, pedestrian," and, Burger feared, there were more such chapters to come. The veteran editor immediately spotted a major problem with Gordon's whole approach. "Those falling skywalks are (to put it bluntly) a terribly tough act to follow." This, if anything, was an understatement for anyone writing the Hyatt story. What ensued in the manuscript, he believed, was "anticlimactic," particularly "if the ins and outs of legal maneuvering are gone into too exhaustively." Burger devised a strategy though: "The chapters leading in to the disaster and the event itself are excellent. . . . I'd be in a stronger position if I took the proposals and just those pieces of the book to publishers." He intended a multiple submission to five houses, carefully avoiding any that might have a business connection to Hallmark. Then, just as quickly he walked that idea back, "but that wouldn't be playing entirely fair since so much of the actual book will consist of Gordon's efforts to bring Hallmark to account." Burger understood the dilemma they collectively faced: "I know this is more than a book about falling masonry; it's about how the system breaks down." He hoped that this obstacle could be overcome if Gordon would only give him and Byrne, longtime partners with a proven track record, "a relatively free hand." This permission never came.[14]

Nevertheless, Byrne worked rapidly and brought Gordon up to speed on his progress. He had rewritten nine chapters so far. Not avoiding a confrontation, he also enclosed a copy of Burger's above acerbic letter after receiving the agent's permission to do so. Byrne asserted his own concerns with "*your version*" of the manuscript (italics mine). Specifically, "Knox is worried that the last part of the book will be too legalistic. I'm worried that the first part will be too technical."[15] As Burger reviewed the rewrites, he followed with his own bits of advice: Shorten the first chapter. Boil down the legal details. "Don't tell when you can show." Avoid "hopped up . . . hyper prose." He mentioned the "almost unrelievedly high pitch" of Gordon's voice. The tutorial continued: "Your outrage is thoroughly understandable, and undoubtedly justified, but your repetitions, your insistence on the enormity of Hallmark's crimes, has [have] a cumulative hard-breathing effect that is . . . somewhat exhausting, and one longs for a touch of coolness of restraint, of seeming objectivity." Burger now pulled no punches: "I see a man obsessed. . . . And that tone, that constant shrill high coloration. . . . Let me repeat, and in deadly earnest, I fully understand your feelings; you've been immersed in this enormity"—that word again—"for what is it? Three years now? The case seems to me, from what I know, unique in the annals of corporate malfeasance, cynicism, and heartlessness—and not just Hallmark, but those venal construction people, and those terrific members of the legal fraternity."[16]

In the midst of this harsh but honest letter, let us pause and ask of Gordon and his book project: When does tenacity end and obsession begin? Had Gordon crossed that line, and if so, could he ever return? Knox Burger used some powerful words to describe his client—"immersed," "outraged," and "obsessed"—and did not do so lightly. He knew that the state of his author's mind was critical to the project, and having to use those blunt words gave him no assurance of its success. Great books about obsessive behavior, lost causes, and tilting at windmills had been written, think Melville's *Moby-Dick* and Cervantes's *Don Quixote*, but one did not confuse their great themes with personal descriptions of their authors. Gordon was in a dangerous place.

Then the old editor abruptly returned to his role as wise, gentle teacher to Gordon's stubborn student: "You and RB [Robert Byrne] can compromise on the tone. . . . Isn't it best to compromise the matter for now, in these early chapters we're going to submit, and then rely on an editor's outside judgment, after his publisher has come up with a contract and a meaningful advance? . . . We're selling a book that can become a huge best seller." He concluded frankly, "I hope my candor doesn't disturb you, but I can't sit here and say you're right and RB is wrong because I don't believe it."[17]

In his next letter, even before the dust had settled from the last, Burger piled on. "You have not yet discovered the manifest virtues of understatement." The proposal should be "deadpan." The goal was basic: "It should be a hell of a story—and let some big-name lawyer reviewing it for the *N.Y. Times* or wherever tell us the lessons to be drawn from it. . . . I fear you want to lean so hard on the moral and legal lessons learned that interest in the book won't be as intense as it ought to be."[18] In everything he said to Gordon, even at this early stage, Burger was on the mark and would be proven right.

Byrne and Burger worked in tandem to get Gordon back on course. By mid-February Byrne had written six versions of the book proposal and gone through seven hundred pages of manuscript, described as "the first part top-heavy with civil engineering and the last with legal arguments." He also sent Gordon a thirteen-page letter of "guidance." Byrne criticized the stiff, stilted dialogue, a shifting viewpoint, and a vast parade of characters. Byrne escalated, "Your obsession with the case and your emotional involvement must be kept in check. . . . The book should not come across as 'A Lawyer's Revenge.'" Furthermore, "There is an unstated feeling in the book that every little detail about Hallmark is fascinating and that therefore its dereliction in building the hotel is astounding and unbelievable and outrageous." (Gordon's marginal note was simply "true.") He continued, objecting to Gordon's tone, "You are in effect being given the opportunity to present the case against Hallmark.... You have to be fair and even generous if you want to keep the support of the reader." He spoke about "objectively unrolling the facts," a statement that to this lawyer, a merchant of "facts," and the man who had toiled countless, thankless hours among the documents, must have grated. "The facts do not need much explaining and certainly not lurid coloring.... Let the facts speak for themselves.... Let Knox supply the hard sell." Gordon's response was a flurry of objections in the margins, which he copied and sent to Burger.[19] He responded likewise, a hail of marginal objections, after Byrne enlisted Martin Cruz Smith, a friend and the novelist of the best seller *Gorky Park* (1981), who graciously read and commented on the manuscript. Rather than being receptive to expert criticism, the likes of which few rookie authors ever enjoyed, Gordon undoubtedly felt ganged up on by all.[20]

Byrne trudged on. Later in the month, he sought approval for the material he had "consolidated" in the sample chapters destined for publishers. He implored Gordon to quit burying both him and Burger with supporting documentation, "all unnecessary at this stage." Pleaded Byrne, "We aren't simply trying to get a book published; we are trying for a blockbuster."[21]

The project had barely commenced, and tempers were fraying. The work on the book proposal dragged on. Byrne informed Gordon, "Here is a compromise between my last version of the proposal, which Knox was ready to present to publishers, and your last version.... I beg you with tears in my eyes not to attack this again.... Let Knox try it on a few publishers. It makes no sense at all for you and me to keep going back and forth on a document that will never be published." By late March Byrne was ready to plow through the first ten chapters again.[22]

Gordon shot off to Byrne, "I am not pleased with the present situation. In short, you don't like what I write. And I don't really think that what you rewrite is always an improvement." A couple of days later he was still upset, complaining about "all the pressure I feel to write the skywalks' story." Ever the professional, Byrne prioritized in his reply, "The serious matters you raise about the trouble we are having with our collaboration I'll respond to in a week or so. Right now, I'd like to continue working on a leaner version of the first fourteen chapters."[23]

Burger jumped into the fray. He described a particular sample chapter of Gordon's as "very windy and expository." To Gordon he said, "If this book is to achieve the success it deserves, labored descriptive passages of this sort must be ruthlessly pared." But on the plus side, Burger casually mentioned that he had sent the revised proposal to Random House, a leading New York publisher.[24]

The book proposal fell flat. In March the legendary Robert D. Loomis, whose Random House authors included Maya Angelou, William Styron, and Kansas City's own Calvin Trillin, declined to make an offer and bluntly gave his reasons to Burger. "He [Gordon] seemed to be insisting that I be appalled at this and worried about that and incensed about something else." Loomis questioned the book's format: "By the time I reached the point where the lawyer began his narrative, however, I felt as though I pretty much understood what the problems were and where all the skeletons were buried. I frankly did not look forward to his discovering it all over again." In sum, the manuscript needed serious reworking.[25]

Burger forwarded the Loomis rejection to Gordon and appended, "I find it hard to disagree with much of what he says." Burger thought the section relating to the 1979 collapse should be "drastically telescoped." If Gordon insisted on including all the legal details, "we will have a very difficult time with the project." Finally, he advised, "I'm afraid we better regroup before going out to other houses."[26] After this early rejection, taking a breather seemed a wise move.

Readily apparent to all parties but one (Gordon), the problem lay not with a reluctant publisher but with an obstinate author. Gordon did not take this Random House rejection well: "I agree that somehow we have nothing to show for 28 months of my labor, as well as over $100,000 in out-of-pocket expenses." (Presumably, Gordon was referring to the costs of copies, research assistance, secretarial help, and Bob Byrne's fee.). He continued his rant: "So far I have received nothing at all from him [Byrne] for nearly two months. In fact, all in all, I have not received much of anything. . . . I am pissed. I now have 1,000 pages of typed manuscript that I have prepared. Apparently, none of it has been revised by Bob. Would you like for me to send it to you directly and just forget about California [Byrne's residence]? I realize it's not the book you envisioned."[27] After this outburst and after only three months into the association, the principals did, indeed, need to "regroup."

IT WAS APRIL 1985, AND THREE MONTHS REMAINED ON THE BYRNE contract. The writer had gone through the first fourteen chapters "still trying to come up with at least a few chapters that you will approve of and that will excite a publisher." Byrne's new version, he reported, would be ready in a week or two, but he warned that his slant differed from Gordon's agenda, which was "to heap all possible blame on Hallmark and Don Hall." In addition, Byrne could not resist giving Gordon more "guidance," candidly stating, "I want to tell a story, and you want to try a case." Gordon let this last comment pass and gave his approval to what Byrne was working on.[28]

Byrne was well aware of the looming June 30 deadline, warning Gordon, "If my work on the book is not complete after six months, we'll have to talk about [what] we should do." Gordon was doing nothing to help ease the impending time crunch, and a clearly exasperated Byrne made it clear to Gordon that he was "not all that thrilled to get another 110 pages of class action pros and cons, but I'll see what I can do with it."[29] Gordon went around Byrne to Burger to make his case, enclosing a chapter. "The last half of it almost completes the class action struggle," Gordon noted, "and if you chop as much as you say you intend to, well you're really ripping out the only high spot of the first half of the book." He apologized for "placing you in the role of umpire."[30]

Burger, an editor first and foremost, did not heed Gordon's pleas to preempt the red pencil, nor did Byrne, who in mid-May reported that, as one example, he had shortened fifty-five Gordon pages to fifteen.[31] Gordon found any cutting of his text intolerable, even if it came from professionals at the top of their game. Maybe they were the first two persons to ever try to edit Robert Gordon. They would not be the last.

Things were not going well on the publisher front either, where a consensus of sorts was being reached about the tone and structure of the book. Although Peter Guzzardi of Bantam Books, Stephen Hawking's editor of *A Brief History of Time* (1988), was "very taken with the *idea* of this book [italics mine]," he expressed nothing but reservations to Burger: "The simple facts themselves present a very damning image of Hallmark, reaching right up to the top of the corporation. Therefore, the more objective the tone of the book, the more reportorial the style, the more powerful the book will be." He suggested starting with the chapter when the skywalks fell. Guzzardi continued, "It's a very powerful (and horrific) story of corporate malfeasance, with the potential to reach a wide audience. But this has to present a more even-handed approach to events and to the people who played a role in them. The objective truth is the most devastating indictment of all."[32] Much later, Gordon followed Guzzardi's advice and moved the skywalks chapter to the front.

The June 30 deadline came and went, and on July 10, Gordon sent Burger forty chapters, presumably a mix of Byrne's rewrites and Gordon's frantic, eleventh-hour compositions. Burger spent two weeks reviewing the material before crafting a response. His well-earned reputation as a curmudgeon was echoed in his reply: "The manuscript is still too windy and polemical, too loaded with heavy finger pointing and breast beating; what could be effective as dry, flat statement, perhaps inflected with irony, too often makes us writhe because you turn it into heavy-handed sarcasm. . . . You do not have a writer's ear for speech." Gordon's marginal notes to himself were, as one would expect, defensive: "But one man can only do so much, and I thought my goal was to finish the book." It is unclear if he sent this marked-up letter to Burger, although by now it no longer really mattered.[33]

On August 1 Burger called it quits. "We are at an impasse." He described the style and tone of the manuscript as "flat" and "combative" and "loaded." Plus, they had failed with seven big-name publishers—Atheneum, Bantam, Houghton Mifflin, Random House, Simon & Schuster, Warner Books, and William Morrow. "It's just not in shape for me to send to publishers." Notwithstanding this last, devastating critique, and ever the stereotypically encouraging editor, he ended on a positive note: "The raw material has great potential, and the account of the actual disaster is still riveting. . . . There's a hell of a story here." He made his last, generic recommendation: "You may want to find some other agent . . . or you may want to find a writer . . . or you may want to send the manuscript around yourself."[34]

Gordon had finally received a wake-up call, although his immediate response failed to reflect any contriteness. "Your letter was, well, quite a blow," he replied, and asked for the return of all his materials. In lieu of a farewell, he said, "I still would like to meet you someday." To Byrne he struck a stoical note: "Contrary to what I may have said in a moment of rage, I do not hate, detest & or even dislike you. . . . Perhaps we were six months out of sync to start with." Gordon intended to soldier on: "I shall push on to finish. . . . My recent chapters aren't quite as dreadful as Knox's letter may indicate (I hope) but even if they are, I simply cannot abandon my Viet-Nam." He asked Byrne too for the return of all materials, which included "fifty pounds of photostats, clippings, and 900 pages or so" of manuscript.[35] Burger later picked at the scab when he callously sent Gordon a recent cover of *Publishers Weekly*, the industry's leading trade journal, that showed the new book *Winning through Integrity* that carried a prominent blurb by Don Hall. Burger inserted a note: "I thought you would be amused in a grisly sort of way."[36]

With this whimper, so closed Gordon's best window of opportunity, the time when his book could have made its greatest impact in the marketplace, as well as in the political, business, and cultural arenas. Four years had elapsed since the skywalks disaster, two years since the courtroom debacle. He had apparently lost his big chance or, at the least, postponed it indefinitely. Now was truly the time for Gordon to regroup.

It is also the time to pause and look at this first manuscript. Was it a "dreadful" polemic filled with bitterness, outrage, and sarcasm? Or was it a "hell of a story" that took too long to tell, buried under an avalanche of detail and legalese? What exactly had those New York publishers declined to accept?

12

The Gordon Thesis

The surviving typescript of "When They Didn't Care Enough," the predecessor to "House of Cards," is worth examining, particularly the first ten chapters of a book over which Byrne sweated, Burger growled, and publishers turned up their noses. These initial chapters totaled 189 typed, double-spaced pages before segueing clumsily to chapter eleven's tea dance.[1] The following chapters of the manuscript's first part ended with the federal court's formation of the class in January 1982.[2]

The thread that ran throughout the beginning chapters was Gordon's detailed and carefully assembled explanation of why the skywalks inevitably fell. The actions by a host of secondary, faceless figures after the atrium roof collapse were the crux of the story. He homed in on the hotel construction's poor project management, the connections, both literal and figurative, between the atrium roof and skywalk collapses, and the warnings that Hallmark failed to heed.[3] These were the bare bones of the "Gordon thesis," as a later critic dismissively termed his argument. The early chapters introduced several characters who appeared later, the latecomer Gordon being a notable exception, and foreshadowed to a limited extent the "legal maneuvers" that exhausted all readers but him. So far so good. Only after the skywalks fell did Gordon insert himself in the story, which he may have felt unavoidable, but the maneuver jarringly switched the viewpoint from an omniscient narrator to "first person stuff," as Byrne derisively called it.[4]

The typescript's first page carried that clunky title, about which Knox Burger once opined, "I could give you two solid pages on why I think yours is wrong." But the matter was not urgent: "Forget the title problem for now. We're not selling a title. We're selling a book that can become a huge best seller." The title page also carried a 1984 copyright date, which is when these chapters were penned and possibly before others heavily edited them, beginning with Byrne's arrival in 1985.[5]

Gordon spelled out in his introduction the purpose of the book: "to set forth the truth about exactly what—and who—caused this unprecedented disaster." Reassembling the story in its proper order may have been in the lawyer's wheelhouse, but telling it in a clear, compelling manner proved more difficult for a novice nonfiction writer. Although the "how" was a settled question, both the "what" and the "who" were controversial and confusing. He looked beyond faulty supports ("things") as the reasons for the failure and included bad management of the overall project ("people"). He explained, "The technical cause of the collapse was a failure of communication about an obvious design problem during a 'fast-track,' 'time is money' approach to the project's design and construction." This included, in the broadest sense, all top decision makers and therefore widely expanded the blame—far beyond a couple of structural engineers—to extend to and include the head of the entire project. Explaining this dynamic required a deft touch at scene setting and character sketching that Gordon lacked.

The author overcompensated by employing the equivalent of a lawyerly opening statement. "The party principally responsible for the skywalk slaughter," by which Gordon meant collectively the Hallmark corporation, its officers, its top executives, and their business associates, "managed to avoid ever having to face a jury for what it had done." He intended the book to show "how, and why, one company intentionally began taking a calculated risk with the skywalk's safety a year and a half before their final collapse." The company had exhibited "the intentional disregard of a number of unmistakable warning signs." Gordon asked the reader, now his judge and jury, "Why were known design defects allowed to go uncorrected?" It cannot be overstated how radically these statements flew in the face of the general orthodoxy, and Gordon knew it. "So far, these facts have been hidden from the public."[6] As any good lawyer, he intended to present the facts in order to make the greatest impact, but the bigger question was whether he could he do so effectively as an author.

Gordon opened chapter 1 on October 14, 1979, the day of the atrium roof collapse, by tracking the activities of one minor and two major characters. He set the scene with newly appointed federal judge Scott O. Wright heading off to work, then moved to "an elderly watchman," making his nightly rounds at the hotel construction site, followed by Don Hall, whose property the watchman was protecting.[7] Only Wright garnered a favorable portrait—a former, battle-hardened Marine Corps aviator who some thought resembled the "Popeye" cartoon character: earthy, direct, a free spirit given to speak his mind and spout country witticisms. This colorful view of the judge mirrored that of others who crossed his path in court or in his chambers or on Kansas City streets as he zipped by them in his sporty convertible in winter with the top down.[8] Until he inserted himself in the story, Gordon made Judge Wright his main protagonist.

Skipping quickly over the night watchman, Gordon's sketch of Hallmark's leader was less flattering. As opposed to Wright, the Hall scion was an indifferent Ivy League graduate, tight-lipped and aloof, who thought himself something of an expert on architecture. Hall had reached the pinnacle of business success through birth, not merit. His new hotel, coming as it did on the heels of Joyce Hall's comparable development project, gave the son the opportunity to author his own success, if not surpass its predecessor, and emerge from his father's shadow. Gordon made much of this competitive father-son dynamic. He, too, had lived with a dominating patriarch of whom "he never spoke favorably," a man he described as obstinate, hard-headed, and unwilling ever to listen to advice. When he once mentioned these traits to his wife, she thought, "And you're exactly the same!"[9]

Gordon pointed out that Joyce Hall had once written, not all that benignly, "Today we are building a second hotel. . . . [It will be] for Donald and his management team to make it as beautiful and successful as 'my' hotel."[10] These strands all came together in a weird way with the Hyatt Regency, particularly their iconic skywalks. When Gordon wrote that Don Hall "wanted these skywalks to be made 'as thin and invisible as possible,'" the descriptor revealed the significance of this one architectural feature above all others.[11] The skywalks were always intended to reflect the son's grander vision, superior design sense, and mastery of modern construction. Perhaps they also symbolized his hubris, the result being that Don Hall owned the skywalks in more ways than one. Before the initial chapter ended, Gordon had his antagonist. Awkwardly, he then had to leave his primary characters and tell his story through the words and deeds of his antagonist's indistinguishable minions.

THE NEXT NINE CHAPTERS OF THE MANUSCRIPT, WOEFULLY SHORT OF sympathetic characters with few exceptions, were told through the recorded words and reconstructed actions of (in order of appearance) Richard C. Heydinger, Jack D. Gillum, Tom Terrebone, Arnold Waxman, Fred Havens, William S. Johnson, Keith Kelly, Bob Berkebile, Karl Eldridge, Laurence Poisner, James C. "Jim" McClune, and Jerome W. "Jerry" Sifers. Gordon used this extended cast, chiefly consisting of individuals in the Hallmark orbit, to carefully craft his thesis about the collapse of the atrium roof and its direct relationship to the doomed skywalks. He started with the men in charge and how they operated after "the bad news had traveled swiftly throughout the project's extensive hierarchy."[12] Collectively the members of this group, none of whom jumped off the page as compelling characters, came across as company men of the best sort and drones of the worst. The telling clue might be their initial reaction to the roof collapse: how much would the repairs cost, and who would pay for it? Not surprisingly, in a world of the bottom line, an insurance man came to the fore.

Richard C. Heydinger was the corporate official responsible for "making sure that there was adequate insurance coverage on all Hallmark assets." His job was "to anticipate the financial exposure to Hallmark from anything which could reasonably be expected to cause damage to property or harm to individuals." In the immediate aftermath of the atrium roof failure, Heydinger saw a simple case of, in his words, "conspicuous shoddy workmanship" and concluded it was all "a straight-out, man-made collapse."[13] Others concurred, and Gordon took pains to always emphasize this in his text.

Jack D. Gillum, who headed the outside structural engineering firm on the job and who ultimately took the fall, surveyed the site and called the steel-to-concrete connections "abominations" loaded with "deadly defects." To Gillum's trained eye, "almost nothing had been built correctly." Heydinger calculated that further investigations and repairs could add six costly months to the project, plus $200,000 to $400,000 in additional expenditures, which did not include the huge loss of hotel revenue from a delayed opening.[14] If accurate, the estimate by this numbers guy of time and money lost could cripple the economic viability of the entire project. Both had to be shaved down.

Another insurance man, an outsider, weighed in. Tom Terrebone represented Kemper Insurance, Hallmark's insurer for the project, and the St. Louis–based official offered his "high priority risk report" of the accident. To his credit and Gordon's admiration, Terrebone chalked up the cause to "gross incompetency" and cited three factors for the roof collapse: bad design, bad installation, and lack of expansion joints to accommodate the recent cold weather, which had caused contraction of the steel. Kemper Insurance's three-page warning to Hallmark minced no words: "The structural engineer is at fault.... Also, the installing contractor is clearly at fault for a bogus installation job." More importantly, and to avoid a repeat occurrence, "The structural steel system design for the atrium area should be completely reviewed with special attention given to the need for expansion joints and for adequate steel/concrete attachment methods."[15] No matter how this directive was later parsed in sworn testimony, the question would always be whether the owner heeded this early warning to "completely review" the atrium.

To the project managers the roof collapse plainly portended other structural defects. Arnold Waxman, an engineer and longtime construction manager described by others as the "eyes and ears" of the owner, had been informed of the specific problem—the same type of wall anchor bolts and same method of attachment of the fallen roof girders had been used for the support shelves of the skywalks. Ominously, "the skywalks' steel support bolts were also showing unmistakable signs of being over-stressed."[16] To Gordon, who always saw the two collapses as interconnected, these were two points on the same straight line. He concluded that the owner's representatives, particularly Waxman, must have as well, but to be fair, the wall anchors for the atrium roof and skywalk shelves were an altogether different system than the latter's hanger-rod supports. Subsequent debate, usually strained, always became more heated over this apples-to-oranges comparison.

Two months before the atrium roof collapse, Fred Havens, whose steel company was a Hallmark-Eldridge subcontractor, had completed the fabrication and installation of the skywalks. Their description by Gordon in his manuscript reflected a lawyer's matter-of-fact tone, not an architect's soaring prose. He described each skywalk as

> a steel contraption that looked about eight feet wide and spanned the entire one hundred and eighteen feet of the north-south axis of the atrium. . . . The lowest skywalk . . . was suspended about thirty feet above the lobby floor. . . . The second floor bridge hung from the highest (fourth floor) skywalk by three pairs of incredibly slender steel rods only about an inch in diameter. The highest or fourth floor bridge was in turn suspended from the ceiling by a similar arrangement of skinny rods. The third-floor skywalk, which was also suspended from the lobby ceiling by virtue of the same type of long steel rods [and which did not fall in 1981], was horizontally separated from the other two by about twenty feet.[17]

Gordon's use of such loaded descriptors as "skinny" and "incredibly slender" was no accident. One can almost hear them uttered in front of a jury to the defendants' chagrin, if not objection.

News of the atrium roof collapse garnered virtually no attention, which was the obvious intent of William S. Johnson, Hallmark's director of public relations. Johnson soon realized the gravity of the crisis, a potential media nightmare, and immediately undertook damage control. As Gordon rather indelicately described Johnson's situation: "It made as much sense to go out and tell the world the news about this incident as it would for Ford Motor Company to have run an ad showing a Pinto gas tank exploding."[18] But go out he did, willingly and effectively.

A few years later, Johnson gave his public "end-of-a-career sentiments" at the time of his retirement, an occasion of which Gordon was apparently unaware. If he had been present at the gathering, he could have heard Johnson express a conventional, persistent image of Hallmark Cards and the Halls that the audience shared and the public accepted: "This company, this family, the people and the corporate culture are nonpareil in the American business community. You would have to occupy the vantage point I enjoyed for so long to fully measure the excellence of the organization. It gives a spiritual strength to our city, to our nation. It epitomizes decency and integrity, and many other old-fashioned values."[19]

But Gordon did see how, in his words, this "extraordinary reputation for civic leadership" came in handy when that reputation was threatened. It granted Hallmark the "power to influence not only what stories the media does about it, but also how the subject is covered."[20] The atrium collapse was the ideal time to use that power, and Gordon saw how it was done.

Johnson, who had moved to public relations from the journalism world, went directly to the local newspaper with a version of the October calamity that, to put it mildly, understated the seriousness of the collapse. The paper rehashed his press release into a back-page, uncorroborated story of the "incident." The article's title itself minimized the situation's seriousness: "Beam Collapse at Downtown Hotel."[21] The bullet points of the story pointed to a minor, isolated incident: It involved only a "16-foot steel beam." No one was injured. They were assessing the minimal damage. Johnson even succeeded in putting a positive spin on things: construction would not be delayed, and the beam should be back in place within a week. There was no indication of a structural weakness or engineering or design flaw, merely an installation glitch that was easily correctable. The two local newspapers, which in 1979 had a combined reportorial and editorial staff of more than three hundred, most of them officed only five blocks away, did not send anyone to fact-check this story, although a puff piece about the new hotel that followed a day later contained "a reassuring exterior photo of a massive, solid structure" and the "open-air ambiance of a five-story atrium, a Hyatt symbol."[22]

The newspaper article also gave an update: the hotel had "404,000 reservations so far," another indicator of the pressure to open on time. All in all, the hotel project was, to quote Johnson, "a smashing success," which in retrospect seems an unfortunate if not cynical choice of words. Nevertheless, the old PR pro was pleased with his successful misdirection and reported the good news directly to Don Hall. "We did this piece with [Philip L.] Burgert [the *Kansas City Times* writer] and BINGO! Good positive story." In retrospect, Gordon saw the downside to Hallmark's success in media manipulation. The precedent had been set for the time when the stakes became exponentially higher. "It emboldened the company to issue another stream of press releases and planted articles, all of which contained even more brazen lies."[23]

Blowing smoke in public did not change the fact that the project managers in private saw their timetable and budget seriously threatened. This provided the motivation, Gordon believed, for their corner-cutting actions. Keith Kelly, the Hallmark executive in charge of the project's day-to-day management, grasped with the atrium roof collapse "what all this would do to the already tight time schedule for getting the Hyatt completed and open for business." To Gordon, Kelly's solution to his timetable problem was simple. "To survive he had to keep the project moving at its incredibly rapid pace," doubling down on its "fast track" approach to building design and construction. Kelly called for October 19 an emergency meeting of the principals—architect Bob Berkebile of PBNDML, contractor Karl Eldridge, engineer Jack Gillum, and Laurence Poisner, president of the testing company—and gave them Hallmark's hard line on the budget. "Crown Center will not accept the cost for any other item of work associated with this failure and structural inadequacies, neither remedial work, reconstruction work, clean-up nor professional services." Kelly, whom Hallmark would fire in a couple years and fail upward to head the high-profile Union Station renovation in Washington DC, received no pushback from his boss, president of Crown Center Redevelopment Corporation Jim McClune, who reported directly to Don Hall. McClune parroted the on-time-on-budget mantra, especially since, as Gordon noted, his predecessor had been fired in 1974 "because the first hotel built at the complex was completed 'one month late and over budget.'" Those further from the boardroom and its influences expressed their concerns with the shortcomings of fast-tracking, however. Jerry Sifers, Hallmark's representative in the field, later summed it up best: "We never know from one day to the next what would be worked on. That made it practically impossible to schedule inspections or do any checking for quality." None of these individuals with either their lofty job titles or their up-to-their-elbows involvement in the project figured in Gordon's narration as much as the trio of lawyers—Charles J. "Charlie" Egan Jr., Judith Ann Cameron "Judy" Whittaker, and Pam Wight Curran—who entered the scene in his manuscript's fifth chapter. Gordon focused on Whittaker as the character poised to "guide Hallmark safely through the jumbled dangers of potential legal liability" and Curran to record it for history.[24]

CHARLES EGAN SERVED AS HALLMARK'S GENERAL COUNSEL. A PROUD, dedicated, and active alumnus of Harvard University, Egan (AB '54) once served as the president of the local Harvard Club of Kansas City and in 1989 in the same role nationally for the prestigious Harvard Alumni Association. In 2015 the university bestowed the Harvard Medal on the former captain of the Crimson swimming and diving team. His brusque, no-nonsense demeanor reflected, as Gordon noted after deposing Egan in 1982, that of the ex–U.S. Marine Corps officer that he was. Gordon also described him as "articulate and extremely hardworking." One gets the impression that the junior attorney was slightly in awe of the aristocratic corporate lawyer, his military background, and his "Olympian view of the world."[25]

The same regard was not extended to Judith Whittaker, although she may have had the better résumé than Egan. Whittaker graduated first in her class at the University of Missouri–Kansas City School of Law and, as a woman of the time, more than held her own in the dangerous waters of the corporate legal world. She was one of the twelve founding members of the Central Exchange, a groundbreaking organization in Kansas City, where professional women, still excluded from local, high-powered men's clubs, could interact and support one another's careers. Hired in 1972, she served as Hallmark's number two lawyer, its associate general counsel, and by the early 1980s was such a rising star that she was the leading candidate for a judgeship on the U.S. Court of Appeals for the Eighth Circuit. Coincidentally, Whittaker was married to a son of the late U.S. Supreme Court justice Charles Evans Whittaker. Fierce opposition to her possible nomination arose, however, when powerful Missouri Reaganites, who suspected her positions on abortion and the proposed Equal Rights Amendment, forced this "insufficient" Republican out of the running. This rebuff earned a stern rebuke from the *New York Times* editorial staff but to no avail.[26]

Gordon seemed provoked by his female rival as well. While his career was stuck in lucrative but behind-the-scenes, low-satisfaction class-action suits, hers was rising and highly visible, especially in political circles. His behavior often appeared to his peers as erratic and off-putting, hers as calm, measured, and professional. He may have been the idealist, but she was the pragmatist. He was a rule follower even when it was against his self-interest, while she bent and maybe broke the rules when the situation called for it. That galled him. Preserved for posterity in Gordon's writings are the gratuitous barbs that said less about another person and more about his notions of women as workplace equals.

Something about Whittaker got under his skin, and she never again strayed far from his narrative. Gordon introduced "Hallmark's lady lawyer" as "Judy," followed soon thereafter as "Mrs. Whittaker," hardly ever simply by her surname "Whittaker," as his male characters were (and as his editor requested of him to change). Routinely described in purely physical terms, Whittaker was not portrayed as an embattled survivor in the tough old-boys-club of a major corporation but rather as "the sweetly-smiling lady in the tailored, Halston suit and grey leather gloves" with "her meticulous coiffure." For an important meeting in the atrium lobby, she "showed up a few minutes later than everyone else," which was meant to show a propensity for tardiness and not a signal of power. Gordon went so far as to conflate physical attributes when he described her voice as "silky as her raven hair."[27]

Putting aside Gordon's personal insecurities with Whittaker, he did feel grudging admiration for her ability. She regularly outmaneuvered her male adversaries in both tactics and strategy. After the atrium roof collapse, for example, she expertly stonewalled Kemper Insurance's request for documents and refused access to the site to their engineering expert. She remained adamant about not allowing anyone she could not control from poking around either the atrium or, during the discovery phase of the *Federal Skywalk Cases*, her files. When it was safe to whisper her professional secrets, Whittaker laid out Hallmark's successful strategy in the Hyatt litigation. "The real story," she shared, "was not a contest between plaintiffs and defendants [but] between two groups of *plaintiffs* and that conflict ultimately determined the strategy of the defendants."[28] The ultimate goal was getting rid of the federal case and, with it, crippling punitive damages. She expertly played the two sides off each other and achieved an outcome that was, given Hallmark's level of liability, a great victory. Together with Egan, who worked more behind the scenes, Whittaker made a formidable opponent.

Pam Wight Curran, the third Hallmark lawyer, now showed up in the manuscript. An in-house counsel and Whittaker understudy, Curran played an indirect but critical part in the events that followed—and in Gordon's narrative—because she kept meticulous notes for important summits such as the October 16, 1979, meeting held two days after the roof collapse. No longer in his recounting did he have to take unnecessary liberties with reconstructed conversations.

The main point of the October 16 meeting that Gordon wanted the reader to take away was the collective decision to hire an engineer to figure out what happened and, more importantly, whom to blame, the owner exempted. Soon Hallmark contracted the firm of Seiden & Page for the measly sum of $5,000 to "investigate the cause for the collapse of the east portion of the atrium roof" only. This bought a hundred hours of the structural engineers' time. Anything beyond this figure and prescribed location could only be done "as directed by the owner." These narrow and specific restrictions on scope precluded a full search and complete review of the atrium to find where other problems might be lurking. Gordon estimated that, together with the existence of more than 1,400 "connections" in the atrium alone, the skywalks never had a chance of being inspected closely if at all by this "tiny" firm hired to investigate only a portion of a "jumbo-size" problem.[29]

On October 19, Crown Center/Hallmark personnel—Curran, Egan, Heydinger, Kelly, McClune, Waxman, and Whittaker—met with two new secondary characters in Gordon's narrative: Uriel Seiden and Charles R. "Chuck" Page. Recently hired structural experts, Seiden and Page presented their initial report on the atrium roof collapse.[30] For this meeting, Curran again kept detailed notes from which Gordon could credibly construct conversations for his narrative.

A brisk but scattered back-and-forth ensued. Page gave the cause of the collapse. "Some balconies and bridges (skywalks) which were installed without expansion have pulled away at the north end." Was the "pulling away" problem of the skywalks the same as that for the roof? The focus of the conversation, therefore, was on their horizontal end supports, not on the vertical support rods. Egan asked, "What I want to know is what does this 'lack of any plan for expansion' suggest in regard to the safety of the balance of the building's structural strength?'" Page replied that "there is vulnerability at quite a number of points." But in the group, the lawyers and the bean-counters outnumbered the engineers, the latter of whom confined themselves to the expansion-contraction problems of horizontal connections.

Jim McClune was interested in who would pay the additional costs, certainly not Hallmark, he assured the group. Heydinger, the risk manager, voiced his estimate of what Kemper Insurance would pay. Hallmark was in no mood to pursue design flaws in general. The corporation stood to lose a half million dollars in revenue for every month the hotel's opening was delayed. Moreover, "the expense in locating all the design deficiencies was simply not economically justifiable." Heydinger offered a way to "hedge the company's exposure," and subsequently took out an extra $200 million in insurance at the cost of $33,000 a year. The group placed in the crosshairs Eldridge, the general contractor, which at the end of the day "accepted . . . blame for the roof collapse although the contractor had nothing to do with either the design of the roof connection . . . or the installation of the connection that failed to let the steel expand or contract."[31] Gordon learned a lot about Hallmark's decision-making and blame-avoidance process from this meeting, which colored his opinion of the corporation forever.

General Testing Labs successfully avoided getting pinned with the blame, maybe because from the beginning it was an underfunded and overlooked part of the construction process. The subcontractor was supposed to issue daily reports, but the on-site inspector offered up for this critical function was a young college student with little, if any, previous experience. He was pulled from the job in September 1979, probably because he was leaving this summer job anyway. When Keith Kelly, representing the owner, asked Laurence Poisner of General Testing why the problems with the horizontal steel-to-concrete connections had been missed, the latter quibbled that his firm was supposed to only look at steel-to-steel connections. The skywalks and their vertical steel hanger-rod connections received "only about ten minutes" of the novice inspector's attention. Apparently, the owner was aware of the many shortcomings in the inspection department. Sifers, the field rep who reported to Kelly, had the job of monitoring quality control, preparing weekly inspection schedules, and logging the results. Gordon later focused on Sifers's role but always had difficulty in drawing out the extent of his knowledge of General Testing's performance or lack thereof. Within Hallmark's corporate suite, it was probably common knowledge, however, and Gordon pointed out that Don Hall himself received a heads-up on General Testing's "inadequate performance at the Hyatt."[32] Notwithstanding, a chastened General Testing remained on the job.

Soon after this meeting the people who controlled the purse made another fateful decision. On October 29 Jack Gillum, the structural engineering subcontractor, requested a full-time, on-site inspector. Hallmark turned it down.[33] Gillum's request may have been prompted by another disaster unrelated to the roof collapse. Five days earlier, on October 24, 1979, Louis Paul Nold Jr., an Eldridge laborer working away from the atrium, had been hit by a falling beam and killed.[34] Years later, after he lost his engineer's license for the Hyatt debacle, a repentant Gillum said, in a hearing that Gordon attended, that he believed a qualified inspector would have caught the skywalk problems and prevented the 1981 collapse.

On November 8 the same group met again to discuss Seiden & Page's final report on the atrium roof collapse. It was a mere two pages. Hallmark had edited the document beforehand. Later in one of Gordon's all-important depositions, coauthor Seiden testified that he "didn't know exactly what his employer wanted him to say," although the conclusion the hirelings needed to reach was that "installers [the general contractor] had to be blamed for the entire collapse regardless of all the evidence to the contrary." And so they did. Egan again asked about "the adequacy of design in other areas of the hotel," without really wanting or receiving an answer.[35]

On November 12 Curran met with Chuck Page for a tutorial on prepping for the next big meeting. He summarized for her what caused the collapse: when the temperature cooled, an "overstressed" steel-to-concrete connection shrank, and a beam that sat on a steel shelf pulled loose from the wall and fell down, taking down the rest of the steel members. Their discussions and notes, important as they were to Gordon's later reconstruction, were overshadowed by the fact that Curran recorded this meeting, as she also did for the one held the next day.[36] In Gordon's view the next large gathering, held on November 13, 1979, was "the most important meeting in the wake of the initial disaster," a point he stressed for the next decade. The episode was equally important for Gordon's book narrative because he could provide a dramatic, running dialogue by the attendees (what he later called "the very best evidence of who said exactly what"). The group included the aforementioned Bob Berkebile, Pam Wight Curran, Herb Duncan, Jack Gillum, Dick Heydinger, Keith Kelly, Jim McClune, and Judy Whittaker, along with two more secondary characters, Steve Byers and Dan Duncan. Byers was the construction manager for Concordia Project Management, a subcontractor working on the Hyatt project. Duncan was project engineer and Gillum's second at Gillum-Colaco and later shared the blame heaped on his boss and the St. Louis company. Although too late to figure in the *Federal Skywalk Cases*, Halvorson's precious transcript of the cassette tape now proved essential for Gordon's narrative.[37]

During the meeting, Gillum took center stage and took some of the heat, a personal exercise in damage control "by confessing to some of his firm's failures," such as "some extremely shabby design work elsewhere in the atrium," and he offered up some of the subordinates on his miserly payroll for the brunt of the blame. Gillum, however, and his associate Duncan desperately wanted to shift culpability and not become the "fall guy for every problem that later developed."[38]

McClune countered by seeking an admission that "the work done by the hotel's structural engineers had been grossly incompetent." Gillum came back with a shocking soundbite that reverberated throughout later testimony and in Gordon's book: "We were looking at every single connection in the field, and what we find is an abomination. It really is. There's 36 separate connections up there and probably there's something wrong with every single one."[39]

A slide show of his field inspection report that pointed out the "abominations" followed, which Gillum attributed to careless installers. Some of the slides showed "how close the skywalks were to falling off their Teflon pads at the north end of the lobby and crashing to the floor."[40]

Then it was time for General Testing Laboratories' turn in the barrel. Whittaker started out by stating the obvious. "General Testing turned out not to be reliable." The architect Berkebile expanded on this: "They are supposed to be our structural engineer's eyes. . . . A week before the collapse, I heard from Jack Gillum. He told me 'You know it's amazing—in every area that we have a job where General Testing is the inspector, we have an absolutely perfect building. They're not planning perfect buildings anywhere else in the country, but we're getting one here.'"[41]

Gordon set the stage for his reader to accept another tenet in his carefully constructed thesis—that everyone in the room knew that the building inspection at the Hyatt Regency was a sham. But what would they do about it?

Gillum reminded Whittaker that it was the owner who decided how much safety it wanted by saying how much it would spend. Gillum and Duncan suggested load tests. Berkebile said those were not in the budget. Whittaker wanted the structural engineers to admit "they were responsible for choosing which redesign procedures to follow and that they would be responsible for all the consequences of that decision." By "responsible for all the consequences," one assumes nonbudgeted costs, and this was a bridge too far for Gillum-Colaco. Wrote Gordon, reinforced by recorded conversations: "Gillum wanted it known that the decision not to spend the money and to stick with only the minimum safety requirement for all the steel-to-steel connections . . . was Hallmark's. . . . 'In other words, Judy, we didn't talk you into accepting this.' [Answer] 'Okay. I understand that. Yeah.' 'That's right,' Byers also acknowledged."[42]

And with that, all the final decisions on safety had been made. The result was that no load testing was ever carried out, and all the steel-to-steel connections were left at their current minimum local building code standards. The hanger rods, which were later determined not to meet code, were not discussed. Apparently their connections did not fall under Jack Gillum's thirty-six abominations. As Gordon viewed it, everyone owned a piece of the problem and shared in the later blame.

As if demonstrating to a jury, Gordon's narrative put forth one example after another. Havens Steel had "installed second-rate connections." General Testing had missed it all "because either the contract did not require [them] to inspect those type of connections or the owner [Hallmark] had permitted incompetent and untrained people to work as inspectors. Or both." Sifers and Waxman "had accepted those connections." On the west side of the atrium, "errors by Havens in their shop drawings had been 'missed or not picked up by the architects, engineers or anyone else.' This prevented any one party from being totally responsible." The owner refused to pay for redesigning and repairing the "36 abominations," which included the skywalks' end connections. Gillum held firm that "if the owner 'desired a higher safety factor,' a written 'directive to that effect must be given.'" It never came. Byers, the outside project manager, managed to stop this circular firing squad and bring the group back to square one with a current issue. "There was a crisis on the atrium's west side," he said. "The construction workers were refusing to work over there until the skywalks were repaired. All progress has been halted."[43] Who would foot the bill?

In normal situations a claim would have been filed with Kemper Insurance, Hallmark's primary insurer for the new hotel. But a claim would mean an investigation, and Whittaker would have none of it. Whittaker preempted any such investigation by admitting to the cause of the roof collapse, "faulty workmanship, construction, or design," so there was no claim to be filed and no need for a Kemper inquiry. The implications of the roof collapse for the rest of the building were left unsaid.[44]

As the two-hour meeting continued, which problematically took Gordon fifty-five pages to chronicle, Dick Heydinger reported on his attempts to line up a second insurer. Heydinger was stymied in part because he could not find a policy that included punitive damage insurance because such coverage barely existed in the marketplace. He settled for one that "did not specifically exclude punitive damage coverage." The risk manager also made a bad joke, tasteless even in 1979, when he referred to the second company as "our insurer who will be insuring collapses in the future." Whittaker hissed, "Shhh, don't say that again."[45] The recording ensured that both would eventually regret uttering their words and also belied their deposition testimony that they forgot or were unaware the tape recorder was there.

The remainder of the year—and Gordon's account—dealt with the principals, especially the Hallmark lawyers, and the "flood of self-serving papers" that were created to show the company's sudden interest in safety. No one could foresee the disaster a year and a half in the future, but it was a time of talk, not action. The steel fabricator sent a safety warning to Hallmark (or was it a CYA memo?): "There appears to us to be structural problems throughout the entire structure which indicate to us the existence of design deficiencies. . . . We would like to know who has been retained to review this entire design and when a report of all these deficiencies will be made available to us." Apparently, the scant two pages produced by Seiden & Page did not count. More telling was the later memo distributed by Andrew Miller, Hallmark's safety director, who tellingly was not present at the November 13 meeting. Miller provided instructions to others on their writing style "so that possibly the liability could be transferred from Hallmark to a contractor."[46] After such a devastating indictment of corporate cynicism and malfeasance, one can only wonder if Gordon's book collaborators ever really appreciated how its depiction of Kansas City's largest private employer would play locally.[47]

In retrospect, Gordon's 1984 manuscript about Hallmark's mad dash to keep its hotel project on time and on budget was a more powerful narrative than his later effort of 1995. That later manuscript stressed a story of legal maneuvers and cover-up. In the earlier manuscript, Gordon does not appear as a character until much later, which forced him to deal with the facts of the case and not how he discovered those facts. Compared to later writings, his prose was somewhat toned down. He kept to his thesis and wandered less on unnecessary tangents: It was the company's "system" that created the skywalks, a system of pliant managers that cut corners, ignored warnings, and proved incapable of learning from its mistakes. The system, if not destiny, made the collapse of the skywalks inevitable. Afterward a fiction arose that all could have been saved by one good engineer.

In addition to this overarching theme, Gordon had his antagonists, although he probably credited Judith Whittaker with possessing more power than she did and, therefore, made her shoulder too much of the blame. Even so, "If instead she had chosen to use her powers of persuasion to lobby Hallmark for the money needed for a qualified, full-time inspector, or for funds to load test the skywalk connections, there would never have been a Tea Dance Tragedy."[48] Gordon rather effectively made his case that bad project management had led to the first collapse and unheeded warnings to the second. In many respects it was a conventional nonfiction story. Yet, Gordon's unconventional side could never stay totally submerged from the next set of characters who came to work on his snake-bit book.

13

Rinse and Repeat

Begun in 1983 and moving along in 1984 and well into the next year, Gordon's book project had lurched to a stop. He remained undeterred, however. His goal was still to see his work in print, a book with the impact of *All the President's Men*. He was determined to get back on track and drew upon his characteristic tenacity, now tinged with a trace of desperation.

Kathy Robbins, the agent spurned earlier, returned briefly and maybe reluctantly. Gordon contacted her as the association with Knox Burger and Robert Byrne finally flamed out. "I have been pushing myself to complete the book," he wrote, adding disarmingly, "I am concerned and insecure about whether my exposition and analysis are sufficiently professional." Then came the plea: "Everything is on disks, and revisions can be made quickly.—HELP!"[1]

Robbins received the manuscript, reviewed it, and a couple months later joined the swelling ranks of naysayers of its quality. Did she think it possible to submit the material as is? "Simply put, I don't." As another independent voice singing in unison with a growing chorus, she commented, "There's something terribly wrong with the way the book is currently structured." Also, "there are close to 600 pages of infighting among a group of lawyers. . . . I'm not persuaded it makes for very compelling narrative." She continued relentlessly but rightly: "As for any kind of denouement, Hallmark is never brought to its knees. . . . There was no large public trial against Hallmark; therefore, there are no rulings, no judgments, no verdicts, no public record to draw from. Virtually all claims were settled out of court. In terms of this book, that's a real problem."

Robbins's original judgment from two years before still stood. He should "turn these pages over to an independent journalist who would fashion a riveting and important third person narrative from the work. On closer examination, I'm no longer sure I see how the story could be constructed past these opening pages." She closed with "I wish our second try at this had had a different ending."[2]

Undeterred, Gordon forged on. Putting aside his innate obstinance with others editing his work, he grasped what constituted a winning book strategy—assemble a high-powered agent, talented collaborator, and big-time publisher. All he had to do, he concluded, was find and field a better set of players. He began his search, and by the end of the year Gordon miraculously had a new dream team in place. In 1986 the book project entered a new phase but, alas, repeated an old pattern.

In late February that year, Gordon reached out for a legal review to Dewey Ballantine, a prestigious law firm in New York whose alumni included at least one former presidential candidate (Thomas E. Dewey) and a host of past cabinet members. "I need your help," he wrote, as he gave one of their attorneys a helpful update on the status of his project. "The book is tentatively titled 'A House of Cards.' My draft consists of 50 chapters, approximately 2,000 typed pages and about 600,000 words." (This monster was more than double the size of the surviving 1995 manuscript.) Gordon had a new collaborator. "Paul Haskins . . . is editing the book for me. We hope to end up with 25 chapters consisting of about 150,000 to 200,000 words." From this encouraging statement, Gordon seemed to be heeding the calls to boil down his massive tome. And he had a new literary agent to boot—Julian Bach. "We anticipate being ready to submit the book to several publishing firms headquartered in New York no later than mid-April, 1986."[3]

The new team and new hopes reinvigorated Gordon, whose enthusiasm matched his expansive manuscript. He wrote Haskins, "The possibility of your helping with the book gave me such a surge of optimism and energy that I have doubled my prior efforts." Gordon went so far as to discuss the book in person in New York, where Haskins was an editor with the *New York Times*. Haskins thought he could finish editing the book in a mere two months, although his agreement took him to late May. Gordon, whose goal was to see his book out by the end of the year, eagerly responded, "I have set everything else aside and continue to work on this project 14 to 16 hours a day—seven days a week."[4] On the surface Haskins seemed a good fit, although his résumé differed considerably from Robert Byrne's.

Gordon knew Paul Haskins from his previous stint at the *Kansas City Times*. He was a special assignment editor who helped direct the paper's Pulitzer-Prize-winning coverage of the Hyatt disaster. A colleague who remembered both Haskins and Gordon described them as equally intense, the former keeping his office calendar on the "July 17, 1981" page for several months after.[5] Imitating several of his newspaper colleagues, Haskins quickly parlayed this success to a bigger job, in his circumstance a New York copy desk editorship. He prospered in the new setting and later in 1995 received a promotion to assistant national editor. The pair had kept in contact after Haskins's departure from Kansas City. Even in the midst of the courtroom, newspaper, and public relations turmoil that characterized the last stage of the class-action lawsuit, Gordon still found time to reach out to the expatriate to solicit his and his paper's interest in the case. "Although you know I wish you success in New York," wrote Gordon, "we miss you like hell and need you here." Haskins returned the compliment and remained engaged in the hotel tragedy, as illustrated by his "Special to the *New York Times*" that appeared in the aftermath of the federal class-action settlement. He noted in his 1983 piece the "reverberations" felt in the city, whose inhabitants still agonized over how the disaster happened and who was to blame.[6] Three years after penning this follow-up, and the aftershocks now largely stilled, Haskins had the opportunity to once again work on the story.

About the same time that Gordon secured Haskins's services, he snagged Julian Bach as his new agent. Bach enjoyed a long, illustrious career—editor of *Life* magazine before and after World War II and later executive editor of *True* and *Today's Woman*. He left magazine publishing to start his self-named literary agency, which grew to represent an astounding five hundred authors. When he added Gordon to his stable, Bach was seventy-two years old but far from retirement.[7] One of his authors described Bach as "a great character in the New York book scene," who spoke with a "deep, resonant, hearty" voice that reminded one of the Jim Backus character in *Gilligan's Island*.[8] When Gordon joined up, the agent was enjoying one of his greatest triumphs, seeing to publication the blockbuster novel by another author who had spent years immersed in portraying human trauma. Pat Conroy, the southern storyteller and a Bach client, had just come out with his acclaimed work, *The Prince of Tides*. Recalled Conroy about his first, inauspicious meeting with the formidable Bach, "He was as rude as any son-of-a-bitch could possibly be on the telephone."[9] However, their relationship did nothing but flourish thereafter, and they stayed together for years. Relying solely on surviving correspondence between Gordon and Bach, their interactions seemed in comparison far more subdued but, as with Conroy, endured a long time.

The situation became inherently more complicated when the trio of Gordon, Haskins, and Bach grew to a quartet. John Garrity, a Kansas City freelancer and also a Bach client, entered the scene to fill the Byrne role of writer-for-hire. Garrity was a colorful, eclectic sort. The local paper once noted when the former history major won the "Hoover Prize" for an article about Herbert Hoover's prepresidential experiences in China during the Boxer Rebellion. His original treatment for *Pendergast*, a television miniseries to star Ed Asner as the notorious Kansas City political boss, had been recently optioned to Hollywood, although it was never produced. Readers of *Sports Illustrated* enjoyed his frequent contributions, and in a few years Garrity landed a permanent place on its staff to write on golf, a sport that had been a passion since his youth.[10] He already had two books under his belt, a traditional biography of baseball great George Brett and a nontraditional collaboration (to say the least) with his older sister.[11] In 1969 Joan Terry Garrity had published under the pseudonym "J" the explosive, sexually explicit "how-to" best seller *The Sensuous Woman*, a book that reportedly outsold that year's *The Godfather* by Mario Puzo. This enormous success had been followed tragically by years of personal turmoil, heartache, and illness for the author. Her brother John helped write and shepherd to publication in 1984 her even more revealing memoir about "the bitter price of her crazy success" and subsequent recovery. Over the years many more books by Garrity followed but largely kept to the subject of golf. Although a book about a structural disaster may have seemed a departure superficially, the worldly writer, drawing on his wide experiences, possessed skills that fittingly applied to this new job—telling a story that appealed to a national audience and, little did he know, dealing with a troubled soul.[12]

Bach contacted Garrity to tell him that Gordon, of whom Garrity knew not in the least, needed a collaborator and urged him to make the call, which he did in January 1986, and they arranged to meet in Gordon's office. They seemed to hit it off and agreed to a deal that would pay him $750 per week for three months of straightforward writing and editing. It seemed, to the professional writer, "like an easy project." It was one founded on secrets, however, because Garrity never learned of Byrne, his predecessor, or Haskins, his contemporary, and Gordon did not know of his new collaborator's secret coauthorship of an infamous sex manual. Nevertheless, the writer soon learned that his new partner, the lawyer, was "extremely bright," possessed "an amazing mind," and more importantly, was impossible to work with.[13]

It should not have been so because the strengths of Gordon's second team equaled, if not surpassed, those of the first. Gordon already knew Paul Haskins, unlike Byrne, before engaging his services and, long before his entering the fold, had felt comfortable sharing with the newsman sensitive information about the skywalk cases. Haskins was a skilled editor rising in his profession. Julian Bach was at the top of his game, too, and from the evidence of his recent Midas touch with best sellers probably ranked further up the New York publishing pecking order than Knox Burger. Bach also seemed to take a more hands-off approach with the red pencil than did Burger. In Gordon's view he had clearly traded up in agents, at least in approach and temperament if not in skill. In his wisdom

Bach had brought in Garrity, a gifted craftsman, a known quantity, and perhaps most critically, a *local*. Not only was he close at hand, available at all times to the whims of Gordon's crazy work schedule, but he had a Hyatt connection as well. He and his wife had attended Friday night tea dances at the hotel, although not the deadly one, but his friend Mike McKenzie, a sportswriter for the *Kansas City Star*, had been there and had survived the collapse. For the good of the book, however, Garrity held no personal animosity toward Hallmark Cards, although, if pushed, he was critical of its subsidiary that built the hotel.[14] This helped with the book's tone. Somebody on the project needed to appear fair and impartial.

Begun in earnest at the start of 1986, this phase of the Gordon book project was on a tight schedule, and two of its principals, Haskins and Garrity, had limited, defined commitments of time. Issues soon arose between each and Gordon, and if either enjoyed a honeymoon, it did not last long. The beginning of the end may have occurred as soon as the experienced author Garrity received the first pages of the manuscript. His immediate impression was of a hundred pages or so that were written in what he termed "a creative nonfiction, novelistic style." At some point the "voice" abruptly changed from an omniscient, third-person narrator to a dry, legalistic style written in the first person. It was clear to Garrity that two different authors had worked on the manuscript. Gordon, he rightly assumed, was one, but who else? It did not really matter. He thought his job was to cut and condense the existing manuscript and create a narrative that reflected the storytelling style of the first part, while avoiding a boastful tone. He would interview Gordon, often on the phone, as necessary to flesh out any details that might "enliven" the tale. This is the process he followed—or tried to.[15]

They met every couple of weeks in Gordon's office, where Garrity showed him his work. For a while he even had a desk in the reception area. If not meeting in person, Garrity left the latest batch of edited manuscript accompanied by his explanatory notes. He kept what he called "the master." In one example of their fraught collaboration, he brought a revised chapter that he had formed from two of Gordon's original chapters. This did not go over well with Gordon, who had called similar such work "unhelpful and probably a waste of money."[16] Things were going no better with Haskins in New York.

In March Haskins sent Gordon the preface and first three chapters, having revised Gordon's first six chapters. By April Gordon lodged a blistering complaint with Bach on the slow-going: "This is a very agonizing period for me. . . . He [Haskins] took almost five months to produce 58 revised pages of the one part of the book that everyone else thought was already superb." Who this "everyone else" was, Gordon did not name. He was concerned by the threats to the schedule and his checkbook. "The $8,500 word processor/laser jet printing system which I bought him does not seem to have paid off—yet." And his annoyance was not confined to Haskins. "Garrity, meanwhile, continues to dither over how much work he can handle right now."[17]

Gordon was right in one sense—Garrity had more than he could handle. Thirty years later the wounds remained fresh as the writer remembered vividly the frustration of working with Bob Gordon. After he turned over his chapters, he expected feedback from Gordon, preferably the text returned with more notes, something, anything, but nothing ever came back. Gordon, it turned out, took his work, made his own changes, and had his secretary create a second "master." Garrity was well into the project before Gordon sprang this second manuscript on him. Gordon's version contained "tons of material" reinserted and the irritating, lawyerly voice restored. Garrity was flummoxed—"completely lost"—at this point. He felt like he was "writing in the sand on a beach."[18]

In May, as the deadline loomed for Haskins's term of work, Gordon expressed his worry to the editor that the manuscript was "only" clocking in at five hundred typed pages. Gordon suggested to Haskins that he restore some cut text.[19] His partners did not share his concern about the length, and they did not agree to a solution for which no problem existed. Garrity sensed every cut to the manuscript was like a "personal injury" to Gordon.[20]

Haskins probably came to the same conclusion. He defended at length his role, which was to do "what you voiced concern about when you asked me to join you as editor/co-author of this book—to protect the reader from the 'Bermuda Triangle,' i.e., the 'legal give and take.'" As an example, Haskins pointed out a major problem and offered a solution. "It takes almost 500 pages to get from the mention of the [Richard C.] Heydinger file you found till we get to the Heydinger deposition = 13 chapters. Under my proposal it takes 5 chapters and somewhere around 130 pages." Somewhat perversely Haskins shifted the monkey back onto Gordon to make the rewrite: "Only you can do it."[21] Whether Gordon undertook what would have been for him a drastic action is not known, but the question was moot.

The Haskins partnership, described by Gordon as "discouraging and unpleasant," was over by June. It concluded with a mixture of sarcasm, threats, and bad blood. Haskins made an ultimatum. "I will lend you no further assistance in any form until I am compensated by you in a just and fair settlement for the more than four months of work and travail that I went through on your book, a task undertaken on good faith based upon your word." Haskins hoped the response from Kansas City would "involve a settlement befitting the caring and fair Robert Gordon depicted in the book." That approach apparently did not work because Haskins followed up in August with another request for compensation. "The fact that you paid another writer $25,000 to write three chapters before coming to me and that you have not paid me a dime for four times that amount of work is unconscionable on your part." He put Gordon on notice that he intended to file a claim against any publisher with whom Gordon contracted.[22] Gordon responded vehemently in kind, "But for you and all your b.s. promises about how you knew what you were doing and all your fibs about 'meeting deadlines' and all your baloney about being 'a perfectionist,' I would have had the book finished and published. . . . Angry? You bet I am. You have done just as much as [Irving] Younger or [Paul] Wolff or anyone else to put your own interests before everything else and to keep the truth from getting out. . . . May 26 was your absolute final deadline. . . . I got nothing."[23]

Julian Bach, who had been copied in on this mess, came down on his author's side. "Bob Gordon felt he had to hire John Garrity to cut and edit the book after you had missed your deadlines."[24] And there the paper trail of recriminations ended, although one doubts the same for their heated disagreement.

In contrast, the work with the affable Garrity stumbled on and crossed the finish line. He and Bach decided to compromise and work with Gordon's version or, to be more precise, versions. According to the diagnosis by Garrity the amateur psychologist, who personally witnessed Gordon's behavior, the inexperienced author "was so OCD [obsessive-compulsive disorder] about how the words looked on the page that he insisted on justifying both sides, but the word processor couldn't hyphenate automatically. So his secretaries had to go through line by line and insert hyphens. Every time a change was made, all of this formatting would get messed up again."[25] Garrity was also the one who recalled Gordon's collection of precisely equal-length pencils on his office reception desk. His rigidity had certainly made a long-lasting impression.

Somehow in the end, by fall 1986, they "put together some sort of manuscript," although the shell-shocked Garrity did not really remember how they had.[26] And hearkening to Kathy Robbins's caveat, what sort of "denouement" had the story reached? What had changed since the 1983 class-action settlement to create a satisfying conclusion for the reader? Whatever it was, Bach seemed pleased enough, calling the manuscript "very solid" and "thoroughly readable," and neither Gordon nor Garrity demurred.[27]

Pleased or not, it was "a most frustrating project," recalled Garrity, made more so by the Gordon personality in extremis, typified by his "inflexibility to pursue the course that he agreed to," and also by Garrity's gut feeling that the book potentially had real, lasting power. He knew it would be unpopular in Kansas City, but Gordon's argument was compelling and convincing. The cover-up of the first collapse—or, at least, its diminution by the responsible parties—seemed to Garrity the most damning evidence that Gordon had mustered. In Garrity's professional opinion, a strength of the manuscript was the star litigator Irving Younger waltzing into court scenes and Gordon successfully portraying him as a "colossal fraud." What great theater! And even with all his personal flaws, Gordon was not in it for the money, he concluded; that was "the farthest thing from his mind." The court settlement had "buried the truth," and he sincerely admired Gordon's efforts, mishandled as they were, to uncover what really happened.[28] Four decades later, Garrity's assessment remains accurate and true. Gordon's manuscript, great literature or not, was deserving and significant.

With a serviceable manuscript in hand, Julian Bach did his job and before year's end somehow secured Gordon his long-sought-after major New York publisher, along with a hefty advance of $50,000. The contract called for a manuscript of up to 150,000 words (not all that much longer than this book) and a deadline of June 1, 1987, both wildly optimistic as it turned out. Gordon paid off Garrity and awaited the next stage of the process.[29] In every way except actually holding in his hands an actual book, Gordon was officially an author. But as Mark Twain, the consummate writer, once purportedly remarked about how some books refuse to be written, occasional publisher Twain could have added that some refuse to be published.

14

What Might Have Been

The soon-to-be first-time author clutched an order form. His editor had mailed him the promotional piece, and here at last was tangible proof that his book was soon to be published. "Coming in June," the Simon & Schuster marketers announced.[1] How could any bookseller resist their provocative copy? The text led with "From the Company that Cares Enough to Send You the Very Best," a play on that famous corporate slogan and a variant of which the author had once used as his title. Another punchier title had been settled on, the shorter and cleverer "House of Cards." The subtitle carried the heavy load of explaining the book's subject and included two words on which the author absolutely insisted—"truth" and "Hallmark"—and read, "The Truth Behind the Skywalks Collapse and Hallmark's Hyatt Regency Hotel Disaster." It was imperative that the heretofore deferred blame be meted out to the correct corporate entity, Hallmark and not Hyatt. And the assigner of blame and determined truth-teller was, according to the information on the form, the sole author. The only name associated with the 304-page hardcover with eight black-and-white photographs and a list price of $19.95 was Robert C. Gordon.

The author must have been pleased with the three blocks of text, as breathless a prose as any Gordon could have composed himself: "the terrible truth," no, "the whole shocking truth" of "Hallmark's desperate strategy" told ("finally revealed") with "carefully documented proof" in "meticulous and riveting detail." The copywriter likened the collapse of the skywalks in *House of Cards* to the sinking of the *Titanic* in *A Night to Remember*, a best seller of an earlier generation, with similar allusions to "unbelievable chaos and destruction."[2] If one just read the headings of the text blocks, they promised a gripping page-turner: "The deadliest hotel disaster of the 1980s" and "A harrowing true story that reads like a novel" and "The most outrageous cover-up since Watergate." The Washington political scandal still possessed a powerful resonance with the American public. Maybe it would rub off on the story of a Kansas City catastrophe.

The story, however, had become stale. One might think that Julian Bach's success in securing a book contract in late 1986 and Gordon's wrapping up the work-for-hire with John Garrity early the next year meant that "coming in June" referred to 1987. *Au contraire*. The Simon & Schuster flyer came out in 1991, four years later, and ten after the disaster.[3] And if one saw that order form and finally expected to see a copy of *House of Cards* later the same year—or ever—the error would have been compounded. What happened this time?

In December 1992 Fred Hills, an editor for Simon & Schuster who had been attached to the project since 1987, rejected Gordon's manuscript "for length," and in March 1993 terminated their contract. Hills, who during his long, respected career worked with a stunning range of authors, from Vladimir Nabokov (*Lolita*) and William Saroyan to Jane Fonda and Arianna Huffington, finally reached the limit of his patience and "the end of the road," as he put it. "I know you have labored long and hard, and there are assuredly some wonderful sections," he said, trying to soften the blow, "but it is now several years since the original delivery date, and we still do not have an acceptable manuscript."[4] His advice could have been mouthed by any in the host of Gordon's earlier collaborators: "pull yourself together" and "cut it to 600 pages."[5]

To no surprise, during this final period Gordon's book project had suffered several wounds, most self-inflicted. "Bob Gordon the imaginative writer," Hills had astutely observed early on, "is being sunk by his alter ego, Bob Gordon the legal analyst."[6] What all happened at the end of the business relationship, however, is not clear. The surviving correspondence is not nearly as robust as previous years. There are no weekly updates, no diatribes, no pleadings, just long stretches when the sole author worked alone and missed deadlines. More likely, Gordon, the irresistible force, finally met the immovable objects of the editorial and legal departments of a large New York trade publishing house. He also encountered at long last serious pushback from Hallmark lawyers, perhaps because they had been provoked.

In March 1988, in the midst of another legal wrangle with Hallmark, Gordon rather inexplicably sent a four-page harangue to Don Hall, which began, "As you know, I have been working on a book about the skywalks for several years. . . . I would like to interview you concerning what you believe happened, how it happened, and who allowed it to happen." Sixteen sets of questions followed, punctuated with an impertinent reference to Joyce Hall at the conclusion: "I had the privilege and honor of discussing my future career with your dad. . . . Do you believe that Hallmark's handling of the skywalks case comports with your dad's advice?"[7] Hall did not answer any of the questions posed, nor did Robert Sisk, his lawyer, who responded a couple of weeks later.

An undergraduate roommate of Don Hall at Dartmouth University, Sisk had led Hallmark's defense during the *Federal Skywalk Cases*, and Hughes, Hubbard & Reed (HHR) still represented the company, even if it involved such nuisances.[8] As a seasoned veteran of similar skirmishes with the Kansas City eccentric, Sisk knew Gordon's weak spots: "There is even less excuse for such questions today than there was six years ago when you first started down this low road. . . . [Y]our letter is irresponsible and demonstrates a reckless disregard for the truth. . . . [I]f the letter is a preview of the 'book' you have been threatening since the case was settled out from under you. . . . [Y]ou will need to find a remarkably foolhardy publisher."[9]

Perhaps the indiscreet query was prompted by the urgings of Gordon's publisher to solicit the other side's view, but if so, the overly aggressive language and tone of the letter proved self-defeating and promised to generate no other response than this one. But Sisk was not through twisting Gordon's tail.

A follow-up from Sisk's firm came early the next year, a fifty-six-page memo titled "The Fallacy of the Gordon Thesis." No cover letter can be found that accompanied this document, but Gordon cited the memo in his endnotes as "Letter, Hughes, Hubbard & Reed to Simon & Schuster, Feb. 1989." A Simon & Schuster editor confirmed that the publisher received a copy and took it seriously.[10] Although originating from Hallmark's law firm, which claimed it had not seen the manuscript, this preemptive strike does not read like a legal brief, at least by any author other than Gordon. More interest was given to invalidating him than engaging with his arguments. The language is overstated, the tone personal, and Gordon's motives impugned. He is presented as a sore-loser lawyer, his "perverse obsession" a case of sour grapes.[11] The memo provided a good overview of the company's continued position on the hotel disaster—"background" as it was termed—although by now the basic tenets sounded more like rote responses.

Hallmark was targeted because of its deep insurance pockets, the law firm argued, even though Crown Center was the real owner. The atrium roof problem had nothing to do with the skywalks collapse. The structural engineers and their ceiling suspension idea for the skywalks were to blame for the accident, along with the steel fabricator and drafting firm for missing the engineering miscalculation. Architect Bob Berkebile, not Don Hall, coined the term "thin and invisible" and dictated the design concept of the skywalks. (Gordon marked this passage in obvious disagreement.) In an intentional use of the passive voice, the memo continued, "By the spring of 1978, the overall aesthetic design of the skywalks had been established." But by whom? The unacknowledged decider could not have been Hallmark or Hall, the firm contended. Other, more subtle deflections away from Hallmark littered the text: Hallmark's hotel was always referred to as the "Hyatt project." The term "suspended bridges" or just the words "bridges" or "walkways" were used in place of "skywalks," a curious word choice that possibly reflected the latter term's continued toxicity. This assignment and avoidance of blame deliberately missed the point of the "Gordon thesis," which sketched the scenario of a dangerous environment created by a hell-bent-for-leather, design-build project overseen, in Gordon's view, by a dictatorial, hands-on, cheapskate owner. A thorough, comprehensive investigation of the atrium roof collapse would have discovered the problems with the skywalks. The atrium roof and the skywalks, Gordon posed, were merely two stages of a single collapse.[12]

The "smoking gun" tape of the November 13, 1979, meeting was dismissed by HHR as "useless," so unimportant that Hallmark "forgot about it." The memo kept on, "No one at the meeting later recalled that it had been recorded." Such a response was Nixonesque. Tapes, what tapes? Break it up people. Nothing to see or hear here. Move along. The quality of the recording was "unintelligible" and "unenhanceable," or so determined their electronic expert.[13] Hallmark's December 1982 transcript, the one that caused Gordon so much indigestion, "supported and . . . corroborated" their position, which was confirmed, no less, by the *Kansas City Times* reporters who "listened to the tapes and reviewed a transcript."[14] The scattershot attack barely mentioned the Halvorson transcript of the same tape, which was completed by that noted audio expert in late 1983, long after the case was settled, and which, to Gordon, contradicted the earlier transcript. Mentioned in passing, HHR dismissed Halvorson. "The transcripts are similar on the material points." Their dismissal of the tape was as extreme a position as Gordon's was on its consequence.

The Gordon thesis, which HHR simply stated and categorically denied, was that Hallmark knew this hotel was unsafe or displayed gross disregard in allowing it to open, and its officials knew this from the October 1979 atrium collapse and did nothing. According to "The Fallacy of the Gordon Thesis," their key point was "an investigation of the one [the atrium roof collapse] would not logically discover the other [the skywalks collapse]." (Gordon highlighted this on his copy.) The "atrium beam collapse theory" and Gordon's vigorous claims of Hallmark negligence and cover-up were "false and defamatory," HHR claimed. And in words that Sisk himself probably supplied, Gordon's role in the *Federal Skywalk Cases* was gratuitously denigrated, which had to hurt. "Lacking a client with a credible injury . . . he invented his own role." Gordon was engaged in a "vendetta" and "obsessed with fastening moral blame." In all these years, "no one has bought his story," although technically Simon & Schuster had done just that. As an author, he was "no Walter Lord." This final slur was especially cutting because Gordon greatly admired Lord as a best-selling author of nonfiction.

Sisk had once threatened a lawsuit against the book, according to Gordon, during an otherwise cordial lunch in 1986.[15] If Sisk's goal was to sow seeds of doubt, his action may have succeeded with Simon & Schuster. The first half of 1989 saw alternating volleys between the anxious author and his publisher's legal department, which was reading the work and asking for all sorts of supporting documentation. On February 28, for example, Gordon sent "2,500 pages of source documents for my book." Thirty pages of queries came from New York in March.[16] When one goes through the Gordon collection today, dozens of folders relating to the book project are empty, with the exception of a note that reads, "The supporting documentation for this point was submitted to New York in February and March of 1989."

At the same time, Gordon must have believed he was close to the finish line. He merited a brief mention in the regular column of Steve Paul, the *Kansas City Star*'s book review editor, with a helpful reminder of who the author was and how he figured in the Hyatt story. *House of Cards* was finished and coming out in summer 1989, wrote the columnist, and Gordon's editor at Simon & Schuster had confirmed it.[17]

But it did not happen. Another deadline came and went, and the manuscript did not emerge from the legal department until early 1990.[18] The professionals at Simon & Schuster urged Gordon to tone it down, admonishing him to be careful with the loaded word "cover-up." Don't promise more than you can deliver. Prove and document; don't speculate. Stop impugning the motives of others. Remove the holier-than-thou attitude and cut the sarcasm. Soften the characterization of opposing counsel, especially Judith Whittaker. Disarm Hallmark by giving them credit where it is due, which will strengthen your credibility. Do not automatically challenge their words; their deficient actions will speak louder and more convincingly to the reader. "Hallmark might have mouthed interminably about safety, but if they did little or nothing to ensure it," said one wise editor, "then you've got them." Although late in the game, the book's organization was a concern. Gordon told too much too soon about Hallmark's responsibility in the disaster, and the reader needed to reach that point on their own gradually. His writing needed to effect initial disbelief followed by gradual awareness concluding with shock and acceptance.[19]

The cautious publisher's additional scrutiny proved to be warranted, and surprisingly Gordon even jokingly agreed. "'Thank you, H.H.&R. I needed that.' The Skywalks book has been strengthened by research prompted by their letter to S&S."[20] In retrospect, one could construe that the Gordon thesis had been vetted in two distinct ways. Gordon's findings and conclusions had formed the basis for the legal argument that the plaintiffs were going to make in court in the *Federal Skywalk Cases*; this argument was silenced by the out-of-court settlement. Independently the legal department of Simon & Schuster had dissected the manuscript, its theme based on the same thesis.

Yet the interminable editorial back-and-forth stretched out. In 1991 Burton Beals, one of Gordon's Simon & Schuster editors, marked the next step in production, the "final legal review." He noted, though, "that there were several places where you have not made the revisions requested in the legal review. . . . Similarly, there are a number of passages still in the manuscript for which confirmation was required. . . . It goes without saying that it [the narrative] should include only allegations that you can prove and document, not speculations. . . . Are you making any progress [on the notes]?" Beals went on to describe the troubled manuscript as "extraordinarily complex and difficult to annotate. . . . Meanwhile, I will hold the manuscript here and await further word from you."[21]

Another year passed, during which the manuscript ballooned "mysteriously," wrote an editor at his wit's end, from 536 pages to 814 pages. He could only add, "Your Achilles heel is excess."[22] Four months later Gordon came back with a manuscript of 719 pages, still unacceptably long, and 3,023 endnotes. He resisted cutting down the notes but relented to a degree and got them down to 2,660. By then the issue became moot. His luck had run out. The foolishness had ended. Failing to meet his publisher's mandated lengths and exhausting everyone's patience, Gordon lost his contract. For all the later tales of undue influence by Hallmark, Gordon's problem boiled down to having a product that was "too long and too late." For all practical purposes, Fred Hills's notice of termination of March 12, 1993, drew Robert Gordon's ten-year catastrophe to an end.[23]

THIS WOULD NOT BE LIKE EARLIER TIMES WHEN GORDON AND HIS team paused, regrouped, and soldiered on. He had no team, no momentum, no incentive to go on. The book was dead, and he knew it. His chance to tell the story of the Hallmark hotel disaster and make a splash in the only meaningful way he knew how ended with this last gasp effort. Sure, there had been obstacles, but none that a neutral observer would think impossible to overcome. All the people Gordon encountered in the book world were on his side. They wanted him to succeed. But where they saw reasonable compromise, he saw an attack on his integrity. Their "excess" was his necessity. He failed quietly but spectacularly. As to the result, he had no one to blame but himself.

The only reason Gordon could not see the book to completion, it seemed, was his inflexible rigidity. Not one page could be cut, and there were plenty of pages to be cut. Hills recommended a manuscript of no more than 600 pages, but the surviving manuscript clocked in at a whopping 854 pages of narrative.[24] That did not count another 23 pages of densely packed footnotes printed in a microscopic point size. Perhaps this was the lawyer in him, looking for a loophole that kept the manuscript technically under his self-imposed, impractical 1,000-page limit.

A good book lay hidden in those hundreds of pages and twenty-two chapters. Gordon introduced himself in the fourth chapter, where he laid the groundwork for Hallmark's role in the collapse. It was a good chapter with some glitches, nothing libelous that an amateur can see. He was not terribly intrusive in the narrative.

By chapter 5, however, Gordon got more pointed and more adversarial. To his credit, he explained the class-action approach quite well; the early parts of the book showed a largely successful effort to explain the legal system to the general reader. But such clarity faltered as the narrative went on. As Gordon continued in subsequent chapters, the pages filled with more and more Gordon: Gordon at center stage, Gordon against the world, Gordon more strident as events played out against him. By about the two hundredth page, he bogged down, and one wonders at this point if he began to rely too much on his old legal writings—those twenty-page letters, fifty-page briefs, and various court pleadings and confidential memos-to-file. The redundancy in the points he made was staggering. The gratuitous comments flowed unchecked. The result must have made a professional agent, writer, and editor cringe. Plus, he peppered his text with strange metaphors and colloquialisms—not unlike Andy Griffith's character Matlock. Most are just plain goofy. For example, his office colleague Bill Whitaker was "more humidity than humility." An untenable position was "like trying to hide an elephant under a napkin." Another situation was "odder than a three-eyed cat." Sooner or later, one stops trying to figure them out.

But there were some good features. The reader learned more about document discovery, the document depository, and the deposition process. The excerpts from the depositions were persuasive reading. Don Hall's innumerable "I don't recall(s)" during his testimony reminded one of testimony from a reluctant witness in an organized crime or Watergate hearing. In the fourteenth chapter, Gordon did a convincing job of using the depositions to emphasize the impact of the "smoking gun" tape, how it revealed the culture of a system dangerously focused on the bottom line. His account gave a hint at what might have transpired in a courtroom.

The reader was offered Irving Younger in all his glory, cast as the ultimate bad guy in Gordon's story, even more so than Don Hall. Lantz Welch, the ambulance chaser, served as the book's comic relief, popping up from time to time, crazy as a loon (or a fox). Clues pop up that the *Kansas City Times* and *Star*, whose influence in town at that time cannot be overestimated, might have been watching Hallmark's back from the get-go. Little wonder that Gordon never got any traction with the two papers and became increasingly critical of their management. If he learned anything from his dealings with the press, it was that newspapers as fact-finding machines were good when no local politics were involved, much less so if the establishment or status quo was threatened and had time to mount a defense. If that happened, the sympathetic rank-and-file reporter could do little to change the dynamic of the boardroom.

The first five hundred pages of Gordon's final manuscript were flabby, but by and large, they worked. After that, it was a hard slog. The subsequent chapters told the story of Hallmark on the ropes, getting threatened with contempt of court, the class being sold out by Younger, and the abrupt January 1983 settlement. But Gordon slowed the pacing of this flurry of dramatic events to a crawl when he drew on his December 1982 "brief" in all its length, legalese, detail, and redundancy. He stopped telling a story and began the courtroom arguments that he never had the chance to present. What came through was his constant antipathy for his opponents. Ultimately, Gordon proved incapable of divorcing himself from a story that demanded a dispassionate chronicler, not a relentless zealot.

The worn-out writer had even more difficulty in the last half-dozen chapters in how to end the book. As new—but basically irrelevant—developments occurred after the end of the *Federal Skywalk Cases*, he dutifully tacked on more pages and needlessly dragged out the story. He seemed lost, a man in search of an ending.

For the book to work, this key insider and self-made expert needed to come across as a measured advocate, not as a snarky, over-the-top, pitiful obsessive. Actually, the former was to be found there on the page, and his collaborators tried to bring out the storyteller and not the litigator but never succeeded in preventing his darker side from haunting the manuscript. It is still possible, though; the words are all there, backed up by credible sources.

For all its faults, the book started off great. The prologue and first three chapters were compelling nonfiction writing, which may have reflected the professional efforts of all the now-forgotten ghostwriters. Here the narrative was a real page-turner, with only a few minor hiccups. In contrast to the 1984 manuscript, the 1995 version presents the awful night of July 17, 1981, early, which left room for the remainder of the book to dwell on the legal tangles. At first glance this was a clever "hook" for the book, but it may have been a strategic mistake. Thereafter, the novice writer faced a problem with technique—how to keep before the reader the author's deep, enduring empathy for the hundreds of faultless skywalk victims and heroic first responders.

For many chapters the victims vanished from Gordon's story, although with all the distractions and disappointments of his legal and book struggles, he never forgot them, nor can a modern reader when encountering "House of Cards" and the book that might have been.

15

Excerpt

For the dramatic, tragic, heartrending experiences of the victims, survivors, and rescuers, Gordon's narrative was passionate, compelling, and riveting. It hinted at the promise of his book, "House of Cards." The two excerpts that follow, gently edited, are the best evidence of his humanity and, when he could muster it, understated outrage. They begin as the skywalks fell.

THE LAST THING MAXINE RHODES REMEMBERED WAS HEARING "a rumble like a California earthquake."[1] To Kay Kenton, it was "a really loud noise, like railroad cars crashing." The skywalks at the second- and fourth-floor levels hung one beneath the other. Each contained over thirty tons of concrete slabs, steel beams, mahogany hand rails, fancy lights, thick carpeting, glass side walls, and brass decorations. They were divided into several equal parts of hanger-rods. The middle pair of fourth-floor connections pulled apart first, allowing the two center sections of the walkway to break apart, allowing the two center sections of the walkway to break and swing downward like two sides of a trap door. The suddenly increased loads on the remaining connections caused them to fail as well, and the entire upper skywalk tore away from its supports from one end to the other. It plummeted toward the floor forty-five feet below. The lower skywalk, hanging from the one above, mirrored the motion, sagging and breaking open in the middle, then dropping as a unit. The lower skywalk crushed the dancers beneath it, then its cargo of terrified passengers was crushed in turn by the upper one. They came to rest in a long, broken pile.

Mike Lonshar, a salesman who had crossed the upper walkway only moments before, said, "It all looked like a human sandwich with arms and legs hanging out." Some people stayed aboard; others flew off. The last Mary Bottenberg saw of her husband, he was being flipped through the air, mouth wide open, screaming a scream she will hear for the rest of her life. Shirley Stover remembered plunging through the air, certain she was going to die, a scream of terror frozen in her throat. She saw the orange tiles of the dance floor rushing toward her face. She landed on her head and shoulders. Something landed on her. Then it was dark.

Molly Riley, who was standing on the dance floor less than ten feet from the line of impact, was hit by flying glass and pieces of concrete. Her first thought was that there was a fight and someone had dropped a tray of glasses. A sixty-four-year-old World War II Navy hero in a wheelchair, Jeff Dixon, crash-landed with the skywalks. Dixon, who had spent years in hospitals enduring painful skin grafts on seventy percent of his body, was trapped in his mangled chair. A mahogany guardrail from the skywalks fell across his legs, snapping them just below the knee. Jack Cady, a bearded high-school teacher, was on the third-floor skywalk, which hung independent of the other two and had not fallen, though the whole atrium was collapsing. He turned and ran for his life down the narrow walkway, hoping to get off before it also crashed.

Frank Grim must have heard the skywalk collapsing. He pushed his wife, Rosalind, with all his might. She survived; he did not. A man standing well away from the center of destruction was struck in rapid succession by a wooden railing, glass shards, part of a woman's torso, and a blast of wind. An elderly couple, Lily and Willy McClure, was seated in the Terrace Restaurant overlooking the scene with forks in hand, ready to eat the "Chef's Delight." Then a woman's head wobbled across the dance floor below like a poorly thrown bowling ball.

Evelyn Gubar, waiting in the part of the lobby bar called "the pit," saw the bottom of the lower skywalk split apart and drop toward her husband,

Joe. She watched Joe lift his arms and disappear under an avalanche of debris. "The roof is coming down," a woman shouted in her ear, "we'll all be killed!" Evelyn bravely started to run toward her husband, but a wall of wind knocked her headfirst back into the pit. In the same way that a book slammed onto a desk will send nearby papers flying, a powerful salvo of wind and debris shot out in every direction, demolishing tables and chairs, knocking people together, blowing musicians off the bandstand. Forty feet away, it blasted Ray Lopez, who had a serious heart condition, over the four-foot-high registration desk. When he recovered from the shock, he saw that a woman had landed next to him. One of her legs was missing. She asked him his name, and he told her. She asked him to call her children to tell them she would be all right. Lopez promised he would. Then she died.

Debbie Jackson from Salt Lake City, a survivor of the 1980 MGM Grand Hotel fire and still trying to overcome her fear of new hotels, had been in the elevator. When the doors opened and she stepped into the atrium, she saw a churning cloud of debris coming her way and felt her legs being nicked by flying glass. "Fire!" she screamed. "Oh, my God, another fire!"

An instant after Shirley Stover hit the floor, she was buried under a slab of concrete. She could not move her right arm or her legs. Her first sensation was an incredible pain in her right leg, which came in repeated crescendos. She felt sure it had been severed at the knee, but it was too dark in her concrete cavern to see for sure. Nearby a man was crying, "Oh, God, get me out of here, oh, God, get me out of here, oh, God, get me out of here," on and on until the noise and pain and horror of the dark pushed Shirley into unconsciousness.

Herb Newberg and Jean Rose were among the lucky ones. The death that fell from the sky missed them. Herb pulled on Jean's arm and shouted, "Run!" but she wouldn't leave her fiancé, John Tvedten, behind. She broke free and ran back toward the fallen skywalks, resting on top of each other in a pile not as high as her shoulder. "Maybe he got the drinks," she prayed. "Maybe he's looking for us on the edge of the dance floor." When she got close to the rubble, she stopped and stared. Part of the upper skywalk's glass sides had not been shattered, and through them could be seen a woman surrounded by half a dozen bodies. She was in pain and so confused in her glass tomb that she could not hear the shouts of those who said they would get her out. Jean Rose saw what might have been John Tvedten, or at least a body wearing clothes like his.

In a panic an elderly lady had knocked down Linda Lopez, Ray Lopez's daughter. "The lady was on top of me. You know how a cat acts when it's terrified? She was clutching at me like that and wouldn't let go." A concrete gray cloud of plaster particles and dust expanded until it filled the entire atrium.

Dancers and spectators were sprawled across the tile floor, covered with pieces of metal, daggers of glass, splintered tables, chairs, blood, and bodies. Torsos were everywhere, the lower parts of bodies crushed beneath the walkways and separated from their upper halves. Some bodies had exploded; one was split in two lengthwise, another compressed in the shape of a "Z." From the long mound of ruins, body parts protruded every few feet—heads, shoulders, arms, hands, wrists with watches, fingers with rings. A high-heeled shoe dangled from a toe. A naked leg jutted upward like a scrub tree growing from a rock. A man's head rested on his folded hands as if he were asleep. People ran back and forth in front of the ghastly pile calling names. From somewhere in the wreckage came a woman's voice: "Oh, help me! I'm afraid of the dark!" Elsewhere the familiar cadences of the Lord's Prayer could be heard.

Mrs. Regina Weir, who was trapped and could only move one hand, said, "There was a lot of moaning, a lot of groaning." She feared suffocation when all the oxygen was used up. Soon she had another fear. Water pipes that crossed the atrium inside the fourth-floor walkway were ruptured, and a steady plume of water cascaded down the north wall. Those still alive in the rubble now faced the possibility of death by drowning. The water poured steadily on the fallen skywalks, seeping through to the floor. Before long, most of the atrium was covered with a shallow pink lake of water mixed with blood.

Brenda Abernathy and her boyfriend Joe Vrabel, a businessman, had failed to jump out of the way. As he opened his eyes, Joe saw a young woman trying to keep her gray-green intestines inside her ruptured body. She looked embarrassed, as if no one should see that part of her. Brenda, with red ribbons of blood streaking her face and neck, was trying to move over toward Joe, when what she thought must be a corpse begged her for help. Another man was propped up close by, immobilized by a steel beam across his mid-section. Brenda thought his eyes had popped right out of their sockets. She fainted.

Amid the cries and moans, a uniformed Hyatt doorman announced shrilly: "Everything is going to be all right! We'll have this cleaned up in a jiffy. Everything is going to be all right!" Two women, total strangers moments earlier, stood with their arms around each other, shaking and trembling like poplar trees during a thunderstorm. Over and over, they wailed, "God is good! God is good!"

A few of the injured, including a woman who had been cut severely by glass, dragged themselves to the east side of the atrium and lay dying near the gift shop; bloody trails led back to where they had been hit.

Tim Lindgren, the hotel manager who had tried so hard for the past year to have everything corrected or completed, was on the escalator to the terrace when the skywalks fell. He raced to his office to phone Hyatt's corporate headquarters in Rosemount, Illinois. Stunned by the "roar of screams," the KMBC cameraman [Dave Forstate, coincidentally covering the tea dance for a story] finally finished changing battery packs. Frantically he pushed the red button and started filming once more.

Ruby Mae Scanlon, a member of one of Kansas City's oldest and finest families, was so badly crushed that later she could only be positively identified by her exquisitely dainty hands. Gerald Coffey, a retired lieutenant colonel and the divorced father of an eleven-year-old daughter, Pam, had taken her to the dance so that they could spend some time together. Both were crushed. Eugene and Karen Jeter, married two weeks earlier, may have given little thought to the phrase "until death do us part." Now they lay smashed together so completely that only one body bag would be needed to carry them out. Jayne Hayes was five feet, two inches tall when the skywalks fell. Virtually every bone in her body was broken. She survived—two inches shorter.

Both fallen skywalks had false bottoms that were about eighteen inches deep. Many of the buried were still alive, squeezed into contorted positions in a watery blackness. An elderly man was thrust into a sitting position with his chest forced against his knees; another had both ankles behind his neck; a third had his face crushed into his buttocks. A woman was trapped with another woman on top of her who was crying hysterically. She kept telling her to calm down and wait to be rescued. Soon the crying woman quieted. She had died. A claustrophobic, white-haired gentleman under another body flailed his arms and sobbed, "Hurry, get this off me, please!"

When Shirley Stover regained consciousness, she had lost track of time. She could not move. She was wrapped in darkness and pain. She thought of her daughter, alone in a strange city, waiting in front of the theater. The only people she knew in town were here at the Hyatt. And so was Dave, her husband.

Mike McKenzie, a sportswriter for the local paper, had been standing on the bandstand judging the dancers. All he remembered was that his two young daughters were dressed in white. Only a few minutes earlier, the girls had complained that they could not see over the crowd of adults. They had told him that they were going to find "a better spot" on the fourth-floor skywalk. "People were screaming names, all sorts of names," McKenzie said. "I remember someone shouting, 'Les, where are you?' No one answered."

Molly Riley was knocked backward by the maelstrom but managed to stay on her feet. She had to keep her eyes closed against the wind and a rain of glass fragments. She thought of her two-year-old son and hoped that she would be able to hold him just once more. After she could see, Molly found herself near the bandstand and in front of the KMBC cameraman, who was facing westward as though paralyzed. She turned to see why he was transfixed and faced a picture of unbelievable devastation. A jumble of wreckage stretched away to her right. Molly thought the roof had caved in. There was someone in the rubble wearing blue. Was it her friend Gaye? Gaye was wearing blue. People next to Molly stood like ghosts, white with the dust of concrete and plaster. "Run!" someone shouted. "Get out! It's all going to come down!" "I can't run," Molly Riley thought. "I'm a nurse." She steeled herself and walked towards the victims, like hundreds of others who were searching for their loved ones.

Three and a half minutes passed before anyone could function well enough to call for help. At 7:08, a dispatcher for the Kansas City, Missouri, Fire Department took a message from the hotel's front-desk receptionist: "Oh, God. Come to the Hyatt Regency immediately!"[2]

Timeline of the Hallmark Hotel Disaster and Response, July 17–18, 1981

FRIDAY, JULY 17

3:00 p.m.—First arrivals to Hyatt tea dance.

4:30 p.m.—Seating in hotel lobby fully occupied. People begin to assemble on skywalks.

7:00 p.m.—Crowd in hotel atrium estimated to number 1,500–2,000.

7:04 p.m.—Band returns from break and begins to play for dance contest.

7:05 p.m.—Two of the three skywalks collapse.

7:08 p.m.—Kansas City Fire Department (KCFD) dispatcher receives first call for help.

7:09 p.m.—Kansas City Police Department dispatcher receives first call for help.

7:12 p.m.—KCFD rescue squad arrives at scene and calls for additional help.

7:18 p.m.—Seven city ambulances at scene.

7:19 p.m.—Call goes out for cutting tools.

7:23 p.m.—Call goes out for forklift.

7:52 p.m.—More than a hundred firefighters and emergency workers involved in rescue operation with more to come.

8:30 p.m.—First heavy crane arrives.

10:30 p.m.—Cranes moved into position at west wall of hotel atrium.

SATURDAY, JULY 18

3:15 a.m.—First walkway section lifted away by cranes.

4:30 a.m.—Last survivor (Mark Williams) removed from debris.

7:45 a.m.—Last walkway section lifted away. Thirty-one bodies recovered.

Based on a summary of events preceding and following the collapse, in R. D. Marshall, E. O. Pfrang, E. V. Leyendecker, K. A. Woodward, R. P. Reed, M. B. Kasen, and T. R. Shives, *Investigation of the Kansas City Hyatt Regency*

Walkways Collapse, National Bureau of Standards Building Science Series 143 (Washington DC: U.S. Government Printing Office, 1982), 33–34.

RAY WYNN, THE FIRST FIREFIGHTER THROUGH THE LOBBY DOOR, SAID, "There were so many people in need of help all at once. You just didn't know which to go, where to start. A woman nearby was just taking her last breath. Another woman's head 'was off.'"

Within a minute, Battalion Chief Mike Falder arrived. "The farther into the hotel I went, the worse it was." Falder immediately ordered a second alarm sounded, and five more fire trucks joined half a dozen already en route. When other firefighters finally entered the atrium, one of them later recalled, "The more we looked, the worse it got."

Molly Riley used her nurse's training to help those she could. The woman in blue had shards of glass stuck in her chest. Pieces of concrete were crushing her legs, and she was twisted facing the ceiling. Next to her was a woman in pink who was also trapped from the waist down, but facing the floor; her stomach was punctured, and she was having trouble breathing because of the blood running across her face from a head wound. Half of her scalp had been ripped off, probably when her long brown chair was caught in falling debris. For the next two hours, Molly and Phyllis Banks, another nurse who was there, would take turns holding the two women's heads up so they could breathe while the blood dripped into their laps. Molly and Phyllis helped give each of these women sixteen transfusions.

Ed Taylor, a young Black man, wanted to help. He dashed out of the kitchen wearing his flowing white dishwashing apron. The first victim he spotted was an elderly woman. She was sprawled flat on her face, her torso wrapped beneath the skywalks. Gently, Ed took her hands in his and began to pull. A moment later, one of her arms snapped free from her battered body.

At 7:12 p.m., only three and a half minutes after the initial summons for help, the first ambulance arrived on the scene. Paramedic Gary Frank could not get over how many people were covered with blood. "It was as if huge buckets of red paint had been flung at them," he said. The instant

Frank climbed out of his ambulance, he was surrounded by twenty or thirty victims who were either hurt or wanted him to help a relative or friend. "I was trying to do a hundred things at once. I was showing a nearby volunteer how to stop the blood when I heard an old man behind me say he had a headache. Actually, he was missing half an ear."

Despite his training and experience, paramedic Jim Taylor's first view of the atrium staggered him. "I couldn't believe my eyes. There were people chopped in half; there were people with their limbs sheared off; there were some crushed so badly I had no idea whether they had been men or women. There were lots of people still trapped, screaming and pleading for something for their pain. There is no way I can explain the helpless feeling that overwhelmed me. And there I stood. The firemen were doing their damnedest to try to free the victims. Intestines, brains, bones were everywhere. I had to blank out their agony, otherwise I would have gone to pieces myself. We had to help the ones who had a chance to live, or at least try to give them that chance."

In the initial rush of survivors through the exits when the skywalks fell was Dr. Gerhard Schottman, head of St. Luke's Hospital's radiology department. Gripped by panic, the Schottmans did not stop running until they were a block away from the hotel. He then got control of himself and turned back, telling his wife he had to return to help out, even though they both continued to worry that "the whole place might come tumbling down at any moment."

The first newspaper reporter at the scene, young Tom Ramstack, saw people walking around "as if struck dumb, too stunned to cry or scream or even talk."

Paramedic John Jacob reached the hotel about 7:25 p.m. "As soon as I got inside the door, it got to me," Jacob said. "There was no mistaking that smell." It took him only a few seconds to locate the source—the body of a woman a short distance from the debris, lying on her side. A kneecap and a hand were beside her face. "She was so pathetic lying there that I wanted to kneel and cry for her. But I guess I was too stunned to do even that. I've seen dead bodies before, but not like this. Not so many."

When the two skywalks fell, about fifty people were sandwiched between them, and at least a hundred and fifty were crushed and trapped under the combined weight of both. Rescuers looking at the wreckage could see the skywalks' false bottoms, which meant that some of the buried victims might still be alive. A number of firefighters and volunteers made a futile effort to peel back the concrete and steel with their bare hands. One such volunteer was Rich Gale, a pitcher for the Kansas City Royals. "Someone kept yelling, 'You can't help them, you can't do anything with that steel,'" Gale remembered. "Some firemen must have gotten hernias trying. God, we tried. Here I am a big moose of a guy, and I couldn't budge that steel an inch. You have no idea what a helpless feeling that is."

Pat Smith of the Metropolitan Ambulance Service said, "You could stand there looking at the catwalks stacked one on top of the other with parts of people sticking out every couple of feet all the way around, and it just wouldn't register. It just seemed impossible that we couldn't somehow get those people out from under there and soon. But gradually it became clearer and clearer that this was going to be necessary, and that we were going to have to deal with the problems one at a time. Unless great care was taken, additional injuries could easily be inflicted upon rescuers and victims alike. Someone had to decide which sections to begin with and which to leave to be dealt with hours later." Soon everyone settled in for a very long night's work.

Making a ghastly job even worse was the water that continued to pour onto the debris from the broken pipe on the fourth floor. Said one firefighter, "With all the electricity and air conditioning off it must have been a hundred and twenty degrees inside."

Two blocks from the hotel, night-shift crews of the John Rohrer Construction Company were at work ripping out the concrete floors of another Hallmark building. When news of the disaster reached the construction workers, they immediately headed for the hotel with equipment that would be a godsend to both victims and rescuers: jackhammers, air compressors, forklift trucks, floodlights, and gasoline-driven electrical generators.

Outside the hotel, emergency medical technician Gary Frank was emptying every emergency vehicle he could lay his hands on. Soon he had assembled piles of intravenous transfusion tubing and liquids, tracheal tubes, cervical collars, spine boards, and scores of other essentials needed to operate what was, in reality, a battlefield medical station.

War was a frequently used analogy. "It tore your heart out to see how people were suffering," said James Flanagan, a priest who had been a Navy frogman in World War II. "You see them looking up at you alive, mangled, pleading." The enormity of the catastrophe momentarily overwhelmed Father Flanagan. He prayed, "Please, dear God, give me strength." Police Chief Norman Caron said, "The closest thing I can recall to compare to this, God forbid, was Korea." To Gerhard Schottman, the doctor who had initially bolted from the atrium in fear that everything was going to collapse, the scene "was as shocking, or worse, than anything I saw when I was with a M*A*S*H* hospital in Korea."

At 7:35 p.m., the man who would be in charge of all emergency medical care at the Hyatt for the next fifteen hours arrived. A half hour earlier, Joseph "Dr. Joe" Waeckerle, thirty-three, had completed his eighteen-hour shift at Baptist Memorial Hospital, where he was head of Emergency Medicine. Paramedic Jim Taylor was the first to stop Dr. Waeckerle when he arrived. "Wow, are we glad to see you," Taylor said. The emergency medical professionals, almost all of whom had previously worked with Dr. Joe, respected him for his skill and coolness. They recognized him as their natural leader.

Waeckerle's first impression was of electrical sparks that were crackling in the damaged circuits lying in "three or four inches of blood, body parts and excrement scattered about." Waeckerle later said, "Many among the fatally wounded had their limbs naturally amputated. I had to make quick decisions. I did what I had to do." Of the people trapped in the wreckage, there were "some who were going to live only if you hurried to get them out because they were so severely injured, and those who weren't going to live because there was no way to get them out or their injuries were too severe. It was almost dark, except for a few very powerful spotlights and sparks from rescue saws and cutting torches. All around us we heard the roar of compressors and generators, the grinding of concrete cutting saws, and the thumping of jackhammers. With all the smells and sights and sounds, there was the overwhelming feeling of death. It's amazing that anybody was able to function at all."

Dr. John Hunkeler, head of the medical staff at nearby Trinity Lutheran Hospital, was at home having dinner when a phone call brought him the news of the disaster. Within little more than an hour, he had twenty-five physicians on duty coping with an unprecedented onslaught of emergency patients. All fifteen hospitals in the area were involved in the medical effort. The Harry Truman Medical Center was only four blocks away. Dr. Mark Singsack of Truman noted, "We received eighteen victims in the first fifteen minutes. Later, quite a few of the more severely injured were brought to us."

Moen Phillips was on duty at the fire station near Penn Valley Park. It had been an uneventful work shift. When he arrived at the Hyatt, Phillips found one thirty-foot-long section of the upper skywalk that had not fallen flat and was still propped precariously against the south wall of the atrium, forming an angle with the other skywalk below it. He peered into the narrow space between the skywalks with a flashlight and saw a man doubled over, gasping in pain. Phillips crawled into the opening without hesitation. There was no time to shore up the angled section of concrete to make sure it would not fall the rest of the way. Pushing dangerously deep into the blackness, Phillips managed to slip both hands under the man's arm. As he started to pull, the concrete and steel shifted just enough to trap Phillips's left arm in a deadly grip from his shoulder to his elbow. He felt a wave of furious pain. His eyes met those of the victim he was trying to save. Now they were both trapped. From behind, Phillips could hear his fellow firefighters shouting at him to "get the hell out of there before the whole slab comes down," and he felt strong hands close around his ankles and try to pull him free. The yanking was futile and only intensified the pain in his arm. An instant later, the slab above him shifted again, and he was able to wrench his arm loose. "Hang on a little longer," he said as he pulled with all his strength, working against the weight of a steel beam that was pinning the man's right thigh bone to the concrete slab beneath them. Gradually he was able to back out of the hole, dragging the man along with him. For a minute, Phillips could not stand up.

John R. Murphy was an attorney who worked for the Belger Cartage Company, which had an equipment yard at 2100 Walnut, eight blocks from the Hyatt. He had just turned into the driveway at his home when he heard about the Hyatt on the car radio. As his wife, Fran, waved hello, Murphy made a U-turn and sped back to the company headquarters. He had not even hesitated long enough to tell his wife where he was going or why. Fran waved a puzzled goodbye. Murphy sensed that heavy cranes would be needed and knew his company's were the biggest in town.

Still trapped under a steel beam, Jeff Durham was getting IVs in both arms. The bags containing the fluid were being held by volunteer Frank Hashman, a local liquor dealer. Dr. Waeckerle dropped to one knee and gave Durham 120 milligrams of Demerol to ease the pain. Waeckerle could see that the man was doomed if he stayed where he was any longer. He turned to Keith Ashcraft, a pediatric doctor who only minutes earlier had been eating an elegant dinner in the Hyatt's Peppercorn Duck Club. Quietly, Waeckerle said, "Keith, you've got to take that leg off. It's his only chance."

"You're right," Ashcraft said, "but I doubt if he'll make it in any case."

"Try."

While Ashcraft went to the kitchen to find a suitable knife, Waeckerle explained to Durham that he would almost certainly bleed to death if he were not taken to a hospital and that amputation looked like the only alternative. Durham thanked him for his efforts and told him to do whatever he thought was best. It had been years since Ashcraft had done any emergency-room work, and he had some trepidation at first. The amputation took twenty minutes and had to be finished with a chainsaw from a nearby construction site. Frank Hashman stayed at this post throughout, holding the IV apparatus steady despite being flecked with bone particles thrown up by the chainsaw. "I told Jeff," Hashman said, "to keep praying, that God would have mercy on his soul." Durham died half an hour after reaching the hospital. The beam that had trapped his leg would not be raised until eleven hours later.

By 8:05 p.m., all of the living victims who could be seen were receiving attention. The problem now was to find and help those who could not be seen, those who were buried in the wreckage. The rescuers knew they were there because they could hear their muffled cries. There seemed to be little chance that anybody was still alive under both skywalks, but there were obviously survivors sandwiched into the space of a foot or two between the concrete walkway of the upper skywalk and its gypsum-board false bottom. Maybe even some of the people who were trapped in the false bottom of the lowest skywalk could eventually be saved. Creating an access hole required breaking the concrete apart with jackhammers and exposing the steel decking by lifting aside the pieces of broken concrete. Welding torches were used to cut a circle several feet in diameter through the wire mesh and the decking. The workmen handled the hundred-pound jackhammers and cutting torches with such delicacy that they were able to break through the slabs without adding to the injuries of those trapped beneath. "Dr. Joe was usually the first one in," commented John Jacob, the senior paramedic who worked with him. "It was not an easy thing, mentally or physically, to go into one of these holes. But he would go in headfirst and try to lift someone out. I don't know how he got his strength."

Fire Captain Joe Thomas remembered reaching through an opening and pulling out two dead people and then a tiny girl who was still alive. "She was the most beautiful girl I had ever seen, with long blond hair and blue eyes. She didn't look like she had a scratch on her."

One of the hundreds of off-duty firefighters who raced to the hotel had a personal reason to be there. John Tvedten Jr. remembered that his dad had mentioned going to the tea dance. John worriedly looked around the atrium for his father. When he could not locate him, he began scanning the debris, looking for the cowboy boots his dad always wore when he was off duty.

Twenty-two people were found alive in the sandwich formed by the two skywalks; only nine survived under both.

By 8:30, an hour and twenty-five minutes after the collapse, more than a hundred victims had been transferred to hospitals, and many more were being treated in the triage area in the atrium and outside the hotel's entryway. An emergency morgue had been set up in one of the hotel's exhibition rooms.

All through the night, mutilated bodies in a seemingly endless stream had arrived at the Mount Moriah mortuary. Joe Lister, assistant funeral director, stared at them. The names of many were familiar. They were classmates of his from Ward High School, who had met that night at the Hyatt for their thirty-fifth reunion. If he had not been required to work the night shift, he would have been there with them.

The last piece of concrete and steel was lifted from the atrium floor at approximately 4:30 a.m. As the ten-ton slab was slowly winched skyward, medical crews scurried underneath the wreckage, paramedic John Jacob was the first to reach Mark Williams, the last survivor.

"Nothing we write in this report," emergency officials later cautioned, "can describe what happened. We were there, but except for occasional flashes of comprehension, we can't get a handle on it."

OVER THE YEARS ROBERT GORDON ASKED SEVERAL PEOPLE TO READ snatches of the manuscript in which they figured. He used their testimonials as supporting documentation for the accuracy of his recounting of their stories. One such reader was Molly Riley, his original client and for a while the class representative for the *Federal Skywalk Cases* and, as illustrated by the excerpts in the unpublished "House of Cards," an eyewitness, a victim, a first responder, a rescuer, and a hero on the night of July 17, 1981. Molly's note to Bob read, "What you have stated is honest . . . & true. I hope the story does some good."[3]

16

Interruptions

The logical ending for "House of Cards," reached at page 639 of the typescript, is when the settlement of the *Federal Skywalk Cases* was finalized, logical but not satisfying to Robert Gordon, who had poured his blood, sweat, and tears into the fight. This could not be how the story stopped and his book ended with Goliath having vanquished David.[1] Nor was he open to a graceful exit from the field of battle, although his last courtroom appearance dealing with the case gave him the chance. He did not take it.

It is worth taking another look at that pivotal day. On January 20, 1983, the final hearing on the Hallmark settlement plan was held before a packed courtroom of lawyers, reporters, victims, and their families. Emotions ran high. Jill Tvedten Long, whose father, the fire captain, had died in the skywalks collapse, sat in front, often seen bent over with hands covering her face.[2] As colead counsel, Gordon rated a seat at the plaintiffs' table, where he sat in quiet desperation, struggling to accept defeat and contain his mixed emotions about Wright, who had been almost a father figure since the beginning of the case. The judge was a great guy when he was on your side and an object of scorn when he disappointed you, like now when settling the case.[3]

Although nothing was going to stop this freight train, the proceedings did not run on the expected track. All parties were in agreement to the provisions, with the exception of a few trifling details, confirmed when their turns came to speak. Robert Sisk, Hallmark's New York lawyer, however, pulled a surprise—at least to Gordon—and took this opportunity, this "last chance" as a reporter put it, to absolve his client. Sisk, who claimed he "wanted to bring an end to this tragic chapter," rattled on at length in his "rich, room-filling, baritone" voice. He presented "the evidence which would have been forthcoming" if only there had been a trial. His brazen attempt at a public exoneration for Hallmark, which, he proclaimed, had nothing to do with the skywalks collapse and "has made a living on the subject of quality," was too much for Gordon, who until this point had breathed not a word.[4] He recorded in his diary, though: "Sisk did (as usual) exactly what he had previously told me he wouldn't do, namely he b.s.'d about Hallmark's great record for quality, including the Hyatt Hotel Project, his client's total innocence & non-culpability for any wrong-doing."[5] Sandbagged once again, Gordon could not let these words go unchallenged.

When Gordon gained the floor (on page 56 of the transcript of the proceedings), he began his remarks. "In listening to him [Sisk], I must say I had almost an overwhelming desire to come up here and say, 'to hell with the settlement.'" What followed (for twenty-five pages of monologue) was an impromptu, rambling, disjointed, and impassioned rebuttal before the assembled crowd.[6] With some dramatic license this exchange could have been the final scene in Gordon's book, his own "end to this tragic chapter." But it was not to be. Knowing as we do of what came later in his life, this episode may serve better as a foreshadowing of Gordon's public unraveling.

If only he could have articulated before the assembled crowd what he calmly wrote a few weeks later in his "final report" to the court:

> Of course, the real issue in this case was never whether Hallmark had all of the end connections of the Skywalks (which it knew were "abominations") repaired following the first collapse, but rather what did it do, if anything, to make sure that the only other structural support for the Skywalks, their hanger-rod-to-box-beam

> connections . . . were safe. The heart of the whole case against Hallmark was that it failed to do anything even though it was put on actual notice . . . that the Atrium area and the Skywalks were defectively designed, improperly installed or both. For a grand total of $5,000 paid to H. R. Inspection . . . and an equal amount paid to Seiden & Page Consulting Engineers, which worked only "as directed" by the owner, Hallmark now claims it did "everything possible" to make "triply sure" that the "entire hotel was structurally super safe."[7]

The stressed-out attorney had no power to change the outcome and scuttle the settlement, and he had to give his grudging assent in the courtroom that day. He had done what he could on the fly, which was not to leave the public record "in such a one-sided and, to me, unfair manner." Jill Long may have expressed what was on the average citizen's mind better and more briefly. She left the courtroom having felt she had listened to an account of an unsolved murder. "We know the weapon," she told a reporter, "but we don't know who did it."[8] That view was shared by some in the press.

Art Brisbane, a young, up-and-coming columnist for the *Kansas City Times*, gave a benediction of sorts for the *Federal Skywalk Cases*. He noted pragmatically that the pursuit of truth in the Hallmark hotel disaster "would have come at too high a cost . . . potentially devastating." To whom exactly, Brisbane left to the reader's imagination, but he was an astute observer of Kansas City's "atmosphere" and how all-powerful the Halls were, at least until this moment.[9] In his column he wondered aloud whether the skywalks collapse came as a result of design and engineering mistakes made "casually and without careful thought," or was it—and this was more dangerous ground to tread—"a calculated risk?" (Gordon took his yellow highlighter and marked this phrase on a clipping, which became for a while the title of his yet-to-be-started book.)[10] Brisbane did not offer an answer but took another tentative step forward and posed—but again dared not answer—the central question: Was anyone to blame? With an expedient settlement having replaced an embarrassing trial, the public inquiry basically ended, and he never expected it to resume. Maybe he only referred to himself and his colleagues, who were moving on from this story and were avoiding lingering questions, but his expectation became a self-fulfilling prophecy after the paper disbanded the Hyatt investigative team in March 1983. Gordon never answered to his own satisfaction his questions about the press's role in the Hyatt story: Were the paper's distortions deliberate? Were its shortcomings due to bureaucratic complacency and incompetence or to collusion and cronyism? Was its upper-level management just another cog in the city's booster machine? He came away from the experience with some reporters as friends and, with a couple of possible exceptions, no lasting enemies.[11]

A Hyatt-related story surfaced in the wake of the settlement. After the culmination of its months-old shoe-leather investigation, the paper served up a juicy scandal. The building inspection office in the city's Public Works Department, reporters revealed, was rank with cheating and dishonesty. Reporters had followed the civil servants on their appointed rounds and witnessed them doing anything but their jobs of making sure Kansas City's buildings did not fall down, mostly loafing at home and lounging in bars. Inspection reports revealed that their endemic neglect included the Hyatt Regency under construction. The system was so corrupt that even after the Hyatt shock, the office still would not or could not pull itself together and clean up its act. Thirteen city building inspectors in the Public Works Department, two of whom were directly connected to the hotel construction, were fired for falsified reports and other fraudulent practices. City officials promised reform.[12] Coming as it did on the heels of the *Federal Skywalk Cases* that assigned the blame to no one, the paper's exposé made it simple for the public to draw the line, no matter how thin and invisible, between bad city inspectors and the skywalks collapse. Gordon, long past given to subtlety, commented, "The public inspector scandal served as a convenient whipping boy for the private sector's egregious indifference."[13]

THE LITIGATION RELATING TO THE SKYWALKS COLLAPSE DID NOT cease with the federal court settlement. In skywalk cases heard in state court, multimillion-dollar judgments—$3 million here, $4 million there—grabbed the occasional headline. Because liability was no issue, only the dollar amounts for damages were contested. The always-quotable Lantz Welch successfully argued a $2 million award for one couple. "I naturally wish it had been higher," he said, "and I'm sure the defense wishes it could have been lower."[14] But that paled in comparison to what a jury settled on for his client Sally Firestone, Molly Riley's "girl in pink" and the most severely injured survivor of the collapse. Firestone's emotionally wrenching courtroom testimony of standing on the second-floor skywalk, being crushed by the skywalk above, and valiantly surviving as a quadriplegic ("First I didn't really understand what was wrong with me or how permanent it was. I dreamed of walking and being the way I was before"), combined with Welch's courtroom theatrics, almost guaranteed the outcome—$15 million. After the verdict one juror said he wanted to make sure that "this girl shouldn't have a worry in the world financially or mentally. . . . And I feel damn good about it." The paper's front-page story noted that history had been made: "the largest such award ever rendered in Missouri." In the decades that followed, Sally Firestone stayed in the Kansas City area and became a champion for the rights of the disabled.[15] Welch, her attorney, became even wealthier and more eccentric.

In 1984 Welch made the paper for a stunt outside of the courtroom. He proposed to his future (second) wife at a home football game of the Kansas City Chiefs. His method, long before it became a cliché, was an airplane buzzing above Arrowhead Stadium trailing the banner "Laura—will you marry me?—Lantz." Never a shrinking violet, he documented such adventures in a later memoir titled *Mr. Lucky*, for which, unlike fellow author Gordon, he did not bother with the nuisance of a publisher. Welch just uploaded it to his vanity website, along with countless chance encounters with celebrities that he documented for the remainder of his outsized life. Success bred more success. He quickly followed the Firestone win with two more, unrelated to the Hyatt, one for $17.5 million and another for $49 million. The man who took to calling himself "Lantzlot" devoted a chunk of his huge awards to build a flamboyant, fifteen-thousand-square-foot, King Arthur–themed castle on the shore of a Kansas City lake. Five years after Welch's 2016 death, his heirs finally unloaded "Camelot," the house that Hallmark built.[16]

Gordon was often put out with Welch's antics but held no lasting grudge and mused about whether he would have been a better "captain of the ship" than Irving Younger. "At the risk of sounding like the resident Don Quixote," Gordon said to Welch in 1983, "it still galls me to see those who are responsible for all those deaths and injuries walking away, essentially unblemished, in spite of all of your and my efforts."[17] Whereas Welch moved on to other fights, Hallmark remained a target for Gordon.

In September 1983 the long-anticipated Halvorson transcript of Hallmark's November 13, 1979, taped meeting about the atrium roof collapse finally fell into Gordon's lap, and he wasted little time in sharing its secrets with Judge Wright—with all of the attorney's characteristic verbosity.[18] Gordon dashed off a fifty-five-page letter with exhibits, detailing the discrepancies of the earlier Hallmark transcript supplied to the paper and the sworn testimony by the attendees against this cleaned-up-and-restored "accurate" version. To Gordon, here was "new evidence" and indisputable proof of false testimony, willfully given. "Hallmark's withholding of the most incriminating evidence in the case, followed by the dissemination of what I have just learned were false and misleading transcripts, coupled with a conspiracy to hide all this, is so indefensible," he wrote, "that I am bringing the matter to your attention without another moment's delay." He anticipated the Hallmark response—a rote dismissal as a mere vendetta by Gordon meant to promote a future book. "My complaint against Hallmark," wrote Gordon, "is limited to a very few of its officers," and that complaint was perjury. He clearly had Judith Whittaker in his sights. On the last page of the letter to Wright, Gordon dropped the tidbit that he had sent a copy to the U.S. Attorney's Office in Kansas City.[19]

Gordon brought up how this new development had distracted him from his book, but he chose not to mention how a criminal investigation might provide the ending that his story so desperately needed. If he expected either the district court or Robert G. Ulrich, U.S. attorney, and Robert B. Schneider, assistant U.S. attorney, to provide him with that satisfaction, however, he was sorely disappointed, as he was with Albert

Riederer, Jackson County prosecutor, who also nosed around the skywalks case for a few months.[20] Despite his constant suggestions-assistance-nudging-nagging, their grand jury investigations went nowhere for reasons a disappointed Gordon never fully fathomed. The inquiry seemed to focus on a scenario of explicit foreknowledge of the skywalks collapse, the existence of which the grand jury apparently discarded, rather than one of rank indifference or gross negligence leading up to it. The federal inquiry decided, therefore, that the 1979 atrium roof collapse had no link to the 1981 skywalks collapse.[21] Gordon, who testified before the grand jury, saw his evidence ignored and theory rejected but continued to beat this dead prosecutorial horse for a couple more years, even going over the heads of local officials to their bosses in the Department of Justice in Washington.[22] This desperate tactic made him no friends on either end and also proved fruitless. As for Wright's thoughts on the matter, Gordon was just not listening. The judge, sympathetic but glad to be shed of the *Federal Skywalk Cases*, had been publicly quoted as saying, "I think that it's important that this case be finished and that we go on to something else." Wright intentionally did not file and hence make public Gordon's October letter because—and he said this to Gordon's face—"The case was over with, and that was it."[23] These efforts by Gordon to engage those in the criminal justice system provided additional pages to his tome but no satisfactory, upbeat conclusion, only more time-wasting distractions to the book's completion.

A separate investigation, one without Gordon's direct involvement, did gain traction. Two structural engineers fought in the courts for their professional lives and became the poster boys for inattention and carelessness in the Hyatt project. In 1984, following a probe by the Missouri Board for Architects, Professional Engineers, and Land Surveyors, the Missouri attorney general brought charges against Jack Gillum and Dan Duncan of Gillum-Colaco. Duncan had served as the project engineer who "designed the single rod concept and approved the fatal change to the two-rod connection," while Gillum, his boss and the engineer of record, signed off on the flawed structural drawings.[24] The judge who oversaw the public hearing, held across the state in suburban St. Louis and an ordeal of twenty-six days that Gordon in part attended, found the pair alone responsible for the structural design and, hence, the building collapse. After a lengthy series of appeals, the engineers were stripped of their licenses.[25]

Gordon supported the charges faced by Gillum and Duncan, weighed the evidence presented in court (which introduced to Gordon's delight the all-important Halvorson transcript and the playing of an enhanced tape of the November 13, 1979, meeting), and agreed with the judge's verdict against the pair. Everyone understood the impact of the decision. "Until now," stated a St. Louis newspaper, "no individual has been blamed in the Hyatt collapse." Hallmark and to some extent the architects saw the verdict as their "total exoneration," whereas Gordon said, in effect, "now wait a minute." He detected an overemphasis on the narrow role of the engineers, negligent as they were. In his opinion it was but one issue in a "whole spectrum of screw-ups" by the design review team.[26] Buried in the weeds of shop drawings and their fatal revisions from a single- to a double-hanger-rod connection made in February 1979 was the broader question of flawed project management.[27] The shop drawing review process needed a proper airing, but regarding the other issue, he argued, Hallmark officers or employees should have been called to testify. The hearing, however, did not venture into the subject of whether the owner, the supreme entity that wielded the power of the purse and the calendar, had taken all reasonable measures after the atrium roof collapse. "The owner," wrote Gordon later, "never contracted for or paid for a full design review of its atrium," although it had the resources and clout to do so.[28] Guilty though the engineers were, Gordon believed their mistakes could have been caught by a more responsible employer, and he remained frustrated with a system that did not believe the same.

The formal blame game may have ended, but who could have left the St. Louis proceedings and not wondered who else was culpable? The two sanctioned engineers were the most obvious, the weakest links, but only two of those in the skywalks chain. It merely requires a long, hard look at Gordon's "cast of characters" to spot other likely candidates. If any grand conclusion can be reached about this sad affair, it is that for each of the 114 Hyatt hotel fatalities, one could draw from Gordon's list and nominate an equal number of persons who flopped beforehand—architects, engineers, project managers, steel fabricators, installers, general contractor—from the lowly, twenty-year-old construction "inspector" to the person perched on the top of the pyramid, the hotel owner, and everyone in between. And let us not forget the many hands involved in the concept, design, fabrication, installation, and inspection of the "thin and invisible" skywalks, none of whom could recall their fathering of this orphan of a failure.[29] They were followed by others whose job seemed only to muddy the waters. All share the blame.

Pointing fingers can be done in a more artful way, as exemplified by The Rainmakers, a Kansas City rock group of the time with national aspirations. The band captured the local zeitgeist of frustration and cynicism in the first track of their big label debut. The lyrics of the up-tempo "Rockin' at the T-Dance" told anyone paying close attention how the blame game was really played:

> . . . They let the monkey go
> And blamed the monkey wrench.[30]

THERE WAS NO END TO THE SELF-IMPOSED INTERRUPTIONS, NONE bigger than Gordon's continued legal pursuit of Hallmark. He still did not have an ending to his book, but one was coming and a bitter one. In the mid-1980s he filed two more lawsuits against the corporation, rematches that, he hoped, would wash away the bitter taste of the earlier setback and maybe please a publisher. Somehow, he managed to find the time to resume the quest while in the midst of his book project, the account of which ended up only being tucked away into a solitary, sad chapter.[31]

In August 1984 Moen Phillips, represented by Gordon, filed a lawsuit against Hallmark Cards for $426 million in compensatory and punitive damages, one that sought to "reopen the question of responsibility for the accident."[32] Unlike the *Federal Skywalk Cases*, only a single defendant was targeted. Bolstered by the new evidence in the Halvorson transcript, Gordon maintained, "Hallmark exercised almost absolute control over the construction of the hotel and was lax in failing to ensure the safety of the skywalks." Like his previous case, Gordon asked for a class to be formed but this time filed in state court because all prospective members were Missourians and no geographic diversity existed. He dangled the prospect that, if a massive judgment came their way, its beneficiaries would also include the Hyatt killed and injured. In response, a Hallmark lawyer gaslighted the newspaper with his assertion that "the company was not involved with the construction of the hotel and was not responsible for the collapse." The news story of the filing noted in passing that Gordon was writing a book but did not make much of it.[33] His new client would certainly appear in Gordon's updated narrative, and what a sad tale it was.

Moen L. Phillips, a member of the Kansas City Fire Department in his early thirties, had responded with his truck company to the Hyatt Regency minutes after the collapse and, among his other sights and actions that awful night, had helped perform an emergency amputation of the leg of a victim trapped under the rubble.[34] An obvious and severe case of post-traumatic stress disorder followed, and his fellow firefighters reached out on his behalf and, in some instances, their own. From their several meetings, beginning in February 1984 and their many logged calls, Gordon pieced together the story of Phillips's skywalks experience, as well as the mental anguish that trailed in its wake. This included further trauma: the destruction—purportedly by chainsaw—of the interior of his home, several months spent in a mental ward of a hospital, and a recent divorce.[35]

The defendant said that all this did not matter given that Phillips and his colleagues were firemen, and their work fell under the "fireman's rule," state law that barred recovery of damages during the course of their work, however dangerous or traumatic. Hallmark argued that any injury, physical or mental, that might have resulted did so within the scope of a fireman's employment, in other words, in the line of duty. Gordon countered that what Phillips and other rescuer-victims had seen and done in the horrendous aftermath of a collapse caused by negligence was so psychologically traumatic that it was outside their range of usual experiences, in other words, *above and beyond* the call of duty.[36]

The Jackson County Circuit Court concurred with the defendant and threw out the case, citing the fireman's rule. Gordon appealed to the Missouri Court of Appeals, which in April 1986 ruled in his favor, two justices to one, the majority opinion being "a fireman is not required by the law to assume all risks that he may encounter."[37] Being a split decision, the defendant could and did appeal, and in December 1986 the Missouri Supreme Court unanimously upheld the circuit court's ruling to dismiss the case. Firefighters (and police officers) must assume such risks in their jobs and cannot sue, the justices decided.[38] Another defeat for Gordon, his second against Hallmark.

In June 1986, with the five-year statute of limitations looming, Gordon filed yet another lawsuit on behalf of other rescuers, *John Jacob v. Hallmark Cards, Inc.*[39] He was back in federal court, requesting a class to be formed of *civilian* rescuers who had come to the site voluntarily and worked the collapse—doctors, nurses, emergency medical technicians, and other good Samaritans with no medical background—thereby bypassing the fireman's rule. On paper this looked promising as both legal strategy and a potentially upbeat ending to "House of Cards." It proved neither.

The three class representatives included an off-duty paramedic and two security officers employed by the hotel. John Jacob worked for the Metropolitan Ambulance Services Trust and heard about the skywalks collapse on television. He rushed to the hotel and worked through the night. His primary job was "crawling in and out between the two walkways, and point[ing] out alive and deceased patients."[40] Larry Lantz, a Hyatt guard, received a frantic call at home from his mother and left for the hotel immediately. Lantz helped carry out the wounded to waiting ambulances. He would never forget the ankle-deep, blood-mixed water in the hotel lobby. Adam Wilson, another guard who worked at the hotel, was called in from home minutes after the disaster and worked on "general rescue." Wilson testified, "I have had nightmares, flashbacks ever since. . . . I can't stand to look at raw meat." All three men worked through the night and well into the next day. Jacob left after the removal of the last living victim.[41]

The cause was probably lost from the get-go. First, Judge Wright recused himself, and Gordon drew another federal judge, D. Brook Bartlett, who expressed little sympathy or encouragement to the plaintiffs and maybe was even hostile to the issue. Gordon suspected the judge's close ties to the defendants because he came from one of Kansas City's wealthiest families, had been a law partner at Stinson, Mag, the local powerhouse that still represented Hallmark, and was identified as a staunch Reagan Republican. The impolitic Gordon did himself no favors when he filed a document that "accused Hallmark and its lawyers of lying," and Bartlett responded in turn, calling Gordon's words "scandalously defamatory" and striking the document from the record. The judge made a point to emphasize, and a reporter dutifully repeated, "When an attorney's emotional involvement in a client's cause interferes with the exercise of the professional judgment which the client expects from an attorney, an important premise of our justice system is threatened." Among Bartlett's other edicts were to deny Gordon's request to disqualify himself from the case and to deny any new discovery in the case, the lawyer's bread-and-butter work for any class-action case.[42]

To no real surprise, outside of the courtroom the local paper made no bones about where its sympathies lay and came out against both lawsuits, even going so far in an editorial as to ridicule the plaintiffs as opportunistic, shameful, and cleverly maneuvering for a big payday. One local columnist—or his editor—coined the clever headline "First You Rescue, Then Sue." Others in the newsroom piled on and did not spare their mocking of the "lawyers encouraging plaintiffs to seek absurd damage amounts."[43] Shades of Lantz Welch! The tarnished Gordon now traveled the same low road, at least in the eyes of the general public, as any ordinary ambulance chaser. But the damage to his self-esteem only worsened.

Hallmark wasted no time in its tried-and-true strategy of class destruction. The company quickly settled with about fifty trained emergency professionals and potential class members, "nuisance value settlements," as its lawyers termed it, but anything to increase the opt-outs and decrease the "numerosity" of the class.[44] An outmanned and outlawyered Gordon could only watch in despair in late 1986 and early 1987 as the events of the case passed him by with little to show for it. Although it pained him to do so, he commenced settlement talks at least as early as May 1987. They continued through the spring and summer with at least nine drafts of proposals passing between him and the defendant's lawyers. Arthur Miller, his old mentor, consoled him: "It is a difficult case, at a difficult time, before a difficult judge."[45] Obviously frustrated, Gordon committed his feelings to his diary: "Prepared five-page class memo to media to explain why settlement makes sense and to point out, in answer to their charges that I have 'gone soft on Hallmark,' that this was the best I could do; that if anyone thinks he can do better, he is welcome to try." By September Hallmark had effectively "gutted the class," as Gordon put it, "by settling individually with 63 rescuers for about $1.3 million." Few persons with serious injuries were left in the class, and it came as no surprise that in December the parties reached a settlement, which was approved by Bartlett on behalf of the 190 remaining class members. Class representative Jacob expressed some relief. "Much too much was written about the procedural aspects of the case, and almost all of it ridiculed or belittled us, our cause, and the attorneys who helped us."[46]

This third and last defeat for Gordon turned out to be the most humiliating. He took some comfort in the fact that, due to the pressure of his lawsuit, the Hyatt rescuers would each receive a payout from Hallmark of more than five times the $1,000 check that the tea dance attendees had cashed in 1983.[47] Hallmark again avoided the pain of punitive damages or the stigma of adverse public opinion. The pain and suffering seemed to be confined only to Gordon. In his last court appearances, the attorney looked and sounded troubled. At a February 1989 hearing Judge Bartlett asked him several times if he was "feeling okay." Replying in the affirmative, Gordon summoned the strength to give "long answers to short questions," as well as to publicly beat himself up. When it was his turn to speak, the judge allowed him to ramble at length: "If I did anything wrong, it was I didn't get enough facts. I don't know what limit there is to facts to know about this, the worst catastrophe in our city's history. . . . Why did we have to have the facts ready to go? Why did the case have to be prepared? It's because otherwise they never would have settled. It's as simple as that."[48]

What followed, the awarding and broadcasting of Gordon's fees, was the last straw. He felt little consolation that the amount came out of Hallmark's corporate coffers and did not affect the judgment. But to the public, goaded by the paper, the fees looked huge, inappropriate, and even obscene, and indeed to any ordinary, hardworking Kansas Citian they were hefty.[49] For his more than six thousand hours working the case (1984–88), Gordon received a Crown Center Redevelopment Corporation check for $594,614.64. This came on top of the several thousand hours he expended and the $450,000 he earned in 1983 from the *Federal Skywalk Cases*.[50] Gordon knew how his feast-or-famine life must look to others and once said facetiously, "I probably look like a drug dealer because some years I have a seven-figure income and some years I have nothing."[51]

Bartlett's initial determination of a dollar figure met with an acrimonious reaction by another plaintiffs' lawyer who had helped with the case, and a hearing on the matter of class counsel fees and expenses could not be avoided, much to Gordon's dismay.[52] He had accumulated enough media savvy by now that he knew that airing one's dirty laundry in public "provides an opportunity for unbalanced and unfair coverage" by the press. The March 1989 hearing, close on the heels of the February spectacle, did not disappoint, devolving into nothing more than an unseemly squabble, which greatly embarrassed Gordon.[53] The other lawyer disparaged Gordon's approach to the case—piling up hours—and his motivation. "It's about the writing of a book. . . . That's the irony of it, Your Honor, that he's seeking money from the persons that he's going to be writing the book about." In response, the overwrought Gordon uttered, "I don't want to be here today," and as one reads the seventy-nine-page transcript of the hearing, one believes it, painfully so. "Sometimes when I speak up," pleaded Gordon, "it's wrong and when I don't speak up it's wrong. That I can never figure out." But now he spoke up, maybe for the last time in his career on such a public stage:

> Hallmark had done a very fine job, I must say. It's hard for me to say that word because it's a very grudging admiration because I was on the short end of it and I got beat by it, but they had done

> a very fine job. . . . A lot Hallmark didn't have to do. There's a very serious question about whether an emergency room doctor who goes down to save people should turn around and sue anyone for anything. I understand that. They were able to focus the issue in on something like that instead of what had the defendant done but meanwhile was killing the rescuers who were embarrassed by this sort of thing, and it was ignoring those who were non-professional rescuers, the waitresses, the bellboys, the Bill Ulmanns [Allman] who comes running with a jackhammer and works for ten and half hours down there and then goes in the VA hospital for six months. People like Larry Lantz and Adam Wilson who[m] you never met, Judge, but were also class representatives. They weren't cops. They were just security guards, just had a uniform on. They carried bags up to people's rooms. They didn't have a gun, couldn't even arrest anybody. Those people had never seen such horrors. They were terrified by it.[54]

Taken aback by the pathos of the day's events, Bartlett concluded, "I hope if anybody is writing a book that they end it before this stage."

A few days later Bartlett coldly reconsidered his original calculation and knocked down Gordon's fee, reducing his hours to a "reasonable" amount. Shaming him further, Bartlett criticized his legal acumen for not using less expensive paralegals for a chunk of the basic work.[55] The scene was painted even worse in the paper, which made much of greedy lawyers squabbling over sums of money that dwarfed the awards that individual victims received. Bartlett minced few words in his comments to Gordon, which the paper made certain to share with the world: "Gordon's persistence in behalf of the class crossed into an obsession with the Hyatt disaster and with obtaining revenge against those he believes responsible. This obsession clouded his ability to make rational decisions about what should be done to further his clients' cause."[56]

The recrimination, justified or not, and the public humiliation, real or perceived, were too much for the brittle man. He said to anybody who would listen: "I can't believe that I did too much. I feel badly I didn't do enough."[57] Thereafter, the deflated idealist withdrew from the law and "simply remained at home" and, one presumes, alone with his manuscript, which at this time the legal department of Simon & Schuster was rigorously scrubbing.[58]

17

Finales

Hallmark Cards Inc. had bigger problems than Gordon's nuisance suits. A post-skywalks narrative was forming among the city's elite, and it did not necessarily follow the Hallmark scenario that Don Hall expressed in a rare interview given in early 1983. Speaking to a *New York Times* reporter, he had said, "I think the company has been able to get its dobber back in good shape." Dobber? The *Times* did not provide a definition of the word, and a search of the *Oxford English Dictionary* refers to "dobber" as a large marble used in children's games. Dictionaries that specialize in modern slang provide a long list of inappropriate nouns, some sexual in nature.[1] If Hall meant "mojo," then it might have been wishful thinking on his part.

In 1987, as a counternarrative, Gordon interviewed John Kreamer, among the city's leading lawyers, as well as one of its most influential civic leaders. How Gordon managed to get this ultimate insider and friend of the Hall family to speak to him is a mystery. Perhaps it was because Kreamer's theme—"how the reigning family of K.C. was disserved by their advisers"—was meant as a ploy to get Don Hall off the hook:

> "Don't quote me on this," said Kreamer. "A corporation gets so big. Hallmark would have handled this [the disaster] substantially differently 20–25 years ago because of people like J. C. Hall. . . . It would

> not [have] devolved upon what I would call the technicians, the hired hands. And you get to the point where you are . . . so much bigger than anyone dreamed it would be . . . with all the layers of bureaucracy and all the calcification that sets in the joints and makes it unable to move. . . . He (Don) didn't have the ability to act himself; instead he acted only on the advice of hired guns, the HH&R [Hughes, Hubbard & Reed law firm], the CE [Charles Egan] and the JW [Judy Whittaker] who, in some cases, I guess, Judy was protecting her own ass, too."[2]

"Hired hands," one might say, were now supposedly running the company. In 1983, shortly after the Hyatt settlement, Irvine O. "Irv" Hockaday Jr. left his lofty position as the head of Kansas City Southern Industries, the railroad conglomerate headquartered in Kansas City, to become Hallmark's executive vice president. Hall gave up the presidency to David H. Hughes, the previous executive vice president, and moved up, if that is the correct direction to term it, to the titular position of chairman of the board. An anonymous source close to Hall explained to a reporter that the hotel disaster "had taken a lot out of Don." His day-to-day management of the family business appeared over. After a respectable time, the carefully groomed Hockaday replaced placeholder Hughes as president and Hall as chief executive.[3]

The game of musical chairs in the executive suite did not stop there. In June 1983 Hallmark announced Bob Kipp as the new president of Crown Center Redevelopment Corporation, a natural fit, it seemed, since one journalist once styled him as a "taller, somewhat snappier version of Donald J. Hall."[4] He replaced Jim McClune.

It did not matter that Kipp had left under pressure his job as the longtime city manager of Kansas City, Missouri. The building inspector scandal had permanently stained his reputation of efficient administration of city services and made him a toxic issue in that spring's mayoral campaign. Mayor Berkley, running for reelection, expressed no confidence in the official who in 1981 had stymied his attempts to stop Hallmark's removal of the third skywalk and to form his citizens' investigation of the Hyatt collapse—although he took care not to say that. After Berkley's victory at the polls, the embattled bureaucrat wasted little time in submitting his resignation. Shortly thereafter Hallmark hired Kipp at a salary several times his city wage. Robert Gordon, who now knew how things worked in the world, probably bit his tongue and wondered to himself if Hallmark had repaid a long-standing debt. A Hallmark board member might as well have been parroting Gordon when he said that new hire Kipp understood "how Kansas City operates."[5]

These smooth transitions aside, cracks in the corporate public image, assaults on the greeting card market, and reservations about Hallmark's vaunted artistic creativity also started to appear, and soon Goliath truly met its David.

In 1985 Hughes jetted to Colorado to meet with the owners of a small, innovative, "alternative" greeting card company that was making a national splash, although Blue Mountain Arts only put out about two hundred cards, in contrast to Hallmark's thousands. Cards by Blue Mountain had a distinctive look and feel: a homemade appearance on roughly textured paper with "deckle" or ragged edges that displayed long messages of emotional, free verse, illustrated by scenes from nature in gentle, pastel colors. The subjects of Blue Mountain cards were not constrained by the demands or needs of special occasions, only by the feelings a person wished to extend toward another.[6]

The Hallmark executive cited the "creative shortage" of his company's unimaginative bureaucracy, liked what he saw in the little company, and hinted at buying it, which the owners, two self-professed "flower children" of the sixties, politely rebuffed. The next year Susan Polis Schutz, one of the husband-and-wife owners, was in a California card shop and, by happenstance, happily spotted her cards prominently on display. At least she thought they were her cards. The one she picked up was on roughly textured, deckle-edged paper whose contents contained a passage of poetry and a nature illustration in pastel. It looked like her card, except for the "by Hallmark" on its back.

Blue Mountain fought back. After a stop-and-desist request was ignored, in 1986 the little company filed a lawsuit in federal court against the "card colossus," which at the time held 40 percent of the multibillion-dollar card market. The suit charged Hallmark with blatant fraud and "trade dress" infringement, that is, copying the look or packaging of a product. Later the company amended its complaint to accuse Hallmark of strong-arming retailers to remove cards of Blue Mountain and other small outfits from their shelves and replace them with Hallmark knockoffs. Hallmark lost the opening skirmish in a federal court in Denver when a judge granted an injunction in favor of Blue Mountain and lost again after appealing the ruling. Robert Sisk, returning as Hallmark's lead counsel, admitted in court to his client's copying others but argued that there was nothing wrong with it. Hallmark later reversed itself on this losing argument and claimed that it had not ripped off Blue Mountain. During the litigation Hallmark lawyers threw up their usual roadblocks, such as slowing down the discovery phase, last-minute document dumps, requesting the judge to recuse himself, and seeking various nagging, expensive delays. As the plaintiff observed, "Hallmark's resources and energy were unlimited, and ours dwindled dramatically every day." But this time their tactics were to no avail. Before their January 1989 trial could convene, the two parties settled. Both kept the final figure of Hallmark's payment confidential, a sizable amount but presumably less than the $50 million that Blue Mountain originally sought.[7]

Kansas Citians did not know quite what to make of the ongoing revelations about its hometown institution, but some of them seriously questioned the company's dedication to high quality in its social expression business. A local columnist placed the offending Hallmark cards under his microscope and used words rarely, if ever, uttered before to describe the company's products: "sappy" and "smarmy" and "sugar-coated sentiments and its cliched, pastel imagery." Hallmark, he decreed, "must forfeit its claim to creativity." It was as if the writer anticipated Hallmark's woeful abandonment of its Emmy-winning "hall of fame" appointment television for its wretched twenty-first-century reinvention of the saccharine, assembly-line Christmas movie.[8]

To add insult to injury, a decade after the Blue Mountain fiasco, Hallmark was still playing catch-up to the demands of popular culture. Still running the company in 2000, Irv Hockaday was asked by a local Chamber of Commerce publication about the impact of the internet on Hallmark. "It's hard to see a major impact so far," he replied. And as to lost business for traditional ink-on-paper cards? "That's not clear at this point, but it is certainly a possibility longer term."[9] Meanwhile the owners of Blue Mountain, flush with Hallmark cash, had been early adopters of electronic greeting cards and online merchandising. For the month of September 1999, their online visitors totaled more than nine million—fifteen times the online traffic of Hallmark. At the height of the turn-of-the-century dot-com boom, Blue Mountain sold its immensely popular website for $780 million, which further illustrated the point that its founders never suffered from a "creative shortage."[10] Gordon could only have envied the neat finale that always eluded him.

As one might imagine, Gordon followed the Blue Mountain case closely, kept in touch with the company's attorney, and reveled vicariously in Hallmark's courtroom and public relations embarrassments.[11] However, he felt no such schadenfreude when he learned of Irving Younger's death in 1988 at age fifty-five. Finding scant litigation success after the *Federal Skywalk Cases*, Professor Younger in his last years had returned to the university classroom. The *Kansas City Times*, which knew of Gordon's antipathy toward his former ally, reached out for a killer quote, and he surprised them with a gracious remembrance instead: "When it came to grasping difficult legal concepts and public speaking, Irving was as good as anyone in the entire country. Irving had a wonderful ability to make complicated legal jargon sound simple. He was a delightful, charming person."[12]

It prompted Rick Alm of the *Times* and a veteran of the skywalk wars to send Gordon a handwritten note: "Bobby, you *have* mellowed. I remember when . . . oh well."[13] Perhaps Gordon was thinking of his own legacy and how others would remember him.

THE LAST YEARS FOR ROBERT GORDON, WHAT ONE MIGHT DESCRIBE as a long tailspin, were disappointing, difficult, and sad. The long, public fight against Hallmark left its repercussions on his marriage. Gordon considered his wife, Josie, as his "wisest adviser." She had heard him out when he came to her early on to ask whether he should initiate the skywalks class action. She did not recommend for or against. Quietly and presciently, she instead cautioned, "I'm worried that no matter how well intentioned you and Arthur [Miller] are, there'll be a lot of people in town who either won't understand or who won't want to go along." Later, considering the consequences of her husband's fateful decision to proceed, Josie wryly noted, "We fell off a few guest lists."

More gravely, Gordon eventually fell into a deep depression, or to be more accurate, he fell to pieces. He responded neither to medication nor to his family's pleas to seek treatment. He stayed in bed and slept extensively. He and the big house fell into great disrepair. After Simon & Schuster dropped the book, the disappointed author did not revert to his previous life as an attorney. Gordon never practiced law again. The sting from a dramatic loss of income was lessened by the benefits of an insurance policy taken out in his salad days. The policy covered professionals, such as doctors and lawyers, who suffered a debilitating disability, in his case a severe case of depression, and could no longer practice. All those close to Gordon saw him as a victim of his own obsession, a dangerous virus they never caught. Counter to wise philosophers, the truth did not set him free; it only shackled him. Gordon could never liberate himself and get past Hallmark and the book. "He would not move on," said Josie, "so I moved on." After twenty-eight years of marriage, their divorce was finalized in 1997.[14]

The idealist harbored no more illusions, only cynicism, reflected by his terrible disappointment in people and the community. If Gordon had been asked, one presumes he would have answered honestly that he was as much disappointed in himself. "He never should have returned to Kansas City," reflected his son, Andy, on this California man. "It ruined him."[15]

In the surviving written records of Robert Gordon's life, few clues emerge about his years as an author after the Simon & Schuster debacle. Documents—those all-important documents—necessary for stitching together a complete story are not there to be discovered, with only a couple of exceptions. A letter from 2000 exists in which Gordon reached out to yet another New York editor, whom he kept ignorant of her predecessors. She read "House of Cards" and independently offered the same professional advice as all had done before: The manuscript was too long, so cut it to five hundred pages. Drop the first-person perspective, so write it in the third person. The legal detail was "mind-numbing," and the narrative was "just not a page-turner," so work with a professional writer, which she could help arrange. All so familiar and disheartening. To a literary agent whom Gordon courted at the same time, he offered a reason for his recent resurfacing: "While the passage of time [almost nineteen years since the disaster] is regrettable, at least it can't be said that I rushed to judgment." He seemed to fudge the reason for the gap in his personal timeline; he explained it away by his having devoted nine years to the litigation and an additional nine to book writing. Neither late-stage, half-hearted overture went anywhere, and it raises the question: did Gordon really want his book published—ever?

If Gordon had wanted to get out the truth—his truth—he could have at any time. In late 1983, in the wake of the Halvorson transcript, he could have held a press conference and touted the new evidence it supplied. In the book project period of 1985–93, when he had a team of professionals from the publishing world on his side, he could have leaned back and let the specialists run with the ball. In 1995, with a clean copy of his manuscript in his hands, he could have self-published the book and done so with no other intermediary than a vanity press. During the new century, at the advent of the digital age and with Lantz Welch as a model, Gordon could have created a website and downloaded his book and an unimaginable array of contextual content. At the end of his life, when one should no longer care about coauthors, agents, editors, publishers, and reviewers—or even Don Hall and Hallmark—he could have made a bequest of his manuscript and the vast record that accompanied it to a responsible, capable historical repository. But he did none of these things. "Ahab is for ever Ahab, man," wrote Herman Melville. Gordon kept his story to himself and, as a result, did no favors to the victims of the Hallmark hotel disaster and to the pursuit of the truth, much less to himself.

Occasionally a glimpse of the old Gordon emerged, although few were around to witness it because his last years were spent rattling around his Mission Hills mansion. Dick Woods, who knew Gordon since the time both were young pup lawyers, visited his good friend at home for a weekly backgammon session. Gordon rarely, if ever, discussed the book project, saying only that he was "not pushing it anymore," and no one else seemed to be pushing it either. Instead, the focus was on backgammon, and for a game with strict rules, accepted structure, and honorable contestants, Gordon still possessed a competitive streak. He manifested it in his usual rule-following manner, the same as he always did throughout his legal career but, in this instance, playfully. "Bob would pour us both some wine," recalled Woods with a chuckle, "but I noticed that he never drank his."[16]

Then came cancer, the final injustice. On February 5, 2008, Robert Gordon died at age sixty-six.[17] His last days were tortured ones, wracked with pain. The cause was colon cancer, a disease that might have been caught earlier if only Gordon had paid heed to friends and family who begged him to consult with a physician. A memorial service was held at the All Souls Unitarian Universalist Church, Kansas City, Missouri. The site may have reflected his general indifference to religiosity or maybe an affinity for Unitarianism's respect for reason and scholarship. In lieu of flowers, the family requested contributions to the Robert C. and Josephine Gordon Endowment scholarship fund at his beloved University of California at Berkeley. He was a California guy to the end.

Gordon's obituary in the paper, one easily imagines, would have set him off and prompted a swift rebuke and demand for a correction. (And it was not because the account made no mention of his book.) The infraction was that, for the most important year of his life, his role was incorrectly labeled as "the lead prosecuting attorney in the Hyatt Hotel skywalk collapse," as if such a job title ever existed. How soon they forget, he would have thought, or more darkly, was the slip intentional? Nevertheless, his passing was noted in the local paper and became a permanent part of the public record.

Like so many of us, Gordon wished to be remembered. He gave this secret away, in a way often done, when he wrote wistfully in 1995 about his own obituary. "'Do you ever wonder what they'll say in your obituary?' a friend asked, sensing my malaise. 'I doubt if they'll print one,' I answered. 'But at least I know I've been here.'"[18]

Those who do remember Gordon—if at all—fall neatly into two camps, their memories either fond or dismissive. "He was the best father," recalled his ex-wife graciously and without prompting a quarter century after their divorce. "He was a nut," exclaimed a retired newspaper editor, who in the 1980s had turned a deaf ear to Gordon's entreaties for attention. The two ends of the barbell are vastly outweighed by all the Kansas Citians in the middle who lived through the skywalk disaster yet retain no memory of Gordon and, at best, only a dim recollection of the players mixed up in the post-collapse legal affair. For Robert Gordon, that seems a shame, if for no other reason than his self-description as "an insider who will say what really happened." Another person, Robert Byrne, the writer, his erstwhile collaborator, and someone who knew the Gordon story, may have said it best: "Of all the skywalk victims, direct and indirect," Byrne told Gordon, "you are probably the only one who volunteered for the role."[19]

INSIDERS, WHETHER THE WORLD SEES THEM AS DECENT FAMILY MEN or perverse obsessives, are valuable commodities when putting together a later, contested narrative, and Gordon deserves to be remembered for history's sake alone. He became an insider on January 25, 1982, when Judge Wright named him colead counsel for the plaintiffs in the *Federal Skywalk Cases*. He became an outsider on March 2, 1989, in Judge Bartlett's court, when he last wielded the law as his weapon to present the truth. To quote a modern novelist with a problematic protagonist, also a lawyer, the law "is there to create a fiction that will help us move past atrocious acts and face our future."[20] Gordon had no intention of creating fiction or applying a soothing balm or moving on as he took up the written word as his cudgel. He proved poorly armed.

Gordon's retreat was total, although he may have taken comfort in the experiences of others. Once, in a long letter to a newspaper editor in defense of Judge Wright, who came under fire by a national magazine for his handling of the skywalk litigation, Gordon drew on the always-quotable Winston Churchill. "To be so entirely correct in a matter of such great importance but not be able to make others heed the warning or accept the clear proof was my most painful experience." The context for Gordon's defense of Wright was that the judge had been "entirely correct" in employing the class-action device, but it was Gordon who had come up short in convincing others to "heed the warning" and accept "clear proof," resulting in "my most painful experience."[21]

Finally, after licking his wounds, many of them self-inflicted, Gordon realized the absurdity of his situation. He wrote on the last pages of his "House of Cards" manuscript, "There are not simple, single-sentence solutions to all of the skywalks' secrets and no resolution of so many absurdities." Yet Gordon dutifully compiled a list of some of them: He went into the case thinking he would be involved for ten months; it turned out to be ten years. He struggled to get the documents to reporters; he saw greater confusion after their appearance in print. He started out working pro bono; he ended up with substantial fees. Gordon admitted, "I quit practicing law. I confess I brooded awhile, but then I got angry at myself for doing that."[22] But he refused to claim victimhood from the Hallmark hotel disaster. "Compared to the 114 tea dancers who would never again live, laugh, and love, I had nothing to gripe about."

Epilogue

The skywalks collapse became a distant memory with each passing year but, thankfully, not to everyone. Every new semester on college campuses across the nation, engineering students are introduced to the Hyatt Regency Kansas City disaster, still considered in the modern era "one of the most significant events in the construction industry." On the curriculum for years at the nearby University of Kansas, for example, was the course "Introduction to Fracture Mechanics." The professor served as drill instructor to his recruits, and the order of the day was "pay attention to the details." With the construction of the Hallmark hotel, it was emphasized, "the details became critical."[1]

Robert Gordon might be disappointed that the knowledge of his labors has been lost, but he would be reassured that the noble purpose of his mission has been achieved—to prevent any further disasters.[2] College instructors have turned the collapse into a case study of the bad things that can happen when structural engineers fail in their jobs. Such sessions become valuable, introspective moments for the engineering community in its attempt to counteract the "diffusion of responsibility" that characterized this particular project. Edward Pfrang, the National Bureau of Standards engineer who headed the federal investigation of *what*—but not *who*—caused the skywalks to fall, summed up the situation best. "In the Hyatt case you had a process of everyone wanting to walk away from responsibility."[3] Today's budding engineers, introduced to the concept of engineering ethics and the unethical actions of the structural engineers on the Hyatt project, learn to do otherwise. This is an unexpected and refreshing development, to see at least one of the fields represented on the Hallmark design-build "team" not shy to accept blame for negligence and own the problem. Nothing but good comes from such intellectual exercises in academia, the revisiting and reexamining of this tragedy. Lessons have been learned.

REMEMBERED IN AMERICAN CLASSROOMS, IT PROVED MORE DIFFICULT in Kansas City to properly commemorate July 17, 1981. It might have been because of the time, before memorials sprang up overnight in the immediate outpouring of emotion after a tragedy, or because of the place, in this instance, a privately owned piece of commercial property. In the wake of the skywalks disaster, nothing appeared like the memorials commonly seen today, say, a small, solitary cross erected along the right-of-way of a busy highway or a massive wall of flowers, teddy bears, and other offerings to a fallen princess outside a royal castle or an outside, urban venue for hundreds of photographs of loved ones lost in the Twin Towers. That type of spontaneous memorialization did not occur at the Hyatt. In the immediate aftermath, good ideas for formal, civic-sponsored memorials were as scarce as sufficient funds.

Some who lived and worked through that nightmare wanted to keep the tragedy a private affair and forget. Others thought healing should not mean forgetting and demanded that the community remember its loss. A core group of survivors and families of victims gradually coalesced and made their desires known for a public acknowledgment, a memorial that took years to form its proper expression.

The Skywalk Memorial Foundation was organized in 2006 after the twenty-fifth anniversary of the disaster. Its purpose was the marking of the event with a permanent memorial. In 2008 the foundation, buoyed by earlier sizable gifts of money from the City of Kansas City and the Hallmark Corporate Foundation, announced that the Hyatt Regency Kansas City also supported its plans. Present at the announcement was

Brent Wright, a memorial foundation member and the son of Karen Jeter, who along with her husband, Eugene, had been crushed to death in the collapse. "It was fresh for a very long time," said Wright of his personal loss. "It has taken this long for people to work through the grief." The resolve of the group hardened as the progress slowed. Three years later on the thirtieth anniversary, the foundation had a designated site—public property at the corner of Twenty-Second Street and Gillham Road, just east and across the street from the back of the hotel—and more than half the necessary funds. "If we don't do this now," implored John Sullivan, a board member who lost his mother, Katy, "nobody else will do it. . . . It's our moral responsibility to finish this."[4] It took the group four more years to reach the finish line, a difficult but uplifting struggle for its participants.

In July 2015, after thirty-four anniversaries had come and gone, ground was broken for the Skywalk Memorial. In November, on a beautiful, crisp fall day, at long last the completed memorial was dedicated before a large, tightly packed group of people, all of whom seemed connected to the 1981 event. The most moving part of the tearful ceremony was the reading of the names of the 114 victims.[5] With that number it took a long time.

The location seemed far removed from the Hyatt, although the building was just steps away. The memorial sat in a small city park behind the hotel, away from the public front where guests today check in and where that night the tea dancers arrived, one more way to acknowledge but not draw attention to the darkest day in city history.

The centerpiece of the compact memorial plaza was a striking, stainless-steel sculpture that rose above the crowd as if an offering to the heavens. The piece sat atop a tall black cylindrical pedestal.[6] On this metal base appeared the engraved names of the killed. After the ceremony one needed to wend through the crowd, still milling about, to find the best angle to view the artwork, titled *Sending Love*. And what did you see? A broken heart? Or was it two tea dancers entwined in a last, affectionate embrace? A statement on the fragility of life? Or a testament to the power of remembrance?

FIVE YEARS LATER, A RETURN TO THE SKYWALK MEMORIAL. IT IS another hot, humid July night in Kansas City, reminiscent of that night in 1981, and it is quiet. No public ceremony marks the thirty-ninth anniversary, and only one couple is present in the small park. From the obstructed vantage point behind the hotel, there is no way of seeing whether the Hyatt Regency, now a Sheraton hotel, is busy. The time is a few minutes before the last tea dance they ever held ended, when the lobby brimmed with people.

The only other evidence this night that others have paid their respects is a solitary memento left on the concrete floor near the base of the sculpture. There are two names handwritten on the plain card, of sufficient weight to hold down the small, partially deflated party balloon attached by a ribbon. The names are of two of the victims, confirmed on the scroll of names below the sculpture. They were a couple, one of the eighteen married couples who died together when the skywalks fell. One's eyes are drawn to the names of the other pairs, partners at their last dance.

It is a time and a place for personal reflection, and nothing intrudes on the moment, except for more questions. Has this memorial served its purpose to the survivors and rescuers, properly sanctified as hallowed ground? And its purpose to the greater community, as a warning to be heeded? And finally, to the family members represented on that card who remembered their loved ones in the most intimate and modest of ways? Questions and more questions. Looking down, the balloon moves slightly in the summer's breeze.

ACKNOWLEDGMENTS

Whether Robert Gordon was a reliable narrator is, at this point, left to the reader's good judgment. But I must confess that my thumb is on his side of the scales, or else I would not have followed this man down this deep rabbit hole. It would have been absurd to do so unless at the end he proved credible as a historical source. At one time he convinced a national law firm and a federal judge to follow his idea of a class-action approach. Several big-time literary agents, editors, and authors believed his story, not because he told it well but because he had the inside scoop and the documents to prove it. Like Gordon, I too believe in the documents, what they reveal, and their power to overturn the understanding of a historical event or, at the very least, to complicate the consensus. Here he succeeded.

To his lasting credit, Gordon saved the documents and left a tangible historical record. He wrote down a previously untold version of the story and, with the foresight and dedication of his family, kept his book manuscript from the shredder or the flames. For a historian, these acts of preservation matter. Many of the persons who constituted his book's "cast of characters"—individuals who could have also created a credible narrative of these disputed events—chose not to do so. They remained silent, and their silence—a modern version of "I don't recall"—speaks volumes about their culpability in the skywalk disaster and its aftermath. This remains a story that needs the contributions of both living witnesses and interested historians.

For my research I have spoken to but a relative handful of persons, focused narrowly as I was on Gordon's failed book project. Those who graciously gave me their time offered considerable insight on the interesting man behind the book. This list of individuals, all of whom I heartily thank, includes those with whom I had meaningful conversations, chats, and email exchanges: John Aisenbrey, Arthur Brisbane, Paul Donnelly, Josephine Pickard (Gordon) Foote, John Garrity, Andrew Gordon, Tracy Gordon, Molly Riley, Ann Rittenberg, Barbara Stillman, Michael Waller, Kent Whittaker, and Richard Woods.

I also wish to thank Joyce Burner, National Archives at Kansas City, National Archives and Records Administration, who has since retired. Joyce took a 2015 call from Andy Gordon, who was trying to find a home for his father's papers, and she referred him to me. The early contact with the Gordon collection by Kara Evans, Kate Hill, and Joanna Marsh has already been chronicled in this book. Of this talented trio of Kansas City Public Library archivists, all there at the beginning, Joanna began the processing work on the collection, and her initial inventory of Gordon's papers proved invaluable to my research project.

Considering my long-standing historical research interests, many of my colleagues were baffled by my interest in this project. I was blessed, however, with several open-minded readers who touched the manuscript at various stages of development: Lori Cox-Paul, Anne Ducey, Chip Fleischer, Paul Hedren, James Leiker, Max McCoy, Dustin Paul, Kerin Tate, and Sam Zeff. All these individuals read the manuscript critically, understood the story I was attempting to tell, and gave me good advice, mostly taken. My conversations with Anne Ducey, a friend, graphic designer, and former KCPL colleague, helped me envision what the book should look like. Kerin Tate brought her considerable copyediting skills to bear on behalf of the University of Nebraska Press. First among equals, though, was Charles Rankin, whose advice and encouragement came in at a critical time when the book's fate was far from clear.

To Clark Whitehorn, acquisitions editor, and the talented staff of the University of Nebraska Press go my sincere thanks for accepting and shepherding this book to publication.

APPENDIX

Selections from the Deposition of Donald Joyce Hall

A former Hallmark Cards executive, quoted in *Forbes* magazine, described Donald Joyce Hall Sr. as "singularly unemotional for a man who sells sentiment."[1] Don Hall was also as tight-lipped as Robert Gordon was verbose. Hall's public utterances in the aftermath of his hotel disaster were minimal. One notable exception came early when he granted a local newspaper an interview the week after the collapse. Lawyers put a stop to that ever repeating itself. The second and much later interview, given to the *New York Times*, came after the settlement of the *Federal Skywalk Cases*.[2] Hall remained mute by choice in the interim, and understandably so, but that privilege was unavailable when he was formally deposed in late August to early September 1982.[3] Gordon pictured the scene a decade later in his "House of Cards" manuscript:

> Donald Hall was questioned at the old Howard Johnson's Motel in downtown Kansas City. Ponick picked it. I know not why. The room was drab and claustrophobic. The walls were chocolate brown, the floor was slanted, and the fluorescent lighting buzzed and hummed like a tilted pinball machine. Blending into the surroundings, Hall showed up wearing a dark brown suit and a nondescript Countess Mara tie. His suit was buttoned up tightly; not once do I remember

him unbuttoning it. His steel-rimmed glasses remained firmly in place. Hall sat at the head of the rectangular table, chain-smoking.[4]

Duke Ponick and Patrick McLarney, "two excellent and experienced lawyers" in Gordon's estimation, led the questioning, Ponick speaking in a distinctive "gravelly, Midwestern drawl."[5] Gordon followed up. His part of the lengthy deposition, less revealing than Ponick's, is not reproduced here.

After the transcripts of the deposition became available, the papers could have run the excerpt that follows, but they did not. It may have been considered prejudicial before the January 1983 court date, even ungentlemanly. Afterward it was irrelevant, although the public might have found the exchange edifying, especially Hall's lack of recall. But it never learned what the owner of the Hyatt Regency Kansas City really had to say about the skywalks collapse, neither from sworn testimony taken by deposition nor from testimony under oath on the stand, another reason Gordon could never let the matter go. Here, Don Hall can speak for himself.[6]

THE DEPOSITION

Monday, August 30, 1982: Examination by Duke Ponick Jr., of Ponick, Amick & Allen, Kansas City, for the Plaintiffs.

Duke Ponick: When did you learn that there were design problems with the structural steel in the atrium?

[Objection by John Townsend of Hughes, Hubbard & Reed, New York, New York, for the defendants Crown Center Redevelopment Corporation and Hallmark Cards Inc. No judge was present to make a ruling for or against an objection made during a deposition. That would have to wait to see if or when the same question was asked later at trial. Until then, this objection and the more than thirty that followed were still part of the record. They interrupt the flow of the question and answers—which might have been the original intent of the deponent's lawyer—and have been generally noted, but the specifics are edited from this excerpt.]

Donald Joyce Hall: I did not learn that there were structural problems in the atrium. I am unable to answer when, that there were structural problems in the atrium, and I am unable to answer when.

Ponick: You don't recall when you learned that there were structural problems in the steel in the atrium?

[Objection.]

Hall: I am afraid I don't understand that question.

Ponick: When did you first learn that there was a risk of danger from the structural steel in the atrium?

[Objection.]

Hall: To the structural steel? I don't think I have known of dangers inherent in the structural steel.

Ponick: When did you first learn that the atrium roof, or a portion thereof, collapsed of its own weight and fell four stories below?

[Objection.]

Hall: I learned of a collapse of a beam in the atrium and subsequent falling of a portion of the roof that was attached to that beam, some distance, I am not sure of how far, shortly after it occurred, and I believe that was in October of 1979.

Ponick: Did that event excite concern within Hallmark about the safety of the structural steel in the atrium?

Hall: That event excited management of Crown Center, and I was, as the person who at Hallmark learned of it, about the safety of that area and the adjacent areas.

Ponick: That included the skywalks?

Hall: The skywalks were not consciously discussed at that point.

Ponick: But your concern extended to all structural steel in the atrium, including the skywalks—

[Objection.]

Ponick: —fabricated of structural steel?

[Objection.]

Hall: The concern of Crown Center management and their reported concern to me, and my concern, had to do with the entire atrium area and more.

Ponick: All right. It would have necessarily included the skywalks?

[Objection.]

Hall: The concern regarding the skywalks was not expressed, but certainly they were within the total area.

Ponick: All right. As a matter of fact, you personally directed that inspection openings be placed at the ends of the skywalks for purposes of inspecting for potential future dangers or hazards associated with the structural steel?

[Objection.]

Hall: Having heard some reporting on the cause of the collapse of the beam in the atrium at a meeting with those people involved in both the installation and the reinspection of the area, I did express some feeling that—I asked the question, rather, could critical structural points be inspected in the future. As I recall, the architect said that if the engineer would indicate those critical points, that he would—that the architect would then be able to design windows to those places; some means of access and an ability to view those points, and so they could be inspected in the future.

Ponick: To your knowledge, were those inspection openings or access ports incorporated in the three skywalks so a safety inspection could be made?

[Objection.]

Hall: I cannot answer as to whether the engineer selected the skywalks as critical points of structure, nor whether they were afforded windows or viewing points.

Ponick: Is it your testimony you didn't know whether or not those inspection openings had been incorporated in the skywalks prior to the time that they collapsed?

Hall: It's my testimony that I did not know the critical points that were outlined by the engineer and did not know whether or not windows were supplied for that purpose, although it was reported to me at some later date that they were.

Ponick: Was that before or after the collapse of the skywalks?

Hall: I am not certain, but I believe my knowledge of the windows having been placed is something that I have heard or something someone has said since the collapse, but I am not certain of that.

Ponick: Assuming there were access openings and ports actually incorporated within the skywalks for safety inspections, as suggested by you, who, as between Crown Center and Hyatt, was supposed to have the responsibility to inspect the bridges?

[Objection.]

Hall: I cannot answer that the skywalks were, again, selected by the engineers as critical points, nor can I confirm that windows were available or abilities to view were made available. It would have been my assumption that some routine would have been arranged with the operator, some normal inspection, periodic inspection.

Ponick: If several inspection openings were provided in the bridges for a safety inspection, I think you have just said that some type of procedure should have been arranged with the operator; is that true?

[Objection.]

Ponick: What is the basis for your assumption that some routine safety inspection procedure would have been set up or provided with the operator?

Hall: Again, I cannot assume that there were windows for the same reasons on the bridge, nor that the bridge was selected as one of those critical areas by the engineer. It would seem only by assumption that the arrangement for inspection would have gone to the operator because, in fact, they would have had possession of the building at that juncture.

Ponick: Did you expect Crown Center or Hallmark employees to sit down with the operator and go over what those procedures would be?

Hall: I didn't define, I think in my own mind—exactly what I meant at that point, but those were—that was a course of action that I thought appropriate, having heard the comments from the engineers and the architects as to the ability to do such a thing. And I would have left it to Crown Center management to effect—

Ponick: With the operator?

Hall: I presume with the operator.

TUESDAY, AUGUST 31, 1982: EXAMINATION BY DUKE PONICK JR.

Ponick: On that date, August 1, 1977, the atrium of the new hotel was discussed, isn't that true?

Hall: On—yes, it's true.

Ponick: The atrium or the public space, as it is commonly referred to throughout these meetings, is that correct?

Hall: The atrium—or the public space/atrium, as it is referred to in these particular minutes at least.

Ponick: All right. You certainly understood by at least that date that the design for the hotel called for some bridges or skywalks through that atrium or public space?

Hall: Yes, according to these minutes, and through my recollection it was—at that time I was aware of bridges through the—this atrium space.

Ponick: Had you seen architectural representations of those skywalks or bridges before August 1, 1977?

Hall: I can't accurately answer that.

Ponick: All right. The atrium or public space was of particular interest to you, isn't that correct?

Hall: The atrium or public space was of interest to me, in that it was the most—the most public, the most apparent space of the hotel. Consequently, it would have substantial impression on a hotel guest, as to the appearance of the hotel.

Ponick: So you would have been concerned with the aesthetic appearance on that date of the atrium and the design elements within the atrium for the reason you have just stated.

Hall: On that date, at that meeting, I would have been interested generally in the atrium space, as a design, as the aesthetic design.

Ponick: And from an aesthetic design point, you wanted to make sure, for your part, that the atrium space and its elements, including the bridges, looked nice or had a pleasing, aesthetic appearance to the eye?

Hall: I would have had an interest on that date in the general atrium space being pleasant, having good aesthetic quality.

Ponick: Would that interest have extended to elements of the space, including the bridges?

Hall: I think it could have. I don't recall elements in discussion at that time.

Ponick: Well, let's see if this quote from that exhibit refreshes your recollection. "The bridges through the space"—the public space/atrium—"connecting the function block to the tower would be made as thin and as invisible as possible to not be distracting." Do you see that language in that exhibit, sir?

Hall: Yes, I do.

Ponick: Does that refresh your recollection that that was the design direction being pointed for the development and the design of those bridges?

Hall: I do not remember that design direction, and this sentence does not refresh my memory.

Ponick: Apart from that, was your personal taste in the matter that they be not distracting to the eye?

Hall: I can't recall an opinion on that any time before the collapse.

Ponick: If, on August 1, 1977, the architect had presented to you an architectural representation either in a drawing or a model or a photograph, showing those bridges being constructed of unfinished timber, would you have had the authority and power, as a Hallmark representative, to veto that on aesthetic grounds?

[Objection.]

Hall: I don't—I can't—I can't say whether I would have veto power or not because it's a power that I never exercised in regard to design of the hotel.

Ponick: Would you have at least spoken your mind on that subject, at that meeting, that you didn't want the bridges through the atrium space to be made of unfinished timber?

[Objection.]

Ponick: Do you refuse to answer that question, sir, on the advice of your lawyers, obviously?

Hall: With the advice of my lawyers, I refuse to answer it.

Ponick: Who present at the August 1, 1977, meeting can say to the architect, "I don't like your design for the public atrium space, and in particular I don't like your bridges, so go back to the drawing board?" Who had that power and authority on that date, of those in attendance?

[Objection.]

Hall: It would seem to me that anyone at that meeting could say I don't like any element that you have designed. But that group was constituted to give advice and counsel to the architects. I don't believe it would be the prerogative of anyone there, outside of the designers, to say it won't be done or it will be done.

Ponick: I'm not arguing with you, but I see a little bit of a contradiction of what you just told me. You are there to counsel and advise the architects on the design, and you are there for Hallmark and the ownership, the people who pay the bills, and you can't stop these architects from doing something you don't personally approve of?

[Objection.]

Ponick: I will withdraw that. Do you see my quandary here, Mr. Hall, that the man who really is the head hog of the whole organization can't say don't build or build something?

[Objection.]

Ponick: I just have a hard time understanding a person of your magnitude and substance at that meeting can't veto something, so my puzzlement is genuine.

Townsend: We will accept that your puzzlement is genuine and even stipulate so on the record.

Ponick: So I understand it correctly, sir, that as of that date, August 1, 1977, the architects could have designed those bridges of any material they saw fit, be it wood, plastic, rope, or steel?

[Objection.]

Hall: Within good building practices, and covered by the codes, they could have used, I presume, various materials. I wouldn't know what those materials were, and I don't know the answer to that directly.

Ponick: So it's your testimony that if you had been presented with a—

[Objection.]

Ponick: —for a swinging rope bridge, through the public atrium space, it would have been accepted on that basis?

[Objection.]

Hall: I will not answer that on the advice of my counsel.

Ponick: Did you ever make any site inspections of the hotel during its construction?

Hall: At various times during construction, I visited the construction site. The term "site inspection" would be a little more formal than my curiosity in seeing the status of construction at a given point.

Ponick: How many separate occasions did you visit the site of the Hyatt Regency Kansas City Hotel project before it was open for business on July 1, 1980?

Hall: I would have no very good guess on that topic.

Ponick: Did you ever go as a group, with the design review committee, for purposes of examining or inspecting or acquainting yourself with the progress of the construction?

Hall: I don't remember precisely, but it seems to me that there was a time or times when that group met at the site to review something particularly. I do recall, for example, looking at the color of the granite that was used on the exterior of the building on site, at sometime.

Ponick: Do you recall going to the site of the hotel for purposes of examining how the atrium was coming along?

Hall: I do not recall during the construction progress going to—excuse me, I'm going to have to ask that be repeated.

[Question repeated.]

Hall: During the design review stages of the construction of the Hyatt, I don't recall specifically going to the hotel site to see how the construction of the atrium specifically was coming along.

Ponick: Did you ever actually look to see whether or not the skywalks had been erected on any visit you made to the hotel for visual or other types of inspection?

Hall: I don't now recall any trip where I specifically was interested in whether the skywalks had been constructed.

Ponick: Did you ever see the skywalks after they had been fabricated and erected, but before they had sheetrock and concrete placed on them?

Hall: I don't recall.

Ponick: Did you ever walk across the skywalks at any time before the sheetrock or the concrete had been placed on them?

Hall: I don't recall doing so.

Ponick: When is the first time you became aware that a double rod had been used on the fourth level of the skywalks as a means of suspension?

Hall: I became aware of that design feature sometime after the collapse.

Ponick: Is that the collapse of the atrium or the collapse of the skywalks?

Hall: Sometime after the collapse of the skywalks in July of 1980.

Robert J. Sisk of Hughes, Hubbard & Reed for Crown Center Redevelopment Corporation and Hallmark Cards Inc.: '81.

Hall: '81. I'm sorry.

Ponick: How did you first learn that a double rod design or fabrication had been used on the fourth level skywalk?

Hall: I'm not sure; it may have been the *Kansas City Star*.

Ponick: After you learned that fact, did you talk with anyone within Hallmark or Crown Center about that subject of the double rodding?

Hall: I don't recall specific conversations about that particular point.

Ponick: Before the collapse of the skywalks, you knew that the skywalks were suspended by round metal rods; is that correct?

Hall: I was—I think by memory, I think I was aware that there—I know I was aware that there were rods, and I was aware that the skywalks were attached on either end.

Ponick: Were you aware that at one time eight-inch steel beams were proposed as a means of suspension for the skywalks rather than these inch-and-a-quarter rods?

[Objection.]

Thomas F. Fisher of Shughart, Thomson & Kilroy for PBNDML Architects: You mean columns, Duke, or beams?

Ponick: Columns.

Hall: I'm not aware of that.

Ponick: Is the only means of suspension that you have ever known about, for those skywalks, the inch-and-a-quarter rods, prior to the collapse?

Hall: Prior to the collapse, I was only aware of the fact that there were rods—I would not know the size—that there were suspending rods and that the skywalks attached at either end.

Ponick: Do you recall seeing models of the skywalks or bridges through the atrium space that would have been presented at the design review committee meetings?

Hall: I recall that I saw models of the Hyatt Hotel and the atrium space, and my recollection is that at least some of those models had some representations of skywalks.

Ponick: Do you recall when it was that the design decision was made to create a fourth level skywalk from the health club to the elevator or tower block?

Hall: I do not recall, nor have any knowledge of when that design decision was made.

Ponick: Do you recall being present at a meeting where that was discussed, namely, moving one of the third level bridges up to the fourth level, or a means of access between a redesigned health club and the north tower?

Hall: I do not recall that discussion as you have described it. I do recall that there was some—I do recall a discussion of the need for access between the hotel block and the function block to provide entry to the pool and the tennis area—health area.

Ponick: Do you recall before that time that there had been one bridge on the second level and two bridges on the third level?

Hall: I do not recall that.

Ponick: Did you ever offer any aesthetic or functional counsel or advice to the architects on the skywalks?

Hall: To the best of my knowledge, I did not offer aesthetic counsel or advice on the skywalks and do not recall any comments or advice regarding the functionality of the skywalks.

Ponick: Did you know that at one time before the rods were decided upon as the means of suspension for the skywalks that box beams were not part of the design for the bridges?

Hall: I do not recall knowledge of that.

Ponick: Do you recall that at one time the design presented to the design review committee for the skywalks was a six-and-a-half- or seven-foot-deep concrete beam . . .

[Objection.]

Ponick: . . . as the design member running north and south?

[Objection.]

Hall: I do not recall that.

Ponick: Do you recall, was the design of the skywalks always the same through the design period we have talked about?

[Objection.]

Hall: I cannot confirm that the design—that the design of the skywalks remained the same, but I remember no alternative design to the skywalks.

Ponick: You don't remember seeing a whole series of different designs for the skywalks or bridges?

Hall: I do not recall that.

Ponick: And don't recall discussing those various design changes at the design review meetings?

[Objection.]

Hall: I do not recall discussion of changes in those designs at the design review meeting.

Ponick: Did you ever walk on the skywalks before it collapsed?

Hall: Yes, many times.

Ponick: Was that before or after the hotel was open?

Hall: It was both before and after the hotel was opened.

Ponick: At any time did you notice anything unusual about the appearance of the skywalks, either before or after it opened?

Hall: I noticed nothing unusual about the appearance of the skywalks, either before or after.

Ponick: Were you aware of any design or construction problem with respect to the skywalks at any time before the hotel opened?

Hall: I don't recall being aware of any design problem with the skywalk, either before or—

Townsend: The question was before.

Hall: Before, before it opened.

Ponick: How about construction problems with the skywalks before the hotel was opened?

Hall: I don't recall hearing of any construction problems regarding the skywalks before the hotel was opened.

Ponick: We talked briefly yesterday about the atrium roof collapse. Do you recall that?

Hall: I recall a discussion of the atrium beam collapse.

Ponick: Did you go over and look at the damage after you were informed that there had been a collapse of some kind over there—

[Objection.]

Ponick: —at the hotel?

Hall: I thought we had covered this before, but, yes, I did, shortly after I had learned of that beam collapse, I did go to the site so that I could better visualize what had happened.

Ponick: Did you look up at the ceiling when you went there, the atrium ceiling, to see how big a hole was up there, following the atrium collapse, obviously?

Hall: Following the beam collapse in the atrium, I think I recall observing the amount of ceiling that had been attached to that beam, and which had fallen to the floor.

Ponick: There was approximately 2,700 square feet of roof that had fallen to the floor; isn't that correct?

Hall: I believe I have heard that there was 2,700 feet.

Ponick: Twenty-seven hundred square feet is about the size of a pretty good house, isn't it?

[Objection.]

Ponick: Maybe not your house, but a good average size house.

[Objection.]

Hall: I'm not a good judge of the size of a house.

Ponick: This room, I will tell you, we are sitting in right now is about 900 square feet. With that as a point of reference, do you recall that, when you looked up at the ceiling, you saw a hole that was about three times the size of this room, as a result of this beam collapsing in the atrium?

Hall: I'm sorry. Will you repeat that question?

[Objection.]

Ponick: Sir, do you remember how long after the atrium beam collapse it was before you went over to see the nature and extent of the damage?

Hall: I do not remember precisely. It seems to me it was within one to three days.

Ponick: Were you accompanied by anyone when you went over there?

Hall: I believe that I was, but I do not recall who was with me.

Ponick: Did you become aware after the atrium beam collapse that an inspection disclosed that the skywalks were pulling away from the walls on the north end?

[Objection.]

Hall: I do not recall specifically that I was aware of that.

Ponick: Were you specifically aware of any design or construction problems with respect to the skywalks after the atrium beam collapsed?

[Objection.]

Hall: Between the atrium beam collapse and the—prior to the date of the skywalk collapse, I do not recall being aware of any design or construction problems with the skywalks.

NOTES

ABBREVIATIONS

DTR	Daily time records (1981–83)
FSC	*Federal Skywalk Cases*
JM	Joanna Marsh
MVSC	Missouri Valley Special Collections
NARA	National Archives and Records Administration
RCGC	Robert C. Gordon Collection
REP	R. Eli Paul
RG	Robert Gordon
RG 1984 MS	Robert Gordon, "When They Didn't Care Enough," manuscript (1984)
RG 1995 MS	Robert Gordon, "House of Cards," manuscript (1995)
Star	*Kansas City Star*
Times	*Kansas City Times*
TRSL	Time records—skywalks litigation (1984–88)

PROLOGUE

1. (504 feet) Diana Dawson, "Up to Date in KC, and Getting Taller Too," *Kansas City Star* (hereafter cited as *Star*), December 19, 1984. Skies, on the forty-second floor, closed as a restaurant in 2011, when it was turned into a private lounge for hotel guests. Joyce Smith, "Restaurants to Close," *Star*, October 11, 2011.
2. ("funny") Dewayne Greer, Eldridge Construction foreman, and ("worried") Shorty Williamson, another Eldridge foreman, as quoted in Robert Gordon, "When They Didn't Care Enough" (unpublished manuscript, 1984), typescript, 174, Robert C. Gordon Collection (hereafter cited as RCGC), Missouri Valley Special Collections (hereafter cited as MVSC), Kansas City Public Library, Kansas City MO. This is an early draft of Gordon's book manuscript, a document discussed in detail in a later chapter.
3. Diane Stafford, "Hyatt Hotel Is $50 Million Investment in KC's Future," *Star*, June 29, 1980.

4. "The term 'skywalk' means the suspended pedestrian walkways situated above the main lobby of the Hyatt Regency Hotel, including all structural parts and sub-parts and including the skywalks which collapsed on July 17, 1981, and the skywalk which did not collapse, but which was later removed." "Plaintiff's First Request for Admissions," August 31, 1984, Moen L. Phillips v. Hallmark Cards, Inc., Case No. CV84-18306, Circuit Court, Jackson County MO, RCGC, MVSC, Kansas City Public Library, Kansas City MO.
5. Kevin Murphy, Rick Alm, and Carol Powers, *The Last Dance: The Skywalks Disaster and a City Changed* (Kansas City MO: Kansas City Star Books, 2011).
6. Andy Gordon to R. Eli Paul (hereafter cited as REP), notes of phone conversation, August 23, 2015, author's collection.
7. David Hayes, "Lawyers Criticize Choice of Counsel for Hyatt Suit," *Kansas City Times* (hereafter cited as *Times*), February 23, 1982; John T. Dauner, "Hyatt Judge Rejects Challenge to Law Firm," *Times*, May 19, 1982; articles found in "Compilation, Hyatt Regency Skywalk Collapse, 1981–2001," MVSC, Kansas City Public Library, Kansas City MO.
8. ("calamity") Ron Ostroff, "Lawyers Try to Alter Hyatt Suit: Class Attorneys Seek to Satisfy Appeals Court," *Times*, July 2, 1982; ("clear and striking") Ron Ostroff, "Quick Hyatt Wrap-Up Would Set Precedent," *Times*, May 14, 1982; ("litany") John T. Dauner and Richard A. Serrano, "Class Lawyer Seeks Sanction in Skywalk Case," *Times*, December 4, 1982.
9. Ron Ostroff, "Flurry of Activity Surrounds Hyatt Litigation: Defendants Deny All Charges of Unethical Conduct in Settlement Talks," *Times*, December 18, 1982; ("confusion") Ron Ostroff, "Hyatt Class Attorneys Reject Plan," *Times*, December 23, 1982; ("complex web") Thomas G. Watts, "Legal Ranks Are Divided in Hyatt Case: Proposal to Settle Out of Court Splits Class-Action Team," *Star*, May 3, 1982.
10. For more mentions of Robert Gordon in the "Compilation, Hyatt Regency Skywalk Collapse, 1981–2001," see John T. Dauner, "Lawyers in Hyatt Case Face Contempt Hearing," *Times*, March 6, 1982; John T. Dauner, "Hyatt Lawyers Deny That Court Was Misled," *Times*, May 29, 1982; "Judgment Sought in Hyatt Lawsuit," *Star*, June 9, 1982; Ron Ostroff, "Hyatt Class Dissolution Is Upheld," *Times*, July 13, 1982; John T. Dauner, "Lawyers Offer Plan for Disclosing Hyatt Papers," *Times*, August 26, 1982; John T. Dauner, "Lawyers Seek an Unprecedented Joint Trial in Hyatt Litigation," *Times*, October 16, 1982; Rick Alm, "Attorneys' Offer to Settle with Hyatt Corp. Fails," *Star*, November 19, 1982; John T. Dauner, "Lawyers Ask Ruling against Hyatt Defendants," *Times*, December 7, 1982; and Rick Alm, "Hallmark Offer Sparks Inquiries," *Star*, December 8, 1982. These articles, along with those previously cited, were gathered by John Horner, MVSC, for me.
11. Inventory items nos. 1225, 1262, 3780, RCGC, MVSC.

12. Since that conversation, Kemper left Kansas City for an appointment as the director of the Institute of Museum and Library Services, Washington DC.
13. REP, "Monthly Report, Missouri Valley Special Collections, October 2015," MVSC.

1. THE TAPES

1. Robert C. Gordon, "House of Cards: The Cover-Up Behind the Worst Structural Collapse in American History—Hallmark's Hyatt Regency Skywalks Disaster" (unpublished manuscript, 1995), typescript (hereafter cited as RG 1995 MS), 448–54, RCGC. This is the fullest, most complete iteration of Gordon's book manuscript, the version he intended for publication. For this study, I treated its contents as the "last word" on Gordon's thoughts on the events he chronicled. Daily time records (hereafter cited as DTR), October 5–6, 1982, RCGC; "Transcript of Proceedings," October 5, 1982, document no. 1,510, *Federal Skywalk Cases*, filed in the U.S. District Court of the Western District of Missouri, Record Group 21, National Archives at Kansas City, National Archives and Records Administration, Kansas City MO (hereafter cited as *FSC*, NARA). Many of the documents filed in the federal case were assigned numbers and appear in numerical order in the court docket. NARA archivists kept that original order in their arrangement.
2. RG 1995 MS, 277–83, 445, 451; "Plaintiffs' Consolidated First Requests for Production of Documents from Defendants," August 27, 1981, no. 136, *FSC*, NARA. The interrogatories generated by the plaintiffs went out the same day. "Plaintiffs' Consolidated First Set of Interrogatories to All Defendants," August 27, 1981, no. 137, *FSC*, NARA; "Motion Requesting Defendants' Liaison Counsel to Show Cause Why They Should Not Be Held in Contempt," March 4, 1982, no. 649, *FSC*, NARA; "Order," March 5, 1982, no. 651, *FSC*, NARA; ("obstructionist behavior") "Motion Requesting Sanctions Against Defendant Crown Center/Hallmark," September 24, 1982, no. 1,248, *FSC*, NARA. Hallmark replied. "Motion for Protective Order," October 5, 1982, no. 1,280, *FSC*, NARA.
3. RG 1995 MS, 447, 457; ("the whole bit") RG 1995 MS, 468, 541; "Plaintiffs' Reply to Defendant Crown Center/Hallmark's Suggestions in Opposition to Rule 37 Motion," October 11, 1982, no. 1,299, *FSC*, NARA; Joe Henderson, "Hallmark Accused of Hiding Tapes," *Star*, October 11, 1982; Richard A. Serrano, "Hallmark Releases Tapes of Hyatt Talks," *Times*, October 12, 1982.
4. RG 1995 MS, 451; "Plaintiffs' Reply to Defendant," no. 1,299, *FSC*, NARA; Henderson, "Hallmark Accused."
5. RG 1995 MS, 452; "Suggestions of Defendants Crown Center and Hallmark in Response to Plaintiffs' Reply, Suggestions on Their Rule 37 Motion," October 14, 1982, Exhibit B, affidavit of Pamela Wight Curran, no. 1,321, *FSC*, NARA. Another attached exhibit was Curran's memo-to-file, "My Understanding of Hyatt Atrium Collapse," her account

of a meeting with Chuck Page of Seiden & Page, consultants. Also attached was Judith Whittaker's sworn statement that she was "unaware" of any tape recorder. Copies of these three exhibits can be found in the RCGC.

6. ("interjected himself" and "lobotomized testimony") "Supplemental Points and Authorities," December 3, 1982, no. 1,554, *FSC*, NARA.
7. RG 1995 MS, 453, 458. To confirm Gordon's suspicion, John Campbell, a lawyer representing Seiden & Page, told Gordon that Whittaker had confided to him that she indeed "had known that tape recordings had been made and what was on them." Gordon could do nothing with this hearsay information, but Campbell intended to use it himself as leverage, if necessary, against Whittaker and Hallmark. RG 1995 MS, 528. In a later, gossipy interview of Gwen Caranchini, who with John Campbell represented Seiden & Page, the Kansas City lawyer confirmed to Gordon's satisfaction that Campbell "knows enuf to have Judy W. 'disbarred.'" Notes of Gwen Caranchini interview, n.d., RCGC. See also Robert Gordon (hereafter cited as RG) to Stephen S. Trott, Assistant Attorney General, Criminal Division, Department of Justice, Washington DC, December 30, 1985, RCGC, in which Campbell "tells me [Gordon] that when he came forward and informed Mr. [Robert B.] Schneider [assistant U.S. attorney and special prosecuting attorney for Jackson County, Kansas City MO] of specific instances of perjury by Hallmark and its Associate General Counsel (Mrs. Judith Whittaker), that his information was totally ignored by the U.S. Attorney."
8. Richard A. Serrano, "Hallmark Releases Tapes." Hallmark also released Pam Wight Curran's notes of the November 13, 1979, meeting at the press conference, and spokesmen said the company had nothing to hide; RG 1995 MS, 467, 474.
9. "Suggestions of Defendants," October 14, 1982, no. 1,321, *FSC*, NARA; RG 1995 MS, 477, 480.
10. "Supplemental Points and Authorities," no. 1,554, *FSC*, NARA; RG 1995 MS, 483.
11. DTR, October 22, 26, 29, 1982; RG 1995 MS, 500.
12. Knut Royce, "The Operators: Chicago's Pritzker Family and Kansas City's Hyatt," *Times*, March 8, 1982; Knut Royce, "The Financial Origins of the Pritzker Empire," *Times*, March 9, 1982; Knut Royce, "Haven in the Bahamas; Pritzkers' Foreign Trusts Caught IRS' Eye," *Times*, March 10, 1982.
13. *Times*, October 30, 1982.
14. Arthur S. Brisbane, "Joyce C. Hall: A Mortal Man in the Realm of Myth," *Times*, October 30, 1982.
15. RG 1995 MS, 500, 713–14; RG to Jim Hale, publisher and chairman of the board, *Kansas City Star* and *Times*, April 16, 1984, RCGC, which was a follow-up to a meeting Gordon had with James H. Hale, the newspaper publisher. Gordon referred cryptically to the story that did not run: "Hopefully, you will explain how one reconciles that policy of 'publish everything' with Mr. [Mike] Waller's explanation to us on Friday

[April 13] regarding his reason for not running the four-page Hallmark story which his own reporters had written."

16. RG 1995 MS, 530; ("just a passive investor") "Supplemental Points and Authorities," no. 1,554, *FSC*, NARA.
17. RG 1995 MS, 510, 521.
18. RG to Paul Wolff, November 2, 1982; RG to Arthur R. Miller, December 10, 1982, RCGC.
19. Little did Gordon's team know at the time, but the other side was in disarray. According to Gwen Caranchini, a lawyer for defendant Seiden & Page, the joint defense "never had a strategy" and "never time to formulate one." She decided that "it didn't matter what we did anyhow" because "we knew HMK [Hallmark] would pay anything to avoid trial." Notes of Gwen Caranchini interview, n.d., RCGC.
20. RG 1995 MS, 517; "Stipulation Concerning Access for the Tape Recordings of Two Meetings Held on November 12 and 13, 1979," November 18, 1982, no. 1,467, *FSC*, NARA; Harold N. Iselin of Hughes, Hubbard & Reed, New York NY, to Nancy F. Preiss of Williams & Connolly, November 19, 1982, correspondence, *FSC*, NARA, in which the two original tapes of the November 12 and 13, 1981, meetings "are delivered herewith," hand-delivered to the DC office. DTR, November 22, 1982, RCGC.
21. "Rule 37" refers to one party's failure of participating in "good faith" during the discovery process, going so far as depriving the other of that information during the course of litigation. Gordon first mentioned working on his Rule 37 motion on November 6. DTR, November 6, 1982, RCGC.
22. "Supplemental Points and Authorities," no. 1,554, *FSC*, NARA; DTR, November 24, December 3, 1982, RCGC.
23. The communication about Gordon's brief traveled from reporter Dauner to editor Robert L. "Bob" Samsote to Hallmark executive Johnson. RG 1995 MS, 558. Gordon noted four phone conversations with Dauner on that day. DTR, December 3, 1982, RCGC.
24. John T. Dauner and Richard A. Serrano, "Class Lawyer Seeks Sanctions in Skywalk Case; Judge Is Asked to Deny Hallmark, Crown Center a Trial Defense," *Times*, December 4, 1982; RG 1995 MS, 560–62.

2. MOLLY RILEY, A CLASS ACT

1. Molly Riley deposition, December 3, 1981, *FSC*, NARA. For drink prices, see Ginny Vineyard, Hyatt Regency Kansas City, to all departments, May 14, 1981, RCGC. Vineyard's memorandum also listed the price of mixed drinks at the first scheduled tea dance as $2. The reference to "seven lobby bars" came from "Defendant Hyatt Corporation's Answers to Plaintiffs' Consolidated First Set of Interrogatories to All Defendants," October 15, 1981, no. 294, *FSC*, NARA.

2. ("dance and visit") Riley deposition, FSC, NARA; Robert Gordon, "Molly Riley" (unpublished vignette, n.d.), 9 pp., RCGC; (lily white) Campbell Gibson and Kay Jung, "Historical Census Statistics on Population Totals by Race, 1790 to 1990, and by Hispanic Origin, 1970 to 1990, for Large Cities and Other Urban Places in the United States," under "Missouri—Earliest Census to 1990," *Population Division Working Paper No. 76* (Washington DC: U.S. Census Bureau, 2005), https://www.census.gov/library/working-papers/2005/demo/POP-twps0076.html; (button) "Defendant Hyatt Corporation's Answers," no. 294, FSC, NARA; ("place to be") Tom Edgerton, tea dancer, quoted in Mark Fraser, "Morgue Keeps Macabre Vigil as Tally of Dead Grows," *Times*, July 18, 1981. The dimensions of the atrium can be found in a National Bureau of Standards report, cited later.
3. "Strike Negotiators Called to Washington," *Times*, July 17, 1981; Mike McKenzie, "'Nothing to Do but React': First, You Can't Believe It's Happening; Then the Terror Begins," *Times*, July 18, 1981; Margie McKenzie, "Dear Mom: 'I Just Want to Cry and Cry,'" *Star*, July 19, 1981; McKenzie, "Royals' Pitcher Gnawed by Frustration," *Star*, July 19, 1981; Joe McGuff, "Horror Continues for Gale," *Star*, July 21, 1981; Laura Knickerbocker, "Hyatt Survivors, Rescue Workers Share Their Pain," *Times*, July 25, 1981.
4. "The Airport of the Future—Now! City Airport Dream Comes True," *Star*, October 15, 1972; "Tables: Top 20 U.S. Metropolitan Areas by Population, 1790–2010," Kansas City, 1960 and 1970, *Historical Metropolitan Populations of the United States*, https://www.peakbagger.com/pbgeog/histmetropop.aspx. An entire section of the paper was devoted to the new baseball stadium for the Kansas City Royals at the Truman Sports Complex. Royals Special Section, *Star*, April 8, 1973; Billy D. Wunsch, "Arrowhead Stadium: Birth of a New Generation of Football Facilities," *Midwest Architect* 1 (August 1972): 6–10; "R. Crosby Kemper, Sr. Memorial Arena," Jackson County MO, *National Register of Historic Places Registration Form*, National Park Service, U.S. Department of the Interior, Washington DC, https://mostateparks.com/sites/mostateparks/files/Kemper%20Arena.pdf; James L. Stratta, *Report of the Kemper Arena Roof Collapse of June 4, 1979, Kansas City, Missouri* (Menlo Park CA: Stratta, 1979).
5. "New Hyatt Regency," *Star*, July 2, 1980.
6. Ron Ostroff, "A Year Later, Hyatt Disaster a Tangle of Legalities," *Times*, July 17, 1982; Bill Norton, "Five Years Later: The Story of Mark Williams, Survivor," *Kansas City Star Magazine*, July 13, 1986.
7. Gordon, "Molly Riley," RCGC; Jacqueline S. Brooks, "Circumstances Forged Link That Bound Death Victims," *Times*, July 20, 1981; "In Memoriam: The 111 [at that time] Who Died in the Hyatt Tragedy," *Times*, July 25, 1981; Tim Weiner, "The Loss Remains; Last Person Saved from Hyatt Makes Painful Comeback," *Times*, January

18, 1982; Associated Press, "Hyatt Victims Tell Rescue Officials of Ordeal," *Times*, June 23, 1982.

8. Riley deposition, *FSC*, NARA. The fallen skywalks were "less than a foot" from her. The Steve Miller band was in the midst of its thirteenth song of that night's program, the Duke Ellington standard "Satin Doll." RG 1995 MS, 37.
9. Riley deposition, *FSC*, NARA.
10. ("small dollar amount injuries") RG 1995 MS, 131.
11. Riley deposition, *FSC*, NARA.
12. Riley deposition, *FSC*, NARA.
13. Riley deposition, *FSC*, NARA. Riley's house, which she owned, was at 2014 West Seventy-Fourth Street, Prairie Village KS, a decidedly middle-class suburb described today, somewhat derisively or enviously, as "Perfect Village." She and her son, Matthew, had only lived at this address since March 1981.
14. Riley deposition, *FSC*, NARA.
15. Biographical information on Whitaker comes from his LinkedIn page, https://www.linkedin.com/in/william-bill-whitaker-27a4342b; "Management Team Biographies," Flow Forward Medical Inc., http://www.flowforwardmedical.com/docs/flowforward-medical-management-team.pdf (site discontinued); and "William Whitaker, Co-Founder," on the "Management Team" page, Artio Medical, https://artiomedical.com/about/.
16. Riley deposition, *FSC*, NARA.
17. Gordon offered up a second, less plausible scenario for the moment when Whitaker put the notion of the class action in his head by stating it occurred the day of his meeting with Riley. RG 1995 MS, 125–26.
18. Gordon, "Molly Riley," RCGC.
19. Gordon, "Molly Riley," RCGC; Miriam Pepper, "A Lost Night Recalled Minute by Painful Minute; Moments Became Hours and Life Was Fleeting," *Star*, July 19, 1981.
20. Gordon, "Molly Riley," RCGC; "Gaye Young, No Condition," listing for St. Mary's Hospital, in "Partial List of Injured in Collapse," *Times*, July 18, 1981; "Gaye Young, Treated and Released from St. Mary's Hospital," in "The Injured; Fair, Good or Released after Treatment," *Star*, July 19, 1981.
21. Gordon had a phenomenal memory for the facts in his cases, plus he was an inveterate collector of newspaper clippings. The years after the Hallmark disaster resulted in an explosion of desiderata in his files, only a tiny portion of which found themselves cited in his own heavily annotated writings or in this work. The same collecting gene could be seen in his extensive assemblage of military memorabilia and personal library.
22. Ron Ostroff, "Lawyers Expecting a Rush of Lawsuits over Disaster; Firms Sued Also Will Take Legal Action to Determine Who Is to Blame," *Times*, July 20, 1981; (twenty-five

victims) James B. Stewart, "Wake of Disaster: Controversy Surrounds Payments to Plaintiffs in Hyatt Regency Case," *Wall Street Journal*, July 3, 1984.

23. ("being a lawyer") Ron Ostroff, "Survivors Face Onslaught of Questions," *Times*, July 22, 1981; James C. Fitzpatrick, "Lawmakers Urge U.S. Probe in Disaster," *Times*, July 25, 1981. See also Ron Ostroff, "Aftermath of Tragedy; Lawyers Investigating Ethics Complaints," *Times*, July 29, 1981.
24. Arthur S. Brisbane, "Disaster's Unhappy Aftermath," *Times*, July 24, 1981.
25. "Victims' Families File Suits," *Star*, July 24, 1981. See also "Band Member's Family Files $1 Million Lawsuit," *Star*, July 23, 1981.
26. ("my involvement") Robert Gordon, "When They Didn't Care Enough," manuscript, 1984, iii, RCGC. Regarding the conflicts of interest and ethical dilemmas that many Kansas City lawyers faced, see Ron Ostroff, "Lawyers Are Forced to Decide Which Side to Take in Hyatt Case," *Times*, July 23, 1981; Ron Ostroff, "Jury Awards $15 Million to Skywalks Victim," *Times*, September 22, 1983.
27. Ron Ostroff, "Lawyers Expecting a Rush," July 20, 1981; John M. Wylie II, "Disaster Suits: Putting Dollar Signs on Lost Lives," *Star*, July 21, 1981.
28. RG 1995 MS, 147–48; "William Finch Hall," obituary, *Star*, October 14, 1971; "W. F. Hall Rites," *Times*, October 15, 1971; Josephine Gordon to Adele Hall, July 18, 1981, RCGC; Adele Hall to Josephine and Robert Gordon, August 17, 1981, RCGC.
29. Editorial staff, "The Halls and Their Crown Center Dream," *Star*, July 21, 1981.
30. Diane Stafford, "Grief Lies Heavily on Family and Firm with a Vision," *Star*, July 19, 1981.
31. John T. Dauner, "Donald Hall Hopes to Leave Sorrow Behind; Haggard Hallmark Chief Vows to Reopen the Hyatt as Soon as Possible," *Times*, July 20, 1981.
32. John A. Dvorak, "Questions Loom as Hotel Designers Search for Cause," *Times*, July 20, 1981. Berkebile was a principal in PBNDML, the Kansas City consortium of architectural firms that executed the Hyatt design. Duncan was an in-house Hallmark architect.
33. Thomas G. Watts and Rick Alm, "Debris Moved as City Presses Probe; Rubble from Hyatt Hauled to Warehouse," *Star*, July 22, 1981. The spokesman for Crown Center was Jim Dawson.
34. Bill Turque and John M. Wylie II, "Road to Settlement of Lawsuits, Insurance Claims Will Be Long," *Star*, July 20, 1981.
35. ("early morning rebuff") Tim Weiner, "Saddened Mayor Expresses Anger in Wake of Hyatt Tragedy," *Times*, July 24, 1981; ("third-floor walkway") Diane Stafford, "Last Skywalk Removed; Critics Cry Foul," *Star*, July 23, 1981.
36. Watts and Alm, "Debris Moved." See also James C. Fitzpatrick, "Berkley Is Warned against Naming Citizens Panel; Sixth Lawsuit to Be Filed Names 12 Defendants, Including Kansas City," *Times*, July 23, 1981. The debris was moved to a Crown Center warehouse at Twenty-Eighth and McGee, the former site of the Major

Cadillac dealership. Regarding the National Bureau of Standards, "The engineers, Edward O. Pfrang and Richard Marshall, arrived in town Tuesday but returned to Washington on Wednesday without viewing the debris, which was moved from the hotel early Wednesday. . . . Pfrang said that he and Marshall viewed the hotel lobby but that their inspection proved to be only 'marginally valuable.'" Stafford, "Last Skywalk Removed"; Weiner, "Saddened Mayor Expresses Anger"; ("public confidence") Stafford, "Last Skywalk Removed."

37. James C. Fitzpatrick, "Survivors Sue Hyatt, Crown Center Firm," *Times*, July 21, 1981; Fitzpatrick, "Berkley Is Warned Against Naming."
38. RG 1995 MS, 95–96, 108, 114. Gordon's likely source for Kipp's presence was John Kreamer, who was also there. Kreamer was a Kansas City lawyer, civic leader, and personal friend of Don and Adele Hall. John H. Kreamer and RG, notes of meeting, April 21, 1987, RCGC.
39. ("secure location") Watts and Alm, "Debris Moved"; ("unannounced removal") Stafford, "Last Skywalk Removed." The plaintiffs' lawyers who were quoted included Max Foust, Lynn Johnson, and Preston Williams, the father of Hyatt survivor Mark Williams.
40. Editorial board, "To Regain Public Trust," *Times*, July 24, 1981.
41. Fitzpatrick, "Lawmakers Urge U.S. Probe." Circuit Judge Keith Bondurant signed the court order. Personal injury lawyer Max Foust, described by Robert Gordon as "tobacco-chewing, tough-talking," filed the first post-collapse lawsuit. RG 1995 MS, 92.
42. Michael Yablonski and John A. Dvorak, "Collapse Baffles Building Code, Safety Officials," *Times*, July 18, 1981. "OSHA conducted a four-day investigation of the building site after the October 1979 accident that killed eighteen-year-old iron worker Louis Paul Nold Jr., of Agency, Mo." See also Thomas G. Watts, "Cause of Collapse Awaits Unfolding of Investigations," *Star*, July 19, 1981.
43. John Carroll, John A. Dvorak, David Hayes, Knut Royce, Richard A. Serrano, Tim Weiner, and Michael Yablonski, "Hotel Lobby Roof Fell during Construction; '79 Damage Documented by OSHA," *Times*, July 23, 1981. For a same-day follow-up to this story, which included a comment from Vernon Strahm of OSHA, see Rick Alm, Roy Wenzl, and John M. Wylie II, "Public Works Chief Did Not Know Extent of 1979 Collapse," *Star*, July 23, 1981. For a comment by Mayor Richard L. Berkley that sidestepped the issue of the 1979 atrium roof collapse, see Weiner, "Saddened Mayor Expresses Anger."
44. "Combined Flaws May Have Led to Collapse; Findings Add Up in Hotel Disaster," *Times*, July 22, 1981. For the supporting opinion of Wayne Lischka, another structural engineer doing consulting work for the newspaper, see Thomas G. Watts and Rick Alm, "Collapse Not Due to Load, Engineer Says," *Star*, July 20, 1981.
45. Carroll et al., "Hotel Lobby Roof Fell."

46. ("high ideals") Editorial staff, "Halls and Their Crown Center Dream"; ("our leading citizen") Weiner, "Saddened Mayor Expresses Anger."
47. Oscar Wilde, *The Importance of Being Earnest* (1895).

3. ROBERT CHARLES "BOBBY" GORDON

1. William P. Whitaker and RG to Molly Riley, July 24, 1981, RCGC; Ron Ostroff, "Lawsuit Seeks to Consolidate Hyatt Claims," *Times*, July 31, 1981.
2. Molly Riley deposition, December 3, 1981, *FSC*, NARA. The year of Riley's birth comes from MyLife, https://www.mylife.com/mary-tomc/e642662164698.
3. Calvin Trillin, *Messages from My Father* (New York: Farrar, Strauss and Giroux, 1996), 53. All these distinguished alumni were mentioned in Edward T. Matheny Jr., *The Rise and Fall of Excellence: The Story of Southwest High School, R.I.P.* (Leawood KS: Leathers Publishing, 2000). Robert Gordon, "Jamboree Diary," July 10–28, 1953, National Jamboree, Boy Scouts of America, Irvine Ranch CA, RCGC; Ellen Bell, "Boy Scout Jamboree on the Irvine Ranch Was First in the West," *Orange County Register* (Anaheim CA), July 24, 2013, https://www.ocregister.com/2013/07/24/boy-scout-jamboree-on-the-irvine-ranch-was-first-in-the-west/; Andrew P. "Andy" Gordon to REP, notes of personal conversation, May 21, 2018, author's collection.
4. "Application of Robert C. Gordon for Allowance of Attorney's Fees and Out of Pocket Expense Reimbursement," March 31, 1983, no. 2,084, *FSC*, NARA. This document was filed *in camera* and remains closed. Fortunately, several drafts exist in the Gordon collection. "History of Boalt Hall," *Berkeley Law*, https://www.law.berkeley.edu/about-us/history/the-school-name/ (page discontinued). Boalt Hall has since been renamed. Gretchen Kell, "UC Berkeley Removes Racist John Boalt's Name from Law School," *Berkeley News*, January 30, 2020, https://news.berkeley.edu/2020/01/30/boalt-hall-denamed/.
5. RG to Walter A. Haas Jr., chairman of the board, Levi Strauss and Company, San Francisco CA, June 17, 1981, RCGC; "News of Kansas City Industries," *The Kansas Citian: A Journal Issued in Behalf of the Business Interests of Kansas City by the Commercial Club of Kansas City* 2 (April 1913): 69; certificate of death for Hyman Naman, April 15, 1951, Division of Health of Missouri, state file no. 12720, https://www.sos.mo.gov/images/archives/deathcerts/1951/1951_00012717.PDF.
6. "M. C. Gordon," obituary, *Star*, March 14, 1984; Richard H. "Dick" Woods Jr. to REP, notes of phone conversation, May 22, 2018, author's collection; Josephine "Josie" Pickard (Gordon) Foote to REP, notes of personal conversation, December 28, 2018, author's collection; RG 1995 MS, 125. Gordon's mother lived until 1992. "Lillian Gordon," obituary, *Star*, April 23, 1992.
7. "Application of Gordon for Attorney's Fees," RCGC; RG 1995 MS, 126, 135.
8. Pickard-Gordon engagement announcement, *The Independent: Kansas City's Weekly Journal of Society* 70 (May 3, 1969): 1; Pickard-Gordon engagement announcement,

Star, May 4, 1969; Pickard-Gordon wedding at St. Paul's Episcopal Church, Kansas City MO, June 28, 1969, *The Independent* 70 (August 23, 1969): 4; "Weddings: Pickard-Gordon," *Star*, June 29, 1969; birth announcement for Tracy Gordon, *The Independent* 72 (April 17, 1971): 4; Marilyn Spencer, "Young Sophisticates at Ease," *The Independent* 73 (June 3, 1972): 4; "In the Garden," *Star*, June 5, 1972. Dr. and Mrs. Nicholas S. Pickard, Josie's parents, donated Pissarro's oil painting *Wooded Landscape at L'Hermitage, Pontoise* (1879) to the Nelson-Atkins Museum of Art, object no. F84-90, https://art.nelson-atkins.org/objects/18273/wooded-landscape-at-lhermitage-pontoise;jsessionid=B71B156736DFD8E6520795D743920C9C?ctx=88b6caff-262e-4d08-82e1-f4c9e1d615da&idx=8.

9. Molly Riley deposition, December 3, 1981. Riley's wages from St. Joseph's Hospital, Kansas City MO, from 1979 to the time of her deposition were "at least $8.77 an hour." Her take-home pay was an estimated $1,080 per month. Information on 2014 West Seventy-Fourth Street, Prairie Village KS, came from Zillow, https://www.zillow.com/homedetails/2014-W-74th-St-Prairie-Village-ks-66208/75528556_zpid/.
10. Information on 2625 Verona Road, Mission Hills KS, came from Zillow, https://www.zillow.com/homedetails/2625-Verona-Rd-Mission-Hills-ks-66208/75594203_zpid/. The former Gordon home sold in 2013 for $2.5 million. ("basset hounds") RG to "Bob" [Robert Byrne?], November 27, 1984, RCGC; (nanny) Elyse W. Allison, "They're Happy Stepping Into Mom's Shoes," *Star*, May 13, 1979, in which the nanny's name was given as Edna Luman; "Cook's Tour," *Star*, May 6, 1980; "The Annual Vanderslice Kitchen Tour and Luncheon," flyer, May 14, 1980, RCGC; "Tours: Leading Us down Garden Paths for Fifty Years," *The Independent* 81 (May 17, 1980): 9; "Fiftieth Annual Wellesley Garden Tour," flyer, May 20, 1980, RCGC; Ray Morgan, "About Town: Wellesley Tour of Gardens Is 50," *Times*, May 19, 1980; (intellectual conversation) Andy Gordon to REP, May 21, 2018; (heard the news) RG 1995 MS, 89–90.
11. ("best dad ever") Foote to REP, December 28, 2018; Hallmark Contemporary Cards, no. 75KB 936-7, Hallmark Cards Inc., RCGC; (pencils) John Garrity to REP and Joanna Marsh (hereafter cited as JM), notes of personal conversation, August 16, 2016, author's collection.
12. ("early foxhole") George H. Gurley Jr., "Behind the Lines: Hyatt Case Obsessing Attorney," *Times*, September 30, 1986; Woods to REP, May 22, 2018; RG 1995 MS, 172; Lea Ann Alexander, manager, Military Collectors Guild Ltd., St. Louis MO, to RG, August 16, 1983, RCGC; ("walking outdoors") Barbara Stillman and REP, notes of personal conversation, July 25, 2016, author's collection; ("Banana Republic") "Fancy Fakes: Midsummer Night's Frabjous Finery," *Star*, July 17, 1983.
13. "Last Will and Testament of Robert C. Gordon," January 19, 1973, RCGC.
14. Woods to REP, May 22, 2018.
15. Gordon Lightfoot, "Don Quixote," 1972.
16. RG to Don Fortune, KCMO–Channel 5, Fairway KS, September 1, 1983, RCGC.

17. Foote to REP, December 28, 2018; RG 1995 MS, 4.
18. Evan S. Connell Jr., *Mr. Bridge* (New York: Knopf, 1969).
19. "Your Old Man" [RG], Berkeley CA, to Tracy and Andrew [Gordon], November 22, 1980, RCGC; "Address at the University of California at Berkeley, Memorial Stadium, March 23, 1962," Speeches, John F. Kennedy Presidential Library Museum, https://www.jfklibrary.org/archives/other-resources/john-f-kennedy-speeches/university-of-california-berkeley-19620323.
20. RG to Tracy and Andrew, November 22, 1980. The Rebar case referred to *Rebar Anti-Trust Litigation*, in which Gordon felt he had overcome great odds to achieve a victory. In his writings he always expressed an unabashed affinity for the underdog.
21. RG, "Bircher Threat," *Star*, July 17, 1964, reprinted in the *St. Louis (MO) Post-Dispatch* as "That's Extremism: Letter to the *Kansas City Star*," n.d., RCGC.
22. RG, "Some Views on the Four-Letter Word Controversy," *Kansas City Bar Journal* 40 (August 1965): 23. For background on the University of California student unrest during the 1964–65 school year, see David Lance Goines, *The Free Speech Movement: Coming of Age in the 1960s* (Berkeley CA: Ten Speed Press, 1993). Gordon expressed similar views in another editorial, "College Discontent Must Be Openly Aired," *Kansas City Jewish Chronicle*, July 2, 1965, where he was identified as a University of California student and the son of Mr. and Mrs. M. C. Gordon.
23. RG, "Power Problem" (honors thesis, Department of Political Science, University of California, Berkeley, 1963), 17, RCGC. This twenty-nine-page document might well be only the introduction to a larger work.
24. Paul Donnelly to REP, notes of personal conversation, August 10, 2018, author's collection. Donnelly, a longtime member of the Kansas City bar, served in the same capacity as a clerk to Judge Becker but years after the Gordon episode.
25. ("dogged") Lanus, "Hyatt Notebook, Part II," 41; ("combative") Andy Gordon to REP, May 21, 2018; ("irrational") Edward J. Essay Jr. of Essay, Wolf & Longan, Kansas City MO, to RG, May 8, 1986, RCGC; ("reckless") Robert J. Sisk of Hughes, Hubbard & Reed, New York NY, to RG, March 23, 1988, RCGC; ("an acquired taste") Kent Whittaker to REP and JM, notes of personal conversation, June 15, 2016, author's collection.
26. John C. Aisenbrey, Stinson LLP, Kansas City MO, to REP, notes of phone conversation, August 13, 2018; RG, "Lunch conversation with John Aisenbrey and Heather Woodson (Attorneys from Stinson, Mag & Fizzell) at Nabil's on May 5, 1988, while they read part of my book and subsequent meeting with John only at the Carriage Club following the hearing on my charitable contribution recommendation to Judge Bartlett," memo-to-file, RCGC. Aisenbrey said in 2018 that he made sure he always had another counsel (Woodson, in this case) with him when he met Gordon about the manuscript.

27. For the most obvious and public example, see Gurley, "Behind the Lines: Hyatt Case Obsessing Attorney." A person who had worked with Gordon observed that this article was "as good a thumbnail portrait of you that could be written without a single mention of Hallmark." "Bob" [Robert Byrne] to "Bob" [RG], October 10, 1986, RCGC. A newspaperman acquainted with Gordon used the term "fanatically obsessed." Arthur S. "Art" Brisbane to REP and JM, notes of phone conversation, July 22, 2016, author's collection.
28. Victims of this "exhaustion" range from Gordon's first representative in the publishing world to archivist Joanna Marsh, MVSC, who meticulously went through and made a preliminary inventory of his papers. Knox Burger, Knox Burger Associates Ltd., Literary Agency, New York NY, to RG, February 16, 1985, RCGC; ("antipathy") RG to "Bob" [Robert Byrne?], November 27, 1984, RCGC.
29. RG to "Mr. Winger," Winger Sports Ltd., North St. Paul MN, June 14, 1984, RCGC.
30. *Peanuts* comic strip clipping, n.d., RCGC; Foote to REP, December 28, 2018.
31. Richard A. Serrano, *Times*, to RG, March 28, 1983, RCGC; ("poring") David Hayes, *Times*, to RG, March 30, 1983, RCGC.
32. Note, n.d., RCGC.
33. Andy Gordon to RG, on his eighth birthday, April 12, 1981, RCGC.
34. Kent Granger to RG, n.d., RCGC.
35. RG 1995 MS, 349.
36. "Revised Stipulation Governing the Establishment and Operation of a Document Depository," October 9, 1981, no. 283, *FSC*, NARA. The depository was located in the Thomas Corrigan Building, 1828 Walnut Street, Suite 630, Kansas City, Missouri, just a few blocks away from both the Hyatt Regency and the headquarters of the newspaper. "Order," September 2, 1983, no. 2,210, *FSC*, NARA, which moved the document depository to another location and discontinued the services of a full-time custodian.
37. RG 1995 MS, 174–75; Robert Caro, *Working: Researching, Interviewing, Writing* (New York: Alfred A. Knopf, 2019), 11.
38. RG 1995 MS, 175, 549. This type of research was not merely serendipitous. The plaintiffs prepared uniform and detailed procedures for the identification and review of "meaningful" documents. Lawyers and paralegals had their eyes open for documents relating to the atrium collapse, the design and building of the skywalks, cost cutting during the project, general problems with the hotel, inspection reports of any kind, and ties between Crown Center Redevelopment Corporation and its parent, Hallmark. "Skywalk Litigation Document Procedures Manual," 8 pp., n.d., RCGC.
39. (seersucker) Lanus, "Hyatt Notebook, Part II," 41. Gordon described himself as "hopelessly unfashionable." RG 1995 MS, 420.

40. As Don Quixote said to his companion before setting off on a great exploit, "For there you see, friend Sancho Panza, thirty or more enormous giants with whom I intend to do battle." Miguel de Cervantes, *Don Quixote*, translation by Edith Grossman (New York: Ecco, 2003), 58.
41. Frederick J. Esposito, "The Friday Five: Make the Timekeeping Honor Roll," *Attorney at Work*, June 14, 2013, https://www.attorneyatwork.com/make-the-timekeeping-honor-roll/; Sam Glover, "How to Keep Track of Your Time," *Lawyerist*, September 1, 2017, https://lawyerist.com/keep-track-time/; Sally Kane, "How to Effectively Bill Time as a Lawyer: Legal Billing Guidelines for Attorney Billable Hours," *The Balance Careers*, January 8, 2019, https://www.thebalancecareers.com/how-to-effectively-bill-time-2164694.
42. "Daily Time Records, December 5, 1981–January 31, 1983, to be filed *in camera* in the United States District Court for the Western District of Missouri, Western Division," RCGC (hereafter cited as DTR). The original document resides at the National Archives and Records Administration in the records of the *Federal Skywalk Cases* but was filed discreetly as a federal court document *in camera* and remains closed to researchers.
43. DTR, February 22, 1982, for the number of hours worked (eleven) on Gordon's own birthday.
44. "Application of Robert C. Gordon for Allowance of Attorney's Fees and Out of Pocket Expense Reimbursement," March 31, 1983, no. 2,084, *FSC*, NARA; also found in RCGC.

4. ONE IN A HUNDRED LAWSUITS

1. "Application of Gordon for Attorney's Fees," RCGC.
2. RG 1995 MS, 147.
3. ("best evidence") RG 1995 MS, 250; ("just and proper") "Application of Gordon for Attorney's Fees," RCGC.
4. "Molly Riley, et al., Plaintiff, v. Crown Center Redevelopment Corporation, Hallmark Cards, Inc., Hyatt Corporation, Hyatt Hotels Corporation, Patty Berkebile Nelson Duncan Monroe LeFebvre Architects Planners, Incorporated, Patty Berkebile Nelson and Associates Architects, Inc., Duncan Architects, Inc., Monroe and LeFebvre Architects, Inc., Eldridge & Son Construction Co., Inc., Gillum-Colaco, Smith & Boucher, Inc., Concordia Project Management, Limited, and Havens Steel Co., Defendants," September 1, 1981, *in re* Federal Skywalk Cases, Class Action Jury Trial Demanded, No. 81-0753-CV-W-3, *FSC*, NARA; also found in RCGC (hereafter cited as "Riley complaint").
5. Scott O. Wright and Larry M. Schumaker, *Never in Doubt: Memoirs of an Uncommon Judge* (Kansas City MO: Kansas City Star Books, 2007), 196.
6. William Whitaker time records, July 30, August 4, 5, 18, 26, 28, 1981, RCGC.
7. Whitaker time records, July 26, August 3, 1981, RCGC.

8. Gordon 1995 MS, 126; James B. Stewart, "Wake of Disaster: Controversy Surrounds Payments to Plaintiffs in Hyatt Regency Case," *Wall Street Journal*, July 3, 1984.
9. "Arthur Miller, Renowned Legal Scholar and Commentator, Named NYU University Professor," press release, New York University, New York NY, May 14, 2007, https://www.nyu.edu/about/news-publications/news/2007/may/arthur_miller_renowned_legal.html.
10. ("wrote the book") Wright and Schumaker, *Never in Doubt*, 197; Charles Alan Wright, Arthur Rafael Miller, and Edward H. Cooper, *Federal Practice and Procedure* (St. Paul MN: Thomson/West, 1969); RG 1995 MS, 132; "Application of Gordon for Attorney's Fees," RCGC.
11. RG 1995 MS, 133; "Application of Gordon for Attorney's Fees," RCGC.
12. RG 1995 MS, 144.
13. *Sachem 1959*, Southwest High School, Kansas City MO, vol. 34: 36–37, 133, 144–45, 162–63, Missouri Valley Special Collections, https://kchistory.org/islandora/object/kchistory%3A128143; "Welcome to Missouri Boys State," https://www.moboysstate.org/.
14. Jeffrey D. Mason, "The Man Who Came to Dinner" (1939), in *The Cambridge Guide to American Theatre*, ed. Don B. Wilmeth and Leonard Jacobs (New York: Cambridge University Press, 2007), 422.
15. "Paul Martin Wolff, Senior Counsel," Williams & Connolly LLP, Washington DC, https://www.wc.com/Attorneys/Paul-Martin-Wolff; Kim Eisler, *Masters of the Game: Inside the World's Most Powerful Law Firm* (New York: St. Martin's Press, 2010), 164–66.
16. ("ultimate conclusion") Eisler, *Masters of the Game*, 35; Robert Pack, *Edward Bennett Williams for the Defense* (New York: Harper & Row, Publishers, 1983), 363; ("consummate insider") "Famed Trial Lawyer Edward Bennett Williams, Who Defended Clients . . . ," obituary, *United Press International Archives*, August 13, 1988, https://www.upi.com/Archives/1988/08/13/Famed-trial-lawyer-Edward-Bennett-Williams-who-defended-clients/2151587448000/; Albin Krebs, "Edward Bennett Williams, Trial Lawyer, Dead at 68; A Brilliant 'Superlawyer,'" *New York Times*, August 15, 1988; ("hottest trial firm") Evan Thomas, *The Man to See: Edward Bennett Williams, Ultimate Insider; Legendary Trial Lawyer* (New York: Simon & Schuster, 1991), 306; ("tornado") "Edward Bennett Williams, 'Contest Living' Exponent," *Associated Press Archive*, August 13, 1988, https://apnews.com/e3289f818a43f3d4e6ededa58f3f5d4b.
17. Stephen Labaton, "Irving Younger, Lawyer, 55, Dies; Judge, Law Professor and Author," *New York Times*, March 15, 1988; Irving Younger and Michael Goldsmith, *Principles of Evidence* (Minneapolis MN: National Practice Institute, 1984); a seventh edition of this classic appeared in 2019. More than thirty years after its recording, Younger's lecture (maybe better described as a performance), "The Ten Commandments of Cross-Examination," can be found on YouTube, https://www.youtube.com/watch?v=dBP2if0l-a8.

18. RG 1995 MS, 152. For the Welch reaction, see Wright and Schumaker, *Never in Doubt*, 197. (flamboyant) Thomas, *The Man to See*, 439, who had nothing good to say about Younger in the scant pages he devoted to him in the Williams biography.
19. RG 1995 MS, 146–47, 250–51.
20. Whitaker time records, July 28, August 3, 4, 13, 17, 20, 24, 25, 27, 31, 1981, RCGC; ("already decided") "Application of Gordon for Attorney's Fees," RCGC.
21. RG 1995 MS, 144–46, 149, 160, 169; Riley complaint, *FSC*, NARA. The complaint was signed by William P. Whitaker, John Anderson Jr., and Kenton C. Granger for Anderson, Granger, Nagels, Lastelic & [Robert] Gordon, chartered; and by Irving Younger and Paul Martin Wolff for Williams & Connolly. Ron Ostroff, "Hyatt Sues for Answers to Insurance Disputes," *Times*, October 10, 1981.

5. HALLMARK'S KANSAS CITY

1. Richard A. Serrano, "Doors Open at Hyatt after Panel Calls It Safe," *Times*, October 2, 1981; Richard A. Serrano and Mark Fraser, "Roof Truss Concerns Hyatt Panel; Members Seek Hotel Owners' Reassurance," *Times*, October 1, 1981; ("un-Hallmark things") Paul Gigot, "Kansas City Hotel Disaster Breeds Suspicions about Hallmark Family," *Wall Street Journal*, August 6, 1981.
2. A perfectly timed look at Kansas City's first century was Henry C. Haskell Jr. and Richard B. Fowler's *City of the Future: A Narrative History of Kansas City, 1850–1950* (Kansas City MO: Frank Glenn, 1950).
3. "Story to the Nation," *Star*, June 3, 1950; ("stronger civic conscience") RG 1995 MS, 148.
4. RG 1995 MS, 3.
5. Kansas City's population woes, as enumerated in the 1980 U.S. Census, are examined in James R. Shortridge, *Kansas City and How It Grew, 1822–2011* (Lawrence: University Press of Kansas, 2012), 103, 150.
6. Joyce C. Hall with Curtiss Anderson, *When You Care Enough* (Kansas City MO: Hallmark Cards, 1979), 164.
7. "Crown Center Historic District," Jackson County MO, *National Register for Historic Properties Registration Form*, National Park Service, U.S. Department of the Interior, Washington DC, https://mostateparks.com/sites/mostateparks/files/Crown-Center-Historic-District.pdf; Robert A. Kipp, "Crown Center: An Emerging Vision for Urban Development," April 20, 1995, Charles N. Kimball Lecture Series, Western Historical Manuscript Collection, Kansas City MO, 10; Hall and Anderson, *When You Care Enough*, 126; ("agent of change" and "85 acres of blight") Patrick Regan, *Hallmark: A Century of Caring* (Kansas City MO: Andrews McMeel Publishing, 2010), 164, 178.
8. Shortridge, *Kansas City and How It Grew*, 130.
9. Shortridge, *Kansas City and How It Grew*, 133, 135.
10. Shortridge, *Kansas City and How It Grew*, 116, 141, 142.

11. Kevin Fox Gotham, *Race, Real Estate, and Uneven Development: The Kansas City Experience, 1900–2000* (Albany: State University of New York Press, 2002), 101.
12. Joe Louis Mattox, "'Horror at the Hyatt': A Disaster Movie in Real Life," *The Call* (Kansas City MO), July 24–30, 1981. *The Call* was published weekly. Mattox was named after Joe Louis, the great heavyweight boxer, and his name usually appeared elsewhere as "Joelouis." For years, historian Mattox was a fixture in the local history and library communities, where I often had the occasion to speak with him (without realizing his Hyatt disaster connection). Knowing of his intense curiosity and strong will, I think it fits perfectly with his character that Mattox would go to the hotel to learn for himself about the racial situation with Hallmark. See also Glenn E. Rice and Matt Campbell, "KC's Joelouis Mattox Remembered for His Passion for Local History, Teaching Others," *Star*, March 27, 2017; Steve Wieberg, "An Appreciation: Joelouis Mattox," Kansas City Public Library, Kansas City MO, February 6, 2018, https://kclibrary.org/blog/library-life/appreciation-joelouis-mattox.
13. Arnett Williams directed the massive rescue operation during the post-collapse hours. He was someone of whom, according to Mattox, "the black community can be proud." Mattox, *The Call*, July 24–30, 1981.
14. Rick E. Abel, "Skywalks' Collapse Shocks City; 111 Dead, No One Admits Blame," *The Call*, July 24–30, 1981. A later issue reported that Nancy Irvin (actually spelled Ervin), a Hyatt waitress, had been injured and was still hospitalized. "Vice Principal at Southeast Jr. Among Hyatt Disaster Victims," *The Call*, July 31–August 6, 1981; Mike McGraw, "Hyatt Worker Relives Terror, Confronts 'Guilt Feelings,'" *Star*, October 29, 1981.
15. RG 1995 MS, 1, citing Hallmark press release, "Donald J. Hall, President, Hallmark Cards, Inc.," November 14, 1972.
16. "Crown Center Historic District"; Kipp, "Crown Center," 9. My use of the term "magic kingdom" is intentional. Walt Disney advised his friend Joyce Hall to not let the Crown Center development site get "hemmed-in" as had his Disneyland in California.
17. James C. Fitzpatrick, "Crosby Kemper Hits Grand Avenue Plan," *Times*, July 26, 1988. Robert Gordon followed up with a personal "attaboy" that Kemper acknowledged. R. Crosby Kemper Jr., 1010 Grand Avenue, Kansas City MO, to RG, September 30, 1988, RCGC.
18. Shortridge, *Kansas City and How It Grew*, 135.
19. "Response to Public Sentiment of Hyatt," Jim Dawson, vice president, marketing, Crown Center Redevelopment Corporation, to Bryan Putman, July 24, 1981, copies to Frederick Bokun, Steve Doyal, and James McClune, RCGC. Biographical information on Dawson can be found in "TMC [Truman Medical Center] Announces New Hire; Jim Dawson Named Vice President of Strategic Business Development," *Star*, August 21, 2007. Putman was Hallmark's director of advertising and public

relations. "F. Bryan Putman, a Former Reporter and War Correspondent," *United Press International Archives*, May 18, 1984, https://www.upi.com/Archives/1984/05/18/F-Bryan-Putman-a-former-reporter-and-war-correspondent/2500453700800/. Bokun was manager of public relations at Hallmark. "Frederick John Bokun," obituary, *Racine (WI) Journal Times*, December 1, 2013, https://www.legacy.com/obituaries/journaltimes/obituary.aspx?n=frederick-john-bokun&pid=168254716&fhid=12105. Doyal retired in 2014 as a Hallmark senior vice president; biographical information can be found at https://journalism.missouri.edu/alum/steve-doyal/.

20. Richard A. Serrano, *Times*, October 2, 1981; John Carroll and Tim Weiner, "Hyatt Panel Plans Testing of Structure," *Times*, August 15, 1981; Rick Lyman and Deborah Singer, "Hyatt Tour 'Reassures' Committee," *Star*, August 27, 1981; Rick Atkinson, "Grim Days Kept in Background at Subdued, Optimistic Opening," *Times*, October 2, 1981.
21. ("highest levels") Richard A. Serrano, *Times*, October 2, 1981; ("mausoleum") Atkinson, *Times*, October 2, 1981.
22. "Plaintiffs' Motion for Class Certification and Memorandum in Support of Class Action Certification," October 27, 1981, no. 315, *FSC*, NARA; ("far exceed") "Application of Gordon for Attorney's Fees," RCGC.
23. The epithet "carpetbagger" was hurled by the irrepressible Lantz Welch. RG 1995 MS, 152.
24. R. D. Marshall, E. O. Pfrang, E. V. Leyendecker, K. A. Woodward, R. P. Reed, M. B. Kasen, and T. R. Shives, *Investigation of the Kansas City Hyatt Regency Walkways Collapse*, National Bureau of Standards Building Science Series 143 (Washington DC: U.S. Government Printing Office, 1982). See also Rick Alm and Thomas G. Watts, "Hotel Owners Snag Federal Investigation; Federal Officials Allowed Access Only to Debris," *Star*, August 6, 1981; Rick Alm and Thomas G. Watts, "Investigators Given Access to Documents," *Star*, August 9, 1981; Richard A. Serrano, "Hyatt Investigators to Weigh Skywalks; Lawyers Notified of Test," *Times*, August 21, 1981; "Government Engineers Weigh Sections of Hyatt Skywalks," *Star*, September 3, 1981; Andrew C. Miller, "Skywalk Beam Replicas Tested in Public; Withheld Debris Needed for Complete Report, Bureau of Standards Says," *Star*, October 14, 1981.
25. Marshall et al., *Investigation of the Kansas City Hyatt Regency*, 54–56; Rick Alm and Thomas G. Watts, "Federal Agency Seeks Skywalk Segments for Tests," *Star*, September 21, 1981. See also David Hayes, "Agreement to Allow Tests on Skywalks," *Times*, October 24, 1981; David Hayes, "Lawyers Act for Completion of Skywalk Probe," *Times*, October 28, 1981; Thomas G. Watts, "Skywalk Samples Removed; Federal Agency Gets Clearance for Debris Tests," *Star*, November 3, 1981; David Hayes, "Federal Agency Wants to Test Support Parts of Hyatt Walkways," *Times*, December 4, 1981.
26. Lewis V. Judson, *Weights and Measures Standards of the United States: A Brief History*, National Bureau of Standards Special Publication 447 (Washington DC: U.S.

Government Printing Office, 1976 revised); ("neutral," "independent," and "experienced analyst") John A. Dvorak, "Federal Officials Examine Rubble for Cause," *Times*, July 29, 1981.

27. Marshall et al., *Investigation of the Kansas City Hyatt Regency*, 246, 249, 253–56.

28. ("looking at everything") Thomas G. Watts, "Standards Bureau Works Hyatt Puzzle; with a Caution for Detail, Agency Seeks Answers," *Star*, September 3, 1981; Hayes, "Federal Agency Wants to Test." Detailed explanations by outside experts of the structural failure of the skywalks regularly appeared in the newspaper while the NBS was in the midst of its field investigations. David Hayes, "Skywalk Data Show Weight Led to Failure; Experts Also Point Out Design Couldn't Handle It," *Times*, September 26, 1981.

29. John A. Dvorak, "Chamber Puts Together Hyatt Review Panel as Council Compromise," *Times*, July 30, 1981; Thomas G. Watts, "Chamber Promises Exhaustive Probe," *Star*, July 30, 1981; John A. Dvorak, "Relief Is Tangible as City Takes Action after Hotel Disaster," *Times*, July 31, 1981; Editorial staff, "The Hyatt Investigations," *Times*, August 3, 1981; Rich Hood, "Berkley's Firmness on Hyatt Contrasts Council's Hedging," *Star*, August 5, 1981; John A. Dvorak, "Hyatt's Owner Hires Engineers to Inspect Hotel," *Times*, August 8, 1981; John A. Dvorak, "Hyatt Committee Invites People to Submit Questions about Disaster," *Times*, August 11, 1981; Carroll and Weiner, "Hyatt Panel Plans Testing"; Deborah Singer, "Chamber's Hyatt Panels Get Little Public Input," *Star*, August 18, 1981. This pointed headline appeared in the state edition for Greater Missouri and contrasted to the one that appeared in the city edition: "Chamber Gets Post-Hyatt Comments." The former drew a stiff rebuke from the Greater Kansas City Chamber of Commerce.

30. Lyman and Singer, "Hyatt Tour 'Reassures' Committee"; photograph by Fred Blocher, "Construction Site Toured," *Times*, August 27, 1981.

31. Richard A. Serrano and David Hayes, "Truss Installed to Strengthen Hyatt Roof as Reopening Nears," *Times*, September 30, 1981; Richard A. Serrano and Fraser, *Times*, October 1, 1981; "The Hyatt Reopening; Panel Finds 'No Valid Reason' to Question Safety of the Hotel," special section, *Times*, October 2, 1981; ("studied for safety") Rick Alm and Thomas G. Watts, "Panel Reports the Hyatt Is Safe," *Star*, October 1, 1981; Serrano, "Doors Open at Hyatt"; Thomas G. Watts, "Improvements at Hyatt Preceded Its Reopening," *Star*, November 2, 1981.

32. Rick Lyman and Deborah Singer, "Quiet Reopening of Hyatt Being Planned for October 1," *Star*, September 20, 1981.

33. Diane Stafford, "People Are the Answer, KC Chamber Told," *Star*, November 3, 1981; Richard A. Serrano, "Report on Hyatt's Safety Expected in Two Weeks," *Times*, October 21, 1981; David Hayes, "Engineers Report Hyatt Flaws Fixed," *Times*, November 3, 1981; John A. Dvorak, "Panel's Report on Hyatt Based on Thorough Groundwork," *Times*, November 3, 1981. See also "Report of the Technical Committee of the Chamber

of Commerce of Greater Kansas City concerning the Hyatt Regency Hotel, Kansas City, Missouri, November 2, 1981," typescript, 17 pp., RCGC.

34. "Application of Gordon for Attorney's Fees," RCGC. Gordon wrote this report in mid-1983 and persisted in the view that absolved Hyatt of responsibility for the disaster, which he was not reluctant to share with the head of the corporation himself. "In my opinion, Hyatt, which had the least to do with the situation, ended up getting the worst black eye in the general public's mind." RG to Jay A. Pritzker, Chicago IL, December 23, 1983, RCGC. One of those black eyes came from the *Kansas City Times* when it did a well-timed, three-part "hatchet job" on the Pritzker family, Chicago's Hyatt Corporation, and its reputed connections to organized crime. Knut Royce, "The Operators: Chicago's Pritzker Family and Kansas City's Hyatt," *Times*, March 8, 1982; Knut Royce, "The Financial Origins of the Pritzker Empire," *Times*, March 9, 1982; Knut Royce, "Haven in the Bahamas; Pritzkers' Foreign Trusts Caught IRS' Eye," *Times*, March 10, 1982. Hyatt took great exception to these stories and later shared with Gordon the corporation's sharply worded letters to the editor. Stanley Sporkin, Chevy Chase MD, to editor, *Kansas City Times*, April 20, 1982, RCGC. Sporkin disputed the paper's implication of mob ties to the Pritzkers from his vantage point as a former director of enforcement for the Securities and Exchange Commission who had investigated the matter for the federal government. Edward H. Levi to editor, *Kansas City Times*, April 5, 1982, RCGC. Levi, a former president of the University of Chicago and U.S. attorney general in the Ford administration, described the articles as "character assassination." Neil A. Lewis, "Edward H. Levi, Attorney General Credited with Restoring Order after Watergate, Dies at 88," *New York Times*, March 8, 2000; ("hatchet job") Jay A. Pritzker to RG, January 10, 1984, RCGC; RG to Pritzker, February 9, 1984, RCGC.

6. THE DEPONENT

1. Other lawyers in the room included Dale Lee Beckerman, Thomas F. Fisher, James R. Goheen, Joel Goldman, Ann Hagan, George E. Kapke, Joseph W. Lampo, Suzanne K. Loseke, Patrick Lysaught, Patrick McLarney, Sheila O'Brien, Duke W. Ponick Jr., Frederick H. Riesmeyer, Edward Ruzicka, and Lawrence R. Tucker. Molly Riley deposition, December 3, 1981, *FSC*, NARA. Bill Whitaker, representing Riley, received a notice of her deposition on November 23 and began preparation on November 24. They met again on December 2, the day before the deposition. Whitaker clocked ten hours on the day of Riley's deposition. Whitaker time records, RCGC.
2. Riley deposition, *FSC*, NARA. Whitaker's ex-wife, Kathy Whitaker, was listed as having been treated at Baptist Memorial Hospital. "Partial List of Injured in Collapse," *Times*, July 18, 1981. See also William Whitaker and RG to Molly Riley, Prairie Village KS, July 24, 1981, regarding *Riley v. Crown Center Redevelopment, et al.*, which served as a "contract of employment by you for our services."

3. Riley deposition, *FSC*, NARA. A stark contrast to this line of questioning was the deferential approach taken with Don Hall during his deposition the next year. See the appendix of this book, "Selections from the Deposition of Donald Joyce Hall."
4. RG 1995 MS, 170; RG and Lawrence M. "Barney" Berkowitz, notes of phone conversation, June 8, 1988, RCGC.
5. Riley deposition, *FSC*, NARA.
6. Riley deposition, *FSC*, NARA.
7. Riley deposition, *FSC*, NARA; ("high pressure job") Richard A. Serrano, *Buried Truths and the Hyatt Skywalks: The Legacy of America's Epic Structural Failure* (West Lafayette IN: Purdue University Press, 2021), 233. For further details of the day's events, see RG 1995 MS, 220–21.
8. DTR, December 6, 8, 10, 1981, RCGC.
9. ("absolute master") Wright and Schumaker, *Never in Doubt*, 197; John T. Dauner, "Lawyers Battle over Status of Hyatt Suits," *Times*, December 11, 1981; "A Washington, D.C. Attorney Said Victims of the Hyatt . . . ," *United Press International Archives*, December 11, 1981, https://www.upi.com/Archives/1981/12/11/A-Washington-dc-attorney-said-victims-of-the-Hyatt/3042376894800/; ("persuasive") "Application of Gordon for Attorney's Fees," RCGC.
10. DTR, January 20, 1982, RCGC.
11. "Order," January 25, 1982, no. 572, *FSC*, NARA; Wright and Schumaker, *Never in Doubt*, 197.

7. THE *FEDERAL SKYWALK CASES*

1. RG 1995 MS, 369. The actual quote referred to spring 1982: "The last few weeks had seemed like several lifetimes." But the term fit with any number of "last few weeks" in Gordon's frenetic year.
2. RG 1995 MS, 242.
3. Thomas G. Watts, "Firms Agree on $151 Million Fund for Hyatt Settlements," *Star*, January 17, 1982.
4. RG 1995 MS, 242–43; Kenton C. Granger of Anderson, Granger, Nagels, Lastelic & Gordon, Overland Park KS, to Paul Wolff of Williams & Connolly, Washington DC, April 8, 1982, RCGC.
5. Patrick McLarney, Max N. Foust, and John Shamberg, plaintiff intervenors, to Scott O. Wright, U.S. District Court of the Western District of Missouri, February 1, 1981, correspondence, *FSC*, NARA; Thomas G. Watts, "Hyatt Decision Leaves Legal Dilemmas," *Star*, February 3, 1982.
6. RG 1995 MS, 253, 284. Oral arguments before the Eighth Circuit were on March 12, 1982. DTR, March 12, 1982, RCGC.
7. RG 1995 MS, 219, 361; "Transcript of Proceedings," April 17, 1982, no. 891, *FSC*, NARA. On the same day of her deposition, Riley was forced to resign from her job as a nurse

at St. Joseph's Hospital, where coincidentally she had been treated on the night of July 17, 1981. Gordon, "Molly Riley," RCGC.

8. "Order," January 25, 1982, no. 572, *FSC*, NARA; DTR, January 25, 1982, RCGC; RG 1995 MS, 231–32, 240; James B. Stewart, "Wake of Disaster: Controversy Surrounds Payments to Plaintiffs in Hyatt Regency Case," *Wall Street Journal*, July 3, 1984; "Application of Robert C. Gordon for Allowance of Attorney's Fees and Out of Pocket Expense Reimbursement," March 31, 1983, RCGC. Riley's replacement was Shirley Stover, an Iowan. Watts, "Hyatt Decision Leaves Legal Dilemmas."
9. RG 1995 MS, 255.
10. RG 1995 MS, 353.
11. Gordon came to the same conclusion about Hallmark's "distancing" efforts as Ed De Vilbiss, an architect and expert witness on safe building practices for the state plaintiffs. RG 1995 MS, 275–76.
12. RG 1995 MS, 258–59, 267. Gordon cited a couple of examples of the press confusion about the defense's settlement strategy. Watts, "Hyatt Decision Leaves Legal Dilemmas"; Thomas G. Watts, "Ruling Expected on Hyatt Legal Snarls," *Star*, February 11, 1982.
13. David Hayes, "Lawyers Criticize Choice of Counsel for Hyatt Suit," *Times*, February 23, 1982; ("excellent") "Application of Gordon for Attorney's Fees," RCGC. Gordon's 1983 application for attorney's fees listed his prior class-action work. The questioning of his qualifications for such legal work remained a sore subject for him throughout the case. For an example, see RG to Rick Serrano, December 13, 1982, correspondence, *FSC*, NARA; also found in RCGC.
14. The pejorative term "to swift boat" someone came into popular usage in the 2004 U.S. presidential campaign and came to mean dishonestly twisting an opponent's strength into a perceived weakness or failing.
15. ("punitive damages") Eileen Ogintz, "Scars of Sky Walk Tragedy Hard to Heal," *Chicago Tribune*, March 21, 1982; ("character assassinations") John T. Dauner, "Hyatt Judge Rejects Challenge to Law Firm," *Times*, May 19, 1982.
16. Andy Gordon to REP, May 21, 2018.
17. RG 1995 MS, 281; "Application of Gordon for Attorney's Fees," RCGC.
18. ("get cracking") DTR, January 26, 1982, RCGC; ("soon") RG 1995 MS, 256.
19. RG 1995 MS, 243–46, 249; "Transcript of Proceedings," April 17, 1982.
20. John A. Dvorak, "Federal Officials Examine Rubble for Cause," *Times*, July 29, 1981.
21. Marshall et al., *Investigation of the Kansas City Hyatt Regency*, vi, 245. See the "estimate of walkway occupancy at time of collapse," 36–39.
22. RG 1995 MS, 269–74, citing "Press Briefing, Report of Investigation of the Kansas City Hyatt Regency Walkways Collapse," February 25, 1982, National Bureau of Standards, Gaithersburg MD, RCGC.
23. "Press Briefing," February 25, 1982, RCGC.

24. Ed De Vilbiss to Robert Schneider, August 10, 1983, excerpted in RG 1995 MS, 665; "Edward A. De Vilbiss," obituary, *Star*, April 5, 2001.
25. RG 1995 MS, 272–74.
26. 8yearhawk, "Thought I would clear up a couple things since there are some misconceptions about what went wrong," March 5, 2016, comment on "Hyatt Regency Walkway Collapse: 35 Years Ago This July," 247 Sports, https://247sports.com/college/kansas/board/103726/Contents/Hyatt-Regency-Walkway-Collapse-35-years-ago-this-July-71245094/.

8. SETBACK

1. RG 1995 MS, 278–79, 281; "Motion Requesting Defendants' Liaison Counsel Why They Should Not Be Held in Contempt with Suggestions," March 4, 1982, no. 649, *FSC*, NARA; "Order," March 5, 1982, no. 651, *FSC*, NARA, which stated "that the Defense Liaison Counsel show cause by noon on March 8, 1982, why they should not be personally held in civil contempt of this court." John T. Dauner, "Lawyers in Hyatt Case Face Contempt Hearing," *Times*, March 6, 1982, which reported on the defendants not answering all interrogatories and "allegedly denying class action lawyers access to witnesses and documents in violation of court orders" during the discovery process. DTR, March 9, 1982, RCGC.
2. RG 1995 MS, 280, 303; "Order," March 9, 1982, no. 661, *FSC*, NARA, which stated, "The Court's Show Cause Order of March 5, 1982, is vacated on consent." ("give-and-take") Dauner, "Lawyers in Hyatt Case Face Contempt Hearing."
3. RG 1995 MS, 283. From March 17, 1982, "since Federal Plaintiffs' counsel first complained about defendant's failure to produce documents," until December 17, 1982, Hallmark/Crown Center Redevelopment Corporation deposited a total of 46,600 documents at the document depository. Barbara Stillman, "Affidavit," December 31, 1982, exhibit no. 1,874, *FSC*, NARA.
4. RG 1995 MS, 304–30, 335–41; Richard C. Heydinger depositions, March 19, 23, 24, 1982, nos. 1,057, 1,058, 1,059, *FSC*, NARA; Arnold Waxman deposition, March 30–April 22, 1982, RCGC; DTR, March 19–20, 24–26, 30–31, April 1–2, 8–9, 12–13, 22–23, 1982, RCGC; ("lobotomized memories") RG to Paul Wolff, August 7, 1982, RCGC.
5. Jeannette Lee deposition, June 3, 1982, no. 1,907, *FSC*, NARA.
6. ("entire categories") "Transcript of Proceedings," March 31, 1982, no. 844, *FSC*, NARA; RG 1995 MS, 250, 308, 348.
7. RG 1995 MS, 334–35; "Transcript of Proceedings," April 17, 1982.
8. RG 1995 MS, 311–12, 315.
9. RG to Judge Timothy D. O'Leary, Sixteenth Judicial Circuit of Missouri, Circuit Court of Jackson County, Kansas City MO, June 10, 1982, RCGC.
10. RG 1995 MS, 312–13, 327–28, 330.
11. RG 1995 MS, 299, 300, 349, 351.

12. Clipping with notations, David Lauter, "Younger v. The Kansas City Bar," *National Law Journal*, February 8, 1982, RCGC; RG 1995 MS, 254. See also William Tavoulareas, *Fighting Back: The Story of How the President of Mobil Took on the Washington Post in One of the Most Sensational Libel Cases in Legal History* (New York: Simon & Schuster, 1985) for another author's description of Irving Younger's failings, an account that brought Gordon much self-satisfaction and vindication.
13. RG 1995 MS, 264.
14. RG 1995 MS, 342, 344, 346, 355, 360; RG to O'Leary, June 10, 1982, RCGC.
15. Ron Ostroff and John T. Dauner, "Quick Hyatt Wrap-Up Would Set Precedent," *Times*, May 14, 1982.
16. "Application of Gordon for Attorney's Fees," RCGC. A tense, face-to-face meeting between Gordon and Younger on April 22, 1982, brought to light these concerns of Gordon. RG 1995 MS, 342–47, 358; DTR, April 22–23, 1982, RCGC.
17. RG 1995 MS, 359; Thomas G. Watts, "Legal Ranks Are Divided in Hyatt Class-Action Suit," *Star*, May 3, 1982.
18. "I find it particularly galling to be accused of opposing the settlement proposal because of personal 'greed.'" RG to O'Leary, June 10, 1982, RCGC; RG 1995 MS, 362–64.
19. Donald D. Jones, "Clarification," *Star*, May 12, 1982.
20. RG 1995 MS, 346, 365; Thomas G. Watts, *Star*, May 3, 1982; ("cover up") Ron Ostroff and John T. Dauner, *Times*, May 14, 1982.
21. RG 1995 MS, 367; ("yea") Irving Younger to RG, May 17, 1982, RCGC; "Notice of Intent Not to Serve as Lead Class Counsel and to Otherwise Withdraw," August 23, 1982, no. 1,160, *FSC*, NARA; submitted by Kenton C. Granger on behalf of Anderson, Granger, Nagels & Lastelic.
22. RG to O'Leary, June 10, 1982, RCGC; Kenton Granger of Anderson, Granger, Nagels & Lastelic, Overland Park KS, to Paul Martin Wolff of Williams & Connolly, July 13, 1982, RCGC.
23. RG to O'Leary, June 10, 1982, RCGC; ("disgorge") RG 1995 MS, 369.
24. "Order," May 28, 1982, no. 958, *FSC*, NARA; John T. Dauner, "Hyatt Lawyers Deny That Court Was Misled," *Times*, May 29, 1982.
25. "Petition for Mandamus/Application for Immediate Temporary Stay," U.S. Court of Appeals for the Eighth Circuit, June 7, 1982, no. 1,109, *FSC*, NARA; "Judgment Sought in Hyatt Lawsuit," *Star*, June 9, 1982; RG 1995 MS, 369; Ron Ostroff, "A Year Later, Hyatt Disaster a Tangle of Legalities," *Times*, July 17, 1982.
26. RG 1995 MS, 371–72.
27. William D. Tammeus, "Editorial Notebook: A Year Can't Begin to Erase Memories of Tragedy," *Times*, July 3, 1982. Gordon was so taken with Tammeus's column that he sent a fan letter. RG to Tammeus, *Kansas City Times*, Kansas City MO, July 13, 1982, RCGC.

28. Ostroff, "A Year Later." Gordon's quote was lifted word for word from the concluding sentence in his motion filed earlier. "Plaintiffs' Motion for Allowing Disclosure of Documents in Depository and/or Alternatively for Filing Depositions and Exhibits in Clerk's Office," July 12, 1982, no. 1,061, *FSC*, NARA.
29. Ostroff, "A Year Later."
30. ("handle it" and "We need that hotel") Mark Fraser, "Few Scars Visible One Year after Hyatt Disaster," *New York Times*, July 18, 1982; Paula Maynard, "The Hyatt Regency Hotel Disaster: A Year Later Survivors Still Dance," *United Press International Archives*, July 17, 1982, https://www.upi.com/Archives/1982/07/17/The-Hyatt-Regency-Hotel-disaster-A-year-later-survivors-still-dance/8186395726400/.
31. ("low ebb") Kenton Granger of Anderson, Granger, Nagels & Lastelic, Overland Park KS, to Paul Martin Wolff of Williams & Connolly, July 13, 1982, RCGC.
32. Ron Ostroff, "Lawyers Try to Alter Hyatt Suit; Class Attorneys Seek to Satisfy Appeals Court," *Times*, July 2, 1982; RG 1995 MS, 278, 369, 419, 459.
33. "Motion to Modify Plaintiffs' Case," July 1, 1982, no. 1,026, *FSC*, NARA.
34. "Motion to Modify Plaintiffs' Case," *FSC*, NARA.
35. Ostroff, "Lawyers Try to Alter."
36. Thomas G. Watts, "Hyatt Decision Leaves Legal Dilemmas," *Star*, February 3, 1982; DTR, August 5, 1982, RCGC. Gordon's full, passionate quote was "I predicted on August 5 that the defendants would try to destroy the class by buying off the class representative.... I've spent the last year on this case, and I'm going to keep working whether it's a class or a consolidated trial. I would do it 10 times over." "Transcript of Proceedings," August 5, 1982, no. 1,127, *FSC*, NARA; (buy off) John T. Dauner, "Judge Refuses to Certify a New Hyatt Class Action," *Times*, September 18, 1982.
37. Lawrence M. Berkowitz of Stinson, Mag & Fizzell to Irving Younger, September 21, 1982, copied to Scott O. Wright and Robert L. Collins, correspondence, *FSC*, NARA, which provided details about the Stover settlement and the defendant's continued denial of a payoff. "At no time was Mrs. Stover's refusal to act as class representative discussed as a condition . . . of her settlement." However, according to the defendant's position, "if the Stover claims have settled, the Stovers [mother, father, and children] could not be class representatives." Interestingly, before the Hyatt case put them on opposite sides, Berkowitz was a close friend of Gordon, even serving as a groomsman at his wedding. The friendship did not survive the year. See also "Plaintiff's Reply to Defendants' and Plaintiff-Intervenors' Suggestions in Opposition to Certification of a Class Action," September 10, 1982, no. 1,212, *FSC*, NARA.
38. Of the estimated total, only $750,000 consisted of a lump sum payout to Stover. The bulk of the settlement was structured via monthly payments calculated by actuarial estimates to reach the overall $3.25 million figure. Berkowitz to Younger, September 21, 1982, *FSC*, NARA. Gordon learned about the Stover settlement on September 10.

DTR, September 10, 1982, RCGC. "Order and Memorandum," September 17, 1982; Dauner, "Judge Refuses to Certify"; RG 1995 MS, 419.

39. Lawrence M. Berkowitz to Robert L. Collins, Houston TX, August 6, 1982, RCGC. A veiled threat from Irving Younger to Collins regarding the latter's legal fees brought a blistering reply from Collins. Younger to Collins, August 17, 1982, RCGC; Collins to Younger, August 30, 1982, RCGC. His fees, wrote Collins, were "none of your business. . . . I will respond decisively to any further efforts by anyone to interfere in these matters. . . . I will aggressively respond to any further tortuous interference on the part of you or anyone else." Younger persisted in his desire for part of Collins's fee for the Stover case and reached out to Judge Wright to intercede on behalf of the plaintiffs' counsel. Younger to Wright, October 12, 1982, correspondence, *FSC*, NARA. Gordon took no part in the money grab. Collins to RG, October 21, 1982, RCGC, in which Collins had the last word with Gordon when he dismissed the pair: "Younger and Wolff . . . claim to be our allies and friends and then do everything they can to harm us."

40. ("irritants") RG to Paul Wolff, August 7, 1982, RCGC, in which, referring to Younger, Wolff, and Paul Mogin, he wrote, "None of you have done squat in the discovery in this case." DTR, September 26, 29, October 6, 1982, RCGC.

41. "Plaintiff's Motion for Reconsideration of Motion for Certification of a Class Action," September 22, 1982, no. 1,241, *FSC*, NARA; "Suggestions of Defendants Crown Center Redevelopment Corporation and Hallmark Cards, Incorporated in Opposition to Appointment of Deborah Jackson as Class Representative of a Rule 23(b)(3) Class," October 22, 1982, no. 1,359, *FSC*, NARA. Deborah Jackson was represented by Kansas City attorney Arthur Stoup, who also served with Robert Gordon as an assistant class counsel on the plaintiffs' legal team. "Order," October 29, 1982, no. 1,391, *FSC*, NARA, which also contained biographical information on Jackson; John T. Dauner, "Judge Certifies Voluntary Class Action in Hyatt Case," *Times*, October 30, 1982; RG 1995 MS, 495. For details of the MGM Hotel fire, see the Clark County, Nevada, report from 1982, https://web.archive.org/web/20131109190735/http://fire.co.clark.nv.us/%28S%28gtgop1ers1xz2gkadvhp1w1u%29%29/Files/pdfs/MGM_FIRE.pdf.

42. RG 1995 MS, 254, 266.

43. ("slant") RG 1995 MS, 255. The Kansas City reporters included (along with a tally of mentions in Gordon's diary for this five-month period): Rick Alm (11), John T. Dauner (17), Paul Haskins (13), David Hayes (16), Richard M. "Dick" Johnson (5), Danice Kern (13), Marty Lanus (30), Micheal Mahoney (7), Ron Ostroff (25), Richard A. "Rick" Serrano (22), Jan Smith (10), and Thomas G. "Tom" Watts (5). Absent from this list is John A. Dvorak, whose full name and surname does not appear. Gordon often used initials in his diary, and the frequent appearance of "J. D." has been interpreted here as belonging to John Dauner. The editors overseeing the aforementioned print reporters and with whom Gordon conversed were

Mike Davies, Roger Moore, Robert L. "Bob" Samsote, and Mike Waller. The *Wall Street Journal* reporters who came to Kansas City were Tom Petzinger and Woody Klein. DTR, June 1–October 31, 1982, RCGC. Lanus, Kern, Mahoney, and Smith were television reporters, and of this cohort, Gordon considered Lanus "the fairest of the group." RG 1995 MS, 283. Mahoney was on site covering the tea dance when the skywalks fell. Gordon made a point in his later writings to express a high regard for Alm, Hayes, and Johnson and a low one for Dauner and Watts. RG 1995 MS, 374. Serrano, who numerically was in greater contact during this period than all but one of the other print reporters, was not mentioned, which may be explained by a falling-out between the two in December 1982 and is covered later in this chapter.

44. ("only vehicle") RG 1995 MS, 373. See also Joe Popper, "The Prize: The Inside Story; How the *Star* and *Times* Covered the Hyatt Disaster, Part 1," *Kansas City Magazine* 8 (November 1983): 42–47, 63–69; Joe Popper, "The Prize: The Investigation, Part 2," *Kansas City Magazine* 8 (December 1983): 50–53, 82–84. For examples of the paper standing up to unnamed "community leaders" opposed to the ongoing coverage of the Hyatt story, see Mike Waller, *Blood on the Out-Basket: Lessons in Leadership from a Newspaper Junkie* (Kansas City MO: Kansas City Star Books, 2011), 71–73; Popper, "The Prize, Part 1," 69.
45. For more on the Pulitzer win by the *Star* and *Times*, see Popper, "The Prize, Part 1," 42–47, 63–69; Popper, "The Prize: Part 2," 50–53, 82–84; Waller, *Blood on the Out-Basket*, 46–55, 71–73, 141nn.
46. RG 1995 MS, 271, 275, 348.
47. On July 2, 1982, Gordon held a conference with Scott Whiteside, the subject of which could only have been the document depository. DTR, July 2, 1982, RCGC; "Plaintiffs' Motion for Allowing Disclosure of Documents," *FSC*, NARA; RG 1995 MS, 374; John T. Dauner, "Class Action Lawyers Ask Judge to Open Hyatt Case Documents to Public," *Times*, July 13, 1982.
48. "The Hyatt Documents," editorial, *Times*, July 15, 1982.
49. Dauner, "Class Action Lawyers Ask Judge"; "Defendants' Memorandum in Opposition to Plaintiffs' Motion for Pretrial Disclosure of Information Obtained through Discovery," July 26, 1982, no. 1,095, *FSC*, NARA; John T. Dauner, "Lawyers Offer Plan for Disclosing Hyatt Papers," *Times*, August 26, 1982; ("speak for themselves") Scott Whiteside, general counsel, *Kansas City Star* and *Kansas City Times*, Kansas City MO, to Scott O. Wright, August 3, 1982, RCGC; Thomas G. Watts, "Judge Orders Hyatt Data to Be Released," *Star*, August 5, 1982; RG to Jim Powell, New Canaan, Connecticut, December 27, 1985, RCGC.

9. BETRAYAL

1. DTR, August 30, 31, September 1, 2, 3, 1982, RCGC; Donald Joyce Hall deposition, August 30–September 3, 1982, RCGC. The four volumes of depositions total 829

pages. ("coached") Notes to Donald J. Hall deposition by RG, n.d., RCGC; ("I don't recall") RG 1995 MS, 333.

2. Notes to Hall deposition, RCGC.
3. Thomas G. Watts, "Cause of Collapse Awaits Unfolding of Investigations," *Star*, July 19, 1981.
4. Hall deposition, September 3, 1982, RCGC.
5. One detects the defense team's solid front to avoid delving into the area of project management. As just one example, when a plaintiffs' lawyer finally moved from the subject of "structural judgment" to "management" with a deposed Hallmark architect, the question was immediately objected to. Deposition of Herbert E. Duncan Jr., August 2, 1982, no. 2,039, *FSC*, NARA.
6. Notes to Hall deposition, RCGC; Hall deposition, RCGC; RG 1995 MS, 433, 436.
7. Hall deposition, RCGC. Hall did concede that the "parent company [meaning Hallmark, but not him personally] did have a high interest and concern that the project be completed within budget and on time."
8. One of the purposes of the deposition, according to Gordon, was "to dispel any lingering notion that Hallmark and Crown Center could be considered independent of one another." RG 1995 MS, 421, 431.
9. "Notes of Defendants found after 9/3/82—D.J.H.," RCGC; RG 1995 MS, 436. Gordon devoted an entire chapter of his manuscript to the Don Hall deposition, awkwardly titled "Edifice Complex." RG 1995 MS, 418–44.
10. ("rush of events") "Order," December 9, 1982, no. 1,585, *FSC*, NARA, which may be Judge Wright's words or, more likely, coined by Joseph Colussi, his clerk.
11. DTR, September 20–21, 24, 1982, RCGC. The team for "The Hyatt Papers" included reporters Rick Alm, Dave Hayes, Dick Johnson, and Rick Serrano and editor Roger Moore, although the actual bylines for their articles read "Staff of the Kansas City Times and Star."
12. "Inspection Problems Plagued Hyatt Construction, Records Show," *Times*, October 2, 1982; "Signals of Trouble Were Missed at Hyatt," *Star*, October 3, 1982. The paper provided more cover for Hall in this article, with his only vague references, such as "despite warnings from top Hallmark officials to ensure the structural safety of the entire hotel." "'Thin, Invisible' Walkways Were Last of Many Plans," *Star*, October 3, 1982. Regarding who made the critical decision, the reporters came up with this innocuous phrasing: "Eventually the designers and owners settled on a skywalk system to span the hotel lobby." These three articles cited the depositions of twelve individuals: Robert Berkebile, Steve Byers, Herbert Duncan, Daniel Hafley, Donald Hall, Keith Kelly, James Lucas, Joe Thomas Martin, Laurence Poisner, Harry Rogers, Jerry Sifers, and Arnold Waxman. RG 1995 MS, 492–94.
13. DTR, September 22–23, 1982, RCGC; Thomas Petzinger Jr. and Heywood Klein, "Haunted Hotel: Building Snags Dogged the Kansas City Hyatt That Collapsed in 1981; A Roof

Beam Fell in 1979; Design Change Preceded Plunge of the Skywalks; A Contractor Short of Cash," *Wall Street Journal*, October 8, 1982. Petzinger and Klein were based in the *WSJ*'s Chicago bureau. Their article cited the depositions of six individuals: Duncan, Hall, Kelly, Lucas, Sifers, and Waxman. DTR, October 9, 1982, RCGC.

14. DTR, October 7, November 4–5, 8, 11, 1982, RCGC.
15. "Supplemental Points and Authorities Regarding Plaintiffs' Pending Rule 37 Motion," December 3, 1982, no. 1,554, *FSC*, NARA; DTR, November 24, December 3, 1982, RCGC.
16. ("those who have lived" and "evasively responded") John T. Dauner and Richard A. Serrano, "Class Lawyer Seeks Sanctions in Skywalk Case; Judge Is Asked to Deny Hallmark, Crown Center a Trial Defense," *Times*, December 4, 1982.
17. ("pattern") John T. Dauner, "Judge Outlines a Plan to End Hyatt Conflicts," *Times*, December 21, 1982; ("the one person") Dauner and Serrano, "Class Lawyer Seeks Sanctions."
18. ("long-running farce") "Supplemental Points and Authorities," *FSC*, NARA, in which Gordon admitted "that we have said harsh things in this Memorandum." He went so far as to mention Don Hall's 1982 trip to Beverly Hills (taken hypocritically, one was led to conclude), to receive "an Emmy award for 'Quality.'"
19. "Supplemental Points and Authorities," *FSC*, NARA; RG 1995 MS, 543, 545, 552–53, 558. Hallmark had been asked for "sound recordings" as early as August 1981 through discovery requests by the personal injury lawyers.
20. "We apologize to the Court for the length of this report," Gordon wrote, but it was necessary "to substantiate with sufficient detail." Intractable to the end, "To no one else do we own any apology." "Supplemental Points and Authorities," *FSC*, NARA.
21. RG 1995 MS, 563; DTR, December 6, 1982, RCGC; John T. Dauner, "Lawyers Ask Ruling against Hyatt Defendants," *Times*, December 7, 1982; Rick Alm, "Hallmark Offer Sparks Inquiries," *Star*, December 8, 1982.
22. RG 1995 MS, 566–71; DTR, December 7, 1982, RCGC.
23. RG 1995 MS, 566, 572, 576; John T. Dauner, "Judge Demands Notice," *Times*, December 8, 1982; "Suggestions of Certain Defendants in Opposition to Plaintiffs' Motion to Hold Defendants in Civil Contempt," affidavit of Robert J. Sisk, December 17, 1982, no. 1,664, *FSC*, NARA.
24. "Suggestions of Certain Defendants in Opposition," affidavit of Patrick McLarney, December 16, 1982, and affidavit of Max W. Foust, December 17, 1982, *FSC*, NARA; "Affidavit of Max W. Foust," December 31, 1982, no. 1,842, *FSC*, NARA; "Affidavit of Patrick McLarney," December 30, 1982, no. 1,843, *FSC*, NARA; DTR, January 3, 1982, RCGC.
25. Notes of interview of Scott O. Wright, spring 1984, RCGC. See also Ron Ostroff, "State Class Settlement Approved in Skywalks Case," *Times*, January 7, 1983.
26. Richard A. Serrano, "Hyatt Owners Were Told Skywalks Were Safe; Load Problems Were Discussed in 1979 Meeting with Engineers," *Times*, December 11, 1982. In RG

1995 MS, 577, in which Gordon referred to the Serrano article: "And in a prominent page-one statement, the paper undercut my whole discovery sanction request." In his piece Serrano correctly noted, however, "Details of the November 13 [1979] meeting are at the heart of a brief filed last week by Robert C. Gordon."

27. "Tape Transcript Gillum-Colaco Meeting, 2:00 p.m., Crown Center 11/13/79," Hallmark transcript, December 1, 1982, 144 pages, RCGC. After learning of the transcript's existence, a Williams & Connolly lawyer requested a copy. Nancy F. Preiss of Williams & Connolly to Robert L. Driscoll of Stinson, Mag & Fizzell, copied to Judge Scott O. Wright, December 14, 1982, correspondence, *FSC*, NARA; Driscoll to Preiss, copied to Wright, December 20, 1982, correspondence, *FSC*, NARA; Preiss to Driscoll, copied to Wright, December 23, 1982, correspondence, *FSC*, NARA. Not to belabor the point about obfuscation, but even the title on the cover page of the transcript deflected away from Hallmark and toward its structural engineering firm.
28. This absence of contact is confirmed by Gordon's diary. His last phone conversation with Serrano was December 3, eight days before the article appeared. DTR, December 3, 1982, RCGC.
29. Richard A. Serrano, "Hyatt Owners Were Told Skywalks Were Safe." No clear candidates for these "other attorneys" appeared in Gordon's diary around this time. The possibilities might include Richard Routman and Paul Wolff, with whom Gordon had phone conversations. DTR, December 13, 1982, RCGC.
30. RG to Rick Serrano, December 13, 1982, copied to Mike Davies, Mike Waller, and Bob Samsote, correspondence, *FSC*, NARA; also found in RCGC; DTR, December 13, 1982, RCGC; RG 1995 MS, 576–78.
31. No immediate mention of Serrano appeared in Gordon's diary before the article's appearance. He spoke with Rick Alm of the *Times*, however, on December 6 and 11. DTR, December 4–11, 1982, RCGC.
32. Gordon concluded the letter with a request for Serrano's return of his office keys. See also Rick Serrano to RG, December 17, 1982, RCGC.
33. Gordon spent an estimated four to five hours in the *Times-Star* newsroom with Dauner and Serrano. The lengthy entry reads, "To K. C. Star at [Rick] Serrano's request to explain some points . . . questions from [Bob] Samsote & other editors from 5:20 p.m. until 10:00 p.m.; complaints by me that paper was not fairly explaining sugg. [suggestions] re: default judgment by ignoring lack of due process which victims suffered & focusing in only on the specious claim by [Charles] Egan that HMK [Hallmark] would be deprived of its due process if it didn't get to go to trial (also fallacious because request is for default as to issue of liability only, not for any money award; thus, HMK would not be deprived of any property by virtue of granting of the 37(b)(2)(C) request)." DTR, December 3, 1982, RCGC.
34. DTR, December 13, 1982, RCGC. Johnson, the Hallmark spokesman and forever tarnished in Gordon's eyes by his deceptive characterization of the massive roof collapse at

the Hyatt in 1979 as merely a "fallen beam," had "personally delivered a thick manila envelope to one of his favorite people at the *Times*. It purported to be an accurate transcript of the November 13, 1979, tape." By the time he wrote of this episode years later, Gordon left unnamed in his vignette that "favorite" person and the author of the scorned December 11, 1982, newspaper story. RG 1995 MS, 576–78.

35. Serrano, the primary recipient of the December 13, 1982, letter, dismissed the incident in a couple of sentences and notes in his 2021 book, as he generally did with Robert Gordon's contribution to understanding the skywalks story. Richard A. Serrano, *Buried Truths*, 317, 403.

36. The final tally was 1,592 $1,000 checks. RG 1995 MS, 578–79, 584, 626.

37. DTR, December 14, 1982–January 9, 1983, passim, RCGC; "Meeting of November 13, 1979," Halvorson & Associates transcript of cassette recording, n.d., 76 pp., RCGC; RG 1995 MS, 606, 613; "Response of Defendants Crown Center Redevelopment Corporation and Hallmark Cards, Incorporated to Supplemental Points and Authorities Regarding Plaintiffs' Pending Rule 37 Motion," December 20, 1982, no. 1,700, *FSC*, NARA. Not to be outdone in rhetoric, Hallmark lawyers referred to Gordon's brief as "the long-awaited sequel to the semi-hysterical attacks made upon Crown Center, Hallmark, and their counsel in court on the morning of October 11, 1982." Gordon received the Hallmark response to his December 3 brief on the same day it was filed. DTR, December 20, 1982, RCGC. In early January Gordon filed "Suggestions in Opposition to CCRC/HMK's Brief in Response," January 5, 1983, no. 1,874, *FSC*, NARA.

38. DTR, January 7, 1983, RCGC; John T. Dauner, "Trial Date Draws Near in Hyatt Skywalks Suit; Federal Settlement Talks Continue," *Times*, January 8, 1983; ("pardoned Nixon") Rick Alm, "Many Issues in Hyatt Trial Outstanding in 11th Hour," *Star*, January 9, 1983; "Negotiators Still Seeking Settlement in Hyatt Case," *Times*, January 10, 1983.

39. DTR, January 10, 1983; "Hotel Disaster Trial Averted with a $10 Million Accord," *New York Times*, January 11, 1983.

40. Gordon mentioned settlement talks occurring on Friday, January 7, "which I am excluded from," but did not share any identities of the negotiators. DTR, January 7, 1983, RCGC. The talks became common knowledge. John T. Dauner, "Trial Date Draws Near"; "Negotiators Still Seeking Settlement," *Times*, January 10, 1983; Ron Ostroff, "Long Chapter in Hyatt Story Ends Abruptly; Charities to Benefit in Federal Settlement," *Times*, January 11, 1983.

41. "Minute Sheet," January 10, 1983, no. 2,001, *FSC*, NARA; "Proposed Settlement Letter," January 10, 1983, no. 2,002, *FSC*, NARA. Gordon learned details of these weekend negotiations later from Joe Colussi, Wright's clerk, who was present and took notes. Joseph A. Colussi of Eckert Alcorn Goerring & Colussi, Madison IN, to RG, November 3, 1986, RCGC.

42. ("mixed feelings" and "closure") Wright and Schumaker, *Never in Doubt*, 200. The remaining members of the federal class included twenty-four persons: Brenda J.

Abernathy, Jack L. Berlau, Jeanne F. Brand, Jozef A. Brand, Senta W. Brody, Joan H. Disney, Marian D. Farris, Joseph R. Fleming, Loralee Frelich, Esther Gilbert, Sandra Ann Goodrich, Deborah T. Jackson (the final class representative), James W. Jackson, Carolyn L. Lucas, Charles E. Lucas, Francis P. Meeks, Dwight Lee Noble, Paul Wayne Noble, John A. Peterson, Charles H. Richardson, Molly Riley (the former class rep), William C. Thomas Jr., Joseph E. Vrabel, and Susan I. Ward. "Order and Memorandum," *in re* Federal Skywalk Cases, U.S. District Court, W.D. Missouri, Western Division, January 31, 1983, 97 F.R.D. 380 (W.D. Mo. 1983). This list is also found in "Order and Memorandum," January 31, 1983, no. 2,048, *FSC*, NARA, which contained the "fair, reasonable, and adequate" passage.

43. Rick Alm, "Hyatt Plaintiffs Settle Suits Out of Court," *Star*, January 10, 1983; Ostroff, "Long Chapter in Hyatt Story." See also "Legal Notice of Proposed Settlement," *Star*, January 16, 1983, which contained a claim form to be filled in, clipped out, and mailed to the clerk of the federal district court. "Order and Memorandum," *Federal Skywalk Cases*, 97 F.R.D. 380.
44. James C. Fitzpatrick, "Pact Can't End Victims' Pain," *Times*, January 11, 1983. Gordon also spoke to Riley on the day the settlement was announced. DTR, January 10, 1983, RCGC; RG 1995 MS, 622–23.
45. DTR, January 11–13, 1983, RCGC.

10. WRITER

1. RG 1995 MS, 330, 636. Even the principal lawyer for the defense, Robert Sisk, so stipulated that the case had been settled out from under Gordon.
2. RG to Knox Burger, Knox Burger Associates Ltd., Literary Agency, New York NY, April 29, 1985, RCGC; ("no fear") "When They Didn't Care Enough" book proposal, RG to James Landis, senior vice president and editorial director, William Morrow & Company, New York NY, April 5, 1984, RCGC; ("unvarnished skywalks story") RG 1995 MS, 642.
3. This was Robert Sisk of Hughes, Hubbard & Reed. RG 1995 MS, 629; DTR, January 20, 1983, RCGC; "Transcript of Proceedings," January 20, 1983, no. 2,049, *FSC*, NARA.
4. "Order and Memorandum," *Federal Skywalk Cases*, 97 F.R.D. 380; Ron Ostroff, "Blame for Skywalks Disaster Debated at Hearing; Judge to Rule on Proposed Settlement in 'Very Near Future,'" *Times*, January 21, 1983; Toni Cardarella, "Hotel Tragedy Settlements Nearly Complete," *United Press International Archives*, January 23, 1983, https://www.upi.com/Archives/1983/01/23/Hotel-tragedy-settlements-nearly-complete/8799412146000/; ("penance") "Editorial Review: The Hyatt Regency Settlement; Absence of Certainty Means All Parties Share Collective Responsibility," *Times*, January 24, 1983, originally printed in the *St. Louis Post-Dispatch*.
5. Gordon referred to his solely authored sanction reports of September 24, October 11, December 3, 1982, and January 3, 1983. "Transcript of Proceedings," *FSC*, NARA; "Motion

Requesting Sanctions Against Defendant Crown Center/Hallmark," September 24, 1982, no. 1,248, FSC, NARA; "Plaintiffs' Reply to Defendant Crown Center/Hallmark's Suggestions in Opposition to Rule 37 Motion," October 11, 1982, no. 1,299, FSC, NARA; "Supplemental Points and Authorities Regarding Plaintiffs' Pending Rule 37 Motion," December 3, 1982, no. 1,554, FSC, NARA; "Plaintiffs Memorandum in Opposition to Motion to Disqualify the Court and Counsel and for Other Relief," January 3, 1983, RCGC. The last document was Gordon's response to Hallmark's "Response of Defendants Crown Center Redevelopment Corporation and Hallmark Cards, Incorporated to Supplemental Points and Authorities Regarding Plaintiffs' Pending Rule 37 Motion," December 20, 1982, no. 1,700, FSC, NARA; RG 1995 MS, 602–3, 633–34.

6. "Suggestions of Robert C. Gordon in Opposition to Motion for Reconsideration of the Court's Order of May 4, 1983, for Expenses and Award of Attorney's Fees," May 27, 1983, no. 2,172, FSC, NARA; RG 1995 MS, 371, citing an article by David Lauter, *National Law Journal*, June 21, 1982, 1, 14–15. A more conservative source dropped the cut of the personal injury lawyers to a still substantial $30 million. James B. Stewart, "Wake of Disaster: Controversy Surrounds Payments to Plaintiffs in Hyatt Regency Case," *Wall Street Journal*, July 3, 1984.
7. "Order and Memorandum," *Federal Skywalk Cases*, 97 F.R.D. 380; DTR, January 31, 1983, which was the last entry in Gordon's skywalks diary. Lawrence M. Berkowitz of Stinson, Mag & Fizzell to Scott O. Wright, U.S. District Court, March 17, 1983, correspondence, FSC, NARA; Berkowitz to Wright, April 11, 1983, FSC, NARA. See also "Motion and Suggestions to Remove Case from Accelerated Civil Joint Jury Trial Docket, Filed by Molly Riley," April 15, 1983, no. 2,104, FSC, NARA; "Stipulation for Dismissal (Molly Riley)," May 3, 1983, no. 2,135, FSC, NARA; "Order (Approving Stipulation for Dismissal of Molly Riley)," May 6, 1983, no. 2,137, FSC, NARA.
8. Molly Riley to REP, notes of phone conversation, January 21, 2022, author's collection.
9. RG to Arthur R. Miller, Harvard Law School, Cambridge MA, February 26, 1983, RCGC. At the time of this post-settlement letter, the number of injured was given as 239. Another 1,029 persons had received $1,000 checks for being present in the lobby area when the skywalks fell. Rick Alm, "A Few Claims Still Linger over Hyatt," *Star*, January 16, 1983.
10. ("preferred") Paul J. Haskins, "Collapse of Hotel's 'Skywalks' in 1981 Is Still Reverberating in Kansas City," *New York Times*, March 29, 1983; ("Watergate legends") RG 1995 MS, 642.
11. "Application of Robert C. Gordon for Allowance of Attorney's Fees and Out of Pocket Expense Reimbursement," March 31, 1983, no. 2,084, FSC, NARA; "Order," May 4, 1983, no. 2,136, FSC, NARA, which awarded fees. Judge Wright also ordered that Gordon be paid $121,308.85 in expenses. Williams & Connolly received $725,000 in fees and $319,736.79 in expenses. Bill Whitaker, Gordon's office mate, received

$190,000 for his work, and Anderson, Granger, Nagels, Lastelic & Gordon was allotted $175,000, of which Gordon was entitled to a share for his work up to his June 1982 departure. John T. Dauner, "Judge Awards Fees to Lawyers of Hyatt Plaintiffs," *Times*, May 5, 1983. The contentiousness between Gordon and his former firm over fees continued through the year. "Application of the Law Firm of Anderson, Granger, Nagels & Lastelic for the Allowance of Attorneys' Fees," January 19, 1983, RCGC; Kenton C. Granger, Overland Park KS, to RG, January 25, February 21, 1983, RCGC; Granger to Wright, May 7, 1983, RCGC; "Suggestions of Robert C. Gordon in Opposition," *FSC*, NARA; "Order," June 3, 1983, RCGC, in which Wright denied reconsideration of his award of attorneys' fees.

12. The party was held at the home of Lee V. and Pamela K. Landon, 6517 Aberdeen, Mission Hills KS, half a mile away from the Gordons. Pam, the wife of a local real estate developer, was celebrating her fortieth birthday. Biographical information from https://www.linkedin.com/in/lee-landon-27948362 and https://nuwber.com/person/563a2179a219445d52617d87. Details on the evening's events come from a memo. Robert Gordon to the Confidential File, "Events of July 25, 1983, concerning Mr. Michel Scrivan," RCGC. ("hot, humid") Florestine Purnell, "Thunderstorms Interrupt Power to 20,000 KCP&L Customers," *Star*, July 25, 1983.
13. Kathy Sawyer was the mutual acquaintance who provided the introductions.
14. Mike Fish, "Tarnation; It's Another Battle with Umpires for Royals," *Star*, July 24, 1983; John T. Dauner, "U.S. Attorney Joins Hyatt Case Investigation," *Times*, July 13, 1983.
15. Scrivan was indeed a low-profile individual considering his high status in the corporation. A search of the *Kansas City Times* and *Kansas City Star* for these years turned up only one passing mention. "Letters from City's Hyatt Hotel File," *Times*, October 2, 1981, letter to Michel Scrivan, Crown Center Redevelopment Corporation, from Mario G. Salvadori, Weidinger Associates, regarding a checklist for Hyatt Regency attached to the letter of August 11, 1981, of Myron Calkins, P.E., director of public works, Kansas City MO.
16. Deirdre Coakley, Hank Greenspun, and Gary C. Gerard, *The Day the MGM Grand Hotel Burned* (Secaucus NJ: Lyle Stuart, 1982); Charles B. Cannon, *The O'Hare Story* (New York: Vantage Press, 1980).
17. Gordon originated a variant of this "bookends" metaphor. RG 1995 MS, 284.
18. Richard A. Serrano, "Eldridge Alleges Walkway Flaws Spotted Earlier," *Times*, December 18, 1982. At the time of this article a Hallmark spokesman did not dispute the claim about the skywalks support system but said that it had been the manager's (Hyatt's) responsibility to carry out inspections and maintenance, not the owner of the building (Hallmark).
19. In 1983 *Forbes* magazine estimated the Hall family wealth at $400 million. N. R. Kleinfield, "Forbes's List of the Richest," *New York Times*, September 28, 1983; Diane Stafford, "Business Beat," *Star*, October 23, 1983. By 2015 the family's estimated wealth

had grown to $2.8 billion. Forbes List, "America's Richest Families, 2015 Net Worth," July 1, 2015, https://www.forbes.com/profile/hall/#4a1f4752217f.

20. The address of the Scrivan residence was 6114 Mission Drive, Mission Hills KS.
21. F. Scott Fitzgerald, *The Great Gatsby* (New York: Charles Scribner's Sons, 1925), 216.
22. Gordon solved the dilemma of what to do with the Scrivan episode by leaving it out of the final version of his manuscript.
23. RG to Burger, April 9, 1985, RCGC; ("chapter title") Notes to Donald J. Hall deposition by RG, n.d., RCGC; Author's questionnaire, Simon & Schuster, New York NY, June 14, 1988, RCGC; ("rest of the year") RG to Robert L. Collins, Houston TX, March 8, 1983, RCGC.
24. Charles Stanford, Department of English, University of Missouri–Columbia, to RG, June 1, 1983, RCGC; Kathryn Anne Miller, Lawrence KS, to RG, September 9, 1983, with résumé, RCGC; Kathryn Anne Miller to RG, September 1983, with an annotated list of persons that Miller had interviewed on Gordon's behalf, RCGC. Her list included Pat deWitt, Evelyn Gubar, Mary Hanks, Caroline and William Kelly, Jeff Kuhn, Billie Miller, Frank Millich, Molly Riley, and Jean Rose.
25. Index to RG files, December 10, 1983, RCGC, which Gordon considered "also sort of an overall [book] outline for me."
26. Thornton Wilder, *The Bridge of San Luis Rey* (New York: Grosset & Dunlap, 1927), 15–23, 211, 217. One editor who crossed Gordon's path even advised that his characters, especially the victims, "should be as real and important to us as the characters in *The Bridge of San Luis Rey*." Frederic W. Hills, Simon & Schuster, to RG, February 3, 1987, RCGC.
27. ("disaster maven") Review of *Mannequin* by Robert Byrne, *Kirkus Reviews*, July 15, 1988, https://www.kirkusreviews.com/book-reviews/robert-byrne-2/mannequin-2/; ("building's flaws") Jacket copy for Robert Byrne, *Skyscraper* (New York: Atheneum, 1984); interview with Robert Byrne, author of *Skyscraper*, "News of Atheneum Publishers," May 1984. Robert Byrne authored in relatively quick succession *The Tunnel* (New York: Harcourt Brace Jovanovich, 1977), *The Dam* (New York: Atheneum, 1981), and *Skyscraper* (1984).
28. Robert Gordon, "When They Didn't Care Enough," manuscript, 1984 (hereafter cited as RG 1984 MS), ix, RCGC; Alan J. Dershowitz, *The Best Defense: The Courtroom Confrontations of America's Most Outspoken Lawyer of Last Resort, the Lawyer Who Won the Claus von Bulow Appeal* (New York: Random House, 1982).
29. Faculty profile of Alan J. Dershowitz, Harvard Law School, Felix Frankfurter Professor of Law, Emeritus, https://hls.harvard.edu/faculty/directory/10210/Dershowitz; Review of *The Best Defense* by Alan J. Dershowitz, *Kirkus Reviews*, May 1, 1982, https://www.kirkusreviews.com/book-reviews/alan-m-dershowitz-4/the-best-defense-3/; Evan Mandery, "'What Happened to Alan Dershowitz?': How a Liberal Harvard Professor Became Trump's Most Distinguished Defender on TV, Freaked Out His Friends and

Got the Legal World up in Arms," *Politico*, May 11, 2018, https://www.politico.com/magazine/story/2018/05/11/alan-dershowitz-donald-trump-what-happened-218359; Connie Bruck, "Alan Dershowitz, Devil's Advocate," *New Yorker*, August 5, 12, 2019, https://www.newyorker.com/magazine/2019/08/05/alan-dershowitz-devils-advocate.

30. RG to Paul Haskins, *New York Times*, New York NY, February 10, 1983, RCGC; RG to Landis, April 5, 1984, RCGC; David McClintick, *Indecent Exposure: A True Story of Hollywood and Wall Street* (New York: William Morrow, 1982).
31. Bob Woodward and Carl Bernstein, *All the President's Men* (New York: Simon & Schuster, 1974).
32. Robert Byrne to RG, March 22, 1985, RCGC, in which Byrne objected to the night watchman scene as "wholly imaginary."
33. DTR, December 26, 1981, RCGC. Gordon created his "cast of characters" initially "for filing purposes & for depo. [deposition] program." RG, "Cast of Characters," typescript, 5 pp., RCGC.
34. RG, "Cast of Characters," RCGC. Gordon credited the "relief act" quip to Lantz Welch. Notation on clipping, Ron Ostroff, "Magazine Examines Hyatt Case; Attorneys, Press Are Evaluated in Law Review," *Times*, February 13, 1984, RCGC.
35. RG 1984 MS. The Hallmark slogan still appears today on their website. "Building a Brand: 1930s–50s," Hallmark, https://corporate.hallmark.com/about/hallmark-cards-company/history/building-brand-1930s-50s/.
36. OCLC WorldCat entry for Robert C. Gordon, *House of Cards* (New York: Simon & Schuster, 1989), manuscript, 1995, RCGC. The assigned ISBN was 067164453x/9780671644536, and the title page read, "House of Cards: The Cover-Up Behind the Worst Structural Collapse in American History—Hallmark's Hyatt Regency Skywalks Disaster." Gordon's use of this title obviously predated the 2013 American television show, as well as the 1989 British novel and 1990 British television series of the same name.
37. Jill Tvedten Long, Wichita KS, to RG, June 16, 1984, RCGC.

11. HOUSE OF CARDS

1. "When They Didn't Care Enough" book proposal, RG to James Landis, senior vice president and editorial director, William Morrow & Company, New York NY, April 5, 1984, RCGC, which mentioned Gordon's conversation with David McClintick. Regarding James David Landis, see Roger Cohen, "The Media Business, Top Editor at Morrow Quits, a Personality Clash Is Cited," *New York Times*, April 12, 1991. Hillel Italie, "'Zen and the Art of Motorcycle Maintenance' Author Dead," *Associated Press News*, April 24, 2017, https://apnews.com/article/46037d15b30944518e16b4f529b8a33f; Robert M. Pirsig, *Zen and the Art of Motorcycle Maintenance: An Inquiry into Values* (New York: William Morrow & Company, 1974).

2. RG to Landis, April 5, 1984, RCGC. By "personal diary," Gordon was referring to the "daily time records" that he kept while working on cases—the detailed document that enabled him to figure out billable hours.
3. Landis to RG, May 2, 1984, RCGC. Landis also recommended agents Michael Carlisle, Gail Hochman, and Perry Knowlton.
4. Kathy P. Robbins to RG, September 9, 1984, RCGC; Linton Weeks, "The Secret Agent's Life," *Washington Post*, February 3, 1996.
5. RG to Robbins of Robbins & Covey Associates, New York NY, September 5, 1984, RCGC, in which Gordon stated, "I am still waiting for your list of possible co-authors." It is unclear whether Robbins ever supplied a list or, if she did, whether Byrne was on it. To James Stewart, another correspondent, Gordon reported that the manuscript was "now about 75–80% completed." These status reports helped keep other authors at bay. RG to James Stewart, *Wall Street Journal*, October 11, 1984, RCGC. In the realm of life's "what ifs," one wonders what would have happened if James Stewart, future Pulitzer Prize winner and *New York Times* columnist, the author of critically acclaimed examinations of Disney, Wall Street, and Washington DC, had somehow taken on Hallmark Cards Inc. as a subject. No good, critical history of Hallmark has ever been written, which has left a narrative vacuum in Kansas City history.
6. Bob Byrne, "Knox Burger," *Ed Gorman's Blog*, February 11, 2010, http://newimprovedgorman.blogspot.com/2010/02/knox-burger-by-bob-byrne.html; "Robert Byrne," *Encyclopedia Dubuque*, http://www.encyclopediadubuque.org/index.php?title=BYRNE,_Robert.
7. Paul Kenton, "Troubled Waters Threaten Young Engineer," *Star*, May 20, 1981.
8. Byrne, San Rafael CA, to RG, September 7, 1984, RCGC.
9. ("terrific impact") Byrne to RG, September 7, 1984, RCGC; Byrne to RG, November 12, 1984, RCGC; RG to "Bob" [Robert Byrne], November 27, 1984, RCGC; RG to Byrne, January 3, 1985, RCGC, in which Gordon referred to an "express package" of December 9 that included "another copy of the Agreement." This letter indicated that some sort of financial arrangement had been reached. RG to Robbins, November 27, 1984, RCGC, in which Gordon sent part 1 of the manuscript.
10. ("lack of attention") RG to Robbins, December 18, 1984, RCGC; ("client and agent") Robbins to RG, December 28, 1984, RCGC; ("time and effort") RG to "Kathy" [Robbins], January 2, 1985, RCGC, which was handwritten because "my secretary was fired for incredible incompetence. (I would accuse her of being on Hallmark's payroll but for the fact that she was too stupid for them to trust.)" Gordon made another incredibly sexist comment when he clumsily stated that Robbins would distract him as an author and "the book would end up sounding as if I had won the great case—when actually I was demolished."

11. Byrne to RG, December 12, 1984, RCGC. Regarding Byrne's offer to do more research, see Byrne to RG, March 19, 1985, RCGC, with Gordon's marginal notes ("Please don't misuse your talents"). For occupational salaries, see Earl F. Mellor, "Weekly Earnings in 1985: A Look at More than 200 Occupations," table 1, "Editors and Reporters," *Monthly Labor Review* 109 (September 1986): 29, from the Bureau of Labor Statistics, Department of Labor, https://babel.hathitrust.org/cgi/pt?id=uiug.30112104136939;view=1up;seq=1.
12. Byrne to RG, January 11, 1985, RCGC, which detailed their process: "Here is my version of the horror scene. . . . When I get editorial suggestions from you and Knox [Burger] on the pages you have now seen, I'll redo them as needed, redo the proposal the way Knox wants it, and then submit it all to you again. That will be the package Knox takes to the publisher or publishers." ("crusty" and "discovered and encouraged") Bruce Weber, "Knox Burger, Agent and Book Editor, Dies at 87," *New York Times*, January 12, 2010; Charles J. Shields, *And So It Goes: Kurt Vonnegut, a Life* (New York: Henry Holt, 2011), 105–7; (curmudgeonly) Byrne, "Knox Burger." More Robert Byrne correspondence can be found in the Knox Burger Collection, MSS 078, Fales Library and Special Collections, Elmer Holmes Bobst Library, New York University, New York NY.
13. Knox Burger, Knox Burger Associates Ltd., Literary Agency, New York NY, to Byrne, January 30, 1985, RCGC, with marginal notes and underlining by Gordon.
14. Burger to Byrne, January 30, 1985, RCGC.
15. Byrne to RG, January 31, 1985, RCGC.
16. Burger to RG, February 16, 1985, copied to Byrne, RCGC.
17. Burger to RG, February 16, 1985, RCGC.
18. Burger to RG, February 17, 1985, copied to Byrne, RCGC.
19. Byrne to RG, February 18, 1985, RCGC, which contained Gordon's marginal notes of February 22. Byrne straightforwardly says, "Part of what I say may strike you as abrasive, but we all know the danger [of] being surrounded by yes-men."
20. Byrne gave Martin Cruz Smith, another author represented by Burger, two hundred pages of manuscript to read. Smith returned it with many comments and questions. The margins of Byrne's letter are filled with Gordon's defensive responses. Byrne to RG, March 12, 1985, RCGC.
21. Byrne to RG, February 28, 1985, RCGC.
22. ("compromise") Byrne to RG, March 1985 (exact date not given), RCGC. One version of their book proposal, titled "Skywalks," illustrated Byrne's penchant for one-word, snappy titles. Book proposal, "Skywalks: The Kansas City Hyatt Regency Disaster," March 4, 1985, RCGC; Byrne to RG, March 22, 1985, RCGC.
23. ("not pleased") RG to Byrne, March 25, 1985, RCGC; ("all the pressure") RG to Byrne, March 28, 1985, RCGC; ("our collaboration") Byrne to RG, March 29, 1985, RCGC.
24. Burger to RG, March 9, 1985, RCGC.

25. Robert D. Loomis, vice president and executive editor, Random House, New York NY, to Burger, March 19, 1985, RCGC; Aaron Welborn, "A Conversation with Legendary Editor Bob Loomis, October 24," *Duke University Libraries Blog*, October 16, 2018, https://blogs.library.duke.edu/blog/2018/10/16/a-conversation-with-legendary-editor-bob-loomis-oct-24/.
26. Burger to RG, March 20, 1985, RCGC.
27. RG to Burger, April 9, 1985, RCGC. Gordon's mention of "28 months of my labor" would date the beginning of the book project to January 1983, the month of the settlement of the *Federal Skywalk Cases*.
28. ("try a case") Byrne to RG, April 3, 1985, RCGC; RG to Byrne, April 5, 1985, RCGC, with a PS by Gordon that he had received the April 3 letter from Byrne.
29. Byrne to RG, April 9, 1985, RCGC.
30. RG to Burger, May 1, 1985, RCGC. Gordon signaled this move when he told Byrne, "I'm happy with Knox, but I'm very disappointed with you." RG to Byrne, April 24, 1985, RCGC.
31. Byrne to RG, May 10, 1985, RCGC.
32. Peter Guzzardi, senior editor, Bantam Books, New York NY, to Burger, May 15, 1985, RCGC, with Gordon's underlining; Guzzardi, "A Brief History of *A Brief History of Time* by Stephen Hawking," *The Guardian*, March 14, 2018; Stephen Hawking, *A Brief History of Time: From the Big Bang to Black Holes* (New York: Bantam Books, 1988).
33. Burger to RG, July 26, 1985, RCGC, with many marginal notes by Gordon.
34. Burger to RG, August 1, 1985, RCGC; RG to Burger, September 18, 1985, RCGC.
35. ("quite a blow") RG to Burger, August 6, 1984, RCGC; RG to Byrne, August 8, 1985, RCGC; Byrne to RG, August 12, 1985, RCGC. The former partners continued a cordial correspondence through the next year. For example, see "Bob" [Robert Byrne] to "Bob" [RG], January 5, 1986, RCGC; RG to Byrne, March 6, 1986, RCGC; "Bob" [Robert Byrne] to "Bob" [RG], March 17, October 10, November 21, 1986, "Bob" [Robert Byrne] to "Bob" [RG], October 10, 1986, RCGC.
36. Burger to RG, September 18, 1985, RCGC; *Publishers Weekly*, September 27, 1985; Cliff C. Jones, *Winning through Integrity* (Nashville TN: Abingdon Press, 1985).

12. THE GORDON THESIS

1. RG to Kathy Robbins, November 27, 1984, RCGC, with an enclosure of part 1 of his manuscript. Robbins referred to having read "those new pages (paying particular attention to pages 190–291)." Robbins to RG, December 28, 1984, RCGC. This correspondence gave a good indication of Gordon's writing progress to date.
2. RG to Knox Burger, May 1, 1985, RCGC.
3. Gordon went so far as to add an entire section as a recap, introduced by "Hallmark had actual knowledge of the following facts." RG 1984 MS, 186–89.

4. Robert Byrne to RG, April 15, 1985, RCGC. Byrne mentioned the shift to first person took place in chapter 17. Byrne to RG, May 10, 1985, RCGC.
5. Burger to RG, February 16, 1985, RCGC; "I'm closing in on the final three chapters." RG to Byrne, August 26, 1985, RCGC. Gordon sent part 1 to Robbins with this comment, "I think Chapters 11–13 (pages 190 to 291) are pretty darn good," which indicated that chapter 10 ended at page 189. RG to Robbins, November 27, 1984, RCGC. Robbins to RG, December 28, 1984, RCGC. Note the progress to date: thirteen chapters by late 1984 and before Byrne's involvement.
6. RG 1984 MS, iii–vi, xx.
7. Gordon gave two different names for the night watchman: William Champion and Frank Cushman. "Champion" is found in Gordon's notations on a letter from Fred Hills, Simon & Schuster, New York NY, to RG, September 23, 1987, RCGC. "Cushman" is found in RG 1984 MS, 6. Elsewhere, the watchman is identified as Frank Elliott. Richard A. Serrano, *Buried Truths*, 58.
8. Rick Alm, "The Hyatt Judge: Tragedy, Controversy, and Scott O. Wright," *Star*, February 6, 1983; Scott O. Wright and Larry M. Schumaker, *Never in Doubt: Memoirs of an Uncommon Judge* (Kansas City MO: Kansas City Star Books, 2007); Donnelly to REP, August 10, 2018; (Popeye) Book proposal, "Skywalks: The Kansas City Hyatt Regency Disaster," n.d., RCGC; (convertible) Reed Whitaker, Overland Park KS, to REP, notes of personal conversation, January 22, 2019, author's collection.
9. ("favorably") Woods to REP, May 22, 2018; Foote to REP, December 28, 2018.
10. Joyce C. Hall with Curtiss Anderson, *When You Care Enough* (Kansas City MO: Hallmark Cards, 1979), quoted in RG 1984 MS, 42.
11. RG 1984 MS, 7. The full passage from which this phrase came was: "The bridges through the space connecting the function block to the tower would be made as thin and as invisible as possible to not be distracting." Jeannette Lee deposition, June 3, 1982, no. 1,907, *FSC*, NARA, which cited notes from a design review meeting of August 1, 1977. Jeannette Spears Lee was Hallmark's vice president of corporate design. See also RG 1995 MS, 429–30, which cited minutes taken by Steve Byers as another source for the damaging quote "as thin and as invisible as possible."
12. RG 1984 MS, 20.
13. RG 1984 MS, 21–22, 24, 32–34.
14. RG 1984 MS, 24–26.
15. RG 1984 MS, 37–38; T. K. Terrebone, "Special Report," R. I. No. 24-9024, November 20, 1979, RCGC. Terrebone gave the extent of the damaged roof as 2,000 square feet, but a higher figure of 2,700 is more likely. Keith Kelly, "Report to Don Hall for the Period October 1 through October 31, 1979," November 1979, RCGC.
16. RG 1984 MS, 30.
17. RG 1984 MS, 29.

18. RG 1984 MS, 46. Exploding Pinto automobiles captured the news cycle in 1978, when the Ford Motor Company faced massive automobile recalls.
19. William S. Johnson, "Private Thoughts about Public Relations," *Midcontinent Perspectives*, Midwest Research Institute, Kansas City MO, March 24, 1987, 7.
20. RG 1984 MS, 47.
21. "Beam Collapse at Downtown Hotel," *Times*, October 17, 1979. When reporters later excavated this brief article with no byline, its author remained anonymous. Joe Popper, "The Prize: The Inside Story; How the *Star* and *Times* Covered the Hyatt Disaster, Part 1," *Kansas City Magazine* 8 (November 1983): 65.
22. RG 1984 MS, 50–51; Philip L. Burgert, "Looking Up; Hyatt Has Bookings for 1992," *Times*, October 18, 1979. The managing editor mentioned that the combined papers had 320 "journalists" on staff when it covered the Hyatt story in 1981–82. Mike Waller, *Blood on the Out-Basket: Lessons in Leadership from a Newspaper Junkie* (Kansas City MO: Kansas City Star Books, 2011), 55.
23. RG 1984 MS, 52–53.
24. RG 1984 MS, 40–41, 43–44, 56. The consortium of local firms that constituted PBNDML came up with its name from the last initials of its principal architects: R. Bruce Patty, Robert Berkebile, Tom Nelson, Herbert Duncan, John C. Monroe, and Gene E. LeFevre. The group, having served its purpose, only lasted as long as the Hyatt project and ensuing lawsuits.
25. "HAA's Harvard Medal Recipients Announced," *Harvard Gazette*, May 27, 2015, https://news.harvard.edu/gazette/story/2015/05/haas-harvard-medal-recipients-announced/; "Charles J. Egan Jr., AB, LLB," *Marquis Who's Who Top Lawyers*, June 26, 2019, https://marquistoplawyers.com/2019/06/26/charles-egan/ (page no longer available); ("articulate") RG 1984 MS, 113; (aristocratic, "Olympian") Brisbane to REP and JM, July 22, 2016; RG 1995 MS, 96, 387.
26. Fred Barbash, "Protestors Deny Woman Judgeship," *Washington Post*, December 23, 1981; Associated Press, "Woman Off List for Judgeship," *New York Times*, December 24, 1981; "Political Snipers and a Good Judge," *New York Times*, January 7, 1982; Lola Butcher, "Little Deliberation Guides Fast Career of Woman Lawyer," *Kansas City Business Journal*, January 11, 1991. For a history of Kansas City's Central Exchange, see "Our History, Where It All Began," *Central Exchange: Where Women Shape the Future*, https://centralexchange.org/our-history/. Whittaker married Kent E. Whittaker in 1960 and earned her law degree in 1963. For biographical information, see "Judith Ann Cameron Whittaker, Lawyer," *Prabook*, https://prabook.com/web/judith_ann_cameron.whittaker/1241538. She was age forty-three at the time of the vacancy on the Eighth Circuit.
27. RG 1984 MS, 56–58. Gordon's editors at Simon & Schuster instructed him to "avoid 'Mrs.' and 'Ms.'" to which Gordon noted in the margins "NO—*Mrs.* Whittaker." Hills and Burton Beals to RG, n.d., RCGC. ("raven hair") RG 1995 MS, 304.

28. RG 1984 MS, 104; Judith Whittaker, "Skywalk Wars," UMKC *Law Review* 52 (Winter 1984): 296–305; based on Whittaker's address to the Annual Convention of the International Society of Barristers, Marco Island FL, March 1983, and reprinted by the University of Missouri–Kansas City. A copy of the article can be found in the Gordon collection with his marginal notes. See also Ron Ostroff, "Magazine Examines Hyatt Case; Attorneys, Press Are Evaluated in Law Review," *Times*, February 13, 1984.
29. RG 1984 MS, 60–63; ("tiny," "jumbo-size") RG 1995 MS, 305. Heydinger's meeting notes confirmed the account of the methods taken. "It just wasn't reasonable to expect 'our (Crown Center/Hallmark's) engineers (Gillum-Colaco)' to candidly and completely investigate their own work and then 'blow the whistle' on everything that they had done wrong," especially if the costs would come out of their pockets.
30. RG 1984 MS, 67.
31. RG 1984 MS, 68, 75, 77, 83–86, 88.
32. RG 1984 MS, 91, 92, 94, 96–97, which identified the messenger as Robert Stark, group vice president, Hallmark Cards. The name of the hapless, inexperienced inspector was Daniel H. Hafley, who was twenty-one years old at the time of the atrium roof collapse. The Hyatt project was his first full-time job. At the time of his 1982 deposition Hafley was a junior at the University of Missouri–Kansas City majoring in business administration. "Deposition Summary of Daniel Hafley," RCGC. Gordon referred to him as "an honest kid." RG 1984 MS, 93.
33. RG 1984 MS, 99–100. In a 1982 deposition Gillum told under oath the story of his denied request for an inspector.
34. The accidental death of Louis Paul Nold Jr. prompted an OSHA investigation, but one that did not get near, literally or figuratively, the greater problems in the hotel atrium. Robert Engleman, "Ironworker Killed by Falling Beam at Hyatt Hotel Site," *Times*, October 25, 1979; Engleman, "To Be Cited in Worker's Death," *Times*, November 7, 1979.
35. RG 1984 MS, 108, 110, 113.
36. RG 1984 MS, 116; Pam Wight [Curran], "My Understanding of Hyatt Atrium Collapse," memo-to-file, November 12, 1979, RCGC.
37. RG 1984 MS, 121; ("very best evidence") RG 1995 MS, 451. Pam Curran attended five other post–atrium roof collapse meetings (October 19, November 8 and 15, and December 12 and 31, 1979). Gordon suspected the existence of more tapes, but none appeared to bolster his case or his narrative. RG 1995 MS, 484–85. As a personal aside, for anyone who has ever endured design review meetings of owner, architect, general contractor, and subcontractors for a major building project, especially during the inevitable trying times, the Halvorson transcript is familiar reading, almost Kafkaesque. I got acid flashbacks of my past project management experiences from reading the dialogue.

38. RG 1984 MS, 126, 127, 132. Gillum-Colaco employees who worked on the Hyatt project included Ed Jantosik and Greg Luth, among others. Gordon never blamed the underlings involved in the Hallmark hotel disaster as much as he did the bigwigs.
39. RG 1984 MS, 132, 135.
40. RG 1984 MS, 136–37.
41. RG 1984 MS, 145–46.
42. RG 1984 MS, 151, 152, 156, 161.
43. RG 1984 MS, 171–74, which cited the concerns of Shorty Williamson, one of those savvy construction workers. "I didn't mind telling anybody, they [the skywalks] worried the hell out of me. They was [*sic*] too heavy for those skinny little hanger rods."
44. RG 1984 MS, 180–82.
45. RG 1984 MS, 162, 179–80.
46. RG 1984 MS, 183, 185.
47. Isadore Barmash, "Hallmark's Fight to Stay on Top," *New York Times*, December 25, 1983, which numbered Hallmark's employees at fourteen thousand nationally. Six hundred "creatives" alone worked in Kansas City, a fraction of those employed by the company locally.
48. RG 1984 MS, 150.

13. RINSE AND REPEAT

1. RG to Kathy Robbins, August 9, 1985, RCGC.
2. Robbins to RG, August 20, 1985, RCGC; Robbins [to RG?], October 10, 1985, RCGC. The corporation A. H. Robins, responsible for a fatally flawed birth-control device, filed for bankruptcy in 1985. A book by the investigative reporter who originally broke the story came out at the time of this correspondence. Morton Mintz, *At Any Cost: Corporate Greed, Women, and the Dalkon Shield* (New York: Pantheon, 1985).
3. RG to Joe Williams, Dewey, Ballantine Law Firm, New York NY, February 27, 1986, RCGC. "The legal review by Dewey, Ballentine [*sic*] has begun," wrote Gordon, "but we need to talk further about the scope of it since my legal fees could make a substantial reduction in the national deficit." A review of the manuscript by this firm, if ever completed, has not turned up. RG to Julian Bach, Julian Bach Literary Agency, New York NY, February 26, 1986, RCGC.
4. ("surge") RG to Paul Haskins, New York NY, January 16, 1986, RCGC; ("continue to work") RG to Haskins, February 19, 1986, RCGC. This was quite a commitment of time, but Gordon was in the midst of a legal lull at the time. "Time Records—Skywalks Litigation, February 12, 1984, to December 30, 1988," RCGC (hereafter cited as TRSL). This document is not to be confused with Gordon's earlier "daily time records."
5. Brisbane to REP and JM, July 22, 2016.

6. Douglas Martin, "Paul J. Haskins, 62, Editor at *The Times*," *New York Times*, November 25, 2003; ("need you here") RG to Haskins, *New York Times*, New York NY, December 10, 1982, RCGC. Haskins, "Collapse of Hotel's 'Skywalks' in 1981 Is Still Reverberating in Kansas City," *New York Times*, March 29, 1983. See also RG to Haskins, February 10, 1983, RCGC.
7. RG to Bach, January 17, 1986, RCGC. Jim Powell, author of *Risk, Ruin & Riches: Inside the World of Big Time Real Estate* (New York: Macmillan, 1986), recommended Bach to Gordon. Powell's book contained a chapter, "Deadly Oversight," on the Hyatt collapse. "Julian Bach," obituary, *New York Times*, October 1, 2011.
8. John Garrity to REP and JM, notes of personal conversation, August 16, 2016, author's collection. Jim Backus, to whom Garrity referred, played the over-the-top millionaire Thurston Howell III on the equally outlandish 1960s situation comedy.
9. Jonathan Segura, "Pat Conroy Dies at Age 70," *Publishers Weekly*, March 5, 2016; ("rude") Sam Staggs, "The Prince of Tides," *Publishers Weekly*, September 5, 1986.
10. G. Fred Wickman, "Hoover Prize for a Writer," *Times*, December 24, 1985; Biographical note on John Garrity, January 1986, RCGC; Garrity to REP and JM, August 16, 2016.
11. John Garrity, *The George Brett Story* (New York: Coward, McCann and Geoghegan, 1981); Joan Terry Garrity and John Garrity, *The Story of "J": The Sensuous Woman Tells the Bitter Price of Her Crazy Success* (New York: William Morrow, 1984).
12. "J" [Joan Terry Garrity], *The Sensuous Woman: The First How-to Book for the Female Who Yearns to Be All Woman* (New York: Lyle Stuart, 1969); Bill Althaus, "Interview: Terry Garrity," *Kansas City Magazine* 9 (October 1984): 21–26; Amy Wilson, "Rediscovering the 'Sensuous Woman,'" *South Florida Sun Sentinel* (Deerfield Beach FL), December 22, 1988. John Garrity also received credit as a coauthor with his sister for *The Sensuous Man*, a 1971 follow-up. "M," *The Sensuous Man: The First How-to Book for the Man Who Wants to Be a Great Lover* (New York: Lyle Stuart, 1971). This publication did not appear on the previously cited résumé that he supplied to Robert Gordon at the time of their initial discussion, a discreet omission that does not seem all that surprising.
13. RG to Bach, January 17, 1986, RCGC; Notes of phone conversation, RG and Garrity, January 24, 1986, RCGC; ("easy project") Garrity to REP and JM, August 16, 2016. Garrity only learned the names of the other collaborators in the course of this interview.
14. Garrity to REP and JM, August 16, 2016. As an example of his up-front manner, Garrity revealed in a "full disclosure" at the time of his 2016 interview that his daughter worked as an executive at Hallmark.
15. Garrity to REP and JM, August 16, 2016.
16. ("the master") Garrity to REP and JM, August 16, 2016; RG to Bach, February 26, 1986, RCGC, in which Gordon enclosed "revised Chapter 17 which Garrity edited from two of my original chapters. . . . Unfortunately, John's synopses were generally unhelpful and probably a waste of money."

17. Haskins to RG, March 23, 1986, RCGC; RG to Bach, April 10, 1986, RCGC; RG to Haskins, April 11, 1986, RCGC.
18. Garrity to REP and JM, August 16, 2016.
19. RG to Haskins, May 8, 1986, RCGC. "The total number of pages contained in the 10 chapters which you have sent me so far is 182." The other fifteen chapters were expected in "two weeks or less." Interestingly and maybe coincidentally, the first ten chapters of "When They Didn't Care Enough" (1984) totaled 189.
20. Garrity to REP and JM, August 16, 2016.
21. Haskins to RG, May 19, 1986, RCGC.
22. RG to Haskins, June 18, 1986, RCGC. Gordon's handwritten letter reflected both highs and lows. "As discouraging and unpleasant as our present relationship is and as dubious the prospects are of there ever being a Skywalks book, miracles do seem to happen at the oddest times and in the most unexpected ways." ("work and travail") Haskins to RG, June 27, 1986, RCGC, referring to Gordon's letter of June 18, in which the return of photos was requested: "I can only assume you did not comprehend what I was telling you in our last phone conversation, so I will repeat it succinctly here." ("unconscionable") Haskins to RG, August 11, 1986, copied to Bach, RCGC, in which Haskins referred to a Missouri newspaper article of July 20 that stated the book was coming out in December. This correspondence occurred when things were heating up for Gordon with the John Jacob case. The "another writer" was, of course, Robert Byrne. John Garrity only received a fraction of that sum, a total of $16,500, for twenty-two weeks of contracted work. Bach to RG, February 23, 1987, RCGC.
23. RG to Haskins, August 19, 1986, RCGC. This letter to Haskins mirrors Gordon's angry letter to Byrne the year before in which he negatively cited Younger and Wolff and also employed his stock phrase, "Angry? You bet I am." RG to Robert Byrne, May 14, 1985, RCGC.
24. Bach to Haskins, September 19, 1986, RCGC. Bach refuted the points made in the Haskins letter of August 11 to RG and added, "He [Gordon] would still be interested to have you contribute a chapter from your point of view regarding what went on at the paper."
25. Garrity to REP and JM, August 16, 2016. Garrity used a word processing software program called *Executive Secretary*.
26. Garrity to REP and JM, August 16, 2016. See also RG to Garrity, April 4, 1986, RCGC. "You had earlier told me that you would assist with the conclusion of the book. I think I still have a few days coming on the basis of the old agreement." RG enclosed chapters 47 and 48, "the only part that is missing from what you already have." RG to Bach, August 19, RCGC. Gordon detailed the compensation to Garrity. "As I promised, I am enclosing the check to John, although the contract has not been signed." He expressed his concern: "[A] ton of work by him remains unfinished and

in view of his failure to complete what he promised me last January, I worry that he may not give *Skywalks* the time it deserves as soon as the check clears. Please don't pass that on to John." RG to Bach, September 18, 1986, RCGC.

27. Bach to RG and Garrity, August 18, 1986, RCGC. "I think this is a very good manuscript. Very solid. Thoroughly readable. . . . You both should be proud and pleased." Bach has several notes: "'When they didn't care enough' seems to me a good title provided the subheading makes it plain that this refers to the Hallmark-Hyatt disaster." At about the same time, Joe Colussi, Judge Wright's clerk, reviewed the draft for Gordon and felt assured that he would "someday read about you receiving a Pulitzer Prize." Joseph A. Colussi of Eckert Alcorn Goerring & Colussi, Madison IN, to RG, November 3, 1986, RCGC.
28. Garrity to REP and JM, August 16, 2016. See also Bach to RG, February 23, 1987, RCGC, for the state of the collaboration. "Each of you have made known to me a degree of serious dissatisfaction with the other."
29. "Publishing Agreement, Simon & Schuster, Inc., and Robert C. Gordon," with the notation, "Gordon's work copy, 12-12-86," RCGC; Bach to RG, December 19, 1986, RCGC; Bach to Fred W. Hills, vice president and senior editor, Simon & Schuster, New York NY, January 6, 1987, RCGC; Bach to RG, February 23, 1987, RCGC, which notes the official end of the Garrity partnership. "Now that you have received payment of the first half of the Simon & Schuster advance, the time has come to settle financial accounts with John Garrity." To date, Garrity had received $11,000 with a balance due of $5,500.

14. WHAT MIGHT HAVE BEEN

1. Book order form for *House of Cards*, 1991, RCGC.
2. Walter Lord, *A Night to Remember* (New York: Henry Holt, 1955).
3. "After five years of work . . . I finished my book . . . which is set for publication by year-end 1987." RG to unknown, April 20, 1987, RCGC, accompanied by a narrative about Gordon's reaction to the disaster and how he came to be involved in the class action. Burton L. Beals, Simon & Schuster, New York NY, to RG, March 11, 1991, RCGC, which included a book order form: "Coming in June [1991] from Simon and Schuster." Exposing a blown-up publication schedule, the *House of Cards* copy for an S&S catalog destined only for bookstores had been prepared as long ago as June 1988. Frederic W. Hills, vice president and senior editor, Simon & Schuster, New York NY, to RG, October 25, 1988, RCGC.
4. Hills to RG, December 2, 1992, RCGC, which rejected the manuscript for length but allowed "non-official extension until March 1, 1993." The last nail in the coffin was "I'm afraid we have come to the end of the road with the manuscript." Hills to RG, March 12, 1993, RCGC. (biographical information on Fred Hills) Carol Galligan, "Shaped by Wonderful Teachers, Shaping Wonderful Books," *Shelter Island Reporter* (Mattituck NY), September 2, 2010, https://shelterislandreporter.timesreview.com

/2010/09/02/shaped-by-wonderful-teachers%E2%80%A8shaping-wonderful-books-%E2%80%A9/. The issue of the excessive length of "House of Cards" extended for years between Gordon and Simon & Schuster. RG to Elizabeth McNamara, legal department, Simon & Schuster, New York NY, February 28, 1989, in which Gordon admitted, "I must finish reviewing the remaining 12 chapters, which I received from the copy editor on Saturday, and cut approximately 100 pages from the text, per Fred Hills's recent request."

5. Formal termination occurred on March 22, 1993. Hills to RG, March 19, 1993, RCGC. Hills added, "Let Julian [Bach] find you an enthusiastic publisher," which never happened.
6. From the start, Hills had wanted Gordon to "cut the story of the legal battle by half." Hills to RG, February 3, 1987, RCGC; Hills to RG, September 23, 1987, RCGC. Cutting the manuscript became a constant refrain. Hills to RG, February 21, 1989, RCGC.
7. RG to Donald J. Hall, 6320 Aberdeen Road, Mission Hills KS, March 7, 1988, RCGC. Hall lived about six blocks from Gordon's home. Gordon's later description of this missive sounded a bit far-fetched: "It was sent after I thought the whole case [*Jacob v. Hallmark*] was over and wrapped up with. . . . It was a personal letter that I sent a neighbor and also had questions in it." "Transcript of Proceedings," March 2, 1989, no. 163, *Jacob v. Hallmark*, NARA.
8. (roommate) RG 1995 MS, 140; "Robert J. Sisk," obituary, *Hartford (CT) Courant*, August 13, 2004.
9. Robert J. Sisk of Hughes, Hubbard & Reed, New York NY, to RG, March 23, 1988, RCGC.
10. Hughes, Hubbard & Reed, "The Fallacy of the Gordon Thesis," February 1989, RCGC; RG 1995 MS, 758n; Beals to RG, March 31, 1989, RCGC. The timing of this document and its attempt to damage a vulnerable Gordon becomes clearer when the events of chapter 16 are considered.
11. ("perverse obsession") Sisk to RG, March 23, 1988, RCGC.
12. RG 1995 MS, 454, 725.
13. Ken Pattison, a technician with Beatty Recording Studio, Kansas City MO, listened "to a few minutes of one tape and advised us that it would be pointless to try to enhance its quality." John C. Aisenbrey of Stinson Mag & Fizzell, Kansas City MO, to RG, October 8, 1982, RCGC. The plaintiffs' lawyers took up Aisenbrey's offer to try again with a "mutually agreeable expert" under "proper safeguards." Obviously, the results of Halvorson's later work proved this local consultant wrong.
14. HHR was referring to Rick Serrano's involvement with the questionable Hallmark transcript, whose contents came into question by Halvorson's. Richard A. Serrano, "Hyatt Owners Were Told Skywalks Were Safe; Load Problems Were Discussed in 1979 Meeting with Engineers," *Times*, December 11, 1982; RG to Serrano, December 13, 1982, correspondence, *FSC*, NARA; also found in RCGC.

15. Notes of lunch meeting between Robert Sisk and RG, May 31, 1986, RCGC; TRSL, May 31, 1986, RCGC, after which Gordon "prepared memo re what transpired at incredible proceeding." His notes survive, but the memo has not yet turned up.
16. RG to McNamara, February 8, 1989, RCGC. McNamara was reading the manuscript of "House of Cards." McNamara to RG, February 23, 1989, RCGC; RG to McNamara, February 28, 1989, RCGC, in which Gordon enclosed "2,500 pages of source documents for my book." RG to McNamara, March 11, 1989, RCGC, in which Gordon enclosed his "Chronology of Events Preceding Skywalks' Collapse" and supporting documentation, "almost all of which was obtained directly from Crown Center/Hallmark's files." RG to McNamara, March 13, 1989, RCGC, in which Gordon replied to her thirty pages of inquiries via enclosures, which were not attached. See also RG to Steven Manning, legal department, Simon & Schuster, New York NY, May 11, 1989, RCGC, in which Gordon sent four depositions as requested and said, "Please continue to be as demanding of me as you have been."
17. Steve Paul, "Bibliofiles: A Hyatt Book," *Star*, March 26, 1989. He got the schedule confirmation from editor Fred Hills. Paul (no relation to me) served as the newspaper's book maven until his 2016 retirement. Elle Moxley, "Steve Paul Reflects on 41 Years at the Kansas City Star," KCUR 89.3, Kansas City MO, March 25, 2016, https://www.kcur.org/community/2016-03-25/steve-paul-reflects-on-41-years-at-the-kansas-city-star.
18. Beals to RG, January 23, 1990, RCGC.
19. Hills to RG, September 23, 1987, RCGC, which set the stage for later editorial recommendations; Beals to RG, March 31, 1990, RCGC; Beals to RG, May 17, 1990, RCGC.
20. RG to Beals, November 6, 1990, RCGC.
21. Beals to RG, March 11, 1991, RCGC. See also Beals to RG, February 27, 1991, RCGC.
22. Hills to RG, March 9, 1992, RCGC; RG to Hills, July 31, 1992, RCGC; Hills to RG, November 7, 1991, RCGC; RG to Eric Rayman, legal department, Simon & Schuster, New York NY, November 7, 1991, RCGC; Hills to RG, November 13, 1991, RCGC; RG to Hills, November 23, 1991, RCGC; RG to Hills, January 4, 1992, RCGC.
23. Hills to RG, December 2, 1992, RCGC, in which Hills rejected "House of Cards" but gave Gordon an extension until March 1, 1993; RG to Hills, February 11, 1993, RCGC; Hills to RG, March 12, 1993, RCGC; Felice Javit, legal department, Simon & Schuster, New York NY, to RG, care of Julian Bach Literary Agency, March 22, 1993, RCGC, which referred to their contract of December 5, 1986. ("too long and too late") Ann Rittenberg, Ann Rittenberg Literary Agency, New York NY, to REP, July 19, 2018, author's collection. Rittenberg worked for Julian Bach when he served as Gordon's agent and remembered the project but not in detail. In her opinion and that of the professional peers she consulted, she doubted that Hallmark exerted any financial pressure on Simon & Schuster and felt that even if it was attempted, it would not have been effective. "Staff, Ann Rittenberg Literary Agency, Inc.," https://www.rittlit.com/staff/.

24. This is the final page count for Gordon's "House of Cards: The Cover-Up Behind the Worst Structural Collapse in American History—Hallmark's Hyatt Regency Skywalks Disaster," manuscript, 1995, RCGC. The date of 1995 is assigned from a Post-It note in Gordon's handwriting on the first page: "Marsha's yellowed highlights/Feb 1995." (The mysterious "Marsha" remains elusive.) Gordon did not number his endnotes within the main body (like those in this book) but created citations identified by page number and a tagline from the text. The notes added another twenty-three highly condensed pages to the manuscript. Beals to RG, March 11, 1991, RCGC.

15. EXCERPT

1. Excerpt from chapter 2, "Tea Dancing at the Hyatt," RG 1995 MS, 40–48. Gordon's sources for the eyewitness testimony have been gathered in the "Bibliographic Essay" to this book under the categories of "collapse survivors" and "rescuers."
2. The Hyatt doorman may have been Erik Walker, who returned to work when the hotel reopened in October. Richard A. Serrano, "Doors Open at Hyatt after Panel Calls It Safe," *Times*, October 2, 1981, with photo of Walker by John Spink. The Kansas City Fire Department dispatcher who received the first emergency call from the Hyatt was Phillip Wall, who later that night went to the hotel to help in the rescue effort. Robert C. Trussell, "By the Minute, Dispatchers Hear Tragedy Unfold," *Star*, July 19, 1981. John T. "Jeff" Nixon, the hotel's last fatality, died from his injuries on December 1, 1981.
3. Molly Riley to RG, July 8, 1991, RCGC. Two other such notes came from John Carl Jacob III ("To Whom It May Concern," June 12, 1991, RCGC), where Jacob described "this document" as "a fair, accurate and very conservative account," and from Judge Scott O. Wright (to RG, December 26, 1991, RCGC), in which Wright stated, "I have read the excerpts from the transcript of Robert Gordon's book about the Hyatt Hotel Collapse and the subsequent law suit and it conforms to my recollection of the events."

16. INTERRUPTIONS

1. RG to Scott O. Wright, January 19, 1983, correspondence, *FSC*, NARA. Gordon noted that he "delivered letter (13 pgs.) to Judge Wright's chambers (supported settlement because it makes economic sense in view of the few people who were left, but trying to, at least, get some points across & to be sure that record is set straight to best of my ability of [on] some key matters)." DTR, January 19, 1983, RCGC.
2. "Hearing Today on Hyatt Settlement," *Star*, January 20, 1983; Ron Ostroff, "Blame for Skywalks Disaster Debated at Hearing," *Times*, January 21, 1983.
3. A later editor pointed out this dichotomy in Gordon's treatment of Wright in his manuscript, without mentioning or knowing about any possible daddy issues. Burton Beals, Simon & Schuster, New York NY, to RG, March 31, 1989, RCGC.

4. "Transcript of Proceedings," January 20, 1983, no. 2,049, FSC, NARA. Sisk's initial remarks cover pages 25–43. ("rich . . . baritone") RG to Robert Byrne, April 5, 1985, RCGC.
5. DTR, January 20, 1983, RCGC.
6. "Transcript of Proceedings," January 20, 1983, no. 2,049, FSC, NARA. Gordon's rebuttal spans pages 56–81. Gordon, having gathered himself a bit, followed up with written particulars to his rebuttal. RG to Wright, January 28, 1983, correspondence, FSC, NARA, in which Gordon was "unable to agree with some of the proposed Findings of Fact submitted to you on January 23, 1983, by Counsel for Hallmark and Crown Center."
7. RG, "Final Report, Part One," February 18, 1983, RCGC. Gordon sent a copy to the paper, "hopeful that you will publish" it, which they did not. RG to Michael J. Davies, editor and president, *Kansas City Times*, February 8, 1983, RCGC.
8. Ron Ostroff, *Times*, January 21, 1983. See also Toni Cardarella, "Hotel Tragedy Settlements Nearly Complete," *United Press International Archives*, January 23, 1983.
9. Arthur S. Brisbane, "Behind the Lines: A Tragic Question Lingers On," *Star*, January 12, 1983. Including a six-year stint at the *Washington Post*, Brisbane moved up the ranks rapidly in Kansas City, from columnist to editor of the *Star* (1992), then to publisher (1997). He ended his affiliation with the paper after his service as senior vice president for the Knight Ridder chain (2005–6), which had bought the *Star* in 1997. Jeff Hanna, "Arthur Brisbane, Former Public Editor of New York Times, to Teach at W&L [Washington and Lee University]," *New York Times*, March 29, 2013; Arthur S. Brisbane résumé, 2016, author's collection; ("atmosphere") Brisbane to REP and JM, notes of phone conversation, July 22, 2016, author's collection.
10. ("a calculated risk") Brisbane, "Behind the Lines," RCGC. The tentative title also appeared in letters from RG to Davies, February 8, 1983, RCGC. RG to Jay McDonald, Santa Monica CA, February 23, 1983, RCGC; RG to Robert L. Collins, Houston TX, March 8, 1983, RCGC; RG to Dede Thompson Bartlett, New Canaan CT, April 18, 1983, RCGC. Gordon may have concluded from Brisbane's public utterance that here was a kindred spirit, and not long after, he reached out to the journalist as a possible collaborator on his book. Talks got serious, and money and bylines were discussed, but Brisbane in due course wisely demurred. Brisbane, *Kansas City Star* and *Kansas City Times*, Kansas City MO, to RG, June 7, 1983, RCGC. Brisbane later observed that the "agitated" Gordon was on "a futile mission," although "he was probably right, but the process of helping him with this was daunting." Brisbane to REP and JM, July 22, 2016; DTR, January 18, 23, 1983, RCGC, which mentioned phone conversations with Brisbane.
11. Gordon notations on Beals to RG, March 31, 1989, RCGC.
12. Richard M. Johnson and David Hayes, "Taxpayers Lose as Inspectors Cheat; Buildings Often Unchecked; Workers Falsify Records, Loaf," *Star*, January 30, 1983; David Hayes and Richard M. Johnson, "City Suspends Inspectors, Removes Supervisor; Angry Officials Pledge Quick Action in Scandal," *Times*, January 31, 1983; Richard M. Johnson and David Hayes, "City Spends Less on Inspections, despite Promises,"

Times, January 31, 1983; "What Is Happening to Our City Government?," editorial, *Star*, January 31, 1983; "13 Building Inspectors Fired," *United Press International Archives*, February 10, 1983, https://www.upi.com/Archives/1983/02/10/Thirteen-building-inspectors-fired/2159413701200/; Paul J. Haskins, "Collapse of Hotel's 'Skywalks' in 1981 Is Still Reverberating in Kansas City," *New York Times*, March 29, 1983. The two Hyatt-related inspectors were Jack T. Pullman and Dominic A. Serrone.

13. RG 1995 MS, 645.
14. Lewis W. Diuguid, "Injured Woman, Husband Get $2 Million in Hyatt Case," *Times*, July 15, 1983.
15. Ron Ostroff, "Hyatt Victim Hopes to Help Others," *Times*, September 20, 1983; Ron Ostroff, "Jury Awards $15 Million to Skywalks Victims," *Times*, September 22, 1983. The juror quoted was Grover T. Haas of Raytown, a Kansas City, Missouri, suburb. Ron Ostroff, "New Dreams Are Start of New Life for Sally Firestone," *Times*, September 24, 1983. Lawyers for the defendants appealed the amount of the award because, well, they could, but they only succeeded in securing a $2.25 million reduction. Ron Ostroff, "Defense Seeks to Slash Firestone Verdict in Skywalks Case," *Times*, October 22, 1983; Ron Ostroff, "Firestone Agrees to Judge's Cut in Jury Verdict," *Times*, December 28, 1983. Missouri's Supreme Court later stuck their collective thumbs in the appeals court's eyes and restored Firestone's original award. Tom Miller, "Judges Lose Authority to Trim Jury Awards," *Times*, June 26, 1985; Firestone v. Crown Center Redevelopment Corp., Supreme Court of Missouri, en banc., June 25, 1985, 693 S.W. 2d 99 (1985). In recognition of her longtime advocacy work, Sally Firestone received an award in 2016 from the Kansas City organization The Whole Person, People with Disabilities Leading Independent Lives. "Summer Celebrations at The Whole Person," *TWP Connects*, Fall 2016, 1, 3.
16. Jeff Taylor, "Sky-High Proposal at Game Signals Wedding for Couple," *Times*, November 12, 1984; Lantz Welch, *Mr. Lucky*, n.d., memoir, http://lantzlot.com/ebook/MrLucky_ebook.pdf; Lewis W. Diuguid, "Man Awarded $17.5 Million for Brain Injury," *Times*, April 14, 1984; Tim O'Connor, "Jury Gives $49 Million in Chemical Suit," *Times*, December 24, 1985; Ian Cummings and Joyce Smith, "Trial Lawyer Lantz Welch, Known for Big Verdicts and His Weatherby Lake Castle Has Died," *Star*, July 23, 2016; Cynthia Billhartz Gregorian, "Camelot's Tale: How Weatherby Lake's Castle, Now for Sale, Came to Be," *Star*, April 28, 2017. Information on the sale of Welch's home came from Zillow, https://www.zillow.com/homedetails/10000-NW-75th-St-Kansas-City-MO-64152/2499916.
17. RG to Lantz Welch, Kansas City MO, February 16, 1983, RCGC.
18. "Meeting of November 13, 1979," Halvorson & Associates, transcript of cassette recording, n.d., 76 pp., RCGC. The Halvorson transcript came via Williams & Connolly, which had been recalcitrant to return and turn over skywalk documents to Gordon.

19. RG to Wright, October 4, 1983, RCGC. Gordon considered this "letter-report" as the second part of his final report. RG to Wright, November 11, 1984, RCGC. Gordon sent a copy to Robert B. Schneider in the U.S. Attorney's Office, Kansas City MO.
20. RG to Schneider, assistant U.S. attorney and special prosecuting attorney for Jackson County, Kansas City MO, October 12, 1983, RCGC; Robert G. Ulrich, U.S. attorney, by Schneider, to RG, October 18, 1983, RCGC. See also John T. Dauner, "U.S. Attorney Joins Hyatt Case Investigation," *Times*, July 13, 1983, which made a vague reference to a document that was probably Gordon's December 5, 1982, brief; Lewis W. Diuguid, "Grand Jury to Hear Evidence in Skywalks Probes," *Times*, October 6, 1983, which mentioned that the inquiry intended to include possible perjury violations.
21. Rick Alm, "Probe of Hyatt Finds No Evidence of Crime; Grand Jury Ends Investigation of Skywalks Collapse," *Star*, December 16, 1983, which was a page 1, above-the-fold story; Associated Press, "Hotel Disaster Inquiry Ends," *New York Times*, December 17, 1983. U.S. attorney Ulrich and Jackson County prosecutor Albert Riederer put out a joint statement that cited "insufficient evidence" for any criminal charges. Reporter Alm may have had qualms about the end of the criminal investigation. In a later conversation he told Gordon in no uncertain terms, "Hell, Bobby, you & I both saw HMK's memos & letters. They didn't do a single thing w/o calculating beforehand each step of the way. And that's what they did before the skywalks fell. They calculated the whole risk." Notes of a conversation of Rick Alm and Robert Gordon, Putsch's coffee shop on the Plaza, Kansas City MO, October 2, 1986, RCGC.
22. RG to Albert Riederer, prosecuting attorney, Jackson County Courthouse, Kansas City MO, April 7, 1984, RCGC; RG to Riederer, December 13, 1985, RCGC, which referenced other Gordon letters, including April 7, 27, May 2, 21, June 29, 1984, and February 20, 1985. The December 13, 1985, letter was a seven-page argument against Riederer's 1983 decision to close his investigation into the skywalks collapse. Gordon copied Judge Wright. RG to Stephen S. Trott, assistant attorney general, Criminal Division, Department of Justice, Washington DC, December 30, 1985, RCGC. Referred by Charles Breyer, a classmate friend and later federal judge, Northern District of California, U.S. District Court, Gordon sent an eleven-page letter that tried to convince Trott to open a criminal investigation due to the inadequate work by Schneider and David Swartzbaugh, an assistant to the Jackson County prosecutor. TRSL, December 30, 1985, which covered February 23, 1984–December 30, 1988, RCGC.
23. ("finished") Rick Alm, "The Hyatt Judge: Tragedy, Controversy, and Scott O. Wright," *Star*, February 6, 1983; ("that was it") Notes, "Interview with Judge Wright," spring 1984, RCGC. This Gordon interview was distinguished by Wright's frankness: "Well, Bob, I'll tell you something. After they pulled that deal over in State Court, we didn't have anything left. . . . Never in my wildest dreams did I dream that they (the intervenors) would get together with the defendants and cut a deal."

24. ("fatal change") G. William Quatman, "The Hyatt Skywalk Revisited: What Happened? Could It Happen Again?," *Schinnerer's 42nd Annual Meeting of Invited Attorneys*, Victor O. Schinnerer, 2003, https://www.victorinsuranceus.com/ae/Pages/amia-Papers.aspx; David Hayes, "Blame Is Not Likely to Be Established," *Times*, January 11, 1983, in which at this early stage the state licensing board had "focused on two key engineers involved in the design of the walkways." The Missouri attorney general at the time was John Ashcroft, later U.S. senator and U.S. attorney general. "Engineers' Negligence Charged in Kansas City Hotel Disaster," *New York Times*, February 4, 1984. Gordon devoted twenty pages in his manuscript to the Gillum-Duncan hearing and its meaning. RG 1995 MS, 720–40. See also Marty Lanus, "Hyatt Notebook," *Kansas City Magazine* 9 (October 1984): 48–51, 64–67; Marty Lanus, "Hyatt Notebook, Part II," *Kansas City Magazine* 9 (November 1984): 38–41, 63–69.
25. TRSL, July 16–20, August 20–24, 1984, RCGC; Jacob H. Wolf, "Engineers and Firm Negligent in Skywalk Collapse," *United Press International Archives*, November 14, 1985, https://www.upi.com/Archives/1985/11/15/Engineers-and-firm-negligent-in-skywalk-collapse/5145500878800/; Daniel M. Duncan, Jack D. Gillum, and GCE International, Appellants v. Missouri Board for Architects, Professional Engineers, and Land Surveyors, Respondent, no. 52655, Missouri Court of Appeals, Eastern District, Division Three, January 26, 1988, 744 S.W. 2d 524 (1988). The Gillum and Duncan hearing ran from July 16 to August 24, 1984. Judge James B. Deutsch issued his opinion on November 15, 1985, and licenses were revoked on January 22, 1986. After the 1981 collapse, Gillum-Colaco changed its name to GCE International, but before the 1985 ruling it had been taken over by a larger firm and no longer existed as an independent entity. See also "[Report] Before the Administrative Hearing Commission, State of Missouri: Missouri Board for Architects, Professional Engineers and Land Surveyors, Petitioner, v. Daniel M. Duncan, Jack D. Gillum and G.C.E. International, Inc., Respondents," Case No. AR-84-0239 (n.p., 1985), OCLC No. 55182519, 442 pp.
26. ("no individual") Edward H. Kohn, "'Fast-Track' Hyatt Construction Raises Safety Questions," *St. Louis Post-Dispatch*, September 16, 1984; ("total exoneration") Hughes, Hubbard & Reed, "The Fallacy of the Gordon Thesis," February 1989, RCGC; ("screw-ups") RG 1995 MS, 738.
27. For a useful chronology of the events leading to the collapse, put together by and for engineers, see "Engineering Ethics, The Kansas City Hyatt Regency Walkways Collapse," Department of Philosophy and Department of Mechanical Engineering, Texas A&M University, College Station, http://ethics.tamu.edu/wp-content/uploads/sites/7/2017/04/HyattRegency.pdf.
28. ("full design review") RG 1995 MS, 737.
29. As a couple of examples of blame-shifting, when asked, "Who came up with the concept of using rods or cables to support the skywalks?" Berkebile, the principal architect, answered, "I don't know precisely who did it, but I assume it was someone on the

Gillum-Colaco staff." Deposition of Bob Berkebile, July 27–August 2, 1982, nos. 2,028–32, *FSC*, NARA. Herb Duncan, another architect who worked on the project, was asked, "You do not recall who specifically came up with the idea of putting the walkways across the atrium?" His answer was, "I do not." Deposition of Herbert E. Duncan Jr., August 2, 1982, no. 2,039, *FSC*, NARA. Anyone who has worked with top-tier architects would find unconvincing such modesty or lack of knowledge about the authorship of a signature element in a new building.

30. "Rockin' at the T-Dance," The Rainmakers, 1986. Dark rumors persisted years later that the popular song was banned from local radio stations due to outside pressure. Matthew Erich "Mancow" Muller, "How the Hyatt Disaster & Bob Walkenhorst Derailed KC's Rainmakers," *KC Confidential*, May 18, 2012, http://www.kcconfidential.com/2012/05/18/mancow-how-the-hyatt-disaster-bob-walkenhorst-derailed-kcs-rainmakers/. The "big dance floor," as mentioned in the song's lyrics, measured 30 feet by 120 feet and partly extended under the skywalks. RG 1995 MS, 28.
31. Chapter 21, "Danger Invites Rescue," RG 1995 MS, 741–85.
32. Moen L. Phillips v. Hallmark Cards, Inc., Case No. CV84-18306, Circuit Court, Jackson County MO, RCGC; RG to Moen Phillips, May 11, 1984, RCGC, with the attachment of a "Contract for Employment of Attorney"; Rick Alm, "$426 Million Sought for Hyatt Victims," *Star*, September 2, 1984; TRSL, August 31, 1984, RCGC. This document was a continuation of Gordon's habit of creating an informative, at times impolitic daily time record. The entries for this later version generally had shorter entries, which reflected the fewer hours that Gordon devoted to his legal work during his book project period. It commenced on February 23, 1984, with a call from Moen Phillips.
33. Rick Alm, "$426 Million"; RG 1995 MS, 749. The Hallmark lawyer was Charles J. Egan Jr., still the corporation's chief counsel. See also Rick Alm, "Dismissal of Hyatt Suit Sought," *Star*, October 11, 1984.
34. "Attorneys for firefighter Moen L. Phillips said he was one of several persons who assisted in an emergency amputation of a trapped victim's leg with a chainsaw in the hours after the collapse." Rick Alm, "$426 Million." The victim was Jeff Durham. See also RG 1995 MS, 741.
35. Gordon's first meeting with Moen Phillips was February 24, 1984. TRSL, RCGC; Marquis Shepherd, "Fireman's Hyatt Suit Rejected; Rescuers Must Assume Risks, High Court Says," *Times*, December 17, 1986.
36. RG 1995 MS, 743–46.
37. Gordon made his oral argument to the appeals court on November 11, 1985, and heard about its decision to reverse the lower court on April 29, 1986. TRSL, May 13, November 11, 1985, April 29, 1986, RCGC; Dunstan McNichol, "Suit of Injured Fireman Goes to High Court," *Star*, April 29, 1986; ("assume all risks") RG 1995 MS, 751.

38. Phillips v. Hallmark Cards, Inc., 722 S.W.2d 86 (1986), Supreme Court of Missouri, en banc; Shepherd, *Times*, December 17, 1986; TRSL, December 16, 1986, RCGC.

39. "Complaint," June 6, 1986, no. 1, U.S. District Court of the Western District of Missouri, Record Group 21, *John Jacob, et al., v. Hallmark Cards, Inc.*, NARA; "First Amended Complaint," July 16, 1986, no. 19, *John Jacob, Adam Wilson, and Larry Lantz on behalf of themselves, and all others similarly situated, v. Hallmark Cards, Inc., and Crown Center Redevelopment Corporation*, NARA; John T. Dauner, "Class-Action Suit Filed for Rescuers at Hyatt," *Times*, June 7, 1986; RG to John Jacob, Kansas City KS, June 6, 1986, RCGC, which served "as the contract of employment by you for my services." William Dickinson IV, "Lawsuits Filed on Anniversary of Hyatt Disaster," *United Press International Archives*, July 18, 1986, https://www.upi.com/Archives/1986/07/18/Lawsuits-filed-on-anniversary-of-Hyatt-disaster/6746522043200/. Jacob later moved out of state. RG to Jacob, Arlington TX, February 18, 1987, RCGC. Gordon also represented rescuers Larry Lantz and Adam Wilson. RG to Larry Lantz, Roeland Park KS, July 2, 1986, RCGC; RG to Adam Wilson, Kansas City KS, July 2, 1986, RCGC. TRSL, June 5, 6, 11, 26, 1986, RCGC; RG 1995 MS, 752–53.

40. John Carl Jacob III deposition, April 5, 1987, *Jacob v. Hallmark*, NARA; John T. Dauner, *Times*, June 7, 1986; O'Connor, "Hyatt Rescuers Kept Out of the Suit Filed for Victims," *Times*, June 19, 1986.

41. Larry Lantz deposition, April 8, 1987, *Jacob v. Hallmark*, NARA; Adam S. Wilson deposition, April 8, 1987, *Jacob v. Hallmark*, NARA; "Affidavit of John Jacob," Exhibit A, December 23, 1988, no. 144, *Jacob v. Hallmark*, NARA.

42. The document in question was probably a variant of a similar screed Gordon filed earlier in state court. "Memorandum Concerning Intentional Factual Misstatements by Defendant," June 29, 1985, *Moen L. Phillips v. Hallmark Cards, Inc.*, RCGC. In his daily diary Gordon recorded a lunch conversation with Robert Sisk in which the Hallmark lawyer referred to the "Bartlett Factor." Sisk meant that "the whole case has now changed due to the advantage Hallmark gains" from having a judge other than Scott Wright. TRSL, July 7, 1986, RCGC. Gordon hand-delivered a twelve-page letter to the judge's chambers that raised the issue of Bartlett's recusal. TRSL, November 3, 1986, RCGC; "Judge in Hyatt Rescuers' Suit Won't Disqualify Self," *Times*, December 23, 1986; John T. Dauner, "Judge Won't Hold up Action in Hallmark Suit," *Times*, September 10, 1986; RG to Arthur R. Miller, January 15, 1987, RCGC. Gordon prepared a fifty-three-page version of the accusatory document earlier for the state court, what he called "factual refutations of Hallmark's five most egregious fairytales." The defense made a motion to "expunge" the memo from the record, apparently unsuccessfully. See also RG to Robert Sisk of Hughes, Hubbard & Reed, New York NY, April 12, 1985, RCGC; TRSL, January 22, 28, February 4, 1985, RCGC; RG 1995 MS, 762–66.

43. "Just a Commodity for Sale?," editorial, *Times*, July 18, 1986; TRSL, July 18, 1986, RCGC; RG 1995 MS, 759; George H. Gurley Jr., "Behind the Lines: First, You Rescue; Then Sue," *Times*, August 12, 1986, in which the columnist opined: "In our enlightened times, firefighters put out your fire without charge. Then they sue you because they can't sleep." Jerry Heaster, "Value of Psychic Damage Has Its Limits," *Star*, July 21, 1986. With the same measure of ridicule, the paper added a snide editorial cartoon by Lee Judge of a traffic cop casually speaking to a victim of a car wreck. Lee Judge, "Of course, you know if this rescue causes me emotional injury, you're letting yourself in for a heck of a lawsuit," *Times*, July 23, 1986; TRSL, July 21, 23, 1986.
44. RG 1995 MS, 758; John T. Dauner, "Attorneys Make Rules in Hyatt Rescue Suit," *Times*, September 24, 1986. Gordon asked the court to restrict the defendants from contacting potential class members, but the judge again ruled against him.
45. TRSL, May–September 1987, RCGC. For the most part Gordon dealt directly with John Townsend of Hughes, Hubbard & Reed and John Aisenbrey of Stinson, Mag & Fizzell. (nine drafts) TRSL, August 24, 1987, RCGC. RG 1995 MS, 774, which cited a phone conversation between Gordon and Miller, August 28, 1987. Gordon parroted back a similar refrain, "I'm afraid this was the wrong group of plaintiffs, at the wrong time, and before the wrong judge." RG to Miller, September 14, 1987, RCGC. Miller kept going with the rap in triplicate. "This was not an easy case, an easy court, or an easy adversary." Miller to RG, September 18, 1987, RCGC.
46. TRSL, September 1, 2, 4, December 15, 1987, RCGC; RG to Miller, September 14, 1987, RCGC; Joe Henderson, "Skywalks Settlement Proposed," *Star*, September 8, 1987; "Notice of Pendency of Class Action and Proposed Settlement," *Times*, September 16, 1987; Rick Alm, "Deadline in New Hyatt Settlement," *Star*, September 16, 1987; Rick Alm, "190 File Damage Claims in Hyatt Collapse Case," *Star*, November 4, 1987; John T. Dauner, "Judge Approves Final Settlement of Lawsuit Filed by Hyatt Rescuers," *Times*, December 16, 1987; ("ridiculed") "Affidavit of John Jacob," Exhibit A, December 23, 1988, no. 144, *Jacob v. Hallmark*, NARA.
47. John T. Dauner, "Rescue Lawyers Get $1.1 Million; Hallmark Will Pay Bill," *Times*, February 8, 1989; RG to Jacob, August 17, 1987, RCGC. "Please find enclosed the Hallmark proposed Settlement Agreement. It's not perfect, but I recommend that you accept it." RG to John Aisenbrey of Stinson, Mag & Fizzell, September 24, 1987, RCGC, which gave Gordon's settlement demands for John Jacob ($29,235.50), Larry Lantz ($8,220), and Adam Wilson ($8,289.50). Jacob settled for less ($10,250). Heather S. Woodson of Stinson, Mag & Fizzell to Jacob, copied to RG, November 18, 1987, RCGC.
48. "Transcript of Proceedings," February 7, 1989, no. 157, *Jacob v. Hallmark*, NARA.
49. John T. Dauner, *Times*, February 8, 1989. It is unclear whether the paper ever printed for comparison the legal fees received by Gordon's opponents, an estimated $1.8 million charged by Hughes, Hubbard & Reed and $600,000 by Stinson, Mag. RG to Miller, February 9, 1989, RCGC.

50. Aisenbrey to RG, March 14, 1989, *Jacob v. Hallmark*, NARA; RG 1995 MS, 775.
51. "Transcript of Proceedings," March 2, 1989, no. 163, *Jacob v. Hallmark*, NARA.
52. Gordon complained, "Despite the small amount of work he actually performed, he wants a percentage fee equal to at least one-third of the total recover." RG to Miller, October 8, 1988, RCGC. To himself he wrote that the other lawyer "used the wrong method of calculation," along with a "failure to devote enough time to this case." TRSL, October 22, 1988, RCGC. The lawyer in question was James Jeans, who served as cocounsel for the plaintiffs. Professor Jeans taught at the University of Missouri–Kansas City School of Law from 1966 to 1994. "James W. Jeans Sr.," obituary, *Star*, November 5, 2006. In Gordon's estimation, he rivaled only Irving Younger for his interest in doing the least amount of work for the most amount of money. RG 1995 MS, 773–80. Jeans maintained that they had an understanding that shares of fees would be split equally rather than based on hours expended, which Gordon disavowed.
53. ("unbalanced") TRSL, December 14, 1988, RCGC. Gordon's attempt to avoid a fee and expense hearing took much of his time in December. See entries of December 9–27, 1988. "Transcript of Proceedings," February 7, 1989, no. 157, *Jacob v. Hallmark*, NARA; "Transcript of Proceedings," March 2, 1989, no. 163, *Jacob v. Hallmark*, NARA.
54. "Transcript of Proceedings," March 2, 1989.
55. "Order Vacating February 7, 1989, Award of Attorneys' Fees and Making Final Award of Attorneys' Fees Pursuant to Settlement Agreement," March 10, 1989, no. 160, *Jacob v. Hallmark*, NARA; RG 1995 MS, 778, 782. Judge Bartlett reduced Gordon's "reasonable" hours to about 3,600 and placed nearly 1,000 hours to his total under the category of "quality paralegal" at a much-reduced hourly rate. Bartlett also cut in half Gordon's reimbursable expenses.
56. John T. Dauner, "Judge Lowers Fees for Lawyers in Hyatt Rescuers' Suit," *Times*, March 13, 1989. In this and earlier articles the paper never quoted John Jacob, who said in court, "Mr. Gordon has rendered to me an invaluable service." "Transcript of Proceedings," February 7, 1989.
57. RG 1995 MS, 782–83; ("feel badly") "Transcript of Proceedings," March 2, 1989.
58. RG 1995 MS, 782–83.

17. FINALES

1. Haskins, *New York Times*, March 29, 1983; ("dobber") *Oxford English Dictionary*, 2020, https://www.oed.com. Gordon was under the impression that Haskins was proceeding with another Hyatt-related story, but this apparently did not happen. RG to Haskins, April 7, 1983, RCGC.
2. ("how the reigning family") These are Gordon's words. Notes of meeting, John H. Kreamer and RG, April 21, 1987, RCGC. Kreamer was so highly esteemed that his death in 1992 garnered a front-page story and a follow-up editorial about this "friendly man

of compassion." Bill Norton and Joseph Popper, "John Kreamer, Civic Leader, is Dead at 69," *Star*, May 30, 1992; "Kansas City's John Kreamer," editorial, *Star*, June 1, 1992.

3. ("taken a lot out") "Outsider Joins Hallmark as a Senior Executive," *New York Times*, May 21, 1983, which reported Hockaday's initial departure from Kansas City Southern; Walt Potter, "Hockaday at Hallmark: Cards to Be Firm's Mainstay as It Carefully Branches Out," *Times*, November 27, 1985; Kenneth N. Gilpin and Todd S. Purdum, "Business People: Hallmark Will Get 3d Chief in 75 Years," *New York Times*, November 27, 1985; Walt Potter, "What's in the Cards for Hallmark?; Changes Come as Market Tightens," *Times*, November 28, 1985.
4. Diane Stafford, "Kipp Gets Top Post at Crown Center Redevelopment Corp.," *Star*, June 7, 1983; ("snappier version") RG 1995 MS, 644, quoting Jeff Coplon, reporter for the *Village Voice*.
5. "'The Race for Mayor'; Their Views and Goals for the Future," *Star*, February 6, 1983; John A. Dvorak and Michael Yablonski, "Divided Council Rejects Resolution Criticizing Kipp," *Times*, February 19, 1983; "Kipp to Leave City Manager's Job on July 1," *Star*, April 28, 1983; Melissa Berg, "Kipp Resignation Stuns KC Leaders; 'Time Has Come' to Step Down, Manager Says," *Times*, April 29, 1983; John A. Dvorak, "Buildup of KC's Problems, Trouble with Mayor Take Toll," *Times*, April 29, 1983; ("how Kansas City operates") Stafford, "Kipp Gets Top Post"; RG 1995 MS, 653–54. The praise of Kipp came from Harold Rice, a Hallmark Cards board member.
6. Unless otherwise cited, the details of the Hallmark–Blue Mountain dispute come from Susan Polis Schutz's memoir, *Blue Mountain: Turning Dreams into Reality* (Boulder CO: Blue Mountain Press, 2004).
7. ("unlimited") Polis Schutz, *Blue Mountain*, 214; "Hallmark Sued over Line of Cards," *Times*, July 22, 1986; "Judge to Hear Arguments against Hallmark Card Line," *Times*, October 24, 1986; Debra Skodack, "Hallmark Must Drop 83 Cards; Injunction Halts Their Sale until Suit Is Settled," *Times*, November 21, 1986; Debra Skodack, "Hallmark Suspends Distribution of Cards," *Times*, November 22, 1986; Debra Skodack, "Hallmark Wanted Card Firm, Owners Say," *Times*, November 27, 1986; Mike Hendricks, "Firm Puts Its Cards on the Table in Suit against Hallmark," *Star*, November 30, 1986; Debra Skodack, "Colorado Card Maker Amends Lawsuit against Hallmark," *Times*, August 1, 1987; Mike Hendricks, "Hallmark Argues It's Legal to Copy Cards," *Star*, September 29, 1987; Mike Hendricks, "Hallmark Denies Copying; View Differs from Statement by Own Attorney," *Star*, October 7, 1987; "Hallmark Card Ban Is Upheld," *Times*, May 25, 1988; Rod Perlmutter, "Hallmark Foe Seeks Quick Trial," *Times*, May 27, 1988; Mike Hendricks, "Hallmark Files Appeal on a Colorado Ruling," *Star*, August 24, 1988; Mike Hendricks, "Hallmark Denied Appeal," *Star*, October 17, 1988; Mike Hendricks, "Hallmark Settles Suit with Colorado Firm; KC Company to Drop Personal Touch Greeting Card Line," *Star*, October 24, 1988; Debra Skodack,

"Accord in Card Suit May Bring Caution," *Times*, October 25, 1988; ("card colossus" coined by Gordon) RG 1995 MS, 249, 790.

8. George H. Gurley Jr., "Behind the Lines: I Just Had to Say This: 'Aaaaack'; Gee the Sap's Running Early This Year, in Greeting Cards," *Times*, November 25, 1986. By the time of Gurley's article, the high-water mark of broadcast television—and maybe Hallmark's contribution to it—had passed. Once an awards juggernaut, the anthology series *Hallmark Hall of Fame* received its last primetime Emmy for an "Outstanding Made for Television Movie" or "Outstanding Drama/Comedy Special" in 1992 for *Miss Rose White*. *Hallmark Hall of Fame*, Awards & Nominations, Television Academy, https://www.emmys.com/shows/hallmark-hall-fame and https://www.emmys.com/site-search?search_api_views_fulltext=hallmark&f%5B0%5D=type%3Ashow; dragonflysuz, "A list of original *Hallmark Hall of Fame* movies starting in 1951," IMDB, April 5, 2016, updated March 2022, https://www.imdb.com/list/ls034889483/.
9. Kate Lee, "Irv Hockaday: Hallmark Renews Commitment to Excellence, Progress, and Community," *Greater Kansas City Business: A Publication for the Greater Kansas City Chamber of Commerce* 1 (December 2000): 12.
10. Chris LaMorte, "Who Wants to Be a Billionaire?," *Westword*, November 18, 1999, https://www.westword.com/news/who-wants-to-be-a-billionaire-5060963.
11. TRSL, November 21, December 3, 18, 1986, January 26, September 3, 9, 10, 25, 27, 28, October 1, 9, 28, November 9, 1987, RCGC; RG 1995 MS, 790–96. Blue Mountain's attorney and Gordon's newfound friend was Harry Melkonian of Los Angeles CA, and they bonded by sharing examples of "parallel shenanigans" allegedly pulled off by Hallmark lawyers against each party.
12. "Lawyer in Hyatt Case Dies," *Times*, March 16, 1988. See also Stephen LaBaton, "Irving Younger, Lawyer, 55, Dies; Judge, Law Professor, and Author," *New York Times*, March 15, 1988.
13. Alm to RG, March 1988, RCGC.
14. ("wisest adviser" and "I'm worried") RG 1995 MS, 136; Josie Foote to REP, June 23, 2016, author's collection; Foote to REP, notes of phone conversation, December 19, 2018; Foote to REP, December 28, 2018; Johnson County (Kansas) District Court, "Divorces," *Star*, April 9, 1997.
15. Andy Gordon to REP, May 21, 2018.
16. Woods to REP, May 22, 2018.
17. "Robert Charles Gordon," obituary, *Star*, February 8, 2008.
18. RG 1995 MS, 784.
19. ("insider") Robert Gordon, "When They Didn't Care Enough," manuscript, 1984, ix; ("volunteered") "Bob" [Robert Byrne] to "Bob" [RG], March 17, 1986, RCGC.
20. Hilary Mantel, *The Mirror & the Light* (New York: Henry Holt, 2020), 728–29.

21. Gordon took some liberties with the Churchill quote, but the meaning remained. Winston Churchill, *The Gathering Storm* (New York: Houghton Mifflin, 1948), 109; Robert C. Gordon, liaison counsel for class plaintiffs, "Skywalks Litigation Story Only Repeats Reckless Gossip," *Times*, August 8, 1983, in response to Ron Ostroff, "Legal Magazine Criticizes Wright for Work in Skywalks Class Action," *Times*, July 15, 1983. Ostroff's article drew on a piece from the *American Lawyer*, July–August 1983. See also RG to Jim Lyons, *American Lawyer*, New York NY, May 20, 1983, copy to Steve Brill, editor in chief, RCGC; RG to Brill, *American Lawyer*, June 1, 1983; RG to Scott Whiteside, July 21, 1983, RCGC; RG to James W. Scott, editor, editorial page, *Kansas City Star/Times*, July 29, 1983, RCGC; RG to Scott, August 9, 1983, RCGC.
22. RG 1995 MS, 853.

EPILOGUE

1. ("construction industry") G. William Quatman, "The Hyatt Skywalk Revisited: What Happened? Could It Happen Again?," *Schinnerer's 42nd Annual Meeting of Invited Attorneys*, Victor O. Schinnerer, 2003; ("pay attention") Rick Montgomery, "Memories, Lessons Live On: Many Are Continuing to Learn from Skywalk Collapse," *Star*, July 15, 2001. For an excellent essay on the approach taken with and value of the Hyatt example in the classroom, see John W. Lawson and Pamalee A. Brady, "Using the Hyatt Regency Skywalk Collapse Case Study in Engineering Education," *ResearchGate*, April 2011, https://www.researchgate.net/publication/265154829_Using_the_Hyatt_Regency_Skywalk_Collapse_Case_Study_in_Engineering_Education.
2. RG 1984 MS, iii.
3. ("diffusion of responsibility") "The Hyatt Settlement," editorial, *Times*, January 12, 1983, which wagged its finger at the studied avoidance of blame by "designers, builders, owners, operators, and inspectors." The drumbeat continues on this point of engineering responsibility. Robynn Adracsek, "Why Engineers Must Remember the Kansas City Hyatt Tragedy," *Engineering News-Record*, December 16, 2015, https://www.enr.com/articles/38400-why-engineers-must-remember-the-kansas-city-hyatt-tragedy; ("walk away") Montgomery, "Memories, Lessons Live On"; see also Rick Alm, "Hyatt Collapse a Spur to Safety Manual," *Times*, June 23, 1988; RG 1995 MS, 171–74.
4. Associated Press, "Hyatt Regency Supports Plans to Build Skywalks Memorial," July 19, 2008; ("the grief") Dirk Johnson, "For Many, a Memorial to Victims of a Hotel Skywalk Collapse Is Long Overdue," *New York Times*, July 27, 2008; ("moral responsibility") James C. Fitzpatrick, "The Hyatt Regency Skywalks Memorial: It's Going to Happen; It Must," *JimmyCsays: At the Juncture of Journalism and Daily Life in KC*, July 17, 2011, https://jimmycsays.com/2011/07/17/the-hyatt-regency-skywalks-memorial-its-going-to-happen-it-must/; Matt Campbell, "Thirty Years after the Hyatt Skywalks Disaster, a Reminder to Never Forget," *Star*, July 17, 2011.

5. Kyle Palmer, "Ground Broken on Memorial for 'One of the Worst Tragedies in Kansas City's History,'" KCUR 89.3, July 17, 2015, https://www.kcur.org/news/2015-07-17/ground-broken-on-memorial-for-one-of-the-worst-tragedies-in-kansas-citys-history; Laura Spencer, "Three Decades on, a Memorial for the Victims of the Hyatt Disaster," KCUR 89.3, November 12, 2015, https://www.kcur.org/community/2015-11-12/three-decades-on-a-memorial-for-the-victims-of-the-hyatt-disaster.
6. Rita Blitt of Kansas City was the sculptor of *Sending Love*. Rita Blitt, "Sending Love at Skywalk Memorial," November 1, 2015, https://ritablitt.com/news/2016/11/15/skywalk#:~:text=Sending%20Love%20was%20installed%20in,the%20Blitt%2012%2Dfoot%20sculpture.

APPENDIX

1. RG 1995 MS, 12, citing "Progeny of Genius," *Forbes*, February 10, 1986, 92.
2. John T. Dauner, "Donald Hall Hopes to Leave Sorrow Behind; Haggard Hallmark Chief Vows to Reopen the Hyatt as Soon as Possible," *Kansas City Times*, July 20, 1981; Paul J. Haskins, "Collapse of Hotels 'Skywalks' in 1981 Is Still Reverberating in Kansas City," *New York Times*, March 29, 1983.
3. Donald Joyce Hall deposition, August 30–September 3, 1982, 4 vols., RCGC.
4. RG 1995 MS, 420.
5. RG 1995 MS, 419, 420.
6. Hall deposition, 150–59, 227–36, 295–307, RCGC.

BIBLIOGRAPHIC ESSAY

Without the Robert C. Gordon Collection there would be no *Skywalks*. Gordon's many manuscripts, daily musings, and extensive correspondence, along with his copies of the legal documents of the *Federal Skywalk Cases*, many of them annotated in his hand, were fundamental to this book. The proof can be found in the notes.

His archival collection resides safely in the Missouri Valley Special Collections of the Kansas City Public Library, Kansas City, Missouri, and amounts to about 180 boxes at this writing. Although in a raw state, the collection is usable by historians. Early on, a responsible MVSC archivist went completely through the mass of material, did some consolidation and organizing, and created a "box inventory" of their contents. On a 2017 spreadsheet the collection consisted of 11,457 items, most of which take the form of folders and individual documents. The Gordon collection awaits its next stage as a historical collection with a detailed processing and orderly, logical arrangement, accompanied by a complete, exhaustive finding aid. This will be a massive project for the future but one the library is dedicated to finishing.

Nearly as important to my research and to any telling of the hotel disaster story was the *Federal Skywalk Cases*, the sixteen boxes of records from the U.S. District Court of the Western District of Missouri, Record Group 21, held by the National Archives at Kansas City, National Archives and Records Administration. In contrast to Gordon's jumble, these records were pristinely preserved and arranged in their original order. The court docket lists the court documents, numerically arranged, as they were filed with the court. A sizable correspondence accompanies the collection, which, I was told, is uncommon for district court cases. Once again, the value of these records to this project is revealed in the notes.

The Mid-Continent Public Library, a library district that serves nearly eight hundred thousand people in the greater Kansas City metro area, recently bit the bullet and purchased at an astronomical price the online database of the *Kansas City Times* and *Kansas City Star*, 1880 to the present. This occurred in time for this project and was a godsend to a person who cut his teeth on newspaper research an eon ago when that meant hours with one's head stuck in a dimly lit, hand-cranked microfilm reader. The *Times* and *Star* are essential historical sources for the 1980s, when newspapers were giants that walked the earth. The fact that the paper earned a Pulitzer Prize for its coverage of the Hyatt disaster was clear evidence of how print media effectively created the "first draft" of history.

Gordon's literary effort may have dwelled on the legal story, but he did not fail to heed eyewitness testimony of the victims, survivors, and first responders to whom he spoke. The victims of July 17, 1981, and the justice due them were always on his mind, no matter how involved he was in his legal practice and book matters. His version of the tragedy in the "House of Cards" manuscript (1995) was formed in no small measure by speaking and corresponding with the following eyewitnesses. Many of their accounts will be found in the Gordon collection.

Collapse survivors: Brenda Abernathy, Mary Bottenberg, Dorothy Lee Dixon, Sally Firestone, Evelyn Gubar, Jayne Hayes, Deborah Jackson, Micheal Mahoney, Lily and Willy McClure, Herb Newberg, Maxine Rhodes, Molly Riley (also a rescuer), Jean Rose, Shirley Stover, Joseph Vrabel, Karen Watts, and Regina and Thomas Weir.

Rescuers: William "Country Bill" Allman (civilian responder), Gary Frank (paramedic), John Jacob (paramedic), William Kelly Jr. (firefighter), Laura Laiban (civilian responder), Larry Lantz (Hyatt security), Joe Lister (mortician), Steve Maxwell (firefighter), John Murphy (civilian responder), Moen Phillips (firefighter), Ed Taylor (civilian responder), John Tvedten Jr. (firefighter), Joe Waeckerle (doctor), and Adam Wilson (Hyatt security).

My goal with *Skywalks* was to reexamine the existing narrative and to present a short, concise book, honest and true, and with no claim of being comprehensive. Leaving aside Robert Gordon's unpublished tome, when I began the research for this project, no all-embracing account of the Hallmark hotel disaster had yet been published. If it had, my curiosity in the subject might have been slaked. Gordon offered an intriguing point of view that heavily detoured from the generally accepted, "safe" narrative. Gordon's interpretations and conclusions, anything but safe, may be particularly persuasive, but basically his remains a solitary voice, and the historical record could stand a larger chorus, whether they sing the same song or not. If history is written by the victors, what happens when they don't bother? Many members of the "cast of characters" compiled for Gordon's book are now dead, but several "insiders" are still on the scene, and all have important stories to tell, positions to defend, reputations to burnish or salvage, and documents to preserve for history. The Gordon family has done its part in saving a critical part of the historical record. Others need to step up and do the same. It's been more than forty years, and time is running out.

INDEX